Augsburg College
Lindell Library
Minneapolis, MN 55454

**Beyond
Intellectual
Property**

Donated to
Augsburg College
by the Resource Center
of the Americas
November 2007

Beyond Intellectual Property

Toward Traditional Resource Rights for Indigenous Peoples and Local Communities

Darrell A. Posey
and
Graham Dutfield

INTERNATIONAL DEVELOPMENT RESEARCH CENTRE
Ottawa • Cairo • Dakar • Johannesburg • Montevideo • Nairobi • New Delhi • Singapore

Published by the International Development Research Centre
PO Box 8500, Ottawa, ON, Canada K1G 3H9

© International Development Research Centre 1996

Canadian Cataloguing in Publication Data

Posey, Darrell A. (Darrell Addison, 1947–

Beyond intellectual property : toward traditional resource rights for indigenous peoples and local communities

Includes bibliographical references.
ISBN 0-88936-799-X

1. Indigenous people — Legal status, laws, etc.
2. Cultural property, Protection of.
3. Intellectual property.
4. Ethnobiology.
I. Dutfield, Graham.
II. International Development Research Centre (Canada).
III. Title.
IV. Title: Toward traditional resource rights for indigenous peoples and local communities.

GN380.P67 1996   342'.0872   C96-980190-4

A microfiche edition is available.

All rights reserved. No part of this publication may be reproduced, stored in a retrieval system, or transmitted, in any form or by any means, electronic, mechanical, photocopying, or otherwise, without the prior permission of the International Development Research Centre.

The views expressed in this publication are those of the authors and do not necessarily represent those of the International Development Research Centre. Mention of proprietary names does not constitute endorsement of the product and is given only for information.

IDRC Books endeavours to produce environmentally friendly publications. All paper used is recycled as well as recyclable. All inks and coating are vegetable-based products.

Contents

Preface xi

Acknowledgments xiii

Introduction 1

Chapter 1
Who visits communities, what are they seeking, and why? 5
    Who visits indigenous communities? 6
    What are they seeking? 12
    Why is it being sought? 13
    Conclusions. 20

Chapter 2
What happens to traditional knowledge and resources? 21
    Conservation centres for biogenetic resources 22
    The commercial sector 27
    Museums, art galleries, and the trade in works of art 28
    Museums, universities, and human remains 28
    Libraries, archives, and electronic databases 29
    Conclusions. 32

Chapter 3
Who benefits from traditional resources? 33
    The value and importance of traditional knowledge 34
    Publication and the public domain 35
    What constitutes "just compensation"? 37
    Conclusions. 41

Chapter 4
Will the community be informed? 43
    Violations of indigenous peoples' right to be informed 44
    Conclusions. 48

Chapter 5
What right do communities have to say
"yes" or "no" to commercialization? 49
    The effects of trade. 50
    Option 1: say "no". 52
    Option 2: say "yes" 55
    Conclusions. 57

Chapter 6
How can a community take legal action? 59
    Western and indigenous property systems and customary law 60
    Organizational options. 62
    Who are the partners? 63
    Conclusions. 64

Chapter 7
What are contracts and covenants? 67
    Legal agreements 68
    Nonlegal agreements 70
    Covenants and model contracts 72
    Conclusions. 74

Chapter 8
Are intellectual property rights useful? 75
    Patents 76
    Petty patents 81
    Copyright 83
    Trademarks 84
    Industrial designs. 87
    Trade secrets 87
    Plant breeders' rights 88
    Geographic indications and appellations of origin 90
    Certification and labeling 91
    Conclusions. 92

Chapter 9
Can communities develop their own system
for protecting traditional resource rights? 93
    What are traditional resource rights? 95
    Community intellectual property rights. 97
    Model draft community intellectual rights act 97
    The Unesco–WIPO model provisions 99
    Conclusions. 100

Chapter 10
Are legally binding international agreements useful? 101
    The GATT agreement on Trade-Related Aspects of Intellectual Property Rights 102
    The Convention on Biological Diversity. 103
    International Covenant on Economic, Social and Cultural Rights and
        the International Covenant on Civil and Political Rights 111
    The World Heritage Convention 112
    The Rome Convention 114
    Convention on the Means of Prohibiting and Preventing the Illicit Import,
        Export and Transfer of Ownership of Cultural Property 115
    The International Labour Organisation's Convention 169 117
    Conclusions 117

Chapter 11
How can communities use "soft law" and nonbinding international agreements? 119
    What is "soft law" and why is it relevant? 120
    The Universal Declaration of Human Rights 120
    ECOSOC and the Working Group on Indigenous Populations 121
    The Rio Declaration 122
    Agenda 21 123
    The FAO International Code of Conduct for Plant Germplasm
        Collecting and Transfer 124
    Unesco's cultural documents 124
    Conclusions 126

Chapter 12
Are nongovernmental, nonlegal instruments useful? 127
    Indigenous peoples' declarations 128
    Ethical guidelines and declarations 129
    Conclusions 131

Chapter 13
Why are funds and funding guidelines important? 133
    Who are the funders? 134
    The Global Environment Facility 135
    The Fund for Farmers' Rights 137
    Conclusions 137

Chapter 14
What creative strategies and unique solutions have been developed? 139
    Community-based initiatives 140
    Networks 145
    Model laws to implement the Convention on Biological Diversity 147
    Other national laws 150

Chapter 15
Toward protection, compensation, and community development 155

Appendices
1. The Human Genome Diversity Project 161
2. The Covenant on Intellectual, Cultural, and Scientific Resources 175
3. Declaration of Principles of the World Council of Indigenous Peoples 179
4. UN Draft Declaration on the Rights of Indigenous Peoples. 181
5. Kari-Oca Declaration and the Indigenous Peoples' Earth Charter 189
6. Charter of the Indigenous–Tribal Peoples of the Tropical Forests 199
7. The Mataatua Declaration on Cultural and Intellectual Property Rights
   of Indigenous Peoples. 205
8. Recommendations from the Voices of the Earth Congress 209
9. COICA/UNDP Regional Meeting on Intellectual Property Rights
   and Biodiversity 215
10. UNDP Consultation on the Protection and Conservation of
    Indigenous Knowledge 219
11. UNDP Consultation on Indigenous Peoples' Knowledge and
    Intellectual Property Rights 223

Glossary 227

Acronyms and abbreviations 235

References 237

Resource guide 245
  People and organizations 245
  E-mail links 279
  World Wide Web addresses 281
  Annotated bibliography 281

List of boxes

	The Declaration of Belém.	2
1.1	Ethnic tourism in Tana Toraja	7
1.2	The Biodiversity Institute	17
1.3	Forest of the lost child, Naimina Enkiyio, Loita Hills, Narok County, Kenya	18
1.4	The Manu Biosphere Reserve	19
2.1	Members of the Consultative Group on International Agricultural Research	24
2.2	Three patent claims based on the cells of indigenous people	26
2.3	The indigenous knowledge resource centres	30
2.4	The World Foundation for the Safeguard of Indigenous Cultures	31
2.5	Programa de Colaboración sobre Medicina Tradicional y Herbolaria	32
3.1	*Homalanthus nutans*	35
3.2	Shaman Pharmaceuticals and COICA	39
3.3	*Stevia rebaudiana*	40
4.1	Commercial use of human images: an example from Amazonia	46
4.2	Breach of confidence: a court case in Australia	47
5.1	*Bixa orellana*: the Yawanawa Association and the Aveda Corporation	56
6.1	Controls and sanctions in the Kafue River basin of Zambia	61
7.1	Software law as a basis for a licencing agreement	69
7.2	The National Cancer Institute's letters of collection	71
7.3	The Royal Botanic Gardens' memorandum of understanding	72
8.1	What is the World Intellectual Property Organization?	77
8.2	Neem — a traditional and modern biopesticide	80
8.3	Ethiopian endod	81
8.4	Thaumatin — a natural sweetener from West Africa	82
8.5	Bulun Bulun versus Nejlam Pty Ltd	85
8.6	The quick and easy way to own a "rainforest"	86
10.1	Environmental impact assessment	106
10.2	A clearing-house mechanism	107
10.3	Subsidiary Body on Scientific, Technical and Technological Advice	109
10.4	Special protocols on indigenous and traditional technologies based on the knowledge, innovations, and practices of local communities embodying traditional lifestyles	110
10.5	Options for a protocol on biosafety and traditional technologies	111
10.6	The sacred weavings of Coroma, Bolivia	116
13.1	The Protect-an-Acre Program of the Rainforest Action Network	135
A1.1	The Human Genome Organization (HUGO)	162
A1.2	Hoffmann-La Roche, the NIH, and the Aeta	167
A1.3	IPR and human genetic material	170

Preface

The Working Group on Intellectual Property Rights was established in 1990 by the Global Coalition for Bio-Cultural Diversity, whose mission was to to unite indigenous peoples, scientific organizations, and environmental groups to implement a forceful strategy for the use of traditional knowledge, involvement of local peoples in conservation and development strategies, and implementation of alternative, people-centred conservation models.

With the generous support of the World Wide Fund for Nature International, funds were acquired by the working group to establish a mailing list and a database of publications and people interested in intellectual property rights (IPR) and to hold a number of seminars for indigenous peoples on this subject. The seminars were aimed at alerting indigenous peoples to the relevance and urgency of IPR issues in the context of two major global negotiation processes — the United Nations Conference on the Environment and Development (UNCED), or Earth Summit (Rio de Janeiro, 1992), and the General Agreement on Tariffs and Trade (GATT). Another purpose of the seminars was to listen to the concerns of indigenous communities so as to orient the IPR debate toward their needs, expectations, and practical problems.

During the Earth Summit, the Global Coalition organized the Earth Parliament as the principal venue for indigenous and traditional peoples. This forum brought together indigenous leaders from over 80 countries to discuss issues of mutual concern, including IPR.

Since the Earth Summit, dozens of conferences, seminars, and workshops have been held with indigenous peoples to discuss the evolving debate over IPR. These meetings include the ones held for 4 consecutive years by the United Nations Working Group on Indigenous Peoples in Geneva, Switzerland, as well as the United Nations Conference on Human Rights, held in Vienna, Austria, in 1993. This book embodies these efforts and the input of many people over a considerable period of time.

It is organized around a series of questions that we believe might emerge in a community when a visitor arrives to collect information or cultural or biogenetic materials. These questions would be the same whether the community was an indigenous settlement in the Amazon or a village in rural England. Each chapter begins with a summary of the main issues it addresses and ends with options and suggested actions.

The terminology used here is a mixture of scientific, legal, economic, and political jargon — not always easily understood and even more difficult to translate. Yet, the synthesis necessary to develop the sui generis view of TRR bound us to acquaint the reader with as many of these terms as possible. Words and terms defined in the glossary appear in heavy italics where they are first mentioned.

The book concludes with some warnings and suggested actions for local communities. These are intended to help guide communities through the basic questions that they should be asking when confronting those interested in their knowledge, natural resources, or biogenetic materials.

As the legal instruments used to invoke IPR are inadequate to protect the cultural, scientific, and intellectual resources of indigenous peoples, the IPR issue has outgrown its name. The term traditional resource rights (TRR) has emerged to define the many "bundles of rights" that relate to protection, compensation, and conservation. The aim in this book then is to outline the nature of these bundles and suggest how these rights can be made accessible to local communities.

In 1994, the Working Group on Intellectual Property Rights changed its name to the Working Group on Traditional Resource Rights in response to the advice, suggestions, criticisms, and, most importantly, invaluable materials and resources provided by over 450 participants. This book likewise reflects the input of many people over this long process.

Darrell A. Posey
Graham Dutfield
December 1995

Acknowledgments

We thank Ernst Josef Fittkau, director of the Zoologische Staatssammlung in Munich, who kindly provided office space in 1989 and 1990, during which time a fellowship from the Alexander von Humboldt Stiftung made it possible to start the first Working Group on Intellectual Property Rights. During that period, four devoted researchers — Ulrike Hagen-Sautier, Christiane Lambert-Dobler, Sybille Nahr, and Andreas Zeidler — and their assistants helped develop the broad intellectual underpinnings for the concept of intellectual property rights (IPR) and traditional resource rights (TRR).

We also thank Chris Elliot of the World Wide Fund for Nature (WWF) International, who had the foresight to recognize the importance of IPR and conserving biodiversity and who secured the first funds for the working group. His colleague, Michael Pimbert, likewise generously supported these efforts and provided many useful insights, ideas, criticism, and encouragement at critical times.

The Heinz Foundation, through a grant to the University of Pittsburgh's Center for Latin American Studies, provided D.A. Posey with a year's research time to work on IPR issues as they relate to indigenous peoples of Latin America. This handbook has benefited from this research, as it has from a consultancy with the International Union for the Conservation of Nature (IUCN) on the importance of IPR in the *Convention on Biological Diversity* vis-à-vis indigenous and traditional communities. We are grateful to Jeffrey McNeely and Caroline Martinet for this opportunity.

The Institute of Social and Cultural Anthropology (ISCA) of the University of Oxford generously provided office space for the Working Group on Traditional Resource Rights during the preparation of this handbook. We are grateful to Isabella Birkin and to colleagues at ISCA for their support and interest in this project, especially Peter Rivière and John Davis.

We also thank John Muddiman and Michael Freeden of the Oxford Centre for the Environment, Ethics and Society, as well as Dennis Trevelyan, principal of Mansfield College, for their support.

This handbook owes its existence, above all, to the hard work and the intellectual contributions of a considerable number of individuals, nongovernmental organizations, and people's organizations. Some sections of the book were improved significantly as a result of the expert contributions of Kristina Plenderleith, Sarah Laird, and Tom Griffiths, as well as Gernot Brodnig and Eugenio da Costa e Silva. Casper Henderson provided editorial assistance.

The learning process that we needed to go through during the project was enriched by several pioneering individuals and organizations who contributed through discussions, papers, articles, and books and by organizing conferences and workshops. We owe a debt of gratitude to: Julian Berger (United Nations Centre for Human Rights), who provided facilities for workshops for the United Nations Working Group on Indigenous Populations; Stephen Brush and the participants of the Intellectual Property

Rights and Indigenous Knowledge Conference at Lake Tahoe, California, in October 1993; Valerio Grefa, who organized the meeting sponsored by Coordinadora de Organizaciones Indigenas de la Cuenca Amazónica on intellectual property rights and biodiversity in Santa Cruz, Bolivia, in October 1994; the IUCN Task Force on Indigenous Peoples, chaired by Cindy Gilday; Peter Jaszi, Martha Woodmansee, and the participants of the conference called Cultural Agency/Cultural Authority: Politics and Poetics of Intellectual Property in the Post-Colonial Era at Bellagio, Italy; Aroha Mead and participants of the First International Conference on the Cultural and Intellectual Property Rights of Indigenous Peoples in Whakatane, Aotearoa New Zealand, in June 1993; participants at the Intellectual Property Rights, Indigenous Cultures and Biodiversity Conservation seminar organized by the Green College Centre for Environmental Policy and Understanding at the University of Oxford in May 1993; and Dinah Shelton and all the participants at the Montezillon Conference.

In addition, we thank the following people and institutions: the African Centre for Technology Studies and its former executive director, Callestous Juma; Alejandro Argumedo and the Indigenous Peoples' Biodiversity Network; Anna Borioni and Massimo Pieri of Cooperativa Técnico Scientífica de Base; Donna Craig, Macquarie University; Anthony Cunningham, past president of the International Society of Ethnobiology; Elaine Elisabetsky; Andrew Gray; Anil Gupta, Society for Research and Initiatives for Sustainable Technologies and Institutions; Alan Hamilton, WWF, UK; Christine Kabuye of the National Museums of Kenya and president of the International Society of Ethnobiology; Anatole Krattiger and William Lesser at the International Academy of the Environment; Gary Martin, Unesco; Jeffrey McNeely, Caroline Martinet, and Jeremy Carew-Reed of IUCN; Pat Mooney and Hope Shand, Rural Advancement Foundation International; Katy Moran, Healing Forest Conservancy; Dorothy Myers; Vandana Shiva; Marcos Terena; Third World Network; the World Council of Indigenous Peoples; Renée Vellvé and Henk Hobbelink, Genetic Resources Action International; Farhana Yamin, Foundation for International Environmental Law and Development; Durwood Zaelke, David Downes, and Chris Wohl, Centre for International Environmental Law; and Charles Zerner, Rainforest Alliance.

We are extremely grateful to those who kindly sent material and information in response to our questionnaire, especially the following people (in addition to those already mentioned): Janis Alcorn, Biodiversity Support Program, WWF, USA; Patrick Bernard, Fonds Modiale pour le Sauvegarde des Cultures Autochtones; Centre for International Research and Advisory Networks/Nuffic; Shelton Davis, World Bank; Kristin Dawkins, Institute for Agriculture and Trade Policy; Madhav Gadgil, Indian Institute of Science; Stephen King, Shaman Pharmaceuticals; Hector McQueen, Edinburgh University; Patrick O'Keefe; Gordon Pullar, Keepers of the Treasures; Helen Ross, Centre for Resource and Environmental Studies; Abayomi Sofowara; Johanna Sutherland, Department of International Relations, Australian National University; Peter Usher, Inuit Tapirisat of Canada.

Liz Evans (Human Genome Organization) and Keith Howard (School of Oriental and African Studies, University of London) kindly agreed to be interviewed for the book, and the following people and institutions responded to our specific requests and enquiries: R. Anderson, director of the British Museum; Bruno Bath, first secretary, Brazilian Embassy in the United Kingdom; Miges Baumann, Swissaid; Jeroen Breekveldt, NoGen; Cristina Bubba Zamora; Lynne Caporale, Merck; Mac Chapin, Native Lands; Jean Christie, Rural Advancement Foundation International; Jason Clay, Rights and Resources; Stephen Corry, Survival International; José Graça Aranha, consultant of the Development Cooperation and External Relations Bureau for Latin America and the Caribbean of the World Intellectual Property Organization; Henry Greely, Stanford Law School; Charlotte Haynes, International Work Group for Indigenous Affairs, International Service for National Agricultural Research; Byongwon Lee and Judy Van Zile, University of Hawaii at Manoa; and John Murra and Francis Sullivan, WWF, UK.

John Barton (Stanford Law School), Michael Gollin (Keck, Mahin and Cate), Tom Greaves (Bucknell University), Thandi Hurworth (*Intellectual Property Property Bulletin*), and Janet McGowan (Cultural Survival) all kindly reviewed drafts of what became Chapter 8 of this book.

Finally, the we would like to thank Sandra Garland for her painstaking and efficient editing of the final draft.

Darrell A. Posey
Graham Dutfield
December 1995

Introduction

The idea of ***intellectual property rights*** (IPR) first developed in European and North American law as a mechanism to protect individual and industrial inventions. Until recently, it was considered unlikely that IPR could pertain to the collective, transhistorical, and (in Western legal terms) nebulous qualities and assets of indigenous cultures. However, more and more, the traditional lifestyles, knowledge, and biogenetic resources of indigenous, traditional, and local peoples have been deemed by governments, corporations, and others to be of some commercial value and, therefore, to be property that might be bought and sold. At the same time, discussions on the Trade-Related Aspects of Intellectual Property Rights section of the General Agreement on Tariffs and Trade (GATT-TRIPs) and at the United Nations Conference on Environment and Development (the Earth Summit, UNCED), where the *Convention on Biological Diversity* (CBD) was developed, have made it clear to indigenous peoples that IPR law is important to them and is certain to become even more so in the future.

It has been suggested that, if corporations can secure IPR protection for their "inventions" — even those derived from the knowledge systems of indigenous peoples — then indigenous peoples, too, should be entitled to IPR protection. Some indigenous peoples are using IPR law already, at least to a limited extent. However, many more have questioned this approach, saying that even if existing IPR protection and compensation mechanisms were fully applied to traditional knowledge and biogenetic resources, this would not be an appropriate mechanism to strengthen and empower indigenous peoples. Dividing intellectual, cultural, and scientific property into three separate areas is strange and unwelcome to indigenous peoples who see these as part of a whole, more like the Western concept of culture. Communally shared concepts and communally owned property are fundamental aspects of traditional societies. Privatization or commoditization of these entities is not only foreign but incomprehensible as well. However, indigenous peoples and traditional communities are increasingly involved in market economies and are seeing an ever-growing number of their resources traded in those markets.

This book is the result of a long process of consultation that began in 1988 during the First International Congress of Ethnobiology in Belém, Brazil. Indigenous and traditional peoples (those referred to in the CBD as "indigenous and local communities embodying traditional lifestyles") from various parts of the world met with scientists and environmentalists to discuss a common strategy to stop the rapid decrease in the planet's biological and cultural diversity. Major concerns included the unique ways in which indigenous and ***traditional peoples*** perceive, use, and manage their natural resources and how programs can be developed to guarantee the preservation and strengthening of indigenous communities and their traditional knowledge.

The congress produced *The Declaration of Belém*, which outlined explicitly the responsibilities of scientists and environmentalists in addressing the needs of local communities and acknowledged the central role of indigenous peoples in all aspects of global planning. Although the language of *The Declaration of Belém* may seem somewhat antiquated today, it was the first time that an international scientific organization recognized a basic obligation that "procedures be developed to compensate native peoples for the utilization of their knowledge and their biological resources" (Statement 4). Since 1988, dozens of other institutions, professional societies, and organizations have followed suit.

The Declaration of Belém

As ethnobiologists, we are alarmed that:

Since
- Tropical forests and other fragile ecosystems are disappearing;
- Many species, both plant and animal, are threatened with extinction; and
- Indigenous cultures around the world are being disrupted and destroyed;

And given
- That economic, agricultural, and health conditions of people are dependent on these resources;
- That native peoples have been stewards of 99 percent of the world's genetic resources; and
- That there is an inextricable link between cultural and biological diversity;

We, members of the International Society of Ethnobiology, strongly urge action as follows:
1. Henceforth, a substantial proportion of development aid be devoted to efforts aimed at ethnobiological inventory, conservation, and management programs.
2. Mechanisms be established by which indigenous specialists are recognized as proper authorities and are consulted in all programs affecting them, their resources, and their environment.
3. All other inalienable human rights be recognized and guaranteed, including cultural and linguistic identity.
4. Procedures be developed to compensate native peoples for the utilization of their knowledge and their biological resources.
5. Educational programs be implemented to alert the global community to the value of ethnobiological knowledge for human well-being.
6. All medical programs include the recognition of and respect for traditional healers and the incorporation of traditional health practices that enhance the health status of these populations.
7. Ethnobiologists make available the results of their research to the native peoples with whom they have worked, especially including dissemination in the native language.
8. Exchange of information be promoted among indigenous and peasant peoples regarding conservation, management, and sustained utilization of resources.

At the International Society for Ethnobiology's (ISE) 1990 World Congress in Kunming, China, delegates from 52 countries established a global action plan — The Kunming Action Plan — calling for specific and urgent action to stop the destruction of biological and cultural diversity as mandated in *The Declaration of Belém*. Specifically, the Global Coalition for Bio-Cultural Diversity was established to unite indigenous peoples, scientific organizations, and environmental groups to implement a forceful strategy for the use of traditional knowledge, involvement of local peoples in conservation and development strategies, and implementation of alternative, people-centred conservation models.

One of the first tasks of the Global Coalition was to form a Working Group on Intellectual Property Rights. Now called the Working Group on Traditional Intellectual, Cultural and Scientific Resource Rights (or simply the Working Group on Traditional Resource Rights (WGTRR)), it has attempted to build on the concept of IPR protection and compensation, while recognizing that traditional resources — both tangible and intangible — are also covered under a significant number of international agreements. The term "property" in IPR was dropped, because property for indigenous peoples frequently has intangible, spiritual manifestations, and, although worthy of protection, is **inalienable** or can belong to no human being. Instead, the term "traditional resource rights" (TRR) was adopted to reflect the necessity of rethinking the limited and limiting concept of IPR. The term "traditional" refers to the cherished practices, beliefs, customs, knowledge, and cultural heritage of indigenous and local communities who live in close association with the Earth; "resource" is used in its broadest sense to mean all knowledge and technology, esthetic and spiritual qualities, tangible and intangible sources that, together, are deemed by local communities to be necessary to ensure healthy and fulfilling lifestyles for present and future generations; and "rights" refers to the basic inalienable guarantee to all human beings and the collective entities in which they choose to participate of the necessities to achieve and maintain the dignity and well-being of themselves, their predecessors, and their descendants.

The concept of TRR can accommodate a wide range of relevant international agreements as a basis for a ***sui generis*** system of protection for indigenous peoples and their resources — that is, a system that is unique and does not belong to an existing category of IPR. In other words, there may be much more to build upon in the international community than we have realized.

This book is only a broad and, therefore, relatively superficial treatment of the complex range of subjects it claims to cover. However, this breadth must be maintained to reflect a holistic perspective. Maintaining it is indeed the only way to transform IPR into TRR, so that equitable sharing and effective conservation of biological and cultural resources can be attained.

Chapter 1

Who visits communities, what are they seeking, and why?

Outsiders visit indigenous and local communities for many reasons and for various lengths of time. They may be seeking knowledge, renewable and nonrenewable natural resources (such as biogenetic resources and minerals), or goods made by local people. If so, they will approach local people directly or indirectly through a nongovernmental organization, government agency, research institution, or religious organization. Often they will simply search without notifying the local people. Information, resources, and goods may be of great importance to outsiders. They may be used to make money for a company or person, although they may also have wider benefits, such as improving health and nutrition or preventing hunger and famine by increasing food production. Some outsiders will be interested in protecting areas where indigenous peoples live or in managing the local resources.

Who visits indigenous communities?

Visitors may come to help local people. Many others, in pursuing their own interests, do not intend to either help or harm them. However, even without hostile intentions, they may be ignorant of the possible implications of their activities. Others may be planning to take advantage of local people and will probably wish to hide their true intentions. For several reasons, then, it is advantageous to find out who visitors are and why they have come.

Tourists

Tourists are usually short-term visitors traveling in groups, although people may come individually to enjoy leisure activities, like sightseeing, walking, sunbathing, and skiing. Mass tourism channels large numbers of people into certain locations where hotels and other facilities have been developed to accommodate them. But many people in industrial countries are dissatisfied with mass tourism and prefer to travel in smaller groups that come into closer contact with nature or local people.

Tourism can have a profound impact on indigenous cultures. The sale of handicrafts and art can be a useful source of income for many communities, but sometimes the demand leads to mass production, a deterioration in quality, and the production of imitations by outsiders who may deceive tourists about their source (see Blundell 1993 for Canadian examples). Tourists enjoy watching traditional performing arts and ceremonies, but because they are repackaged and commoditized as forms of entertainment for tourists, such performances can accelerate the erosion of a people's cultural identity. Ideally, **indigenous peoples** should have sufficient political autonomy either to ensure that they can control tourists in the way that the Kuna of Panama and the Awa Federation in Ecuador control researchers (see Chapter 14) or to manage tourism themselves (perhaps as part of a local development strategy including an element of **conservation**). Otherwise, they may be exploited as were the Toraja people in Sulawesi (see Box 1.1).

Indigenous peoples are likely to encounter tourism of various types: nature tourism, adventure tourism, and community-controlled tourism.

Nature tourism

Nature tourists travel to see wildlife and landscapes of outstanding natural beauty. The rich animal populations of the national parks and game reserves of East Africa attract tourists from all over the world in particularly large numbers. Unfortunately, the large influx of nature tourists can have a negative impact on the very **ecosystems** they want to enjoy.

In Kenya, the Maasai Mara Game Reserve is one of the most popular destinations in Africa (Loita Naimina Enkiyio Conservation Trust Company 1994). At peak season, revenue from tourist fees can be as high as $18 500 a day.[1] But tourism in the park has

---

[1] All monetary values are expressed in US currency except as indicated.

been allowed to develop with virtually no controls. Too many lodges have been built, too much firewood is being used, and no limits are placed on the use of tourist vehicles. Consequently, the park is being eroded and degraded. The local population is not benefiting from park revenues because the 25 percent of revenues collected at the gates that is supposed to be distributed to the local community actually amounts to no more than 5 percent because of weak administration.

To counteract the negative impact of popular tourism, the concept of ecotourism has emerged. This is a type of nature-based tourism that, in principle, is

- Based on relatively undisturbed natural areas;
- Nondamaging, nondegrading, and ecologically sustainable;
- A direct contributor to the continued protection and management of the natural areas visited;
- Subject to an adequate and appropriate management regime (Valentine 1993).

However, this description reflects an ideal rather than the usual situation. Environmentalists, especially in developed countries, hope that it can help create the necessary incentives for the protection of natural environments. The Costa Rican government, for example, hopes that ecotourism will allow the national parks to become

Box 1.1

Ethnic tourism in Tana Toraja

The Toraja people of Sulawesi, Indonesia, recently became a major tourist attraction because of their spectacular funeral ceremonies, effigy-filled burial cliffs, and elaborate architecture, which are becoming "international icons of a seductively exotic culture." As a consequence of this popularity, tourists complained that the Toraja communities were becoming too commercialized. In response, the local government designated some communities and burial cliffs "tourist objects," and brought in a team of consultants (none of whom were Toraja) to plan a zoning system. One proposal was for the preservation of traditional houses and graves in some zones, which would require the permission of hundreds or even thousands of people associated with each of them. Another was for a "tradition-free area," in which the Toraja would perform their rituals and dances of life and death in front of an audience of tourists, even though the mixing of such rituals is forbidden according to tradition. Through their inability to understand Toraja culture, the consultants provoked resentment and stirred up rivalry between sections of Toraja society. In 1987, several communities refused to accept tourists. However, they soon reopened to continue the trade in souvenirs on which they had become dependent. This example shows how the commercial exploitation of cultural property can become irreversible and can contribute to the loss of a people's autonomy.

Source: Adams (1990, pp. 31, 33)

self-financing (Burnie 1994). However, it has not been demonstrated that tourism, however well intentioned, can generate substantial revenues without an increasingly negative environmental impact. For example, a study of the impact of tourism in Belize reported that "despite some promising results, much ecotourism in Belize merely replicates the problems characteristic of mass-tourism: *foreign exchange leakage*, foreign ownership and environmental degradation" (Wheat 1994, p. 17).

Adventure tourism

Adventure tourists travel to the most isolated regions of the world to enjoy activities like trekking, rafting, wildlife viewing, and visiting "exotic" peoples. Popular destinations include the Himalayas, Southeast Asia, and East Africa.

Even though such alternatives to mass tourism are smaller in scale and claim to be lower in their social and environmental impacts, they may have a greater effect on local communities than mass tourism. This is because the local people may be less acculturated than those in less remote areas and, therefore, less accustomed to influxes of often very curious people who may not know how to interact with their "hosts" in a culturally sensitive manner. Such visitors may "penetrate further into the personal space of residents" than mass tourists (Butler, in Zurich 1992, p. 611). Also, even small numbers of visitors can be highly intrusive in terms of their numbers relative to local residents and their demands for food, water, and firewood. Furthermore, they can act as a catalyst for mass tourism.

Community-controlled tourism

According to one commentator (Swain 19, p. 37), if "an ethnic group has legally recognized power in determining local use of the national infrastructure (education, communication, transportation and health systems), and exploitation of *natural resources*, then it is likely to play a role in its own tourism development." The best option for indigenous peoples may be community-controlled tourism, which may be an independent initiative or one component of a development project funded wholly or partly by outside sources — for example, through an integrated conservation–development project (ICDP) (see Wells and Brandon 1993; Brown and Wyckoff-Baird 1992). ICDPs are community-based projects, both large- and small-scale, that are intended to ensure a balance between conservation and economic development. Examples with a tourism component include the Annapurna Conservation Area Project in Nepal, the Sian K'an Biosphere Reserve in Mexico, and Amboseli National Park in Kenya.

The Mayan organization, Toledo Ecotourism Association (TEA), in Belize accommodates tourists in settlements that local people build using local materials. According to one observer, "Tourists are looked after by the villagers themselves, ensuring that all the financial benefits are kept within the community. Special emphasis is put on preserving their ancient culture and fragile environment ... aware of the danger of their tourism business becoming a monoculture, the TEA members are also developing a firm agricultural base" (Wheat 1994, p. 19; see Young 1995 for examples in Australia and Canada).

The potential benefits for local communities from tourism within ICDPs may be substantial, especially if they are well endowed in terms of natural beauty and wildlife. If not and if they also lack good roads, hotels, and restaurants, the potential is much reduced. It is very important for conservation planners to understand that communities within ICDPs where there is tourism must be able to receive benefits directly and not through a bureaucracy. Zimbabwe has attempted to follow this path with the Communal Areas Management Programme (CAMPFIRE), which allows local communities to own wildlife in their areas and receive money from tourists who wish to take part in hunting expeditions and safaris (Wells 1992, p. 239).

Hobbyists

Some people come to indigenous communities to collect plants, animals, and minerals for personal interest. They might collect flowers, butterflies, attractive stones, or archeological objects. Hobbyists have no commercial interest in collecting and do so as a hobby or pastime.

Collectors

Some visitors may sell the items they collect to companies or other people — perhaps even in other countries. They may be supplying them to botanical gardens, universities with plant collection programs, or private and public research institutes. Some collections may be limited and not have a significant environmental impact; however, in some cases, collections may be so large as to deplete the **resources** being sought. The commercial side of the collecting operation may not be obvious to the community; in fact, the purpose of the collection may not be commercial at all, yet items acquired casually by travelers may later be sold to a gift shop. Indeed, often traders learn of desirable artifacts through tourists' acquisitions.

Extractors

Extractors remove natural resources such as minerals, timber, plants, and animals. These may be nonrenewable resources whose disappearance may radically alter the landscape or renewable resources whose removal may threaten local **biodiversity** and possibly local livelihoods. The scale of extraction can vary enormously because the "extractor" may be anyone from an individual to a multinational company supplying a global market. Some extractors may not be concerned that extraction of renewable resources is taking place at a level beyond the rate at which they are replaced naturally, leading to their depletion or even elimination.

Developers

"Developers" is a rather broad term that can include governments, corporations, or even nongovernmental organizations (NGOs) interested in developing an area (transforming it both economically and socially). Development entails a wide range of possible activities, such as road building, construction, and land colonization schemes, and may be large, medium, or small in scale. Its aims may be to generate wealth locally or to provide wealth for people in other parts of the country. Some development activities can be highly beneficial for local communities, but there may be environmental, economic, and social effects about which communities may not be fully informed.

It may be difficult even for development planners to predict all the consequences, both positive and negative. Planning such activities requires the collection of information about the area being "developed," perhaps as part of an environmental impact assessment or a social impact assessment. These are economic surveys that allow planners to predict as accurately as possible the positive and negative consequences arising from the implementation of a project. Conducting them may sometimes be a condition set by a bank or government that is supplying funds for a project.

Out of a growing realization of the need to use resources wisely for the benefit of present and future generations, new information about traditional cultures, including traditional knowledge as it relates to the environment and to natural resource management, can be of enormous interest to representatives of development planners. For example, in recent years, some governments interested in indigenous knowledge applied to environmental management have been supporting scientific research intended to find out more about such practices and to prove their effectiveness (Ross et al. 1994). NGOs are also extending their activities into learning more about indigenous agricultural practices.

Representatives of NGOs

Nongovernmental organizations may be local, national, or international, small or very large organizations. NGOs also vary in their activities, including development, conservation, and offering assistance, such as medical services, to local people. Some of them may be interested in setting up projects for environmental conservation or development. Others (or the same NGOs) may be interested in helping local people in emergencies like famines, floods, wars, and earthquakes. Some conduct research to influence governments and public opinion, and are sometimes called "pressure groups."

Conservation NGOs, like the World Wide Fund for Nature (WWF) and Conservation International, may be interested in protecting certain areas or particular *species*, and, in some cases, in helping indigenous peoples.

Other well-known international NGOs are Oxfam, Cultural Survival, and Rural Advancement Foundation International (RAFI). Representatives of NGOs can sometimes be useful sources of information for local people. However, NGOs are not usually community-based and are much less accountable to local communities than people's organizations (see Chapter 6).

Government representatives

National governments may send scientists, soldiers, health officials, medical teams, and managers of protected areas, such as national parks, into local communities. They may carry out inventories of the country's natural resources, monitor activities and events taking place on national territory, or secure national borders against people in neighbouring countries. Some of these people may be offering assistance to local communities.

Representatives of religious groups

Missionaries may wish to stay in a local community for a long period to convert local people to their religion or to provide services, such as health and education. Some religious groups stay with local people to learn their language and translate religious texts into it. Missionaries may wish simply to provide material benefits to communities. On the other hand, some religious groups are intent on imposing their spiritual and cultural values on local people and this can cause long-term social problems.

Representatives of corporations

Profit-seeking bodies may be interested in collecting biological material or other valuable resources or in developing an area in a variety of ways. Their aim is to make money from their visits, either directly by selling the things they collect, buy, or extract, or by using them to make other products, such as medicines, or indirectly by investigating the possibilities of commercial development. The profit may be paid to the owners of the business or shared among the people who invest money in the corporation.

Other bodies may not be motivated by the desire to make a profit. They may be charitable foundations that raise money to support activities intended to improve the welfare of people (see Chapter 6).

Researchers

Researchers, such as anthropologists, archeologists, and biologists, may be involved in scientific or cultural investigation. They may be individual academics or they may be employed by companies, governments, universities, botanical gardens, NGOs, or conservation organizations. Some of them may be interested in staying in the area for a long time. They are likely to be sympathetic to local community members but may not necessarily feel any obligation to assist local people by, for example, sharing the products of their work — data, film, artifacts, resources, and profits.

Photographers, journalists, and film crews

Photographers may be tourists who do not wish to sell their pictures or professional photographers, either freelance or employed by a newspaper, magazine, or agency. Journalists are looking for interesting subjects for a news report. Film crews may be filming for a television or movie company, or they may want to sell their film to such a company, or even to an advertising agency. The interest of such people may lie in the local community itself, in events taking place in the area, or in the natural environment. The community may be approached and requested to cooperate, though some photographers, journalists, and film crews may not think it necessary to ask permission or even to respect the privacy of local people (see Chapter 4).

What are they seeking?

Academic researchers, such as anthropologists and ethnobiologists, may be far more interested in the knowledge and culture of people living in an area than in its natural resources. Archeologists try to find ancient artifacts and human remains to learn more about past cultures, perhaps the ancestors of the current inhabitants. Others may be interested in past and present culture for commercial reasons. They may wish to trade in aspects of the cultural heritage of local people, such as manufactured objects, pictures, crafts, or video and audio recordings of songs and performances. Other visitors may be seeking to collect **biogenetic resources** (biological and genetic) or other resources used by traditional communities. Alternatively, they may be compiling information about the area, its people, or the local environment. Such visitors may be very interested in local knowledge. Those seeking biogenetic or mineral resources may not know how or where to find them and may seek local guidance.

Outsiders are not the only ones interested in collecting traditional knowledge and resources; indigenous peoples are also becoming more and more aware of the economic value of their knowledge and resources and are approaching outsiders and outside organizations to explore the possibility of commercially exploiting knowledge and resources on their own terms.

Local people may be asked to provide the following:

- Knowledge of current use, previous use, or potential use of plant and animal species, as well as soils and minerals;

- Knowledge of preparation, processing, or storage of useful species;

- Knowledge of formulations involving more than one ingredient;

- Knowledge of individual species (planting methods, care, selection criteria, etc.);

- Knowledge of ecosystem conservation (methods of protecting or preserving a resource that may be found to have commercial value, although not specifically used for that purpose or other practical purposes by the local community or the culture); and

- Classification systems of knowledge, such as traditional plant taxonomies.

Other categories of possible interest include

- Renewable biological resources (such as plants, animals, and other organisms) that originate (or originated) in indigenous lands and territories;
- Cultural landscapes, including sacred sites;
- Nonrenewable resources (such as rocks and minerals);
- Handicrafts, works of art, and performances;
- Traces of past cultures (such as ancient ruins, manufactured objects, human remains);
- Images perceived as "exotic," such as the appearance of indigenous people, their homes and villages, and the landscape; and
- Cultural *property* (culturally or spiritually significant material culture, such as important cultural artifacts, that may be deemed sacred and, therefore, not commoditizable by the local people).

Why is it being sought?

There are many reasons why knowledge and biological resources are sought — for scientific research with or without a commercial object, such as pure academic research, **biodiversity prospecting**, or agricultural research for commercial development. Resources and knowledge may be investigated to find ways to help conserve them for present and future generations.

Academic research

Research is systematic investigation aimed at the discovery of new facts and the development of new conclusions based on data collected in the field or laboratory. Individuals may carry out academic research to obtain educational qualifications or as part of their academic career at a university. Such research might entail observations of traditional communities and interviews using photos, drawings, or recordings, and may include the collection of plants, animals, soils, and other objects. Noncommercial research may be funded by the researcher, the university, the government, an NGO, a private foundation, or a corporation. In the latter cases, funding institutions receive copies of research data and reports. Funders can dictate the manner in which intellectual and biological materials collected as part of the research are disseminated and frequently claim ownership over final reports.

Biodiversity prospecting for industry

Biodiversity prospecting (sometimes called bioprospecting) is searching for commercially valuable genetic and biochemical resources, with particular reference to the pharmaceutical, biotechnological, and agricultural industries. With technical advances made over the past few decades, the ability of scientists to study the commercial potential of species has improved enormously. Consequently, many companies have initiated or expanded their study of the natural world, particularly the species-rich tropical forests. In carrying out this study, scientists often rely on the guidance of local communities who have sophisticated knowledge of local plants and animals.

Of the 119 drugs with known chemical structures that are still extracted from higher plants and used in industrial countries, over 74 percent were discovered by chemists attempting to identify the chemical substances in plants used in traditional medicine (Farnsworth 1988). Drug companies may investigate not only plants but also animals, insects, and microorganisms in search of material of use to Western medicine.

Botanic research

Botanic research grew as travelers brought home plants that were unknown or different from those growing at home. They were cultivated for ornamental or economic use or added to botanic gardens. The interest in classifying and comparing new species to those already known led to expansion of the science of taxonomy. Taxonomy is vital to botanic research because it provides a universal language by which plant material can be unambiguously described.

Botanic research has several functions based on a need to know and understand plant life. Researchers may wish to understand how plants thrive and reproduce, their biochemistry, and their interactions within a plant community. The goal of this research may be improving health care, increasing crop productivity, industrial development, or pure academic research that may later be used for commercial development. Researchers, therefore, may be visiting a community for various reasons, but their first priority is to catalogue and collect samples of plant material. They may be interested in only one type of tree or plant or in the biodiversity in a particular ecosystem. In any case, they will need the cooperation and knowledge of local people to guide and inform them in the limited time that they have to do their research.

Agricultural research

The aim of agricultural research is to improve the productivity, and resistance to pests and disease, of crop plants to help farmers improve their harvests. During the 1960s, new breeding techniques produced high-yielding strains of maize, rice, and wheat, and farmers were encouraged by the international agricultural research centres (IARCs) to use these varieties instead of traditional ones (see Chapter 2). At the time, this "Green Revolution" was regarded as a landmark in agricultural development; productivity was increased considerably in some areas by planting high-yielding varieties (HYVs) in monocultures on large areas of land. Previously, this land had been used for traditional agriculture, based on planting a diverse range of crops and crop varieties (***landraces***).

The new HYVs require a large input in terms of energy, water, expensive agrochemicals (fertilizers and pesticides), and equipment to maintain their productivity, yet they are still susceptible to disease and pests. The productivity gains of the 1960s and 1970s did not continue into the 1980s and 1990s, and today we recognize that the Green Revolution had many negative economic, social, and environmental effects, including the loss of local varieties, increasing landlessness, unemployment, debt, growing inequalities of income, and degraded soils.

Since the 1980s, a greater share of agricultural research, especially in developed countries, is commercially supported. Companies are developing **biotechnology**, such as **genetic engineering**, to breed new crop varieties that, again, threaten to undermine the diversity of traditional crops.

Agricultural research is dependent on new material from areas where traditional farming practices persist because of the high diversity of crop varieties and environmental adaptations. Although some researchers have become interested in looking at methods of farming and crop improvement carried out by indigenous communities and traditional farmers and in working in collaboration with indigenous groups, most researchers still do not appreciate the effectiveness of traditional agriculture.

Conservation of biogenetic resources

Many biogenetic resources are being rapidly depleted because of irresponsible development and overexploitation. Sometimes inappropriate government policies allow corporations relatively unlimited access to local resources, instead of requiring them to extract material at a sustainable level. Traditional farming techniques — intercropping and developing crops that thrive in a particular location — have maintained the productivity of land over many generations. Unfortunately, some of these techniques are disappearing as large expanses of land are planted instead in cash crops (like sugarcane, bananas, and coffee) for export. This trend has been stimulated by the adoption of HYVs and by the growth in export of agricultural products by indebted countries in accordance with the instructions of the lender governments and multilateral development banks (such as the World Bank and the Inter-American Development Bank).

Many NGOs and even some governments and intergovernmental institutions have become more interested in traditional agricultural practices for various reasons, such as preventing the erosion of crop genetic diversity and solving other problems associated with the spread of monocultures. There are two main types of conservation: in situ conservation and ex situ conservation.

In situ conservation is the maintenance of a species of plant or animal as part of a living ecosystem. One function of protected places is to preserve plant or animal species in their natural habitat so that they may continue to thrive without disturbance.

Indigenous peoples and local communities have an important role to play in conservation. Where farmers have bred crop varieties that are suited to their land and climate, especially under adverse conditions, encouraging those farmers to continue growing and developing specialized crops is the kind of in situ conservation that is essential if growing populations of the world are going to be fed. Ironically, in situ conservation is also important to the seed companies, even though the replacement of landraces by their modern varieties is largely responsible for the erosion of the genetic diversity of traditional crops.

The principle of in situ conservation is upheld in Article 8 of the CBD, especially paragraph j, which directs that the practice should "respect, preserve and maintain knowledge, innovations and practices of indigenous and local communities embodying traditional lifestyles relevant for the conservation and sustainable use of biological diversity" (see Chapter 10).

Ex situ conservation is the maintenance of species of plants or animals away from their place of origin to save them from extinction or because they have a useful trait that researchers want to study. The conservation place may be a research institute, a germplasm bank, a zoo, or a botanic garden. The species may be kept in the country of origin or abroad, but the intention is to protect and conserve them. In the future, they may be reintroduced to their source in response to circumstances like natural disasters and wars that threaten biological diversity. For example, the International Centre for Tropical Agriculture (see Box 2.1), which keeps seed banks of the main crop varieties grown in Rwanda, plans to distribute seeds to Rwandan farmers to replace stocks lost because of war.

Ex situ conservation need not require resources to be kept in an international institution far from the communities where they occur naturally. For example, in Ethiopia the Biodiversity Institute is working closely with farmers to save indigenous crops (see Box 1.2).

Conservation of landscapes

When the United Nations list of national parks and equivalent reserves was first compiled, the main priority was conservation of wildlife and ecosystems. The intention in creating protected areas was to save them for future generations to enjoy, but it is now recognized that many of these places will change or even be impoverished if there is not a continuation of the patterns of use and occupation that have been taking place for hundreds of years. Consequently, the original designation "protected area" has been widened to include human occupation and activities wherever these are compatible with conservation.

However, this does not necessarily result in sustainable land use. In Kenya, the Maasai Mara Park has become so overused by tourists that the local council is seeking to extend the reserved area into the adjacent lands of the Loita Maasai. To do so would disrupt not only a community following a way of life that helps sustain the semi-arid environment but would also desecrate their sacred places (see Box 1.3). Any extension of tourist activities into the lands of the Loita Maasai would have to be carried out with extreme caution and sensitivity.

Box 1.2

The Biodiversity Institute

The Biodiversity Institute (formerly called the Plant Genetic Resources Centre) in Ethiopia provides farmers with germplasm to further their experimentation in crop development. Farmers' landraces are preserved in the **gene** bank and are accessible to them. Community seed production, marketing, and distribution can play a vital part in the multiplication of such varieties using traditional farmer networks for seed trials and selections.

On-farm landrace conservation and enhancement

Since 1988, farmers, scientists, and extension workers have been involved in a program of genetic resource conservation in northeastern Shewa and southeastern Walo, with support from the Unitarian Service Committee of Canada. The aim of the project is to help farmers maintain crop diversity by maintaining cultivars and also by improving their genetic performance. Materials previously collected from surrounding areas and regions are given to farmers to plant and to carry out simple forms of mass selection to improve their characteristics. Farmers are assisted by breeders, and other scientists have access to the farmers' fields to carry out research. Most of the farmers are women and were selected through farmer cooperatives.

Maintaining elite indigenous landrace selection on peasant farms

The Biodiversity Institute, in conjunction with Debre Zeit Research Centre of the Alemaya University of Agriculture, is developing a program to maintain elite indigenous wheat germplasm collected by the Biodiversity Institute over the last 7 years. Various genetic lines are selected for their adaptation to specific environmental conditions, such as stress. After yield testing, two or more superior lines are chosen for further multiplication and distribution to farmers. The farmers multiply and use the stock best suited to their conditions. The Biodiversity Institute maintains representative samples for long-term storage at their gene bank. This enables farmers to experiment with the elite landrace varieties without the threat of losing the old indigenous populations.

At the national level, varieties adapted from local landraces can be released to ensure that farmers have a long-term choice of seeds and can fall back on improved versions of adapted local varieties when high-risk crops fail. This is particularly relevant in areas with marginal growing conditions or extremes of environment, where improved varieties fail to meet the requirements of farmers.

Field gene banks for drought-prone areas

A field gene bank is being developed in collaboration with the Alemaya University of Agriculture at Dire Dawa in eastern Ethiopia, which will test famine crops and involve farming communities in maintaining and evaluating seed. This program is essential for future food production in Ethiopia with its periodic severe droughts, especially as the war and famine in the country in the 1980s gravely damaged the agricultural infrastructure with families forced to eat seed normally saved for the next planting season. In Ethiopia, several wild plants, known as "famine crops," have the potential of surviving droughts where conventional crops perish. The Biodiversity Institute is carrying out experiments on yeheb (*Cordaeuxia edulis*), a drought-resistant perennial bush that grows in the Ogaden region. Its seeds are used by nomads as a highly nutritious source of food.

Source: Worede and Mekbib (1993)

Box 1.3

Forest of the lost child, Naimina Enkiyio, Loita Hills, Narok County, Kenya

One of the last indigenous forests in East Africa is located in the remote Loita Hills. It is protected and venerated by the Loita Maasai who use the forest for their traditional ceremonies and as a source of medicinal plants and herbs.

The Loita Maasai are seminomadic pastoralists who continue to follow their traditional lifestyle, maintaining strong clan and age-group affiliations. There are about 17 000 members of this Maasai subgroup. They hold their land according to **customary law** with no individual rights of ownership. Their efforts to remain independent have been supported by Dutch missionaries who created the Ilkerin Loita Integral Development Project, through which the Maasai received agricultural and community training. Today, the project is managed independently by a board of Maasai elders. Funds are augmented by a Dutch NGO, but more than 50 percent is internally generated.

The lifestyle of the Loita Maasai is threatened because of mismanagement and overexploitation of the nearby Maasai Mara reserve. Although their land is held under customary law, legal title to the Loita Hills is held by Narok County Council in trust for the Maasai, which wants to turn Naimina Enkiyio forest into a nature reserve to attract tourists. Such a designation would exclude the Loita Maasai from their ancestral land, which is not only of great cultural importance to them but provides essential dry-season grazing.

The Loita Maasai are challenging Narok County Council's interpretation of the *Trust Land Act* and are suing them to prevent the Kenyan Minister for Local Government from approving the plan for Naimina Enkiyio. They see their action as a test of Article 8j of the CBD (see above) that has been signed by Kenya.

Source: Loita Naimina Enkiyio Conservation Trust Company (1994)

National parks

According to the United Nations' list (IUCN 1994), national parks are

> Protected areas managed mainly for ecosystem conservation and recreation, ... [specifically] natural areas of land and/or sea, designated to (a) protect the ecological integrity of one or more ecosystems for this a future generations, (b) exclude exploitation or occupation inimical to the purposes of designation of the area and (c) provide a foundation for spiritual, scientific, recreational and visitor opportunities, all of which must be environmentally and culturally compatible.

The first national parks were created in the United States to protect the most spectacular areas of what was perceived by incomers to be wilderness from human interference (Yellowstone National Park was established in 1872). Many countries have followed this concept of preservation and exclusion by working to save areas of outstanding natural beauty, high diversity, or large wildlife populations by following policies that bar people from moving into the protected area or excluding people who may have been living there already.

Box 1.4

The Manu Biosphere Reserve

Although international organizations may believe that they are working to provide protected areas that will also enhance the lives of indigenous peoples, insufficient communication with local communities may have the opposite effect. Unfortunately, damage is most likely to become apparent only after the fact. "Learning by experience" has been the rule in many cases.

The Manu Biosphere Reserve is the largest national park in the world. The Manu National Park was established by the Peruvian government in 1973 and, in 1977, the reserve area was extended when it became an official part of Unesco's biosphere reserve system. In 1986, Manu National Park was declared a world heritage site (see Chapter 10) because of its outstanding natural value. The reserve includes the national park, along with a "reserved zone" and a "cultural zone" as buffers in which traditional subsistence activities by the indigenous population are allowed.

Much effort has been expended by the Peruvian government and international NGOs, such as the WWF, to conserve the area within the Manu reserve, because it is perceived as a unique example of the upper Amazonian ecosystem, which has survived because of its inaccessibility. However, to the local populations the goals of the conservators are suspect because of the "museum mentality" inherent in them (the intention has been to maintain the status quo, disregarding the need for continuing evolution).

It was inevitable that isolated indigenous groups should come into contact with visitors from outside and have their perceptions of life changed by this contact. Repeatedly, contact between the indigenous peoples of the area and groups supposedly working for their interests have been marred by the complete failure of those groups to discover what the indigenous people believe would be in their best interests.

Introduction of the indigenous people to Western culture through contact with missionaries and park guards has undermined indigenous cultures. Health programs in the area have also failed to meet the needs of the people and have undermined their traditional medical practices. Contact with visitors brings disease against which isolated people have little immunity, but the imposition of Western medical practices to fight Western disease has severely disrupted communities by marginalizing and devaluing the shamans and their traditional medicine.

Now, the indigenous peoples are fighting back, working through groups such as Coordinadora de Organizaciones Indigenas de la Cuenca Amazónica (COICA) and the Native Federation of the River Madre de Dios and Affluents (FENAMAD). FENAMAD is demanding that the whole national park be declared traditional indigenous territory to centralize and strengthen indigenous control. They want access to business and commerce for people living in the park. FENAMAD has taken control of the health of the local people through the FENAMAD Health Project, which seeks to promote traditional medicine using only those aspects of Western medicine that complement traditional practice, such as immunization programs. COICA has declared that "the park is not a reality like a people, the park is like a law, changeable, dependent, violable" and has called for the government to recognize and rebuild ethnic territories, because the best protection for a territory is for the indigenous peoples to administer it according to their own culture.

International NGOs should learn from the reactions of the indigenous people living in the Manu reserve so that they can apply the knowledge in the preservation of other areas of outstanding natural value using the sustainable methods that have shaped those ecosystems.

Source: Gradwohl and Greenberg (1988), COICA (1990), A. Gray, Oxford, UK, 1993 (personal communication)

Buffer zones

Since the 1980s when the concept was introduced as part of Unesco's Man and the Biosphere Programme, the most popular means of harmonizing human activity with wildlife conservation has been by establishing a buffer zone. Buffer zones are areas around a protected area, such as a national park, in which only certain activities are allowed. They help preserve the plant and animal life living in a protected area from damage by outside activities, such as large-scale agriculture or settlement by migrants.

Activities allowed within buffer zones are traditional agriculture, for example, or the infrastructure for a small ecotourism industry. These are considered to be in harmony with the protection of the park. However, the philosophy guiding the management of protected areas and buffer zones may create conflicts, especially if governments and NGOs involved with designating and administering them are not sufficiently sensitive to the concerns of the local people (see Box 1.4). In a national park or buffer zone, the local people are likely to encounter several categories of visitor, whose length of stay will vary along with their social and economic impact.

Governments and NGOs involved in the conservation of landscapes may be unaware that such landscapes may have been transformed, over generations, by the activities of local people and are, therefore, not wild landscapes but cultural landscapes (see Chapter 10). Conservationists must be aware that they are not managing wildernesses but a kind of cultural property to which the local people who have inhabited the area for generations have a prior legitimate claim.

Conclusions

Members of local communities must know the identity of their visitors. Interactions with visitors can be highly beneficial. Indigenous people may be able to gain useful information, broaden their knowledge through cultural exchanges, and collaborate in conservation, research, and development projects that could provide monetary, social, and political benefits.

On the other hand, communities may be faced with visitors who intend to take advantage of them and who may use dishonest means to extract information and resources. The following sections of this book explain how local communities can obtain maximum benefit from such interactions and show how they can exercise their rights not to collaborate if they so desire.

Chapter 2

What happens to traditional knowledge and resources?

A large quantity of goods, resources, and knowledge flow from traditional communities. In this chapter, we discuss where plant and human genetic material, knowledge, and articles like works of art are kept for conservation, scientific, and other purposes or, in some cases, traded commercially.

Knowledge, biological resources, manufactured goods, works of art, and even human remains can be sought-after items to be collected, stored, and sometimes bought and sold. Transactions involving these items can take place at great distances from their source, and it can be difficult, or even impossible, to determine their final destination once they have left the source community.

Conservation centres for biogenetic resources

Human, animal, and plant material is needed for research. Researchers must examine and analyze the material they collect and preserve it for posterity. Biological resources (perhaps accompanied by information about them) may be conserved at the site of origin or in another place or country. Ex situ conservation centres may be botanic gardens, museums, seed or gene banks, or laboratories owned by governments, intergovernmental agencies, or corporations.

Plant genetic material

Collection and storage of plant genetic material has been taking place for centuries, as the result of curiosity, for taxonomic research, or for commercial purposes as the global market for *germplasm* has grown. The oldest and the most numerous collections are held in industrialized countries (*the North*). Most of the germplasm in these collections has come from the greatest centres of genetic diversity, which are mainly within the tropics (*the South*) (Kloppenburg 1988a,b; Juma 1989).

Botanic gardens

There are at least 1550 botanic gardens in the world, of which about 800 are actively involved in plant conservation, ensuring that endangered or disappearing plant species do not become extinct. To coordinate their work, botanists working for these gardens share their knowledge through organizations such as the Botanic Gardens Conservation International (BGCI). BGCI sends out reports and information to all its members, as well as operating an exchange of plant species. Most major botanic gardens increasingly collaborate with other gardens throughout the world. For example, the Royal Botanic Gardens (RBG) at Kew, England, is working with the Limbe Botanic Gardens in Cameroon to encourage the conservation of the natural resources of Mount Cameroon by the local population.

Agricultural research centres

Agricultural research centres hold collections of crop germplasm for research and breeding of improved varieties and also for conservation. Conservation has been a minor facet of their work, but the failure of the Green Revolution varieties to maintain their vigour and diminishing pest resistance make it necessary to maintain a plentiful supply of fresh genetic material from which to develop replacements. This can be drawn from landraces held either in collections or on farms. The Consultative Group on International Agricultural Research (CGIAR) is the major international association for the improvement and maintenance of world food-crop productivity. CGIAR's 16 member organizations, or IARCs (see Box 2.1), hold more than 500 000 accessions, which are held "in trust for the world community" (Diversity 1994; Seedling 1994), including up to 40 percent of all unique samples of major food crops held by gene banks worldwide. The IARCs may work within a country in conjunction with national agricultural research centres, or independently. The emphasis on the CGIAR system's collections being held "in trust" is important because it prevents them from becoming absorbed into national collections or owned by national governments or countries in which they are located.

One of the primary centres is the International Plant Genetic Resources Institute (IPGRI) based in Rome, whose objectives are as follows:

- Strengthening national programs;

- Contributing to international collaboration in the conservation and use of **plant genetic resources**;

- Improving strategies and technologies for conservation of plant genetic resources;

- Providing an international information service.

Plant material collected by researchers may be preserved in seed banks, field gene banks, herbariums, or as part of in vitro collections (see below). These may belong to an institution such as a botanic garden, a museum, or a company's seed bank. For example, herbariums may be found associated with universities or museums, and in vitro collections may be held in laboratories by biotechnology companies.

Seed banks are collections of seeds, stored in some central location. Seeds cannot be stored indefinitely because they lose viability after a certain period. Loss of viability varies according to seed type, but in general only **orthodox seed** is suitable for this type of collection.

Field gene banks are of use for collecting species with **recalcitrant seed**, especially those with commercial potential for agricultural use or forestry. Field gene banks are more expensive to maintain and far less efficient in terms of space than seed banks because species are conserved by planting them under carefully controlled conditions to allow seed and plant tissue to be harvested for reuse and for breeding trials. Because the plant is growing and flowering, great care must be taken to isolate the specimens from cross-fertilization with wild varieties; this further extends the area needed for planting. To protect the widest genetic diversity possible, many specimens of different varieties are needed.

In vitro storage of germplasm is the preserving of living plant tissue under laboratory conditions. Samples are stored at low temperatures to inhibit growth, but they do not remain viable over long periods and thus need to be renewed and recultured. In vitro storage is intensive and expensive and requires skilled personnel, making this method less popular than others.

Box 2.1

Members of the Consultative Group on International Agricultural Research

- **Center for International Forestry Research** (CIFOR), Indonesia; founded 1992 — Focuses on conserving and improving productivity of tropical forest ecosystems.
- **International Center for Tropical Agriculture** (CIAT), Colombia; founded 1967 — Focuses on germplasm development (global mandate for beans, cassava, forage crops, and regional mandate for rice) and on resource management research in Latin America and the Caribbean (with research in land use, hillsides, forest margins, savannah).
- **International Centre for Maize and Wheat Improvement** (CIMMYT), Mexico; founded 1966 — Focuses on crop improvement (with research on maize, wheat, barley, and triticale).
- **International Potato Center** (CIP), Peru; founded 1970 — Focuses on potato and sweet potato improvement (with research on potato and sweet potato).
- **International Center for Agricultural Research in Dry Areas** (ICARDA), Syria; founded 1975 — Focuses on improving farming systems in North Africa and West Asia (with research on wheat, barley, chickpea, lentils, pasture legumes, and small ruminants).
- **International Center for Research in Agroforestry** (ICRAF), Kenya; founded 1977 — Focuses on mitigating tropical deforestation and land depletion and alleviating rural poverty through improved agroforestry systems.
- **International Center of Living Aquatic Resources Management** (ICLARM), Philippines; founded 1977 — Focuses on improving production and management of aquatic resources in developing countries.
- **International Crops Research Institute for the Semi-Arid Tropics** (ICRISAT), India; founded 1972 — Focuses on crop improvement and cropping systems (with research on sorghum, millet, chickpeas, pigeon peas, and groundnuts).
- **International Food Policy Research Institute** (IFPRI), USA; founded 1975 — Focuses on identifying and analyzing policies for meeting food needs of developing countries, particularly the poorer groups within these countries (with research on ways to achieve sustainable food production and land use, improve food consumption and income levels of the poor, enhance the links between agriculture and other sectors of the economy, and improve trade and macroeconomic conditions).
- **International Institute of Tropical Agriculture** (IITA), Nigeria; founded 1967 — Focuses on crop improvement and land management in the humid and subhumid tropics and on farming systems (with research on maize, cassava, cowpeas, plantain, soybeans, rice, and yams).
- **International Irrigation Management Institute** (IIMI), Sri Lanka; founded 1984 — Focuses on improving and sustaining the performance of irrigation systems through better management.
- **International Livestock Research Institute** (ILRI), Kenya and Ethiopia; founded 1995 — Focuses on livestock production, disease control, and forage crops.
- **International Plant Genetic Resources Institute** (IPGRI), Italy; founded 1974 — Focuses on conserving gene pools of current and potential food and forage crops (with research in plant genetic resources).
- **International Rice Research Institute** (IRRI), Philippines; founded 1960 — Focuses on global rice improvement in major rice environments: irrigated, rainfed lowlands, uplands, deep water, and tidal wetlands.
- **International Service for National Agricultural Research** (ISNAR), Netherlands; founded 1979 — Focuses on strengthening national agricultural research systems through improvement in their policy planning, organization, and management.
- **West Africa Rice Development Association** (WARDA), Côte d'Ivoire; founded 1970 — Focuses on improving rice varieties and production methods among smallholder farm families in the upland–inland swamp continuum, the Sahel, and mangrove swamp environments.

Source: Ayad (1994), CGIAR (1995)

Herbariums

Dried samples of plants and trees are kept in herbariums for reference, not for propagation or experimentation purposes. Botanic gardens and universities may maintain a herbarium along with other long-term record storage facilities. If well organized according to internationally accepted rules, herbariums can be vitally important in recording the flora of the world. Establishing community-owned and controlled herbariums can also be an important means of informing and supporting peoples' knowledge about their local flora and its uses (see Box 2.5).

A carefully tended herbarium will provide a record of the flora of a locality that may last hundreds of years. Therefore, it is worth ensuring that the collection is made correctly from the outset according to well-established methods. Advice and help in setting up a herbarium can be obtained from national botanic gardens.

Human genetic material

Human cells can be preserved, stored, and even cultivated in vitro in the form of **cell lines.** Cell lines can be stored indefinitely at low temperatures and are capable of reproducing under artificial conditions in a laboratory to provide a constant supply of the full genetic code of the donor organism. Alternatively, human **DNA** from collected human material, such as blood, bones, hair roots, or cheek cell samples can be reproduced indefinitely using **polymerase chain reaction** (PCR) technology, which can be performed in a laboratory. (The process patent for PCR technology is owned by Hoffman La-Roche; see Appendix 1 for further information.) This technique is less expensive than developing cell lines but does not preserve the genetic code in its entirety.

Twenty-six institutions are recognized under the Budapest Treaty on the International Recognition of the Deposit of Micro-organisms for the Purpose of Patent Procedure (administered by the World Intellectual Property Organization (WIPO); see Box 8.1) as depositories of biological material for the purpose of dealing with patent applications. The largest of these is the American Type Culture Collection (ATCC) in the United States, a private nonprofit corporation, where at least three cell lines originating from indigenous people have been stored in connection with patent applications (see Box 2.2). Such deposits are not freely available, even to the donor, until a patent is granted. Human biological material is considered to be patentable in the United States because when it is removed from a human body it is considered by the Patents and Trademarks Office to be nothing more than a chemical, or what patent lawyers sometimes call "a composition of matter."

Work on the Human **Genome** Diversity Project is likely to increase markedly the collection and storage of blood, hair root, and cheek cell samples from members of targeted indigenous groups. The planners of this project appear to take the view that the ex situ conservation of DNA from isolated indigenous groups is necessary because of their "endangered" status. The project itself, as well as the whole idea of patenting human cells and **genes**, has been opposed strongly by indigenous peoples (see Appendix 1).

Box 2.2

Three patent claims based on the cells of indigenous people

The Guaymi patent claim

This claim resulted from a project carried out by the Centers for Disease Control (CDC) of the United States Department of Health and Human Services and the National Institutes of Health (NIH) in collaboration with Panamanian scientists. The project is an investigation of the rare human T-cell lymphotrophic **viruses** (HTLV), one of which (type II) is known to be the causative agent of adult T-cell leukemia and a neurologic disease. For some reason, infection with HTLV type II is common among the Guaymi as well as other Amerindian peoples in North and South America, who have also donated samples.

According to Isidro Acosta, president of the General Congress of the Ngobe-Bugle (Guaymi), "Doctors came to the communities of Pandilla in small groups and started to collect indigenous blood, pretending that the indigenous people were suffering from a mortal disease and that the blood study was necessary to investigate the malformation or type of disease they suffered. Participants were given a small pill to compensate for the loss of blood" (Acosta 1994, p. 48).

One of three local women suffering from leukemia was found to have an unusual capacity to resist the disease. A T-cell line infected with HTLV-II was developed in the United States from blood donated in 1990, and a patent application was filed by the NIH later that year, first in the United States and later worldwide under the Patent Cooperation Treaty (an international agreement that makes it possible for a single patent application to be filed in several countries in which patent protection is desired).

The abstract claimed that this was "the first isolation of HTLV-II from a defined nonintravenous drug using population." The CDC claims that the purpose was to foster greater interest in HTLV-II research and to make the cell line available to researchers. Nevertheless, it would appear that the application was filed without notifying the woman, any other Guaymi person, the project's Panamanian collaborators, or the Panamanian government, and without consideration of the cultural and religious sensibilities of the Guaymi people. Although the CDC claims that the donor gave her "oral informed consent" (Bangs 1993/94), it appears unlikely that she was made aware of the possibility of a patent application or of the implications. Condemnation came from several quarters, including RAFI, which had discovered the patent application, as well as the World Council of Indigenous Peoples and the General Congress of the Ngobe-Bugle. Isidro Acosta wrote to the US Secretary of Commerce asking that the application be withdrawn and to the Patents and Trademarks Office asking it to reject the application. He also denounced the patent claim at the GATT Secretariat and at a meeting of the Intergovernmental Committee on the CBD, saying that making "living cells ... patented private property ... is against all Guaymi traditions and laws." Less than a month later the patent application was withdrawn, allegedly because of the high cost of pursuing a patent claim.

It seems more likely that the real reason the claim was abandoned was the international outcry. As far as Acosta is concerned, the matter is still not closed. He is demanding that the cell line be removed from the ATCC and repatriated. However, according to the Budapest Treaty, the sample must be kept for 30 years.

Box 2.2 concluded

The Hagahai of Papua New Guinea patent claim

This patent application is for a T-cell line developed from a blood sample that came from a member of the Hagahai, a group of 260 hunter-cultivators first contacted by government and missionary workers in 1984. A cell line from a donor's blood was cultured and infected with a local variant of HTLV-I, making it potentially useful in the development of vaccines and diagnostic assays for the screening and treatment of Melanesian people infected with this virus. After it was deposited at the ATCC, patent applications were filed by the NIH. In 1995 a US patent was granted in spite of objections from the Papua New Guinea government.

The Solomon Islands patent claim

This application is similar to the previous one. This time the donors were a woman with a history of hepatitis contracted through a blood transfusion and a man with an enlarged liver and spleen (hepatosplenomegaly). The T-cell line, which was also deposited at the ATCC, contains a local HTLV-I viral strain. Again the patent applicant is the NIH, and two of the inventors are also named in the application. They claim that the two Solomon Islanders gave their informed consent. Nevertheless, the Government of the Solomon Islands has asked the United States government to withdraw the application.

Further information on these patent applications may be obtained from RAFI (see Resource Guide, Canada).

The commercial sector

Traditional knowledge, products, and resources, even genetic material extracted from a donor organism, can become tradable goods. These may be bought and sold in markets or transferred directly to the purchaser, often by prior agreement.

Markets

Markets are a temporary destination of manufactured products, foodstuffs, and biogenetic resources, which may be bought and sold to anybody prepared to pay for them. Foods and biogenetic resources may be traded in their raw state or processed, perhaps several times over. Each time they are processed and the further they are taken from their source, value is added so that they become more expensive. Therefore, the providers of raw materials selling locally receive a small proportion of the price obtained by the seller of the finished article, especially when they are bought and sold many times during their journey from source to final purchaser. Gift shop owners may buy crafts or textiles from local markets very cheaply to sell them, often at inflated prices, in specialist shops in other countries. In many countries, companies that sell natural remedies and herbal preparations also purchase their raw materials in markets. However, companies that produce Western medicines usually buy them directly from professional collectors.

Commercial collections

Plant collections are the most obvious form by which knowledge and biological resources are supplied to those with commercial interests. Those doing the collecting may be individuals who collect for immediate payment, university-based plant-collection programs, botanical gardens supplementing their field-research budgets, private for-profit **brokers**, or private and public research institutes based in developing countries.

Traditional knowledge is an important element in the commercialization of natural products, because it consists of a wealth of information on how these products could be commercialized. Currently, traditional knowledge is supplied to commercial interests through databases, academic publications, or field collections.

Museums, art galleries, and the trade in works of art

Certain objects play an important part in reinforcing a people's cultural identity and have deep religious significance. Nevertheless, these kinds of objects may be appropriated by museums, art galleries, and individuals, and bought and sold, sometimes at high prices, in the international art market. Occasionally they are stolen from indigenous groups or illegally smuggled out of countries. Sometimes individuals are forced, by poverty, to break customary law forbidding the sale of such objects to outsiders. Even then, the sellers will obtain only a fraction of the price paid by a museum, gallery, or private collector. The ethnic art market is a highly lucrative sector, with private collectors paying huge sums of money for individual items valued for the skill and artistry of the manufacturer, their antiquity, or their perceived exotic and "primitive" characteristics.

Museums may display a large range of objects of interest to the public. These may include objects produced by people who lived in the past, but they may also display items manufactured by present-day peoples, including sacred and secret objects. Art galleries display works of art and crafts. They may be large and own several semipermanent displays or small privately owned galleries offering specialist collections, such as textiles or carvings acquired from certain parts of the world. Sacred objects of indigenous peoples have been returned on occasion, a recent example being the sacred weavings of the people of Coroma, Bolivia (see Chapter 10).

Museums, universities, and human remains

Human remains that are not in marked graves are often considered by law to have been abandoned and no longer the cultural property of the descendants of the people who were buried. Instead they become the property of the state, the landowner, or the institution sponsoring the excavation. In some countries, large quantities of skeletal remains have been collected and stored over the years by state or private museums and universities and displayed for public view.

Many of these are not ancient bones found by archeologists; for example, the 25 northern Cheyenne men, women, and children whose remains were returned to their tribe in 1993 by the Smithsonian Institution in Washington were killed during an unsuccessful revolt against the US army in 1879. Army doctors had collected their bodies to examine human skeletal diversity and the effects of modern weapons (National Geographic 1994).

Indigenous peoples are now actively contesting the right of these institutions to own remains of past members of tribes. Until recently, the Smithsonian Institution possessed the remains of 18 000 indigenous people, but the remains of 2000 people have been returned to their descendants in response to demands of indigenous peoples, supported by the 1990 *Native American Grave Protection and Repatriation Act*.

For well over a century, the British Museum has been a major collector of artifacts and human remains from around the world. Its policy is subject to a law that forbids the museum from transferring ownership of objects that it possesses. According to the Museum's Director (R. Anderson, personal communication, 1994), "To 'return' objects would be to break the law." However, the museum does not display human remains of peoples whose descendants, the museum believes, would object to them doing so.

Libraries, archives, and electronic databases

Information about the cultural and biogenetic resources of indigenous peoples discovered by scientists, researchers, and other writers, such as journalists, may be published in books or recorded on audio- or videotape, or as photographs. These may be stored in libraries, archives, or electronic databases. The development of the electronic mail network has opened up a worldwide communication system. Users communicate and have access to information via systems such as the Internet, which offers coverage direct to most continents and via satellite to Africa and the Pacific. Through Internet, users can gain access to universities, library catalogues, databases, and specialist networks such as GreenNet, a global computer communications network for environment, peace, human rights, and development issues. GreenNet, based in the United Kingdom, is part of the Association for Progressive Communications, which has access to more than 20 000 groups and individuals.

Although databases can be protected under copyright law, and users may have to pay for the right to inspect them, it is difficult for the original suppliers of information in databases to prevent data from entering the **public domain** and to control use of such information. One very large database of ethnobotanical information is NAPRALERT, located at the University of Illinois at Chicago, from which information is supplied to companies for a fee.

There has been a proliferation in the amount of indigenous knowledge being stored and disseminated. Usually, access to information is not conditional upon recognition of the IPR of indigenous peoples. However, the case studies described below (Boxes 2.3 and 2.4) are examples of attempts to store traditional knowledge and

> Box 2.3
>
>
>
> ## The indigenous knowledge resource centres
>
> A growing network of indigenous knowledge resource centres is emerging to collect, record, and disseminate traditional knowledge, such as the Center for Indigenous Knowledge for Agriculture and Rural Development (CIKARD) in Iowa, USA, the Centre for International Research and Advisory Networks (CIRAN) in the Netherlands, and the Leiden Ethnosystems and Development Programme (LEAD), also in the Netherlands. CIKARD, for example, "focuses on understanding, recording, preserving, and using the indigenous knowledge of farmers and rural people around the globe, and on making this knowledge available to development professionals and scientists" (Warren (Director of CIKARD) 1990, p. 1). The network now consists of four global centres, two regional centres, and 18 national centres in developing countries. It has a newsletter called *Indigenous Knowledge and Development Monitor*, organizes international conferences, and publishes regional and national databases of indigenous knowledge research. The databases are intended to contribute to sustainable development and to education, while enhancing the status of traditional knowledge.
>
> According to an editorial in the newsletter (vol. 1(3), p. 1), traditional knowledge "should be included, alongside the more usual scientific knowledge, as part of national and international discussions and the strengthening of intellectual capacity."
>
> The prevailing view of the network is that there should be a free flow of information and that this will be of benefit to developing countries and local communities. However, there is no stated policy regarding IPR or TRR. Although indigenous peoples may indeed benefit from increased respect for their knowledge, and from access to new knowledge, their own intellectual contributions to the databases can be freely exploited for commercial purposes by companies with no obligation to compensate communities.
>
> For further information, contact CIRAN/Nuffic (see Resource Guide, Netherlands).

information about indigenous peoples while either trying to enhance the status of traditional knowledge or respect the desire of indigenous peoples to restrict culturally sensitive information.

Control of collections, herbariums, museums, and databases by the community is the best way to ensure that the main beneficiaries are local people and that visitors' access is restricted (see Box 2.5). These systems can be used not only to educate local people, but also to educate visitors so that they are more aware of the rich cultural and intellectual heritage of local people and of the potential economic and scientific benefits of collaborating with them on a more equitable basis.

In Canada, the Dene Nation has a library/archive that includes the following:

— An audiovisual oral history collection in the Dene language;

— A photograph collection;

Box 2.4

The World Foundation for the Safeguard of Indigenous Cultures

This organization, set up in France in 1993, has the following objectives:

- To contribute to the protection of mankind's heritage in full consultation with indigenous organizations;
- To convince individuals, nations, and their leaders of the importance of safeguarding the ethnic cultural wealth of indigenous peoples;
- To keep a record of the knowledge and techniques created by indigenous peoples over the centuries;
- To promote and encourage research and the making of films, recordings, and other documents by indigenous peoples;
- To send teams for field research wherever existing populations and groups want to assert their cultural differences;
- To promote the preparation of such documents on threatened populations about whom little information exists.

Its main activities are listing documents (including publications, films, and recordings), collecting traditional knowledge, conserving it in archives at the organization's headquarters, and making it available on request. Two archives are planned: a public one that will be open without restrictions and a reserved archive containing documents that may "directly or indirectly prejudice the concerned populations ... [and] scientists, film producers, etc., who would have given or lent their documents to the Foundation and the representatives of the indigenous peoples whose memories have been collected will have the right to restrict access to them. Nevertheless the FMCA will be able to release those materials for research, once a written request explaining its purpose has been approved by the Foundation Management Council, or by an appointed or elected Ethics Committee." Thus, the foundation is aware of the fact that some information is sensitive and should not be disclosed freely.

For further information, contact Patrick Bernard, WOFIC/FMCA (see Resource Guide, France).

- Maps, which contain information on treaties, land occupancy, territorial claims, Dene place names, and traditional conservation; and

- Text materials.

The Dene have submitted a proposal to develop the library further and implement a database system for the benefit of the Dene people. They hope that it will be an invaluable educational resource and a provider of employment. (For further information, contact Bill Erasmus, Dene National Chief.)

> Box 2.5
>
> ### Programa de Colaboración sobre Medicina Tradicional y Herbolaria
>
> This organization, PROCOMITH, based in Chiapas, Mexico, was set up to conduct research into the traditional knowledge of local Maya-speaking communities related to the use of plants. Research data are published in the native languages of the people living in the region.
>
> One of PROCOMITH's activities is the establishment of the Chiapas Ethnobotanical Herbarium and local Ethnobotanical Gardens for the purposes of research, public education, and the promotion of indigenous knowledge and culture.
>
> In parallel with the herbarium, ethnomedicinal/ethnobotanical databases are being assembled in local languages. Because these databases will be in multimedia format, they can be made accessible to all local people, even those who are illiterate, as well as to students and visiting scientists. PROCOMITH is thereby helping to provide a resource for a local population that has been unable to create it alone.
>
> For further information, contact PROCOMITH (see Resource Guide, Mexico).
>
> *Source: Berlin (1993)*

Conclusions

Traditional knowledge and resources are frequently stored ex situ in specialized conservation centres, such as botanic gardens, herbaria and agricultural research centres. Sometimes biogenetic resources are bought and sold after they have been collected for scientific purposes. Museums, art galleries, and universities also store collections of resources, artifacts, and even human remains from traditional communities. Whenever communities are asked to provide information and resources they should find out before agreeing to cooperate where and in what form visitors intend them to be stored, and how these visitors and the institutions funding the collections intend to use them afterwards. By doing so communities will be in a stronger position to dictate beneficial terms for accessing, commercializing, and trading their traditional resources. Given that many communities are concerned that knowledge and resources that are of value to them are being lost, the best option may be to conserve them in situ. Community-controlled conservation centres can ensure that protecting knowledge and resources benefits local peoples first and foremost.

Chapter 3

Who benefits from traditional resources?

The value of end-products developed from resources and knowledge of indigenous peoples is usually far greater than the benefits returning to those peoples. Often, collectors of biological resources are unaware of any legal obligation to local people, as are the companies or institutions sponsoring the collections or buying the samples. Just compensation is a moral obligation; it can also be argued that international principles make compensation a legal right. In this chapter we discuss the value and importance of traditional knowledge and explore the notion of just compensation. We also deal with the implications of publishing knowledge and how this can increase the number of potential beneficiaries.

The value and importance of traditional knowledge

It is probably impossible to estimate the full market value of traditional knowledge, but it is certainly enormous and may increase as advances in biotechnology broaden the range of life forms containing attributes with commercial applications. By one estimate, the market value of plant-based medicines alone (many of which were used first by indigenous peoples) sold in developed countries amounted to $43 billion in 1985 (Principe 1989, pp. 79–124). However, only a tiny proportion of this (much less than 1 percent) has ever been returned to the source communities (Posey 1990).

Modern agricultural practices depend upon crop species with characteristics of productivity and disease resistance that can only be maintained and improved with the continuous input of new germplasm. Most of this new germplasm comes from landraces (or folk varieties) bred and conserved by traditional communities over millennia. Agriculture also benefits from plant-based pesticides — some of which may first have been used by traditional communities — as do the companies that produce and sell seeds and agrochemicals. In this way, indigenous and other traditional cultivators subsidize modern agriculture but receive no payment in return except, perhaps, for small payments from local people who agree to supply seeds and other samples to outside organizations (see Boxes 8.2 and 8.3 in Chapter 8 for examples).

The pharmaceutical industry continues to investigate (and confirm) the efficacy of many medicines and toxins used by indigenous peoples (see Box 3.1). Other industries manufacturing personal care products, foods, and industrial oils also benefit from the knowledge and resources of indigenous peoples. However, few companies making such products have shown concern for the fact that traditional knowledge is sometimes lost and resources disappear when land is converted, sometimes to produce more raw materials for these same companies.

Recently the personal care and food industries have both led and responded to a rise in consumer interest in "natural" products and ethically sound harvesting practices. As a result, a number of companies and nonprofit organizations have begun to work with indigenous communities to acquire information leading to the development of new products and to create socially and environmentally sound strategies for acquiring raw materials. However, on occasion companies obtain knowledge and biological material by deception — for example, by sending employees to communities who do not admit that their purpose is to search for knowledge or biological resources that will be of financial benefit to their company.

Traditional knowledge produces more than commercial benefits for others. Academics and scientists rarely become rich by recording traditional knowledge, yet their academic careers may be enhanced considerably by doing such research in terms of improvements in both their status and their salaries.

Box 3.1

Homalanthus nutans

Homalanthus nutans is a rainforest species collected in Western Samoa for the National Cancer Institute (NCI) by Paul Cox of the Brigham Young University. It has yielded the anti-HIV compound prostratin. Collections were undertaken in forests threatened by logging operations. In interviews with local healers, Cox discovered that this species is used to treat yellow fever and thought that it might prove of interest to the NCI as well. Cox has brokered an agreement between the NCI and these communities.

At the NCI, experiments demonstrated effectiveness against HIV-1. This case is unusual in that it is a recent example of pharmaceutical research and development led by traditional knowledge. It provides us with a clear-cut example of traditional knowledge leading to what may be a commercial product. Without traditional knowledge, it is likely that the NCI would never have learned of this plant.

For further information, contact Paul Cox, Brigham Young University, Salt Lake City, UT, USA.

Publication and the public domain

When the knowledge of a traditional community is passed on to an outsider who subsequently publishes it, it becomes difficult for the community to control how the knowledge is used and who else receives it, because it falls into the public domain (it is not secret or protected by law and can be used freely by anyone, including companies that find the knowledge useful and valuable). Even though most visitors to communities are probably not interested in commercially exploiting traditional knowledge, they may unwittingly or deliberately pass on information to people who are. Results of academic research may be passed on through publication or by contributing to a germplasm collection.

Publication

Academic researchers are expected to publish their research findings, and companies have been able to acquire useful information by reading these research reports. In fact, academic literature is commonly consulted by industry researchers, and valuable knowledge (such as ethnobotanical information) can quietly become part of the research and development (R&D) efforts of commercial enterprises. The drug company, Merck, for example, decided to investigate the commercial potential of a tree bark extract used in hunting by the Urueu-Wau-Wau of Brazil after learning about the plant and its characteristics from a magazine article (Jacobs et al. 1990; McIntyre 1989).

An even better known example is that of the rosy periwinkle (*Catharanthus roseus*), which had been used for centuries as a treatment for diabetes by several indigenous peoples around the world. Research into this plant began following a literature search by a US drug company (Eli Lilley) and a Canadian university. This then led to the discovery of two compounds, vinblastine and vincristine, which have since been used to treat certain cancers.

Another common outcome of publication is that even though the book or research report resulted from information provided freely by indigenous people, the researcher, writer, publishing company, or sponsor of the research claims copyright. Government or university sponsors often justify holding copyright because public funds were used to support the research project. For example, a project funded by the European Union to survey the ethnobotany of the Topnaar people of Namibia resulted not only in the export of medicinal plants by the researchers but also in the claim by the European Commission that it owned all research results (Cunningham 1993a). Although plant samples were deposited in Namibia's national herbarium and research results were passed on to the Namibian authorities, these are more likely to benefit the Namibian government than the people whose cooperation made the project successful.

Failure to acknowledge indigenous sources is an issue of which some indigenous peoples have become aware. For example, the New Zealand government published and claimed copyright for two documents on Maori resource management without acknowledging the many Maori informants (Mead 1993, pp. 33–34). Sometimes such problems can be solved easily by making local people principal or coauthors of papers and books, or coproducers of films and videos.

Warning readers of their obligations may be somewhat effective in guaranteeing the proper use of published material. For example, in a Ciba Foundation publication, authors Elisabetsky and Posey (1994) inform readers that the information contained in their article was authorized and freely given by indigenous leaders. In the paper's opening paragraph, readers are advised that by reading the paper they are ethically and morally bound to respect the source of the information and to share any benefits, economic or otherwise, with the indigenous community.[2] Although such a warning may not have legal force in some countries, it nonetheless carries a universal force of moral and ethical standards and obligations. Another possibility is defensive publication, which is a means of blocking patenting (see Chapter 8).

Germplasm collection

Collections of plants and other biological material for academic purposes may be open to commercial exploitation. Neither source communities nor academic researchers may be aware that a commercial product has been developed based on material or information in such a collection. However, in some cases collectors of plants and other biological material for commercial purposes are academics under **contract** to industry. These contracts make it possible for the researchers to continue with their often

---

[2] The statement reads: "The authors of this paper embrace the principles of the Covenant on Intellectual, Cultural and Scientific Property developed by the Global Coalition for Biological and Cultural Diversity. The data were obtained with full consent of the Kayapó people. The paper is published in the spirit of joint partnership with the Kayapó to advance knowledge for the benefit of all humanity. Any information used from it for commercial or other ends should be properly cited and acknowledged: any commercial benefits that should accrue directly or indirectly should be shared with the Kayapó people" (Elizabetsky and Posey 1994, p. 78).

underfunded botanic, pharmacologic, or other academic research, but frequently no practical distinction is made to source communities between collections for academic purposes and those for commercial ends.

What constitutes "just compensation"?

Whether compensation is merited on moral grounds alone or is a legally enforceable right depends on national laws, implementation of principles in international laws (see Chapter 10), and the ability of members of a community to negotiate an agreement with a company or collecting organization that includes compensation. The question of compensating source communities for knowledge and biogenetic resources is problematic and inevitably will vary from case to case, not only in quantity but also in form (monetary or other) of compensation. Collectors often have agreements to supply resources to companies and other institutions, but a comprehensive policy for compensating individuals or communities for their intellectual and cultural resources is difficult to formulate.

To illustrate the complexities that may be involved, Bennett (Laird 1993) describes the difficulty of assigning ownership when communities have exchanged germplasm and ethnobotanic lore for centuries:

The Quijos Quichua name *chiri caspi* (*Brunfelsia grandiflora*) becomes *chini kiasip* in Shuar. Both groups use the plant similarly. The Canelos Quichua probably served as the mediators between the Quijos and Shuar. Who then should be compensated for a drug discovery based on this plant: the Canelos, the Quijos, or the Shuar?

Three questions arise here:

— What quantity of compensation is both just and realistic?

— What form should compensation take?

— How can it be distributed fairly?

How much compensation?

Compensation will vary depending on a number of factors. For example, in the pharmaceutical industry, if knowledge and resources are contributed only during the early stages of research, compensation in the form of percentage of sales (**royalties**) will be quite low (1–5 percent). However, if the knowledge and resources identify an actual product, royalties could be as high as 10–15 percent (Laird 1993, p. 111). To determine the amount of compensation payable by agreement between a community or communities and a company or other institution, certain factors must be taken into account:

— The pharmaceutical, biotechnology, agricultural, and personal care industries draw on genetic, biochemical, and traditional intellectual resources in distinctly different ways. Thus, a product may be very similar to the original resource, or it may result from a process that makes it quite different. Alternatively, it may be derived from several resources.

- Even within the same industry, the relation of final products to the knowledge and resources supplied by local peoples varies considerably. For example, drug companies may buy plants collected randomly, or the material may be preselected in some way, such as by evidence of use by local people. Resources may originate from private lands, national parks, indigenous reserves, or lands held under communal title. The final product may be closely or only distantly related to the original plant compound or traditional use.

- Brokers or intermediary collectors may be involved. They may be willing to negotiate compensation for the community but will expect to receive a percentage of benefits (usually 10–20 percent), thus reducing the percentage received by the community.

- Compensation must be weighed against relative risk and investment in the development of a final product. For example, the pharmaceutical industry will invest many years and millions of dollars in the development of a drug, whereas a personal care company's outlay will be much less. As a result, the return to communities, in terms of a percentage of profits, from a pharmaceutical product is likely to be much smaller than that received from the development of a personal care product.

What form of compensation?

Does the form of compensation reflect the needs and desires of communities or researchers' perceptions of the situation? Money may not always be the most useful form of compensation. What is the ideal process by which benefits are negotiated or determined? Should compensation consist of an "up-front payment" or a percentage of sales or both?

One company that has sought to provide fair compensation is Shaman Pharmaceuticals. This company develops novel pharmaceuticals from higher plants and is committed to returning a portion of the profits from its products to **all** of the communities and countries in which it works. Its management believes that this distributes risk and assures a more rapid return of resources for all of their collaborators, including a portion of profits derived from the product. The company will also create new sustainable natural-product supply industries in the countries in which it operates (see Box 3.2).

Shaman Pharmaceuticals asks groups with whom it works what pressing needs the communities have that could be met by the company. Steven King, vice-president of ethnobotany at Shaman, has said, "A 10-year waiting period for any potential benefits for any particular indigenous group is almost the same as never, as the needs of these families are much more pressing than to wait for some reciprocity." Immediate benefits have included funds for the construction of an extended airstrip that is the main emergency exit for medical patients from a Quechua community. Shaman has also supplied, at the request of the Commission for the Creation of Yanomami National Park, hundreds of doses of methaloquine for Yanomami Indians dying of chloroquine-resistant malaria introduced by gold miners.

Box 3.2

Shaman Pharmaceuticals and COICA

In 1990, Shaman Pharmaceuticals began negotiations with the Consejo Aguarana/Huambisa (CAH) in Peru and COICA regarding long-term supplies of raw material for their products. Staff at Shaman Pharmaceuticals see such collaboration as a major contribution to local economies and livelihoods.

Initial discussions involved negotiations over the details of price and mechanisms of supply, including the costs of transport and export of material, and dealt with concerns regarding the sustainability of supplies, conservation, and the type of benefits that would accrue to local collaborators. On request, Shaman Pharmaceuticals provided the internal airfare and transport for one member of COICA to return to his federation in the northern Peruvian Amazon to discuss Shaman's proposal to obtain material directly from their communities.

Indigenous leaders were adamant about allowing time for discussion among the many federation and community leaders. They suggested that if Shaman Pharmaceuticals was in a great hurry to establish this supply agreement it should go elsewhere. During this time, ecological studies were conducted to determine the quality and quantity of the plant material in the region.

In December 1992, an agreement was signed by Shaman Pharmaceuticals and the CAH. A major concern of the CAH was who would pay the various costs involved in the purchase and transport of the material to a central city for export. Specific terms, along with the purchase price (which was higher than any currently paid by independent commercial go-betweens), were agreed to and written down with the assistance of legal council. The premium price was an important negotiating point for the federation; in turn, Shaman Pharmaceuticals required a guarantee for a minimum level of quality and integrity of the product.

A *letter of intent* was signed by 138 delegates of the CAH documenting these negotiations. Shaman Pharmaceuticals provided the resources for an in-country collaborator to learn the legal export procedures in Peru and pass on the knowledge to CAH. The Aguarana and Shaman Pharmaceuticals worked for over 2 years to develop a workable relationship. In addition to obtaining raw materials from these communities, Shaman is committed to providing resources for conservation management and local community efforts in health care.

Shaman Pharmaceuticals is pursuing similar experimental supply and purchase agreements with other groups in the Peruvian Amazon and in Colombia, Ecuador, and Mexico. Each case has been slow and time-consuming.

Steven King of Shaman Pharmaceuticals believes that one of the benefits of the long gestation period for pharmaceutical product development is that these discussions and negotiations can be conducted in a "rational and thoughtful manner."

One criticism that can be leveled at Shaman Pharmaceuticals has been that although its willingness to engage in lengthy negotiations and to provide immediate benefits may be laudable, the company has yet to make a firm commitment regarding the payment of royalties. In addition, although the company has applied for patents, it does not appear to have considered the possibility of sharing patent ownership with communities or of naming local community members as inventors (Kennedy and Zerner 1994). However, the company argues that it looks for widely used and distributed species and, therefore, such offers might be impracticable.

For further information, contact Shaman Pharmaceuticals (see Resource Guide, USA).

Box 3.3

Stevia rebaudiana

Stevia rebaudiana (Asteraceae) is a shrub native to Paraguay, but it is found throughout warm and tropical America. It contains a compound that is up to 250 times as sweet as sugar. *Stevia rebaudiana* has long been used by indigenous peoples for sweetening drinks and was the chosen sweetener for coffee and tea in Paraguay and southern Brazil long before sugar became popular. A multibillion dollar market for the compound is still growing.

Both indigenous and nonindigenous communities throughout Paraguay and southern Brazil grow *S. rebaudiana* in backyard gardens for family use. However, the extent of local peoples' involvement in the industry is generally limited to employment in plantations.

By the time large-scale commercialization took place, *S. rebaudiana* was so widely used in the region and across national boundaries that no specific claim to ownership of the species or its use could be made, so it is unlikely that a particular community could legally gain rights to any revenue generated from its sale. This does not mean, however, that a portion of the revenues generated from the sale of *S. rebaudiana* could not be used to benefit communities in the region in which it was originally used. For example, companies involved in its production could be pressured into making charitable donations to conservation and development efforts in the area.

For further information, contact Herb Research Foundation, Boulder, CO, USA, or the American Botanical Council, Austin, TX, USA.

Other groups have signed **material transfer agreements** (MTAs) with specific communities in exchange for their biological and intellectual resources. For example, the NCI has signed a letter of collection (which is not legally binding) with the Awa Federation in Ecuador.

How can compensation be distributed fairly?

Ensuring that compensation is shared equitably between and within existing groups and future generations and that it reaches the actual knowledge holders and resource conservers is a challenge. However, although the problem is complex, it is not insurmountable. The case described in Box 3.3 brings up the question of retroactive claims to benefits from the commercialization of biological and intellectual property. It also shows that even though the knowledge and resources being commercialized are widely distributed, benefit-sharing in such circumstances is still possible.

A report from a conference on indigenous peoples and IPR[3] (Working Group on Intellectual Property Rights 1993) suggests three possible means to secure protection

---

[3] The Conference on Intellectual Property Rights and Indigenous Knowledge, Granlibakken, Lake Tahoe, CA, USA, 5–11 October 1993.

and compensation for biogenetic resources and traditional knowledge: IPR, contracts, and funds (see Chapters 8, 7, and 13). It concluded that a system of compensation based on a fund (such as the Food and Agriculture Organization's (FAO) fund for farmers' rights) would be most appropriate when the knowledge is historical, not just recent, and when the resources and the knowledge about them are widely distributed. Therefore, in the case of neem (see Chapter 8), which has been used for centuries by farmers throughout India to protect their crops but is now being commercialized by companies in the United States, an international fund might be the most effective means of sharing benefits. There are three reasons for this:

— Communities may be in a weak bargaining position with respect to other forms of compensation because companies often acquire information from literature searches.

— No individual community has a stronger claim to compensation than others with the same knowledge.

— The original innovators are anonymous and may no longer be alive.

A contract is a legally binding agreement between two or more parties. Contracts may be appropriate if knowledge and resources are not widely known and are not in the public domain, and both parties believe that they can gain advantage through a contract. Before agreeing to sign a contract, parties should always seek independent legal advice. Contracts are discussed in greater detail in Chapter 7.

Conclusions

Local communities should be aware of the importance of controlling the publication of traditional knowledge and information about resource management practices. Researchers will customarily publish the results of their studies in academic journals, books, or even popular magazines to enhance their reputation in the academic community; this is a tremendous incentive for them to report information they have gathered on indigenous cultures, traditional knowledge, and resource management practices.

Researchers must often be educated about the implications of publishing. Many have never given much thought to the fact that once published, indigenous knowledge becomes part of the public domain and beyond the control of the source communities or the scientist. Others may knowingly disregard their responsibilities in this matter.

Professional societies have begun to draft codes of ethics to direct researchers, but communities should be prepared to negotiate with researchers and set terms for their work. Communities should ensure their autonomy by working in partnership in **collaborative research**, by contracting outside researchers to carry out the required research (**community-controlled research**), or by establishing guidelines for equitable research contracts (see Chapter 14).

Chapter 4

Will the community be informed?

Communities have the right to be informed about how their knowledge, life-styles, images, and resources may be used by others. These rights are independent of any sovereignty rights conferred by national law. For example, the right to privacy — to be free from intrusion and unwanted public attention — is recognized as a basic human right in international law. Failure to inform a person, family, or community by full disclosure about what is being sought, how it is being used, and by whom can be interpreted as an invasion of privacy. Because relevant laws may vary widely from one country to another, generalizations are difficult when applied to individual countries. The concept of prior informed consent includes procedures that should be carried out by visitors interested in local knowledge or resources to ensure that privacy rights are respected.

Violations of indigenous peoples' right to be informed

A broad range of abuses inflicted on indigenous peoples can be viewed as violations of their right to be informed. Among these are the following:

- Unauthorized use of tribal names. For example, an automobile manufacturer has named one of its trucks "Cherokee." Also, the words "Hopi" and "Zuni" have been incorporated into trademarks without permission from the tribes concerned.

- Unauthorized commercialization of indigenous peoples' knowledge, seeds, and plants, and extraction of their own biogenetic material without their informed consent. This can be regarded as a form of piracy, and in the case of biogenetic resources, is nowadays being referred to as "biopiracy."

- Public disclosure and use of secret knowledge, images, and other sensitive information. This is commonly practiced by museums. For example, an Australian anthropologist wrote a book containing information divulged in confidence by tribal elders (see Box 4.2).

- Filming and taking photographs without permission. Video images of indigenous peoples are sometimes used for commercial purposes, such as advertising by companies like Shell and American Express. Whether this is inherently exploitative is for indigenous peoples themselves to decide and may depend on the context. Advertising aimed at attracting foreign tourists to a country sometimes depicts indigenous people; for example, Australia, Canada, the United States, Indonesia, and many Latin American countries have featured indigenous people in tourism promotion literature. Guatemala has used photographs of Mayan people and their arts and crafts to attract tourists in spite of the fact that these people have often suffered brutal repression at the hands of Guatemalan governments over many years.

Privacy and the law

Some of the above actions are invasions of privacy. Privacy is a human right according to international law. Article 17 of the *International Covenant on Civil and Political Rights* (ICCPR) states:

1. No one shall be subjected to arbitrary or unlawful interference with his privacy, family, home or correspondence, nor to unlawful attacks on his honour and reputation.

2. Everyone has the right to the protection of the law against such interference and attacks.

Laws protecting privacy vary from one country to another and the advice of a lawyer will probably be necessary to identify the appropriate legal tools available in national laws. A country's legal system may provide citizens with a legal right to privacy, or it might provide more indirect protection against infringements of privacy rights. Many countries have no privacy law as such, but several areas of the law may still protect the rights of people from certain acts that constitute privacy infringements. For example, the following IPR laws may be invoked to protect some aspects of privacy:

- *Copyright:* In some countries authors have **moral rights** (the right to be identified as creators of their work — the right of paternity — and the right to be able to prevent any distortion of the work that would prejudice their reputation as an author — the right of integrity). Some countries may have entrenched more extensive moral rights than these. The law may also protect the privacy of someone who commissions a photograph or film for private domestic purposes (such as a wedding). If the photo or film is protected by copyright, the person who commissioned it may restrict public access to the work or to copies.
- *Trademark:* The use of a trademark can be challenged in courts in some countries if it is insulting to an ethnic group (see Chapter 8).

Legal concepts that exist in some countries, such as theft, trespass, and defamation, may protect those aspects of privacy that may be of concern to a community. Some possibilities and limitations of privacy rights in the protection of indigenous people are illustrated in Box 4.1. It can be difficult to take legal action with reasonable expectation of success. Furthermore, pursuing legal action is likely to be expensive. Therefore, in many cases, creating adverse publicity and, perhaps, threatening legal action may be the best course of action.

Another type of violation of a peoples' privacy is the publication of their secret knowledge without consent. If the group or community had signed an agreement with the recipient of the knowledge that it would not be revealed to others, publication could well be an illegal act: depending on the country's legal system it could be a breach of contract, an invasion of privacy, a breach of confidence, or perhaps more than one of these. However, even without such an agreement, the group or community need not necessarily remain passive victims; legal recourse may still be possible, but legal advice can be costly and the outcome is uncertain. The following example demonstrates that a traditional community may be able to take legal action in cases where secret knowledge is published without its consent (Box 4.2).

Prior informed consent

Prior informed consent (PIC), although not clearly defined, is a concept that exists in international law. Two international legally binding documents use the concept: the 1989 *Convention on the Control of Transboundary Movement of Hazardous Wastes and Their Disposal* and the CBD. Article 15, clause 5 of the CBD states: "Access to genetic resources shall be subject to prior informed consent of the Contracting Party providing such resources, unless otherwise determined by that Party." The International Union for the

Box 4.1

Commercial use of human images: an example from Amazonia

Kukryt Kako Kaiapó, a member of a Kayapó community, was shocked to find that a company had reproduced a photograph of him, his wife, and child on T-shirts and was selling them at the Earth Summit. How does the law stand on such a situation? In most countries (France is an exception) copyright law does not protect a subject's right to prevent subsequent use of his or her photograph for commercial purposes unless, perhaps, it was commissioned by the subject. In Brazil, legal action based on invasion of privacy could be successful under a number of circumstances. For example:

- If the photograph was taken against the will of the subject;
- If the photograph damages the subject's reputation;
- If the company obtained significant profits from exploiting the photograph;
- If the subject is a well-known person, whose personality is being exploited without his or her consent.

In the Kayapó case, the family is not well known in Brazil and may well not have objected to being photographed, yet the company may have made quite a lot of money from selling the shirts. Legal action would undoubtedly be expensive and the decision would not be certain. Therefore, the best strategy in such a case might be for indigenous peoples and their supporters to make their feelings known to the offending company, and also to publicize the case to make companies aware that such behaviour may be offensive and can give the company a negative image. In this case, however, such a course of action would not have been successful, because the company later changed its name to avoid paying taxes and could not be traced.

Conservation of Nature's (IUCN) guide to the CBD (Glowka et al. 1994, p. 105), describes prior informed consent as:

> (1) consent of the Contracting Party which is the genetic resource provider, (2) based on information provided by the potential genetic resource user, (3) prior to consent for access being granted.
>
> [Furthermore,] the PIC requirement gives a Contracting Party the authority to require a potential genetic resource user — whether another Party or, for example, a collector or a company in the private sector — not only to gain its authorization before accessing genetic resources within its jurisdiction, but also to require the potential user to outline the implications of access by, among other things, specifying how and by whom the genetic resources will be subsequently used. This information, or lack of information, may be important for the provider to decide whether, and on which terms, to grant access.

Box 4.2

Breach of confidence: a court case in Australia

In 1976, the Supreme Court of the Northern Territory of Australia decided to ban the sale of a book written by Mountford, a well-known Australian anthropologist, which contained an Aboriginal group's sacred knowledge divulged to him 35 years previously by tribal elders. Even though there was no written confidentiality agreement, the anthropologist's knowledge of these people should have made it clear that it was secret information of a highly confidential nature. Indeed, the book even contained a warning that the book should not be used without consulting local male religious leaders, indicating that Mountford was well aware of the situation.

According to the judge, in referring to the Aboriginal group,

> The revelation of the secrets to their women, children and uninitiated men may undermine the social and religious stability of their hard-pressed community. Despite Dr Mountford's prognosis that their life and beliefs "are so quickly vanishing," there is still an urgent desire in these people to preserve those things, their lands and their identity.

Although Australia (unlike many other countries) has a privacy law, the Court's decision was based on the law of confidence, which Mountford's act of publishing was considered to have been in breach of. This law exists in many countries whose legal systems are based on the British system.

Source: Golvan (1992, p. 230), ECOSOC (1993, p. 22)

Implementation will probably require national legislation in both the country providing and the country using genetic resources. Will this require users of genetic resources on the lands of indigenous peoples to obtain the prior informed consent of the local communities? The CBD can be interpreted to require this.

Prior informed consent is being taken into account in collaborative research agreements and codes of ethics (see Chapters 11 and 14), but what is needed is a definition. The following one is proposed:

> Prior informed consent is consent to an activity that is given after receiving full disclosure regarding the reasons for the activity, the specific procedures the activity would entail, the potential risks involved, and the full implications that can realistically be foreseen. Prior informed consent implies the right to stop the activity from proceeding, and for it to be halted if it is already underway. The following types of activity should be subject to the PIC condition:
> - Medical or other research carried out on a human body, whether or not it involves extraction of material, such as organs, body fluids, etc., and whether or not it is for commercial purposes;
> - Medical treatment, especially where it entails risk;
> - The extraction of biogenetic material and minerals from local communities or the territories of traditional communities, whether or not the communities have legal title to these lands;

- The acquisition of knowledge from a person or people;
- All projects affecting local communities, such as construction works, colonization schemes, and protected areas.

Requests for consent should be accompanied by full disclosure of the following, in writing **in the local language:**

- The purpose of the activity;
- The identity of those carrying out the activity and its sponsors, if different;
- The benefits for the people or person whose consent is being requested and for the sponsors;
- The costs and disadvantages for the people whose consent is being requested;
- Possible alternative activities and procedures;
- Any risks entailed by the activity;
- Discoveries made in the course of the activity that might affect the willingness of the people to continue to cooperate;
- The destination of knowledge or material that is to be acquired, its ownership status, and the rights of local people to it once it has left the community;
- Any commercial interest that the performers and sponsors have in the activity and in the knowledge or material acquired; and
- The legal options available to the community if it refuses to allow the activity.

It is very important that countries which enact laws to implement the CBD make it obligatory for companies or research institutions to obtain the prior informed consent of indigenous peoples as well as, or instead of, the state.

Conclusions

Ensuring respect for the privacy of indigenous peoples and communities is complicated by the fact that relevant laws, being based on Western notions of privacy and confidence, do not adequately reflect the concerns of indigenous peoples. However, legal redress may be possible and indigenous people trained as lawyers and other sympathetic lawyers may be on hand to offer guidance. Exposing and publicizing flagrant invasions of privacy may also be somewhat effective, because individuals and companies may change their practices in response to negative publicity.

Chapter 5

What right do communities have to say "yes" or "no" to commercialization?

Many indigenous peoples have traded with outsiders for centuries, but interest in and potential profits from knowledge and biogenetic resources are now increasing in modern markets. Some pharmaceutical and personal care companies are approaching indigenous communities directly or through intermediaries or brokers. Indigenous peoples often need cash for tools, transport, schoolbooks, radios, medicines, cultural items, legal assistance, and to maintain their own institutions and negotiate with each other and the state. How can the need to secure external sources of income be reconciled with indigenous peoples' wish not to sell, commoditize, or otherwise lose certain domains of knowledge, sacred places, plants, animals, and objects? The decision to enter trade relations with outsiders is important, and many factors must be borne in mind by those making it. They must be aware of their rights under the law and the implications of such a decision.

The effects of trade

Trade can be a two-edged sword. It can bring wealth and independence, but it can also increase dependence on outsiders and vulnerability to exploitation. Many environmentalists (and even some companies) believe that the trade in nontimber forest products (NTFPs), like fruits, nuts, fibres, oils, and exudates from tropical forests (the so-called "rainforest harvest"), can benefit both the forests and their indigenous inhabitants. A well-known advocate of this view is the NGO Cultural Survival, which has assumed an active role as an intermediary between indigenous groups and companies interested in buying products such as NTFPs. Another NGO, Survival International, which has campaigned for the rights of indigenous peoples for more than 25 years, is much more sceptical. In the early 1990s there was a great deal of debate among NGOs, journalists, and academics concerning the theory and practice of sustainable trade in NTFPs. What are the underlying assumptions behind the opposing positions of Cultural Survival and Survival International? It is instructive to see how they respond to the following four statements:

1. *Indigenous people are already part of the world economy and have needs that can only be satisfied through trade.*

    Cultural Survival says its position is one of realism: most indigenous peoples are already locked into the world economic system and cannot simply opt out. According to Jason Clay, former head of the organization's trading operations, "We have not found any groups that are not, in some way, involved with the market economy, nor have we found groups that don't want to get a better price for goods that they are producing" (Clay 1992). Cultural Survival also points out that campaigning for recognition of their rights will require a degree of financial independence by indigenous communities (Clay 1992). In addition, groups need money to buy medicines and other important goods. One might suggest also that it can seem paternalistic to assume that consumption of luxury goods will necessarily weaken a group's cultural identity. For example, the Kayapó, who have had trading links with Cultural Survival and The Body Shop, use video cameras to record their ceremonies and tape recorders to record the promises made to them by company and government representatives. If they cannot gain income from an environmentally friendly source, they resort to other means, such as selling logging and mining rights.

    Survival International claims not to disagree with the statement (Stephen Corry, director general, 1994, personal communication) but says that the new extractivism is far from lucrative and can only benefit a small number of people. The organization has accused Cultural Survival of exaggerating the economic potential of extractivism and its importance as a means of empowering indigenous peoples and of misleading members of the public who believe that they are helping indigenous peoples by buying their products (Corry 1993).

2. *Trading in forest products to supply overseas markets is inherently exploitative.*

Survival International argues that the history of such trade provides strong evidence in support of this statement. For example, quinine, a cure discovered by indigenous Amazonians for a disease introduced by invading Europeans, was overexploited without benefit to the native people. Also, the "rubber boom" of the early 20th century caused enormous suffering to many forest dwellers who were badly treated by traders. Prices of many NTFPs are low and, even when products have a high economic value, local communities seldom receive a fair percentage of the **value added** to products that are processed and transported long distances. Thus, the view that trading in forest products has always been an expression of colonialism at its most rapacious is certainly reasonable, making the whole idea of saving the rainforests by increasing consumption of these products in the North seem contradictory. According to Corry (1992), "It's dangerously ironic that the **increased** consumption in western markets, the cause of much of the destruction, is now hailed as beneficial." Not only is Cultural Survival wrong to embrace it, but it is guilty of a subtle form of neocolonialism, even if its intentions are benign.

Cultural Survival counters with the argument that tropical forests must pay for themselves. Sustainable trade in forest products adds value to a standing forest and creates incentives to conserve them by providing employment and income. The fact that, more often than not, economic value has usually been extracted without any regard to the environment or the lives of forest dwellers does not invalidate the argument. Although Cultural Survival argues that the "use it or lose it" concept points to the need to build international market links of the kind it is promoting, Survival International argues that local communities are already using the forest's resources but that this "subsistence value" is not taken into consideration in the development process. Thus, it is not international trade that will save the forests but securing the rights of forest communities so that planners and politicians will have to recognize this kind of nonmonetary value (Corry 1993, pp. 3–5).

3. *Trade makes indigenous peoples more, not less, dependent.*

According to Survival International, indigenous groups are bound to become victims of the vagaries of market forces if they get involved in selling raw materials for products like confectioneries and cosmetics. Trade in exported products whose popularity may be short-lived will increase dependence on the trade and on the companies that groups work with, making trade-based relations essentially paternalistic. According to Survival International, "The 'harvest' will not empower the rainforest community ... the real effect is to tie the people into exactly the same relationship of dependence and patronage as any of the traditional forms of exploitation through which the wealthy dictate trading terms to impoverished people and countries" (Corry 1993, pp. 6–7).

Cultural Survival is aware of the risks but counters that in the absence of alternative sources of income, the sustainable trade in forest products is a worthwhile activity. According to Clay, "If they [the producers of raw materials] do get more of a return, that will slow or maybe even halt the destruction of a lot of this resource base. It will also help preserve the cultural diversity if these indigenous people have an economic base" (see Lerner 1992, p. 160).

4. *Trade can cause internal divisions within indigenous communities.*

Survival International has claimed that a project in which the UK-based company, The Body Shop, works with the Kayapó Indians of Brazil to extract brazil nut oil for export to Britain has been socially divisive. According to Corry, "It has contributed to internal antagonisms and divisions, not to mention social dislocation and alienation which recently ruptured the community completely" (Corry 1993, p. 2). Certainly, the social impact of sudden wealth, along with quarrels between those who wish to participate in trading and those who oppose it, can be destructive to a community.

Cultural Survival and The Body Shop accept that there are risks but argue that indigenous peoples and their cultures may be far more resilient than Survival International appears to assume. They also point out that Kayapó society has always been riven by disputes: they did not begin with its relationship with Cultural Survival and The Body Shop. According to The Body Shop's chairperson, "The Kayapó are not placid people; their history is one of internal strife and villages breaking into factions, eventually dividing into subvillages" (Roddick 1992). This point of view is supported by most anthropologists familiar with these people.

Whether Cultural Survival or Survival International has the most convincing arguments, local communities around the world are finding it ever more necessary to secure a reliable flow of income so that they can achieve greater self-sufficiency. They may try to earn money by working outside the community, although doing so is seldom lucrative. Another way, and often a more appealing option, is to establish market links. Community members may take the initiative and sell local resources, manufactured goods, and artwork in local and regional markets, as many communities have done for centuries, or they may establish an agreement with a company, perhaps from another country, that is interested in commercializing the community's knowledge, resources, or arts and crafts.

Given the reality that some companies and individuals will enter into such agreements without even asking local communities for their consent, what rights do communities have to prevent unwanted commercialization or to ensure that they have control over commercial activities?

Option 1: say "no"

"Biodiversity prospectors" and biotechnology developers are **not** noted for their ethics and concern for, or experience with, indigenous peoples or local communities. They **are** noted for capitalizing on opportunity. Therefore, there are good reasons why indigenous and traditional peoples should be worried about the commoditization of their cultural, intellectual, and scientific property — not to mention their plants, animals, seeds, and even their own genetic material.

For example, the Guajajara people of Brazil use a plant called *Pilocarpus jaborandi* to treat glaucoma. Although Brazil now earns $25 million annually by exporting the plant, the Guajajara have allegedly been subjected to peonage and slavery at the hands of agents of the company involved in the trade. Furthermore, the supply is being rapidly exhausted (Davis 1993, pp. 8–11).

However, companies and individuals are not the only ones seeking to commercialize resources without the consent of local people; local communities face the serious problem of expropriation of their resources by nation states. Most collection agreements and international exchange arrangements are not with communities but with national governments. Thus, indigenous peoples are often denied by their own governments the basic right to exploit their own resources for commercial purposes.

Two kinds of rights may be asserted to strengthen the ability of indigenous peoples to enforce a decision against commercialization of their knowledge and resources by others: the right to self-determination and inalienable rights.

The right to self-determination

Self-determination is a doctrine of international law that can be regarded as a collective human right. According to two UN agreements — the *International Covenant on Economic, Social and Cultural Rights* (ICESCR) and the ICCPR — all peoples have the right to self-determination, and by virtue of that right, may freely determine their political status and pursue their economic, social, and cultural development (see also Chapter 10).

In spite of its enshrinement in international law, the degree of self-determination conceded by nation states to indigenous peoples varies within the extremes of virtually none to full sovereignty rights. Full sovereignty rights include the right

- To be self-governing;
- To enact legislation;
- To control access to the territory and the resources existing within territorial boundaries; and
- To enter into legally binding international treaties.

In some countries, indigenous peoples have limited sovereignty over their own territories. Perhaps the broadest sovereignty rights for indigenous peoples are exercised by the people of Greenland under the 1979 *Home Rule Act* passed by the Danish parliament (Nuttall 1994; Petersen 1994). The people of Nunavut in northern Canada will soon enjoy similar rights. Many native tribes in North America and the Maori of New Zealand have treaties with their nation states that imply acknowledgment of their right to self-determination. In the United States, native tribes recognized by the federal government have sufficient sovereignty rights to allow tribal courts to adjudicate violations of customary law committed by both Indians and non-Indians (T. Greaves, Department of Sociology and Anthropology, Bucknell University, Lewisburg, PA, USA, 1994, personal communication). If their laws forbid the commercialization and "export" of certain resources, it may be possible to prosecute visitors who break them (although this action may conflict with federal law). Some native American tribes even issue passports.

Without self-determination, including legal title to their territories, it is very difficult for traditional groups to back up their right to say "no" to commercialization. Nevertheless, principles **do** exist in international law that support rights to self-determination of indigenous and traditional communities.

Inalienable rights

In traditional societies, the right to livelihood resources (apart from immediate personal possessions), such as trees, crop species, and medicinal plants, are not usually exclusive (Okoth-Ogendo 1989, p. 11). They are often shared among individuals and social and corporate groups, each of which may have "bundles" of graded rights to the same resources within a given area. Such rights are considered inalienable; they cannot be transferred, either as a gift or through a commercial transaction. As a general rule, knowledge and resources are communally held and, although some specialized knowledge may be held exclusively by males, females, certain lineage groups, or ritual or society specialists (such as shamans), this does not give that group the right to privatize the communal heritage (see also Chapter 6). Thus, customary law may make it illegal for anybody to sell knowledge and resources. Many African countries acknowledge customary law by having dual legal systems, so that crimes and disputes can either be settled within the community or decided in the courts according to local custom. Other nation states, regardless of whether they have conceded sovereignty rights to indigenous groups, may also recognize customary law. For example, the Canadian Royal Commission on Aboriginal People recommended that indigenous customary laws take precedence over federal and provincial laws when they conflict (Richardson et al. 1994, p. 45). In countries where customary law is recognized as part of national law, and local communities have inalienable rights to certain knowledge and resources, legal recourse in national courts should be possible in cases of unauthorized commercialization of knowledge and resources.

Both collective rights and the inalienability of resources are linked to the need for indigenous peoples to secure legal title to their territories and can be used to strengthen their claim to territory. According to Gray (1994):

> Indigenous land rights are based on a people's prior occupation of an area, usually before a state was even formed. In this sense, Indigenous Peoples have a claim to "***eminent domain***" (inalienability) which a state usually considers to be its own exclusive right .... Connected with the concept of inalienability is the collective responsibility which a people has for its territory. This does not mean that individual persons cannot hold lands and resources for their own use, but that personal ownership is based on collective consent. The collective rights to lands and resources of Indigenous Peoples have been acknowledged by many governments of the world in their constitutions and in international provisions.

Option 2: say "yes"

Indigenous groups may have been trading in local resources and in manufactured goods for many years. Others may be less experienced traders and less aware that biogenetic resources and local knowledge about them may serve as the basis for products that can help drug, personal care, and other companies generate profits. Whether an indigenous group chooses to trade independently or to build relations with such companies, legal options do exist. Chapter 8 explains how indigenous peoples can use IPR tools to protect knowledge about resources that they wish to commercialize. In many cases, however, the best way to benefit from trade may be to press for the right to receive fair compensation.

According to Corry (1993, p. 6):

> The best marketing schemes are those which arise from the people themselves and are controlled by them; are appropriate within their economic and social situation; lead to genuine economic independence from exploitative middlemen; promote cohesiveness rather than division within the communities concerned; and are not carried out by outside organizations for their own profit. Profits should belong to the community which should be under no coercion if it wishes to abandon the scheme.

According to Clay (Lerner 1992, pp. 159, 161):

> Every indigenous group that I have worked with, and the vast majority of the rest of them, sells or trades something because they all need to buy things .... We [Cultural Survival] work at figuring out how these groups can make a living in the modern world. We focus on how they can trade, sell, or barter products to get what they need to have better health, better education, or whatever. We are interested in what skills they need in the modern world that will not destroy or degrade their resource base. This requires working with them and providing them with technical assistance.

The right to development

There is at least one principle of international law that grants any people the right to participate in development on their own terms: the right to development. For indigenous peoples this right encompasses

— The right of access to resources on their territories; and

— The right to seek development on their own terms.

This is an important principle because governments may interpret the CBD in a way that gives nation states sovereignty rights to all knowledge and biogenetic resources existing within their borders. Also, government agencies and NGOs concerned with conservation sometimes deny communities the right to exploit and commercialize local resources. The principle of the right to development is enshrined in international law in

Box 5.1

Bixa orellana: the Yawanawa Association and the Aveda Corporation

Bixa orellana (or annatto) is native to and widespread throughout the neotropics. It is a shrub, often cultivated around villages and in yards. It has many traditional uses, such as in folk medicine.

Bixin is a derivative that is traded internationally as a food dye. During the 19th century, the Brazilian Amazon exported significant quantities of annatto powder to Europe. Nowadays, there is renewed interest in annatto among food-processing and cosmetic companies because bixin is safe for consumption and skin application.

The Yawanawa Indians have lived in an area of Acre, Brazil for centuries, but like many indigenous groups have been under extreme pressure from immigrants to the region for over 100 years. The Aveda Corporation, based in Minnesota, has recently begun a joint effort with the Yawanawa to develop commercial products from *B. orellana*. Aveda staff have worked directly with the Yawanawa Community Association in the development of their research program.

The project itself was put together and is administered by the community association with support from local institutions. The Yawanawa association is legally institutionalized and autonomous. Aveda has supplied financing to cover all the costs of establishing "plantations." Financing is spread out according to a schedule determined by the operational and administrative needs of the community. Aveda must approve expenditure reports before supplying funds, and these must match the preapproved plan.

Once larger scale *B. orellana* production is in place, the association can sell or export the material as it wishes, and Aveda will be treated as any other buyer. The agreement between the association and Aveda is not exclusive, nor must Aveda buy all that is produced, although it has made a commitment to help place any excess product in the market. It is thought that the amount produced will exceed Aveda's current needs significantly, but staff at Aveda are researching additional applications for *B. orellana* in their cosmetic line, and local and international demand is significant and rising.

Because *B. orellana* is a widely known and used product throughout the neotropics, and is available in any marketplace there, the agreement between Aveda and the Yawanawa was not based on ethnobotanical leads but deals primarily with assuring a source of raw material for use in Aveda products. Aveda is trying to keep the level of its involvement to a minimum and is taking the lead of the community regarding product selection (within a list of species) and sustainable harvesting.

For further information, contact Aveda Corporation, Rua Marques de Abrantes 148/1104, Flamengo, Rio de Janeiro, Brazil.

both the ICESCR and the ICCPR (Article 1 of both). It is also included in the International Labour Organisation's (ILO) Convention 169, as follows:

> The peoples concerned shall have the right to decide their own priorities for the process of development as it affects their lives, beliefs, institutions and spiritual well-being and the lands they occupy or otherwise use, and to exercise control, to the extent possible, over their own economic, social and cultural development. In addition, they shall participate in the formulation, implementation and evaluation of plans and programmes for national and regional development which may affect them directly. [Article 7.1]
>
> The rights of the peoples concerned to the natural resources pertaining to their lands shall be specially safeguarded. These rights include the right of these peoples to participate in the use, management and conservation of these resources. [Article 15.1]

Whether a group decides to favour or oppose the commercialization of their knowledge, legal options are available, such as contracts and covenants providing for up-front payments, royalties, a legal fund, and arbitration. Also, some companies are developing policies intended to provide benefits for indigenous peoples collaborating with them. The case study in Box 5.1 illustrates the potential benefits of trading links with those, so far few, companies that are willing to collaborate with local communities in a manner that respects their rights.

Conclusions

Deciding whether to commercialize knowledge and resources may be one of the most important decisions faced by a community or group because of the possibility of far-reaching economic and social impacts and the risk that it will result in diminished control over knowledge and resources. Before deciding to get involved in trade, either independently or in collaboration with an NGO or corporation, the community must be clear about how it can act legally. The next three chapters provide information about how communities can do this.

Chapter 6

How can a community take legal action?

*Taking action to commercialize or to prevent commercialization requires understanding of how the administration of property is different in indigenous and local communities than it is in industrial societies. Action may be more effective if local communities or groups are registered as "a **juridical person**" (a legal entity), as a company, NGO or religious community might be. In any collaborative exercise, the outside partners to an agreement will be organizations who send their representatives to visit indigenous groups and collect knowledge or resources in one form or another.*

Western and indigenous property systems and customary law

Strictly speaking, "property" refers to rights to something rather than to the thing that is "owned." Property may take the form of rights to land, manufactured goods, commodities, services, resources, or knowledge. Property rights are normally accompanied by obligations. For example, a landowner may still be obliged to acquire permission from others (such as the government, the local authorities or neighbours) to erect a building or to convert the land use from, say, forest to cropland.

The holder of property rights is entitled by law or custom to restrict access to and use of the property by others. If the property belongs to a juridical person (an individual, a natural person) or a group of people forming a legal person, it is considered private. However, if state-owned, it is public property because the state represents all citizens of the country. Land, goods, resources, and knowledge that are available to local people may be either common (society as a whole owns them) or communal property (local people own them).

In industrial societies, ownership of land, goods, and services can be transferred from one person or corporation to another in exchange for money. Except for personal possessions, property rights (such as IPR) are typically held by legal persons (corporations) rather than individuals. Traditional societies may view such transactions as contrary to their customs and laws. Communal property is the prevailing system used in most traditional societies to control access to basic resources like food and fuel, but rights are multiple in that individuals, elders, women, clans, lineages, etc., each have ownership rights within a given resource area and over specified resources within them. Such rights may vary in their extent from one group to another, but they are inalienable (others cannot take away or undermine them).

In Western societies, the creator of a new song is usually an individual who automatically becomes its owner and has the right not only to sell recordings of the song but also to prevent others from doing so. In a traditional society, however, the "creator" may attribute "authorship" to a member of the spirit world. In any case, elders and lineages may have certain rights to the song. For example, elders may forbid performance of the song in front of women or members of another clan; a clan may have the right to prevent the "author" (or "first performer" in cases where "authorship" is an alien notion or is attributed to spiritual beings) of the song from signing a contract with a record company or, alternatively, to obtain any share of profits.

Even in cases where certain esoteric knowledge is the exclusive intellectual property of individuals, families, shamans, clans, or lineages, these owners cannot necessarily commercialize the knowledge without the permission of the whole community or the tribal elders. The case study in Box 6.1 provides a good example of a complex traditional resource ownership and management system.

The assumption that there exists a generic form of non-Western, indigenous collective property rights ignores the complex nature of indigenous proprietary systems. Specifically, any legal instruments aimed at protecting cultural knowledge must accommodate cultural and local variation in the forms of such systems.

Box 6.1

Controls and sanctions in the Kafue River basin of Zambia

The Tonga/Ila peoples have occupied the lands around the Kafue River, Zambia, since the beginning of this millennium. They live on higher land, using it for cultivation, wet season grazing, and hunting and gathering in the woodlands; the floodplain is used for fishing and dry season grazing.

In response to the unpredictable nature of the ecosystem, the local people have evolved flexible management systems maintained by strongly held and protected rights and obligations reinforced by spiritual beliefs. All land is controlled by clan leaders named after the original owner and inherited through the female bloodline by a person chosen from a pool of contenders. These are known as Owners of the Land.

Woodland products are central to the livelihood of these people and are subject to various traditional laws, which may vary slightly from place to place, depending on the need that a tree or plant fulfills in the local economy, the scarcity of the plant or product, and the degree of respect given to the traditional control systems. No fruit trees, or certain other trees considered to be beneficial to soil or people, may be felled without the permission of the Owner of the Land. In return for permission, a tribute may be paid to the ancestors of the land. However, fruit, bark, leaves, roots, and other tree products are free for communal use, if they are not in a homestead and if taking of the product does not kill the tree. The produce of a tree has no commercial value until marketed or converted into a marketable object. Traditional laws are essential in keeping the use of the ecosystem at a sustainable level.

External pressures on the system, brought about by the damming of the river for hydroelectric power and immigration of the increasing population, make it even more essential that the complex system of controls and sanctions be maintained.

The community has responded by introducing new conservation regulations. A requirement for permission to gather has been imposed on all community members. Women have begun planting the wild plants that they formerly gathered, and saving and distributing seed from the most productive plants. The inhabitants of the flats can find sufficient flexibility within their system of knowledge and beliefs to maintain the productivity of the river basin.

Source: Sorenson (1993)

The most appropriate options appear to lie within customary law. However, indigenous peoples frequently find that their laws are not recognized by nation states; they may be forced to conform to laws with which they are unfamiliar and that may be inappropriate to the point of conflicting with their own laws. In general, customary laws are unwritten and, in some countries, such as Australia and Canada, there has been much discussion as whether customary law should be codified (written down). However, it may not be beneficial to codify customary laws because doing so could freeze them in time and prevent them from evolving. On the other hand, integrating them into the national legal system may require in-depth understanding and analyses that only codification would make possible (Allott 1987).

Organizational options

Juridical persons

If a traditional community, indigenous peoples, tribe, or group becomes a juridical person, it might find that its legal options are much enhanced. The procedures for doing this will vary from one country to another. The same process should be possible for federations of indigenous groups, such as COICA, which has consultative status at the United Nations. A case study involving the Awa Federation in Ecuador is described in Chapter 14. This federation administers the land held under communal title by the Awa people and makes collective decisions regarding its use.

In some cases, becoming a juridical person may not only be beneficial but even necessary for negotiations and signing contracts. For example, income may have to be received and administered by a juridical person representing the local people. Also, legal tenure may require that documents are held by a legally recognized entity (Lynch and Alcorn 1993).

These legal structures would likely involve communities in certain administrative procedures with which they may be unfamiliar, such as filing annual statements and recording minutes of meetings (Lynch and Alcorn 1993). Local people may prefer the entity representing them to have a structure and to follow procedures that conform to traditional community structures and customs but find that national law regarding juridical persons does not easily accommodate this desire. An alternative to becoming a juridical person is to set up an independent **trust fund** to help ensure that local people are not exploited by organizations that they choose to deal with (see also Chapter 7).

Religious structures

In most countries, legal structures that approach parity with states — and are, therefore, able to challenge them — are religious institutions. Although indigenous peoples have frequently suffered from and been alienated by religious institutions and their representatives, the resilience and special status of religious structures may be of interest as a model for organization. For example, "nonconformist" church communities in Scotland can own land and property, have communal rights, and enjoy a relatively independent status under national laws. They are not subject to the rules, laws, and taxes of corporate structures and their members are free to leave the organization as they choose. Furthermore, the community has the right to choose whomever it wishes for membership. The community does have to name a responsible body of elected or selected individuals to represent it but may do this however it wishes.

"Base communities" in Brazil have followed this model, although they retain affiliation with an established church. They are composed of individuals who work together to improve the social, economic, and spiritual conditions of their communities. As a religious structure, however, they have special protection under national law.

There is no necessity to be affiliated with a religious organization in order to appropriate the special legal status of religious structures. The reason for using a religious structure as a model, or organizing principle, is that it may be possible thereby to take advantage of legal privileges as if the community were a religious organization.

Who are the partners?

Representatives of organizations seeking partnership with an indigenous group may be working on behalf of one or several of the potential partners listed below; it must be clearly explained to the group on whose behalf the visitor is working. The community should insist on receiving such information in writing and if possible on audio- or videotape. Promises that scientific data will not be used for commercial exploitation without the consent of the community could also be recorded.

Profit corporations

Profit corporations are commercial bodies dedicated to increasing their income for the benefit of their shareholders or their owners. Their profit is earned by marketing a product, and their interest in making links with indigenous groups will be in channeling indigenous knowledge or resources into the marketplace. For example, companies selling personal care products will be looking for plants and products used by indigenous groups to clean or adorn themselves that can be adapted or developed for the wider global marketplace.

Nonprofit corporations and private organizations

Nonprofit corporations are organizations whose goal is not dedicated to increasing their financial turnover but to furthering a specific aim. They may be charitable foundations or religious groups, owned by a private group or by a trust, government organizations, or departments using funds allocated by a national government. They may receive support from one nation or from an international grouping, and they are likely to fall into the following categories.

Public institutions

Public institutions belong to the governing infrastructure of a country — a botanical garden, a museum, or an educational institution such as a university, dedicated to obtaining and disseminating knowledge. Their representatives will be researchers collecting specific information for use in and by the institution, as well as to further the researcher's career.

Today, owing to the high and increasing costs of education, university research departments are linking with for-profit corporations to increase their funding base. Care should therefore be taken that knowledge given to university researchers or to government data banks is not unknowingly going indirectly to a commercial company.

National government departments are also represented by development specialists who visit developing countries to bring aid in the form of technical assistance or to gather information. Their work may be closely linked to that of NGOs.

There are also international organizations linked, for example, to the United Nations system, which have funds to undertake specific tasks; examples are FAO and the United Nations Development Programme (UNDP).

Nongovernmental organizations

NGOs are supported by donations and grants from fundholders, who may be a government or private persons and groupings. Their mission is generally linked to conservation and development. Since UNCED in 1992, the emphasis of many NGOs has been on development of a kind that is less damaging to the environment, often referred to as **sustainable development**. Pressure groups working for people in developing countries — such as Third World Network in Asia, Genetic Resources Action International and the Gaia Foundation in Europe, and RAFI in North America — publicize information on issues concerning the conservation and sustainable use of biogenetic resources through newsletters, communiqués, and electronic conferencing. Their approach can be described as "bottom up" (working in collaboration with local communities). The larger international NGOs, which have generally made their approach at the government level, are beginning to follow the lead of these pressure groups and listen to voices "on the ground."

People's organizations

People's organizations are groups such as the World Council of Indigenous Peoples, the Cordillera Peoples' Alliance, or smaller local groupings that are formed and run by local peoples to further their own needs. This may be connected to health, marketing, protecting knowledge, or advertising it, but the emphasis is on autonomy. (See the Resource Guide for names and addresses of many people's organizations.)

Conclusions

In the long term, self-determination and the recognition of customary law would help create the most favourable conditions for community-controlled commercialization. However, with or without the advantages that they would bring, it is important to be aware that in collaborating with an outside organization, the community may be at an enormous disadvantage in terms of access to funds and information. Therefore, when deciding to engage in trade and planning to set up an organization to represent the community or group, the following issues should be considered carefully:

- What should be the most appropriate form of organization, bearing in mind national law stipulating how groups can acquire a legal personality;

- The likelihood of highly unequal access to financial support and legal access between the community or group and the trading partner, customer, or broker;
- The difficulties of pursuing legal action if the partner fails to carry out its agreed obligations;
- The possibility that interest in traditional knowledge, goods, and resources may fluctuate so that dependence on trade could lead to financial losses in the future even when current prospects are promising.

Chapter 7

What are contracts and covenants?

Contracts are probably the best understood and most accessible legal instruments. They can be agreed on quickly, they require relatively little legal expertise to implement, and they can be tailored to suit each situation. However, for indigenous peoples to benefit, they must be able to make contracts and take legal action on their own behalf; this may not be possible in some countries. In this chapter, we look at various types of contracts and discuss various options that can be pursued.

A contract is a class of legally enforceable agreement that consists of an exchange of negotiated promises or actions. Contracts for the exchange of knowledge or biological samples generally involve communities agreeing to collect, identify, process, resupply, and in some cases conduct further research in the laboratory on a supply of samples that are then sent to companies for screening. Ideally, communities will control all stages of this process, including the recording of local knowledge pertaining to collected species. However, in some cases collaboration with outside research institutes may prove necessary. Companies, in turn, might agree to provide communities with some or all of the following:

- Per-sample fees;
- Advance payments;
- Their best efforts to screen samples;
- Reports on the results of their research;
- Training for collaborating communities;
- Royalties on any compounds;
- The option of filing a jointly owned patent (copatent) with the community.

Not all written and signed agreements are legally binding. A letter of intent or a *memorandum of understanding* is not a contract, but an agreed to set of statements intended to serve as the basis for a legally binding contract at a later date.

Legal agreements

Material transfer agreements

An MTA establishes standards for the transfer of biological resources for research and possible commercialization in exchange for benefits to the party recognized as the supplier. This might be a government, a collecting organization (such as a botanic garden), or even a local community. Such benefits may be in the form of up-front benefits, a trust fund, or future royalties. In exchange, MTAs usually grant the recipient of the material the right to apply for patents if any of the material has commercial potential.

For example, an MTA was drawn up between the National Biodiversity Institute of Costa Rica (INBio) and the drug company Merck. INBio receives an immediate payment in addition to royalties of about 3 percent of sales if a product is developed from any of the 10 000 or so plant or other biological extracts sent to Merck. However, as is common in commercial contracts, the precise terms of the agreement are secret except to the signatories.

Information transfer agreements

We propose that an alternative term — information transfer agreement — be adopted in the case of agreements made between a traditional community or group and an outside organization interested in the commercial possibilities of local biological resources. The word "material" (in MTA) does not do justice to the intellectual contribution of the community in conserving, nurturing, using, and developing the biological "material" in which the outside organization is interested. The organization (corporation or public institution) must realize that the contract must not only provide compensation for the material provided but also recognize the intellectual property rights of the community. One way to do this might be to name community members as inventors in the patent application or to share patent ownership with the community.

Licencing agreements

A community, institution, or corporation may prefer not to commercialize a product to which it has an intellectual property right (such as a patent) itself, but instead, either sell the patent or sign a licencing agreement with another company that is better equipped to commercialize that particular product. The greater the commercial potential of the patented information or the unpatented **know-how**, the more expensive the **licence** will be. An exception to this occurs when the patent holder is a government agency. For example, the NCI in the United States is not allowed by federal law to commercialize products or to sell licences. Therefore, companies can receive exclusive rights to commercialize a patent-protected product that was developed, at least in part, by the NCI through a free licence.

The example in Box 7.1 illustrates one possible form that a licencing agreement should take, based on the kinds of agreements that computer software companies make with other companies that use and modify the first company's software.

Box 7.1

Software law as a basis for a licencing agreement

Companies producing computer software face the problem that their products can easily be copied and sold by others. Therefore, many software companies have licencing agreements that allow others to use the software and modify it. However, licenced users do not have the right either to copyright their modified versions or to transfer the software to someone else. Ownership of any software derived from the original product remains with the original producer. Computer software licencing agreements often contain the following provisions (Stephenson 1994, p. 183):

- An annual licencing fee, payable by the licencee in exchange for the right to use its modified versions;
- Consulting fees, by which software owners have an on-going advisory relationship with their licencees.

Licencing agreements based on such a model could enable a traditional community to gain an income by sharing its knowledge with outsiders, while at the same time preventing unwanted commercial exploitation. One way to adopt the model would be as a confidentiality clause of a contract involving the transfer of the indigenous knowledge. Contracting parties receiving this knowledge would have to pay fees to the community providing it and to undertake not to transfer the knowledge to others. Stephenson (1994) suggests that before entering into this kind of agreement, a community should be a juridical person (see Chapter 6).

Nonlegal agreements

Letters of intent and memoranda of understanding

Nonlegal agreements, in contrast with contracts, are more likely to be open, particularly where a public institution is involved. Some such institutions may use both legal and nonlegal agreements. The United States NCI, for example, uses an MTA to transfer samples collected earlier to interested companies. But to obtain samples for its own research, it uses a letter of intent (which it calls a letter of collection; see Box 7.2). Letters of intent usually outline the preliminary understanding between parties who intend to enter into a contract. In the case of the NCI, interesting compounds will be licenced to corporations that the NCI expects will then enter into contracts with communities. When letters of intent are signed with communities during collection, the terms continue to apply for an MTA. However, the NCI cannot legally compel a company to pay royalties if the company refuses to do so.

Some institutions employ a memorandum of understanding that, like a letter of intent, is not a binding contract but is similarly used as a statement of intentions and can serve as a starting point for subsequent negotiations (see Box 7.3).

These types of agreements can address issues of confidentiality, the sharing of research results, and the provision of benefits to supplier contractees, but they do not safeguard the rights of local communities and are not necessarily legally enforceable.

Apart from compensation, two important principles often contained in contracts are confidentiality and exclusivity. If a traditional community is willing to supply knowledge or biological material to outsiders but does not wish it to become available to others, it can make an agreement containing a provision for confidentiality. A confidentiality clause can ensure that the recipient will not make knowledge (such as a trade secret) or material available to anyone else without permission of the provider. In return, the other party may request exclusive rights to the information or material supplied. This means that the giver must not pass on the same information or material to someone else during a fixed period. For example, a community may agree to send a number of plants to a company. The latter may demand exclusivity for, say, 6 months. Thus, during this period the community is not allowed to supply the same plants to any other company.

Box 7.2

The National Cancer Institute's letters of collection

The NCI's Natural Products Branch conducts research into plants, microbes, insects, marine organisms, and fungi in its efforts to identify treatments for cancer, AIDS, and other viral infections. It probably has the most extensive natural products collection and screening program in existence.

NCI collections are primarily conducted randomly based on taxonomic data. A small proportion (less than 5 percent) are collected ethnobotanically, through institutions such as the New York Botanical Garden, Missouri Botanical Garden, and some universities. The NCI is interested in any endemic species that, based on local knowledge, are employed for the treatment of cancers, wound healing, and the improvement of health. The NCI relies heavily on the contacts and representative skills of its collectors to ensure that a letter of collection (LOC) is used. As a result, these institutions, and their "country organization" collaborators, play a pivotal role in determining the level of control and resulting benefits local communities receive as a result of collaboration on NCI collections. The LOC states, in part:

- Should the source country government or source country organization(s) have any knowledge of the medicinal use of any plants by the local population or traditional healers, this information will be used to guide the collection of plants on a priority basis where possible. Details of the methods of administration (hot infusion, etc.) used by the traditional healers will be provided where applicable to enable suitable extracts to be made.

- All such information will be kept confidential by NCI until both parties agree to publication.

- The permission of the traditional healer or community will be sought before publication of their information, and proper acknowledgment will be made of their contribution.

Although the LOC clearly acknowledges the utility of local peoples' intellectual contributions, under US patent law if these are not written down, dated, and signed they cannot be considered true inventions as might, for example, the taxonomic input of a collector. The LOC does not include explicit legally binding provisions. It uses terms like "will make the best effort" rather than "will require" because the US government is not allowed "to licence or assign its intellectual property" and it is the policy of the NIH Patent Policy Board "to defer negotiations and agreement upon a specific royalty rate until the specific invention is ascertained."

Box 7.3

The Royal Botanic Gardens' memorandum of understanding

The RBG at Kew, London, has developed a memorandum of understanding for seed collections and another for biochemistry, which outline institutional policy with regard to the return of benefits and the design of equitable arrangements between RBG and its collaborators.

The memorandum of understanding addresses issues of confidentiality, sharing of research results, and the equal sharing of any net profits derived by RBG from commercial collaborations. RBG agrees to send the results of its research to the supplier as soon as they are available. The supplier is required to make its best effort to supply further samples of any material of interest. If a compound looks particularly promising, RBG, with the supplier's agreement, will attempt to develop the work in collaboration with a commercial partner. RBG agrees to split any net profits derived from such collaboration with the supplier. There are no written stipulations on how the supplier's share of the net profits is to be distributed.

The Seed Bank agreements explicitly state that RBG will return 50 percent of any commercial benefits to local collaborators and will deposit herbarium vouchers of all collections in local herbaria. They select their collaborators "carefully," usually working with the national research institute in charge of related research and then rely on them to distribute responsibly any revenues within the country of origin. Recently, the Seed Bank included a caveat in its agreements with recipients of materials that if any commercial activity is proposed, RBG must first be consulted and an agreement negotiated.

RBG has extensive and often long-term relationships with collaborators in over 50 countries, generally with botanic or other scientific institutions. Agreements with the Seed Bank are signed only with institutions (never individuals); these are usually government research institutes. However, because commercial relations to date are based on living or seed collections contained at Kew, ethnobotanic collections are not undertaken as part of commercial agreements.

For further information, contact the Royal Botanic Gardens (see Resource Guide, UK).

Covenants and model contracts

The potential usefulness of contracts compared with the weakness of currently existing ones points to the need to develop model agreements that can be adapted by indigenous peoples to suit their requirements. Covenants serve to establish principles that can lead to a legally binding agreement, but they contain ethical and moral commitments beyond mere commercial agreements. A significant covenant that has been produced recently is described below.

Covenant on Intellectual, Cultural, and Scientific Resources

The covenant produced by the Global Coalition for Biocultural Diversity is based on the view that protecting traditional knowledge is central to any negotiation between local people and outside institutions. Analysis of certain elements of the covenant illustrates what provisions might usefully be included in a contract. The model has been called a *Covenant on Intellectual, Cultural, and Scientific Resources* (reproduced in full in Appendix 2). It is intended to guide negotiating partners into ethical and equitable associations of mutual benefit. The covenant is meant to be more than just a contract. It establishes a basic set of principles to be adopted by all partners, while emphasizing that to strengthen local communities and biodiversity conservation, a long-term commitment is necessary.

Although the covenant deals with equitable trade, any agreement must inevitably encompass protection. Essential elements of the covenant include the following:

- The establishment of immediate benefits, such as a legal trust fund for the local community. In principle, a fund helps to offset the financial handicap of indigenous peoples regarding access to legal assistance and litigation. Up-front payments and advance payments are made to the supplier of resources or information soon after a contract is signed. Up-front payments normally cover expenses incurred before the main activities described in the contract begin. For example, an indigenous organization representing many communities would probably have to consult these communities before entering into an agreement. Therefore, it would be reasonable to ask that the contract include up-front payments to cover the expenses of the consultation process. Advance payments usually cover costs that have to be incurred to fulfill the activities agreed upon in the contract. For example, if a company wishes to purchase clothes from a community, it may have to pay in advance for the equipment needed to produce the clothes.

- An independent monitor to evaluate the agreement and ensure that all parties understand their obligations and comply with them.

- Prior informed consent, full disclosure, and joint planning. These are critical elements (see Chapter 4).

- Concern for the biological and social environment. There is no point in discussing equitable agreements, just compensation, and TRR/IPR if biological diversity is not conserved and ecological concerns are not a priority for all partners. This is explicitly stated in Principle VIII (see Appendix 2).

- Compensation and profit sharing. In the case of drug companies it may take many years for the company to produce a new medicine and, therefore, to make profits. This is why up-front payments are important. However, when they come, profits can be enormous. The usual way to share profits is through royalty payments. A royalty is a payment, usually a fixed percentage per unit sold, to an intellectual property owner established by contract or other agreement.

Royalties may also be payable, if stipulated in the contract, by a drug company to a supplier of biological matter or to the landowner if the material has attributes useful for the development of a new product (drug, agrochemical, cosmetic, food, etc.). An indigenous group that supplies plants to a company or other institution may be able to secure a guarantee of royalties in a contract. However, the percentage will reflect the value of the biological and intellectual information it provides, balanced by the relative amount of intellectual and financial investment a company must make to develop a useful product. In the case of drug companies, this latter investment is usually considerable and will also entail a delay of several years before the product goes on the market and royalties are payable. Also, the community's contractual partner may not be the one that markets the product. Therefore, royalties may have to be shared with this partner. This is the case for several institutions (such as botanic gardens) and companies that make agreements with plant suppliers but then licence the information relating to their research to a manufacturer. It may well be possible, where relevant, for a community to be a copatent holder if it wishes to pursue such an option.

A number of contracts have been developed that might provide background and serve as models for local communities, but most such documents are not geared toward traditional resources but focus instead on randomly collected biological samples. Examples are *The Biodiversity Prospecting Contract* (Downes et al. 1993; see also King 1994) and *The Contract between the Collector and the Government Parties* (for information, contact the Third World Network — see Resource Guide, Malaysia).

Conclusions

Contracts and other agreements can be useful tools for ensuring that local communities benefit from the commercialization of their knowledge and resources. However, those currently in existence are far from satisfactory. Great caution should be exercised by those considering an agreement with an outside institution. This chapter contains information on both provisions that are likely to appear in a contract and provisions that should be included. Even if both parties have legally binding obligations, the community will be much less able to take legal action if obligations of the other party are not met. It will almost certainly be necessary to obtain independent legal advice during the early stages of negotiation, and insisting on the establishment of a trust fund may be the best way to do this. It may also be a good idea to approach NGOs with the expertise to provide sound legal advice or financial assistance to enable the community to acquire such advice (Kloppenburg and Gonzales 1994). It is also critical to find an independent monitor acceptable to both sides to mediate and evaluate the terms and implementations of the agreement.

Chapter 8

Are intellectual property rights useful?

Traditional communities may have their own concepts of intellectual property and resource rights. However, industrializing countries are under political pressure to adopt the European and North American concepts of intellectual property, which, by guaranteeing the right of legal individuals to profit from their innovations, are widely believed to promote development. IPR laws have usually been inimical to the interests of indigenous communities, but there are ways in which these laws can serve the interests of these communities.

IPR laws exist in most countries of the world and Western concepts of IPR usually prevail in national laws. These concepts are based on the idea that innovation is the product of the genius of individuals. Such people, by sharing the fruits of their genius with society, are deemed to be deserving of economic rights granted by the state on behalf of society. These economic rights are collectively known as IPR. In the 20th century, modern societies are increasingly dominated economically by corporations that employ researchers and inventors. As a result, the IPR often go not to individuals but to the corporations, government agencies, or universities that employ them or fund their research.

Various IPR types exist, all of which may have a role to play in protecting indigenous knowledge and in helping indigenous peoples to market the products they decide to commercialize. Some of them may also be useful for the protection of cultural heritage and biodiversity.

However, IPR cannot adequately protect the knowledge and resources of indigenous peoples, nor are they a panacea for the lack of self-determination of indigenous peoples and the inequalities of wealth and power between local communities on one hand and governments and corporations on the other. Furthermore, not only do IPR have to be acquired by a process that can be difficult, time-consuming, and expensive, but they also have to be defended. Acquiring and defending IPR protection requires access to information, good legal advice, and financial resources, all of which may be beyond the reach of many indigenous peoples.

Although IPR laws vary from country to country, international treaties like the Paris and Berne Conventions give them a common basis. The recent TRIPs agreement of GATT will enhance the convergence of IPR national laws in the future (see Chapter 10). Most international conventions pertaining to IPR are administered by WIPO, a United Nations agency based in Switzerland (see Box 8.1).

The following categories are explained and discussed in this chapter: patents, petty patents or utility models, copyright, trademarks, unfair competition, industrial designs, trade secrets, plant breeders' rights (PBR), geographic indications, such as appellations of origin, certification (not normally regarded as an IPR but dealt with here in view of its relevance).

Patents

A patent is a legal certificate that gives an inventor exclusive rights to prevent others from producing, using, selling, or importing the invention for a fixed period (usually 17–20 years). Legal action can be taken against those who infringe the patent by copying the invention or selling it without permission from the patent owner. Patents can be bought, sold, hired, or licenced. A patent application must satisfy the patent examiners that the "invention" is

- *Useful* (have industrial application): ideas, theories, and scientific formulas are not sufficiently useful to be patentable;

Box 8.1

What is the World Intellectual Property Organization?

WIPO was established by a convention in 1967, although its origins can be traced to the Paris and Berne Conventions adopted in 1883 and 1886, respectively. WIPO's primary objectives are to administer international treaties on intellectual property laws; to provide assistance to signatory nations in promulgating intellectual property laws; and to seek harmonization of national laws, aiming to "promote the protection of intellectual property throughout the world." IPR laws are the laws that governments enact to make these international treaties part of national law. WIPO administers, inter alia, the following treaties concerning IPR:

- *Paris Convention for the Protection of Industrial Property* (1883);
- *Berne Convention for the Protection of Literary and Artistic Works* (1886);
- *Madrid Agreement Concerning the International Registration of Trademarks* (1891);
- *Lisbon Agreement for the Protection of Appellations of Origin and their International Registration* (1958);
- *Rome Convention for the Protection of Performers, Producers of Phonograms and Broadcasting Organizations* (1961) (see Chapter 10);
- *Patent Cooperation Treaty* (1970) (see also Chapter 2);
- *Budapest Treaty on the International Recognition of the Deposit of Microorganisms for the Purpose of Patent Procedure* (1977) (see Chapter 2).

Negotiations that might lead to future international IPR agreements are held under the auspices of WIPO (34 Chemin des Colombettes, PO Box 18, Geneva 20, CH-1211, Switzerland).

- *Novel*: the invention should be recent and original, but perhaps most importantly it should not already be known (in the public domain). In most countries (except the USA) the patent is awarded to the first person to apply, regardless of whether this person was the first to invent;

- **Nonobvious**: not obvious to a person skilled in the technology and more inventive than mere discovery of what already exists in nature (such as a gene with no known function). The "invention" must be disclosed to the patent examiners in a detailed way that would enable a skilled technician to make and use it. In the case of an invented process, the patent can cover a nonobvious way of making something already known (previously invented or discovered). In the case of an invented product, the nonobvious requirement does not require it to be made by a novel method.

Several kinds of patent may be granted (Lesser 1991, p. 14):

- *Products*: covers any use of the product including those as yet undiscovered. For example, a new drug patented as a cure for cancer may later be found to cure heart disease; the patent will cover this new use.

- *Uses*: covers a specific use only. Thus, it would cover the above drug only as a cure for cancer and not for any uses that are found later.
- *Processes*: protects the process when used with any product, but does not protect the invention when it can be manufactured by a different process.
- *Products-by-process*: covers only products made by the process described in the application. Therefore, it would cover the drug, but only when made by a specified process.

These should not be regarded necessarily as discrete categories of patent because broad patent claims may include several products, processes and uses.

Not all inventions that meet the above conditions can be protected by patent. In many countries, medicines and genetically modified organisms (plants, animals, or microorganisms containing a gene transferred artificially from another organism) cannot be patented at all. In part the differences in national patent laws are due to the fact that each country prefers to define what inventions may be patented in accordance with its perceived national interest.

It can easily take over 2 years to obtain a patent from the day that an application is filed and the invention is disclosed to the national patent office (the priority date). The patent office carries out a search to ensure that the invention really is new and nonobvious. When it is satisfied that this is so, the application is published and an in-depth examination follows. In the case of an invention derived from a natural product, the examination might include the obligation to describe the source and location of the natural product (Gollin 1993, p. 166) and demonstrate that the prior informed consent (see Chapter 4) of suppliers of resources and information was obtained. To obtain patents in other countries, it is usually necessary to file a different application in each country, preferably within 12 months of the priority date. However, a number of international agreements (such as the *Patent Cooperation Treaty* (PCT)) simplify this process by requiring a single international application to be prepared. In the case of the PCT, this application is then submitted to a receiving office from where it is distributed to national patent offices designated by the applicant. It is very important that inventors do not disclose their invention before applying, except in the strictest confidence. If they do, the patent might be invalidated.

Is indigenous knowledge patentable?

Three questions now arise:

1. *Can indigenous people patent their own knowledge?*

A product patent cannot be obtained for a naturally occurring organism or a gene that has not been isolated. This rules out the patenting of much potentially useful indigenous knowledge relating to naturally occurring organisms. Nevertheless, some traditional medicinal or other preparations from natural substances could be regarded as patentable modifications or combinations (processes), and process patents may be obtainable for them.

However, this is possible only in the case of new inventions and as long as individual people can be cited as the "inventors." To this extent, indigenous people may be able to patent a certain amount of their own knowledge. One major obstacle is that the process of acquiring a patent, which includes payments for filing, the examination, and the grant, is expensive and time-consuming. Furthermore, the patent will need to be renewed annually. Indeed, the expense may be beyond the means of many communities.

2. *Can companies obtain patents based on indigenous knowledge?*

This is certainly possible. Frequently, companies have investigated useful attributes of a biological substance known to a traditional community. Although normally a product patent cannot be obtained for a naturally occurring organism, chemical, or gene, in some industrial countries patents can be obtained for one that has been altered in some way. Therefore, after isolating the active principle of a substance, the company can modify it or use it in the design of a new synthetic compound that may be more stable or less toxic than the original substance. Such an "invention" can then be patented by the company. Boxes 8.2, 8.3, and 8.4 describe three cases in which this has happened.

3. *What can be done if someone copies an invention without permission?*

One of the biggest problems that would face an indigenous community with a legal personality (see Chapter 6) that obtained a patent is the danger of others infringing the patent by copying it. The community might not know about it, and even if it finds out, legal action can be very expensive. Whereas corporations have their own lawyers and financial resources to provide effective legal support, local communities rarely have such resources or advocates. Even if a case does go to court, the company may well succeed in convincing the court that its product, use or process is sufficiently different from the original to constitute an invention.

Are patents useful for local communities?

Some traditional knowledge is patentable, although the expense of a patent application may be prohibitive. Also, the indigenous group would have to prove that the invention was novel by convincing the patent examiners that it was the only group with the knowledge. This might be difficult and would probably be incompatible with the indigenous peoples' practice of sharing knowledge. The cases cited above suggest that patent law is bound to favour companies rather than local communities.

An indigenous group could still contest the right of others to patent an invention based on information acquired from the group and used without its authorization (Gollin 1993, p. 167; also see neem case described in Box 8.2). Some NGOs, such as RAFI and Swissaid, have played a useful role by checking patent applications in various countries for cases in which indigenous peoples may have been exploited. In most countries (the United States is an exception) copies of patent applications can be seen by members of the public on application to national patent offices before the patent is awarded. (These NGOs discovered the applications based on the cell lines of indigenous peoples described in Chapter 2.) The very possibility of a challenge to a patent

Box 8.2

Neem — a traditional and modern biopesticide

Seeds of a species of neem tree (*Azadirachta indica*) have been ground and scattered on fields by Indian farmers for centuries to protect their crops from insect pests. However, the neem tree has many other uses: it appears to be effective against malaria and internal worms; the leaves are used to protect stored grain from pests and clothes from moths; neem oil is used to make candles, soap, a contraceptive, and can even fuel diesel engines; and 500 million Indians reportedly use neem to brush their teeth. Most of these discoveries were first made by members of Indian rural communities.

As a pesticide, neem has great potential as a cheap and environmentally friendly alternative to commercial synthetic pesticides. Two companies, W.R. Grace and Agrodyne, recently obtained patents in the United States for derivatives of neem developed in their laboratories, even though the insecticidal, human nontoxic, and biodegradeable properties of neem are far from novel and nonobvious to millions of Indian farmers.

Another patent has been granted in the USA for an extract of neem bark effective against certain types of cancer. W.R. Grace is now producing neem-based pesticides with an Indian company called PJ Margo at a new facility in India. They estimate that the global market for their product may reach $50 million annually by the year 2000 (*AgBiotechnology News*, February 1993, p. 4). Agrodyne Technologies now has US government approval to sell neem-based bio-insecticides and has applied for registration of its products in several European and Latin American countries.

These companies (and the Indian companies that also hold patents related to neem) stand to gain from the insights of Indian farmers. Nevertheless, the farmers are in a weak position to demand compensation, because the knowledge is widespread and in the public domain. India, too, has a weak claim because the tree is native also to neighbouring countries and is now grown around the world.

Recently, the patent held by W.R. Grace has been challenged in the United States courts on the basis that knowledge of neem as a pesticide was already in the public domain when the patent was granted. If the patent is revoked, many other patents that also relate closely to traditional knowledge could also be challenged with highly significant outcomes.

For information about the neem antipatent campaign, contact the Research Foundation for Science, Technology and Natural Resource Policy (see Resource Guide, India).

application would make companies more willing to consider compensating indigenous people in some way to avoid an expensive out-of-court settlement, a damaged reputation, or even a rejected patent application.

If an inventor is not interested in obtaining a patent but wishes to ensure that no one else can obtain one, he or she may publish a thorough description of how to practice the invention. In the United States, this is called "defensive publication." The published material forms part of the ***prior art*** that a patent office is obliged to search; thus, after the date of publication, any patent claim for the same invention will be invalid. This might be a useful way for indigenous peoples to prevent others from patenting inventions derived from indigenous knowledge and resources.

Box 8.3

Ethiopian endod

Berries of the endod or African soapberry plant (*Phytolacca dodecandra*) have long been cultivated by Ethiopians, mainly for use as a detergent. In 1964, an Ethiopian scientist, Aklilu Lemma, discovered that snails carrying the fluke causing schistosomiasis, a disease that afflicts 200 million people and kills 200 000 people a year, were killed in streams where people used the soapberry to wash their clothes.

Lemma and Legesse Wolde-Yohannes of Addis Ababa University undertook the preparation of a low-cost molluscicide based on endod. With support from the Netherlands government, Wolde-Yohannes was able to identify the most efficacious endod variety, E-44, and toxicity studies were carried out. Unfortunately, Ethiopia does not have the capacity to conduct trials and toxicologic studies to the standards required for international recognition, and Lemma failed to secure financial backing for further research. Up to now the only molluscicidal product recommended by the World Health Organization is Bayluscide, which costs as much as $25 000 per tonne.

Subsequent research by Lemma in collaboration with a US biologist, Harold Lee, at the University of Toledo confirmed that endod was also effective against zebra mussels, and the name lemmatoxin was given to the active ingredient. Zebra mussels, accidentally introduced in the Great Lakes, now foul water intake systems, disrupt shipping, and threaten the fishing industry.

A few months after this discovery, the University of Toledo applied for a patent for its use as a control agent for the zebra mussel, with Lemma, Lee, and another scientist named as inventors. If a company is granted a licence by the university to market endod, the University will share the royalties with the three scientists. Ethiopia and the local people whose use of endod had attracted the attention of Lemma will receive no benefits and will still have to import Bayluscide. Ethiopia can only benefit by supplying the berries, but if it tries to raise the price, the companies that produce endod may find it cheaper to synthesize the active principle, thereby eliminating the market for berries.

For further information, contact RAFI (see Resource Guide, Canada).

In many cases, however, it is inappropriate. For example, Indian farmers would have had to isolate and name the active ingredients of neem, then publish the details to prevent companies from applying for patents. Also, publication might simply attract the attention of companies and provide them with a useful lead for a new product. (See also Table 1.)

Petty patents

Petty patents (also known as utility models) differ from conventional patents in several ways:

- The nonobvious requirement is far less stringent and may even be discarded in favour of a less demanding "***inventive step***";

- The period of protection is shorter;

Box 8.4

Thaumatin — a natural sweetener from West Africa

Thaumatin is a natural sweetener derived from the berries of a shrub called the katemfe (*Thaumatococcus daniellii*), which grows in west and central African forests. The protein, which is about 2 000 times sweeter than sucrose, was discovered by researchers at the University of Ife, Nigeria. The berries had apparently been in use for centuries as a sweetener and flavour enhancer, although in some areas only the stalks and leaves are used and the berries are considered waste.

In recent years it has been used by food and confectionary industries in a number of countries, sometimes marketed as a low-calorie sweetener. It is also used as an animal feed. For several years, the British sugar company, Tate and Lyle, has marketed the product under the name Talin. As the plant will not bear fruit outside its natural surroundings, the company imports the fruit from its own plantations in Ghana, Côte d'Ivoire, Liberia, and Malaysia.

Because the method of extraction is expensive, a number of companies attempted to use **recombinant DNA** technology on the gene responsible for producing the thaumatin protein. Beatrice Foods obtained a patent in the USA for the process of cloning the gene in yeast. It has been estimated that the company could gain substantial royalties, amounting to $25 million.

Researchers from the Lucky Biotech Corporation and the University of California have received a US patent for all transgenic fruits, seeds, and vegetables containing the gene responsible for producing thaumatin. The competitive nature of biotechnological research into thaumatin indicates the potential value of the genetic information as perceived by the companies involved. In fact, the market for low-calorie sweeteners in the USA alone is estimated to be $900 million a year. It is highly likely that katemfe plantations will soon no longer be necessary; if so, the countries where katemfe is grown will not even be able to benefit from exporting the berries.

Source: Sasson (1989), Walgate (1990, p. 161), Myers (1993), Shand (1993, p. 1), A.A. Elujoba, Department of Pharmacy, Obafemi Awolowo University, Nigeria, 1994 (personal communication).

- The patent examination is either deferred or replaced by a registration system (as with trademarks).

Petty patents vary more than other IPR types because there are no international agreements or conventions covering them.

Can indigenous knowledge be protected through petty patents?

It is likely that some indigenous knowledge or know-how, particularly that related to medicinal preparations derived from plants, would meet the inventive step condition. Although a plant extract and the method used to obtain it may be "obvious," it could still be novel, useful, and an inventive step beyond anything already in the public domain (Gollin 1993, p. 173). This point is reinforced when we consider medicines prepared by unique methods and from mixtures intended to achieve synergistic effects or to mitigate harmful side-effects. Significantly, Kenya recently passed a law that allows petty patents for traditional medicinal knowledge ("herbal as well as nutritional formulations which give new effects" — *The Industrial Property Act* 1989).

Are petty patents useful for local communities?

Petty patents could become a useful tool to protect indigenous knowledge (Table 1). However, as yet only a few countries (such as Brazil, China, Germany, Japan, and Malaysia) accept them, and there are no international agreements, like the PCT, to simplify the effort of applying in several countries. Indigenous peoples might gain from efforts to increase international recognition of this IPR type. Uncovering and publicizing the actions of companies and institutions seeking to apply for patents based on information disclosed in foreign petty patent applications may also be worthwhile actions.

Copyright

Copyright gives authors legal protection for the following types of work:

- Literary works (such as books, film scripts, and even private correspondence);
- Dramatic and musical works (such as plays and music compositions recorded in the form of musical notation);
- Artistic works and works of applied art (such as paintings, ceramics, carvings);
- Maps and technical drawings;
- Photographic works;
- Motion pictures and sound recordings (such as movies, documentaries, and interviews);
- Computer programs and databases.

Copyright law is intended to protect authors by granting them exclusive rights to sell copies of their work in whatever tangible form (printed publication, sound recording, film, broadcast, etc.) is being used to convey their creative expressions to the public. Although registration is not usually necessary, it is advisable for authors to place their name on the work. However, legal protection covers the "expression" of the ideas contained, not the ideas themselves, which are not actually required to be novel at all. Copyright gives owners exclusive rights, usually for the life of the author plus 50 years. In the case of sound recordings, copyright is usually conferred for 50 years and is available to the person or company responsible for making the recording. Copyright owners have the legal right to stop others from

- Copying or reproducing the work;
- Performing the work in public;
- Making a sound recording or motion picture of the work; and

— Broadcasting, translating, or adapting the work.

Others who wish to exploit copyright material in these ways must usually seek the permission of the copyright owner or an organization that represents copyright owners in a particular industry. Permission is likely to require payment of royalties. In some countries, copyright owners may have the legal rights to be identified on their work and to object to distortions of the work. These are known as moral rights and remain with the author even if the author transfers the copyright to somebody else.

Can indigenous peoples' folklore be protected by copyright?

Indigenous peoples may be concerned about outsiders reproducing their arts, crafts, songs, and designs without permission and either neglect to acknowledge the source of the creativity or *pass off* works as genuine indigenous art when they are not. The main limitations of copyright as an IPR tool to protect indigenous culture are as follows:

— Copyrights are assigned to individuals or companies, whereas indigenous people are more likely to desire protection of the rights of the community or tribe, even in cases of recent individual authorship.

— The protection of folklore should ideally be in perpetuity.

— Among some indigenous groups, many expressions of folklore are not fixed but are passed on orally from generation to generation. This excludes such expressions from eligibility for copyright protection.

Is copyright useful for local communities?

Conventional copyright is limited in its usefulness as a tool for preventing the exploitation of folklore, although a number of countries have sought to incorporate folklore into their national copyright laws (see Table 1). In Australia, Aboriginal artists have successfully sued on the basis of copyright (see box 8.5). Copyright law is also being used by the Dene of Canada, as well as several other indigenous groups worldwide, to control documentation of their traditional knowledge (Greaves 1993, p. 7).

Trademarks

A trademark is a marketing tool that is often used to support a company's claim that its products are "authentic" or "distinctive" compared with similar products from another trading entity. It consists of a distinctive design, word, or series of words, usually placed on the product label and perhaps displayed in advertisements. For example, Coca Cola is a trademark that can only be used on goods manufactured by the Coca Cola Company. A trademark does not have to be registered, but doing so enables owners to sue

Box 8.5

Bulun Bulun versus Nejlam Pty Ltd

Aboriginal art is now a major source of income for many communities in Australia. The art industry provides employment for thousands of people, including artists and employees of art centres where the works are sold. Many of these people are not indigenous. Retail sales amounted to more than AU $18 million in 1988 (1.315 Australian (AU) dollars = 1 US dollar), of which AU $7 million was received by the artists. According to Golvan (1992), "The works of Aboriginal artists have become our national artistic symbols. It has become inconceivable for any major public building to be opened today which does not feature some Aboriginal art."

Unfortunately, there have been many cases of non-Aboriginal people producing distorted and trivialized versions of Aboriginal artworks. In 1989, John Bulun Bulun, who had discovered that a T-shirt manufacturer had printed shirts displaying an unauthorized reproduction of two of his paintings, sued for copyright infringement. The company and two shops that had sold the T-shirts agreed in court to withdraw them from sale. Later, 14 other artists brought claims against the same company. These cases were settled out of court with the artists receiving AU $150 000 in compensation and to cover their costs.

A positive outcome of this attempt by Aboriginal artists to use the law to protect their rights was that the practice of making unauthorized reproductions of Aboriginal designs on clothes came to an end. Nevertheless, it has not completely stopped people making and selling crude imitations of Aboriginal designs. The most important consequence is that these indigenous people have become aware that the law is not necessarily inimical to their interests but can even be used to further them. Their biggest obstacle, however, is securing the financial resources necessary to take a company to court.

Source: Golvan (1992), ECOSOC (1993, p. 35).

infringers and to licence use of the trademark. The *Madrid Agreement Concerning the International Registration of Trademarks* enables an applicant to obtain coverage in several countries with a single trademark application. About 30 countries have signed this agreement.

Can indigenous peoples' cultural heritage be protected by trademarks?

Indigenous peoples' handicrafts and artworks are desirable products in some countries, but reproductions made by nonindigenous people may undermine the market. If tribal names had trademark protection, people might prefer to buy goods bearing such names, perhaps at higher prices because they value authenticity. Also, imitators might be deterred by the possibility of legal action. The sale of reproductions passed off as genuine indigenous handicrafts is also a violation of the rights of consumers; thus, other legal instruments may be applicable, too.

Nowadays, many people choose to buy goods that appeal to their ethical values. A trademark can be designed to indicate that purchasing goods carrying the mark supports a good cause. The Body Shop registered the word "rainforest" to help make it fashionable to buy the company's tropical forest products (see Box 8.6). Many customers believe that by buying products with this mark they are helping to protect the forests. However, another company selling similar products risks trademark infringement if it uses the word "rainforest" in advertising or on the product labels. This points to an opportunity for a company to encourage other companies to trade ethically. Such a company with a trademark has the right either to ignore infringements or to register users when it believes that this will further the cause of ethical marketing (C. Haynes, director, Rainforest Foods, London, UK, 1994, personal communication). In the absence of a trade association controlling the use of certification trademarks, a company could follow the example of Cultural Survival, which allows companies to use its trademark "Forest Flavors" and the Rainforest Seal of Approval palm frond logo in exchange for a percentage on raw materials or sales (Snead 1992). The money is then used to support forest peoples and the in situ conservation of the genetic base of the raw materials.

Better still, a trade association or indigenous alliance consisting of representatives of different communities selling similar products could register a trademark that could be used by all participating communities. This trademark could then become a kind of certification mark (see "Certification," below).

Box 8.6

The quick and easy way to own a "rainforest"

It is possible for traders to monopolize use of the word "rainforest" to distinguish their products from similar ones on the market. The commercial advantage comes from its fashionable exotic and "green" connotations (as long as the goods are not made of mahogany).

Trademarks apply not to any goods but to classes of goods. Thus, if a company registers "rainforest" for cosmetics, as The Body Shop has done, rival companies are forbidden to use the word to inform customers of the rainforest source of ingredients, except in the small print on a label or advertisement. Similarly, no confectionery company can place the words "rainforest crunch" on product labels except the one that already owns this trademark, which is Ben and Jerry's.

Although companies might claim to be the first to market tropical forest products ethically and would understandably not wish to see other companies that are unconcerned about sustainability and fair trade using the word, other ethical companies will also be prohibited from using the word "rainforest" to sell similar products. This is perhaps not the best way to expand the sustainable and equitable trade in tropical NTFPs.

Trademarks can be a useful tool to promote rainforest marketing, but monopolizing the use of trademarks that are successful at attracting buyers may be counterproductive.

Source: C. Haynes, Director, Rainforest Foods, London, UK, 1994 (personal communication)

In some countries, a trademark may be challenged in the courts if it insults an ethnic group. Indeed, legal action is being taken against the Washington Redskins football team for this reason (T. Greaves, Department of Sociology and Anthropology, Bucknell University, USA, 1994, personal communication).

Are trademarks useful for local communities?

Trademarks can not only help indigenous peoples wishing to commercialize certain products but can also support claims of "unfair competition," defined in the Paris Convention as

- Acts of such a nature as to create confusion by any means whatsoever with the establishment, the goods, or the industrial or commercial activities of a competitor;
- False allegations in the course of trade of such a nature as to discredit the establishment, the goods, or the industrial or commercial activities of a competitor;
- Indications or allegations the use of which in the course of trade is liable to mislead the public as to the nature, the manufacturing process, the characteristics, the suitability for their purpose, or the quantity of the goods.

However, legal action on the basis of unfair competition does not require that goods be already protected by trademark or other forms of legal protection (see Table 1).

Industrial designs

Industrial designs are defined in the Paris Convention as "the ornamental or aesthetic aspect of a useful article" and may consist of the shape, pattern, or colour of the article. For example, the pattern on an article of clothing or pottery could be protected. The designs must be original and reproducible by industrial means. The period of protection is not indefinite but may be for 5, 10, or 15 years up to a maximum of 25 years. Like trademarks, registering a design is cheaper and less time-consuming than applying for a patent. It also gives owners the right to take legal action against infringers.

Trade secrets

Know-how is practical information that may give a person or company a competitive advantage. As long as it is known only to a few people, such information can be legally recognized and protected as a trade secret even though it fails to fulfill the criteria of patentability. A claim for protection of know-how as a trade secret requires that efforts be made to prevent disclosure. Agreements between indigenous peoples and others to respect the confidential nature of information disclosed and strictly enforced access restrictions are examples of such efforts. Law makes the taking without permission of a trade secret an illegal act but not the discovery by proper means (by independent discovery), accidental or actual disclosure, or by *reverse engineering*.

Can traditional knowledge be protected as trade secrets?

The knowledge or know-how of an individual or the whole community might be protected as a trade secret as long as the information has commercial value and provides a competitive advantage, whether or not the community itself wishes to profit from it (see Table 1). If a company obtains such information by illicit means, legal action may be used to force the company to share its profits (Gollin 1993, p. 164).

Conceivably, a considerable amount of indigenous peoples' knowledge could be protected as trade secrets. Restricting access to their territories and exchanging information with outsiders through agreements that secure confidentiality or economic benefits would be appropriate means to this end. Trade secret law can be used to facilitate the drafting of contracts with companies that oblige "recipients to obtain regular patent protection and to share royalties" (Axt et al. 1993).

It has been suggested that knowledge shared be all members of a community may not qualify as a trade secret, but "if a shaman or other individual has exclusive access to information because of his status in the group, that individual or the indigenous group together probably has a trade secret" (Axt et al. 1993).

Plant breeders' rights

The *Union for the Protection of New Varieties of Plants (UPOV) Convention* provides for rights commonly known as PBR. According to the latest 1991 revision of the convention, breeders are people who breed, discover, or develop crop varieties. PBR prevent other breeders from breeding and selling the same plant varieties. The convention has force only in its 20 member countries, all of which are developed countries except Argentina, South Africa, and Uruguay. A few developing countries have national forms of PBR.

To be eligible for protection, the plant variety must be

- *Distinct* (the most important requirement): distinguishable by one or more characteristics from any other variety whose existence is a matter of common knowledge;

- *Stable:* remain true to its description after repeated reproduction or propagation;

- *Uniform:* homogeneous with regard to the particular feature of its sexual reproduction or vegetative propagation;

- *Novel:* not have been offered for sale or marketed, with the agreement of the breeder or his successor in title, in the source country, or for longer than 4 years in any other country.

An application for plant variety protection requires a written description of the variety and deposition of samples in the form of seeds, a dried plant, or a live plant for the examination and conclusive demonstration of stability and homogeneity through propagation trials. Protection is for 15–20 years.

Until 1991, exclusive rights were given by the UPOV Convention to prevent the sale of the reproductive or vegetative propagating part of the plant and commercial production for the purpose of marketing the variety. However, the 1991 revision extended protection from the propagating part of the variety to the whole plant. It also made two other important changes from the previous version regarding two exemptions:

- The research or breeders' exemption allowed people to use a protected variety as an initial source of variation to create their own new varieties and then to market them as long as repeat use of the original variety was not needed.

- The farmers' exemption, or privilege, permitted farmers to keep seed of a protected variety for use as seed in subsequent seasons, but not to sell it.

The 1991 UPOV revision eliminated the first of these and made the second optional rather than obligatory for signatory nations. The revision appears to be an attempt to make the protection as strong as that of a patent. So far, only the United States has signed the new agreement, but several countries are drafting new legislation in line with the 1991 convention.

Can indigenous peoples use PBR to protect their own plant varieties?

The UPOV Convention is of limited relevance because it has so few member states. In theory, it is certainly possible for indigenous peoples to obtain a plant variety certificate for some of their crop varieties, and possibly some nondomesticated plants that are utilized by them (Gollin 1993, p. 164), although the intravariety genetic diversity common to traditional cultivars might make many of these ineligible. Indeed, indigenous peoples actually prefer varieties that possess variability and adaptability and therefore breed for these qualities.

The community or group would presumably have to demonstrate that it was the only one that had bred the cultivar or used the landrace. Fulfilling all the above legal requirements is less expensive than applying for a patent, meaning that PBR could be a useful tool for indigenous peoples. However, carrying out the field trials and recording results to demonstrate to the examiners that the variety is eligible for a certificate might be difficult if not impossible to achieve (Table 1). This is one reason why it has been much more common for professional breeders to breed new varieties based on landraces and obtain legal protection for these new varieties. Professional breeders also have greater financial resources, legal experience, and scientific facilities. As long as professional breeders have such advantages over traditional farmer-breeders, the convention is more likely to undermine the rights of traditional communities than support them.

Table 1. Advantages and disadvantages of various IPR mechanisms for local communities.

Mechanism	Advantages	Disadvantages
Patents	Can safeguard knowledge legally Available in most countries	Limited term of protection Applications expensive and require legal advice Protect knowledge of individual inventors, not collective knowledge of communities Difficult and expensive to defend
Petty patents	Can safeguard knowledge legally More traditional knowledge may be protected than under patent Compared with patents, less expensive application procedure and shorter and less stringent examination	Available only in a few countries No international agreements to facilitate application in different countries Shorter period of protection than patents
Copyright	Easy to obtain Long period of protection	Protects expression of ideas but not knowledge itself Protection period not indefinite Subject matter must be in a physical form
Trademarks	Inexpensive Indefinite protection period, although may have to be renewed periodically May attract more customers to products of indigenous traders and trading organizations	Does not protect knowledge per se
Trade secrets	Can protect traditional knowledge with commercial application Can protect more knowledge than the other IPR types Can be traded for economic benefits by contract Inexpensive to protect	Available in fewer countries than patents and copyrights
Breeders' rights	Less expensive than patents Many folk varieties (landraces) may be eligible	Only available in UPOV convention signatory countries, which are few in number Difficult to demonstrate eligibility criteria

Geographic indications and appellations of origin

Geographic indications "identify a good as originating in the territory [of a member], or a region or locality in that territory, where a given quality, reputation or other characteristic of the good is essentially attributable to its geographical origin" (Article 22 of GATT-TRIPs). One well-known type of geographical indication is the appellation of origin.

Appellation of origin was originally a French geographic indication applying to products considered to be distinctive due to a combination of traditional know-how and highly localized natural conditions (ECOSOC 1993, p. 35; for more information on geographic indications, see Moran 1993). In France, a government agency validates Appellation d'Origine Contrôlée (registered designations of origin), so that producers of wines, cheeses, and other foodstuffs, whose goods are renowned for their distinctive qualities and geographic origins are protected from those who would undermine their good reputation by making similar, but false, claims (Bérard and Marchenay 1993). For example, wines from the Champagne region of France are protected this way; local producers acting collectively have prevented the use of the word "Champagne" on bottles of perfume, English wine, and German shampoo (Freedman 1994, p. 14).

In British trademark law, local manufacturers can set up their own association and register a collective "certification trademark," although the applicant association cannot itself trade in the product. The makers of a well-known British cheese, which must be produced in or near the village where it originates (Stilton) according to a certain recipe and process, is protected in this way. The European Union has a register of products protected by geographic indications.

Although so far the use of this method has been confined mainly to certain foodstuffs, it could conceivably be extended to protect expressions of folklore (see Unesco–WIPO model provisions, Chapter 9). This would most likely work if regional associations of indigenous peoples, with government recognition, set up their own appellations of origin or certification-issuing entities (see also below).

Certification and labeling

Certification and labeling are used simply to make a claim about a product that may be of interest to the customer. Certification can be used in a way that protects the environment and ensures that resources, such as timber, are used in a sustainable manner. For example, wood may have a mark to certify that it came from a sustainably managed forest or a handicraft may be marked in some way to show that it is authentic. Tuna fish cans are often labeled "dolphin friendly" to indicate that dolphins were not killed as a result of the method used to catch the tuna. Certification means that claims are authenticated by an organization independent of the individual or company making or selling the product. This could be a regional association of indigenous peoples (as above). Sometimes imitators label their products in a misleading manner. Certification should help buyers distinguish between fakes and genuine products and can make it possible for traders to take legal action against others who use the mark without authorization.

In Canada, it has been claimed that labels such as "handmade," "handcrafted," and "authentic" that are not authenticated by an independent body confuse buyers and compete with products made and sold by indigenous peoples (Blundell 1993, p. 69). In response, Canada has introduced official certification marks to authenticate indigenous peoples' works (Blundell 1993; ECOSOC 1993, pp. 34–35). For example, Inuit soapstone carvings are labeled with a mark certified by Indian and Northern Affairs Canada (Blundell 1993, p. 78). A certification scheme is also being developed in Australia to authenticate Aboriginal products.

However, labeling has been unsuccessful in some US states in terms of promoting trade in indigenous peoples' products. This may be because customers are not aware of the marks or do not care whether the articles they purchase are genuine (Axt et al. 1993, p. 46). They may also be confused by the labels. These problems illustrate the difficulties likely to arise from the use of certification and geographic indications for manufactured goods and artwork. Nevertheless, they can be successful marketing strategies, especially if traders have a clear understanding of why people wish to buy their articles.

Certification is also being used as a means to encourage trade in sustainably harvested tropical timber. For example, an independent organization — the Forest Stewardship Council (FSC) — consisting of foresters, timber traders, and environmental groups dedicated to sustainable forestry — has been set up with the authority to certify groups around the world who comply with principles it has drawn up. Among its principles are that ownership of a forest must be clearly defined and the traditional rights of indigenous people must be protected.

Conclusions

IPR laws are generally inappropriate and inadequate for defending the rights and resources of local communities. IPR protection is purely economic, whereas the interests of indigenous peoples are only partly economic and linked to self-determination. Furthermore, cultural incompatibilities exist in that traditional knowledge is generally shared and, even when it is not, the holders of restricted knowledge probably still do not have the right to commercialize it for personal gain.

Various indigenous communities and ethnic groups that have occupied similar environments may possess the same, or similar, technical knowledge regarding a specific resource and its use. Therefore, payments to one community could engender conflict between indigenous groups and result in protracted legal battles. This potential conflict between groups calls into question the wisdom of using IPR mechanisms in attempting to award retroactive payments for indigenous knowledge.

Furthermore, the lack of economic self-sufficiency of indigenous peoples and the unequal power relations between themselves and the corporate world would make it very difficult for communities to defend their IPR. Preventing companies from infringing their IPR, for example, by applying for patents based on knowledge derived from, but not identical to, that of the community, presents serious difficulties because of the potentially high cost of litigation.

Indigenous organizations, such as COICA, are becoming more aware of IPR issues and understand that although use of the IPR types described above may under certain circumstances be beneficial, it is necessary, as the title of this book suggests, to look beyond IPR and consider alternative systems of protection, compensation, and self-determination. The statement resulting from an international meeting organized in Bolivia in September 1994 suggests numerous strategies for raising awareness of the potential and the (much greater) limitations of existing IPR laws, and for creating and implementing alternative systems (see Appendix 3 for the full statement).

Chapter 9

Can communities develop their own system for protecting traditional resource rights?

Given the inappropriate nature of IPR as a means of protecting the rights of indigenous peoples, a number of models and concepts are emerging. These are intended to help people develop new, appropriate bases for future legal systems to protect their knowledge and resources. A number of these alternatives to IPR are analyzed in this chapter.

As discussed earlier, IPR may be of use to local communities, but they are basically inadequate and inappropriate to provide the necessary protection of and compensation for indigenous peoples' individual and collective rights to their knowledge, their culture, and their resources. They are, in fact, more likely to be inimical to their interests. In recent years pressure from the Northern countries, in part through the GATT negotiations discussed in the next chapter, has meant that national IPR laws in developing countries are becoming more and more like those in the United States and Europe, which are much more supportive of high-technology corporations. Among the industries that benefit most are the pharmaceutical and seed industries, which are dependent on biological resources originating from the territories of traditional communities.

Therefore, not only are many communities concerned that this situation is inherently unfair, but the governments of developing countries have also been expressing their criticisms. They commonly use two arguments:

- The biotechnology industries, which are mostly based in the North, rely on the availability of free biological resources from South. Patent law protects corporate investments in R&D and enables companies to charge monopoly prices until the patent expires. On the other hand, the biodiverse countries of the South, which provide these resources without charge, must pay these monopoly prices and are expected to conserve the sites of origin of resources that made the manufacture of the products possible.

- Northern countries frequently complain about IPR piracy in the form of infringements of patents, copyrights, and trademarks by manufacturers in the South and have pressured Southern countries to prevent the copying and sale of IPR-protected goods. However, countries of the South are realizing that their biodiversity is a potential source of great wealth, while Northern countries insist that their access to biodiversity should not be unduly restricted. If corporations from the North continue to have access to biological resources without having either to pay a fair amount for the right or to share the benefits of their research, then Southern countries argue that Northern institutions are guilty of "biopiracy."

At the Third World Patent Convention in New Delhi, India (March 1990), one of the areas of concern was the negotiations taking place regarding the TRIPs agreement of the GATT treaty and its unsuitability for protecting the traditional customs of farmers and indigenous peoples. The New Delhi Declaration included the following statement:

> There can be no uniform set of standards and norms of equal validity or relevance applicable to a wide range of developing countries which are obliged to respond to the imperative of their respective cultural and socioeconomic needs. The holding of a global monopoly of patents representing a massive stock of science and technology by a group of industrialized countries is no justification for common standards and norms to be demanded from the developing countries, or a price for being admitted to a global multilateral system of trade and exchange.

Even though the concerns of Southern governments and local peoples regarding IPR may appear to be similar, their interests are not necessarily the same. Therefore, local communities themselves should be involved in the development of a more appropriate sui generis legal regime. Several promising new concepts and model laws have been developed. One of the most promising is TRR, which consists of rights, obligations, and concepts already existing in "hard" and "soft" law instruments (see also Chapter 11).

What are traditional resource rights?

Knowledge and traditional resources are central to the maintenance of identity for indigenous peoples. Therefore, control over these resources is of central concern in their struggle for self-determination. The term TRR has emerged to define the many "bundles of rights" that can be used for protection, compensation, and conservation (Posey 1994; Posey et al. 1995). The change in terminology from IPR to TRR reflects an attempt to build on the concept of IPR protection and compensation, while recognizing that traditional resources — both tangible and intangible — are also covered under a significant number of international agreements that can be used to form the basis for a sui generis system. "Traditional resources" include plants, animals, and other material objects that may have sacred, ceremonial, heritage, or esthetic qualities. "Property" for indigenous peoples frequently has intangible, spiritual manifestations, and, although worthy of protection, can belong to no human being. Privatization or commoditization of their resources is not only foreign but incomprehensible or even unthinkable. Nonetheless, indigenous and traditional communities are increasingly involved in market economies and, like it or not, are seeing an ever-growing number of their resources traded in those markets.

TRR is an integrated rights concept that recognizes the inextricable link between cultural and biological diversity and sees no contradiction between the human rights of indigenous and local communities, including the right to development and environmental conservation. Indeed, they are mutually supportive since the destiny of traditional peoples largely determines, and is determined by, the state of the world's biological diversity. TRR includes overlapping and mutually supporting bundles of rights. These rights and the international agreements that support them are detailed in Table 2.

TRR can be implemented locally, nationally, and internationally. They can guide international law and practice and national legislation. Furthermore, they can provide a source of principles to guide the process of dialogue between indigenous and local communities and governmental and nongovernmental institutions, for example, through innovative contracts providing benefits from the transfer of traditional resources, new codes of ethics and standards of professional conduct, socially and ecologically responsible business practices, and holistic approaches to sustainability.

TRR go beyond other sui generis models in that they seek not only to protect knowledge relating to biological resources but also to assert the right of peoples to self-determination and the right to safeguard "culture" in its broadest sense.

Table 2. Traditional resource rights.

Category	Supporting agreements[a] Legally binding	Not legally binding
Human rights	ICESCR, ICCPR	UDHR, DDRIP, VDPA
Right to self-determination	ICESCR, ICCPR	DDRIP, VDPA
Collective rights	ILO 169, ICESCR, ICCPR	DDRIP, VDPA
Land and territorial rights	ILO 169	DDRIP
Right to religious freedom	ICCPR, NLs	UDHR
Right to development	ICESCR, ICCPR, ILO 169	DDRIP, DHRD, VDPA
Right to privacy	ICCPR, NLs	UDHR
Prior informed consent	CBD, NLs	DDRIP
Environmental integrity	CBD	RD
Intellectual property rights	WIPO, GATT, UPOV, NLs, CBD	
Neighbouring rights	RC	
Right to enter into legal agreements, such as contracts and covenants	NLs	
Cultural property rights	Unesco–CCP, Unesco–WHC, NLs	
Right to protection of folklore		Unesco–WIPO, Unesco–F
Right to protection of cultural heritage	Unesco–WHC	
Recognition of cultural landscapes	Unesco–WHC	
Recognition of customary law and practice	ILO 169, NLs	DDRIP
Farmers' rights		FAO–IUPGR

[a] Definitions: **CBD**, UN *Convention on Biological Diversity* (1992) — 108 states parties as of 31 December 1994; **DDRIP**, UN *Draft Declaration on the Rights of Indigenous Peoples* (formally adopted by the UN's Working Group on Indigenous Populations in July 1994); **DHRD**, UN *Declaration on the Human Right to Development* (1986); **FAO–IUPGR**, *International Undertaking on Plant Genetic Resources* (1987 version); **GATT**, *Final Document Embodying the Results of the Uruguay Round of Multilateral Trade Negotiations* (1994); **ICCPR**, UN *International Covenant on Civil and Political Rights* (1966) — 129 states parties as of 31 December 1994; **ICESCR**, UN *International Covenant on Economic, Social and Cultural Rights* (1966) — 131 states parties as of 31 December 1994; **ILO 169**, International Labour Organisation *Convention 169 concerning indigenous and tribal peoples in independent countries* (1989) — 7 states parties; **NLs**, national laws; **RC**, *Rome Convention for the Protection of Performers, Producers of Phonograms and Broadcasting Organizations* (1961) — 47 states parties as of 31 December 1994; **RD**, Rio Declaration (1992); **UDHR**, *Universal Declaration of Human Rights* (1948); **Unesco–CCP**, *Convention on the Means of Prohibiting and Preventing the Illicit Import, Export and Transfer of Ownership of Cultural Property* (1970) — 79 states parties as of 1 January 1994; **Unesco–F**, Recommendations on the Safeguarding of Traditional Culture and Folklore (1989); **Unesco–WHC**, *Convention Concerning the Protection of the World Cultural and Natural Heritage* (1972) — 135 states parties as of 1 January 1994; **Unesco–WIPO**, *Model Provisions for National Laws on Protection of Expressions of Folklore Against Illicit Exploitation and Other Prejudicial Actions* (1985); **UPOV**, *International Union for the Protection of New Varieties of Plants Convention* (1961, revised in 1972, 1978, and 1991) — 27 states parties as of 31 December 1994; **VDPA**, UN *Vienna Declaration and Programme of Action* (1993); **WIPO**, World Intellectual Property Organization (administers international IPR agreements such as the *Paris Convention for the Protection of Industrial Property* (1883, revised most recently in 1967) — 129 states parties as of 31 December 1994; the *Berne Convention for the Protection of Literary and Artistic Works* (1886, revised most recently in 1971) — 111 states parties as of 31 December 1994; the *Madrid Agreement Concerning the International Registration of Trademarks* (1891, revised most recently in 1967) — 43 states parties as of 31 December 1994; the *Lisbon Agreement for the Protection of Appellations of Origin and their International Registration* (1958, revised most recently in 1967) — 17 states parties as of 31 December 1994; and the *Patent Cooperation Treaty* (1970) — 77 states parties as of 31 December 1994).

Community intellectual property rights

Community IPR developed to counter what Shiva (1994a) calls "the colonization of the seed" by multinational companies selling seeds and agrochemicals. Community IPR would enable farmers to assert their "rights to seed" by claiming that any corporation using local knowledge or local resources without the permission of local communities is engaging in intellectual piracy.

The Crucible Group (1994, pp. 67–68) has said that for community IPR to be effective:

- They would have to be entrenched in appropriate national legislation with reciprocal recognition in other countries;
- An international database would have to be created for tracing germplasm, possibly through the CGIAR system; and
- A "public defender" would have to be appointed in the shape of an internationally recognized mediator or ombudsman.

At a meeting on Methodologies for Recognising the Role of Informal Innovation in the Conservation and Utilisation of Plant Genetic Resources, which took place in Madras, India, in January 1994, it was proposed that IPR legislation relating to plant genetic resources should provide for both breeders' rights and farmers' rights. To establish community IPR effectively, members of The Crucible Group suggest the following:

- Plant varieties developed by communities should be deposited in germplasm banks along with registration data: date, place, and location of origin (including names and addresses of communities). Community IPR applications would have to include all this information.
- All germplasm currently existing in germplasm banks should be covered by such legislation.
- National IPR offices and the international secretariat for each IPR convention should have an office to investigate complaints by local communities and governments, and a tribunal should have the power to revoke IPR.
- Fees derived from IPR should be used to fund this office and to give legal aid to local communities involved in disputes.

Model draft community intellectual rights act

A model community intellectual rights act was suggested in a Third World Network discussion paper (Nijar 1994) as a means of bringing about the evolution of new criteria for claiming patent rights compatible with cultural values and practices of indigenous peoples. It could be used in the context of the GATT-TRIPs call for sui generis forms of

IPR protection and is in accord with the requirements of the CBD, particularly Article 8(j).

The purpose of the act would be to prevent the "privatisation and usurpation of community rights and knowledge through existing definitions of innovation." It would assert the existence of knowledge that is communally owned and shared, given that ownership of property is not a concept accepted by many indigenous peoples. Therefore, a more suitable form of description for knowledge that is of value, not privatized, and cumulative would be "community intellectual rights" (CIR).

To meet the novelty or innovation requirement of regular patent protection criteria, indigenous peoples are described as "innovators" because the knowledge they have accumulated has been unknown to the outside world. Two legal bases are suggested for "vesting in local communities custodianship rights of an innovation":

- *Constructive trustee*: local community leaders are nominated or appointed to act for the whole community as trustees for the beneficiaries (the community).

- *Higher trust*: this builds on the concept, declared in the CBD and UNCED documents, that government, in possessing sovereign rights, is in fact holding those rights in trust for the community (see Megarry 1977). It also refers to FAO Resolution 5/89, on farmers' rights being vested in the international community "as trustees for present and future generations of farmers." As suggested by the concept of farmers' rights (see Chapter 13), the right is to be held in perpetuity because knowledge and practice will evolve as a community evolves.

Section 5 of the model CIR act suggests the creation of a **registry of invention**, in which a community might register its innovations as a simple method of declaring their existence to the world. The idea is similar to copyright law, in which protection generally arises with no need for formal acceptance by a registering authority, and the mechanism is more flexible than filing a patent. Failure to register does not surrender the innovation rights, but doing so may block a patent application for an identical or similar "innovation" (see also "Defensive publication" in Chapter 8).

A similar possibility is for communities to develop a **community register**, in which local people document all known plant and animal species with full details of their uses. Community members would then be in a position to refuse access to the register or set conditions under which access would be allowed. It is even possible that a community could use a community register as evidence of intimate knowledge of the local environment to support a claim to legal title of its territory. Although community registers would be kept locally, they could be components of regional and national registers containing information freely available to communities. This would keep such information in the public domain.[4]

---

[4] For further information about community registers, contact the Foundation for Revitalisation of Local Health Traditions or Ashish Kothari (see Resource Guide, India).

The Unesco–WIPO model provisions

In 1985, the United Nations Educational, Scientific and Cultural Organisation (Unesco) and WIPO produced *Model Provisions for National Laws on Protection of Expressions of Folklore against Illicit Exploitation and Other Prejudicial Actions*. The intention was to go beyond conventional copyright by protecting intangible expressions as well as fixed works. The document avoids a definition of folklore, but in Section 2 does explain what the term ***expressions of folklore*** should encompass:

- Folk tales, folk poetry, and riddles;
- Folk songs and instrumental music;
- Folk dances, plays, and artistic forms of rituals;
- Drawings, paintings, carvings, sculptures, pottery, terracotta, mosaic, woodwork, metalware, jewellery, basket weaving, needlework, textiles, carpets, costumes, musical instruments, and architectural forms.

Although not stated, a law that implements the model provisions could include traditional genetic resources as "expressions of folklore" to be protected if national law-making bodies wished to approve such an interpretation.

According to the model provisions, certain uses of expressions of folklore are subject to prior authorization by a competent authority or the community itself if they are "made both with gainful intent and outside their traditional or customary context" (Section 3) and would therefore constitute "illicit exploitation" if used without this authorization. "Traditional context" here means remaining "in its proper artistic framework based on continuous usage by the community" (WIPO 1989, p. 6). "Customary context" means in accordance with the practices of everyday life in the community. Four other types of "prejudicial action" may be subject to criminal sanctions (Section 6):

- Failure to indicate the ethnic and geographic source of an expression of folklore in printed publications and other communications to the public;
- Unauthorized use of an expression of folklore where authorization is required;
- Deliberately deceiving the public about the ethnic source of a production;
- Any kind of public use that distorts the production in a manner "prejudicial to the cultural interests of the community concerned."

A "competent authority," which could be the communities themselves, would be set up to deal with applications for use of expressions of folklore and perhaps to fix and collect authorization fees.

The rights covered in the model provisions have some of the characteristics of copyright law, in that they protect the (community) creators of artistic expressions, and neighbouring rights (see Chapter 10), in that they can protect performances. However, compared with both these mechanisms, the model provisions have some advantages:

- They protect both fixed and unfixed works of folklore, which is rare in national copyright laws.

- The period of protection is indefinite.

- The protection goes beyond neighbouring rights, which only prevent performing, recording, and broadcasting works, and includes rights similar to the moral rights that exist in some copyright laws (see Chapter 8) and even appellation of origin.

- The provisions recognize the need to balance protection from abuses of folklore against "freedom and encouragement of its further development and dissemination."

However, the model provisions make it possible for a state agency to collect fees from users; this may be a problem if the agency cannot collect fees efficiently or misappropriates those it does collect. A number of African countries, such as Nigeria, have enacted legislation based, at least in part, on the model provisions. Elsewhere, there has been little response from national legislatures.

Conclusions

The concepts of TRR, community IPR, CIR, and the model provisions are alternatives to IPR that accommodate more adequately the concern of traditional communities to prevent others from privatizing their knowledge and resources. However, the TRR concept goes furthest in a number of respects:

- It emphasizes the right to self-determination, including territorial and human rights.

- It covers a broad range of rights to protect, not only knowledge and biogenetic resources but also cultural property, folklore, and even landscapes.

- It does not reject IPR outright but instead includes them as one of a whole bundle of rights.

Chapter 10

Are legally binding international agreements useful?

This and the following two chapters outline the various legal and nonlegal instruments that may become useful tools in the struggle to establish TRR. In this chapter, we discuss the nature and scope of major legally binding international agreements containing rights, principles and concepts of relevance to the protection of indigenous peoples' knowledge and resources.

Given the fact that governments often refuse to sign international agreements that they perceive to be against the interests of the country, or fail to carry out international legal obligations that they have agreed to, it may not seem worthwhile analyzing international legal instruments. However, they contain important rights, principles, and concepts that can be valuable in the building of the sui generis TRR system. In this chapter, we examine these instruments and provide answers to the questions: what useful provisions do these legal instruments contain? and how can indigenous peoples exploit the fact that such provisions exist?

The GATT agreement on Trade-Related Aspects of Intellectual Property Rights

In a 1986 meeting, government ministers from around the world launched the Uruguay Round of the GATT negotiations. The Ministerial Declaration on the Uruguay Round (GATT doc. MIN.DEC, 20 September 1986) called for the formulation of a multilateral agreement on minimum levels of protection for IPR, thereby increasing awareness of the importance of intellectual property in international trade.

IPR were included in the GATT negotiations at the request of the United States and its supporters to harmonize the treaty for two reasons (van Wijk et al. 1993):

- Negotiations on IPR were linked to international trade negotiations, making developing countries' access to export markets in industrialized countries contingent upon advances in IPR recognition or establishment.

- GATT contains an effective dispute-settlement mechanism that could be used to take action rapidly against any countries violating any GATT agreement on intellectual property.

The TRIPs section of GATT may be the most ambitious multilateral agreement ever made in the area of intellectual property. Divided into seven parts and 73 Articles, it covers issues of copyright and related rights, trademarks, geographic indications, industrial designs, patents, layout designs of integrated circuits, trade secrets, control of anticompetitive practices in contractual licences, as well as provisions on enforcement, acquisition, maintenance of IPR, and dispute-settlement mechanisms.

The TRIPs agreement includes a provision (Article 27 (3b)) that excludes from patentability

> Plants and animals other than microorganisms, and essentially biological processes for the production of plants or animals other than nonbiological and microbiological processes.

The same provision also guarantees

> The protection of plant varieties either by patents or by an effective sui generis system or by any combination thereof.

This provision has been viewed as a threat to community rights because it would create legal monopolies on common resources, but it may also provide opportunities.

There is a threat in the sense that although developing countries have a grace period of 4–10 years, these countries are being pressured into accepting protection of plant genetic resources and limitations to access, which are contrary to their customary practices. Specifically they are expected to introduce either patent protection for plant varieties or a sui generis system protection based on the 1991 UPOV Convention (see Chapter 8). The main issue is the imposition on developing countries of a regulation that overturns a centuries-old custom of sharing seeds and community innovations in favour of a system that sections of the population do not necessarily believe is to their benefit. Vandana Shiva (1994b, p. 12), a well-known critic of GATT-TRIPs, speaks for Indian farmers when she says:

> [TRIPs] has failed to recognize the more informal, communal system of innovation through which Third World farmers produce, select, improve and breed a plethora of diverse crop varieties.

There is an opportunity in that a sui generis system, developed in accordance with Article 27, could be designed that would serve the interests of local communities. Also, even if indigenous peoples themselves cannot obtain IPR protection for plant and animal materials, they can still demand that governments prohibit multinational pharmaceutical companies and others from patenting such material found on their lands. Although, it is uncertain whether governments would agree to do so, indigenous peoples should be aware that such action is possible under international law.

Most countries of the world have signed the 1994 GATT, which also establishes the World Trade Organization (WTO), and will thus be obliged to comply with Article 27 of TRIPs. However, if developing countries are able to resist pressure from the United States and Europe, it may be possible for them to enact legislation aimed at protecting traditional knowledge and processes related to plant life if national legislatures and governments are prepared to explore such a possibility. Shiva (1994b) advocates such efforts by calling on India to respond to the GATT and emphasizing the need for communal knowledge to be acknowledged:

> Our challenge now is to use the clause for evolving a sui generis system to push for the protection of collective innovation and the protection of the creative potential of our people and our country.

The Convention on Biological Diversity

Article 1 of the CBD states:

> The objectives of this Convention are ... the conservation of biological diversity, the sustainable use of its components and the fair and equitable sharing of the benefits arising out of the utilization of genetic resources, including by appropriate access to genetic resources and appropriate transfer of relevant technologies, taking into account all rights over those resources and to technologies, and by appropriate funding.

The logic behind these objectives is that biodiversity can only be conserved if resources are used in a sustainable manner, particularly by the biotechnology industries, and the economic benefits of such use flow back to conservation activities, particularly in developing countries. States retain sovereign rights to their biological and cultural resources and are responsible for ensuring that the benefits flowing from their use reach the citizens.

Indigenous peoples, who have been largely marginalized by such processes in the past (if not totally excluded), are understandably sceptical of the view that this time things will be better. However, for the first time, at least indigenous and local communities embodying traditional lifestyles are expressly mentioned in the CBD, and their central contributions to biodiversity conservation are recognized. Signatories to the CBD have pledged to

> Respect, preserve and maintain knowledge, innovations, and practices of indigenous and local communities embodying traditional lifestyles relevant for the conservation and sustainable use of biological diversity and promote their wider application with the approval and involvement of the holders of such knowledge, innovations and practices and encourage the equitable sharing of the benefits arising from the utilization of such knowledge, innovations and practices. [Article 8(j)]

This opens the door for farming communities, for example, to claim IPR, not only for the benefits they receive from biological resources but for the part they play, or can play, in conservation of resources in situ and ex situ. However, it also gives government priority where there is a conflict of interest between indigenous peoples' needs and those of conservation, which will depend on government's interpretation of specific cases.

The language of the CBD, the Rio Declaration, and *Agenda 21* (see Chapter 11) is vague and will be molded by future political and economic actions. Given that indigenous peoples are recognized as having specific rights and benefits and that economic livelihood is linked to development and conservation of natural resources, as much energy and effort as possible should be put into activating the sections relevant to indigenous rights — especially the recognition and protection of, and compensation for, intellectual property. GATT negotiators, FAO, the WTO, and WIPO will all have to accommodate to this reality in future because the vast majority of countries are signatories of the CBD.

The CBD contains several provisions that, if implemented, could provide ways to secure a greater degree of community empowerment. Article 6 calls for strategies, plans, and programs for conservation and sustainable use of biological diversity. Indigenous peoples should be actively involved in these national studies, not only as participants and executants but intellectually through the development of their own criteria and value systems. Likewise, Article 7 calls for identification and monitoring of biodiversity, which should include criteria set by indigenous peoples and include their full participation.

Article 8 deals with in situ conservation, which in effect calls for support of indigenous and local communities, as they are an intricate part of the overall ecosystem. Article 8(j) specifically deals with indigenous peoples (see above). Effective implementation of Article 8(j) requires at least the following measures:

– Indigenous land demarcation and guarantees of security;

- Support for indigenous-based and designed conservation and sustainable development efforts;
- Research centres to develop strategies and models to apply traditional technologies in a larger context;
- Support for and strengthening of indigenous organizations, including local, regional, national, and international indigenous alliances, councils, federations, unions, etc.;
- Creation of enforceable international legal structures to develop mechanisms for protection of, and equitable sharing of, benefits from indigenous and traditional knowledge, innovations, and practices.

Article 10(d) states that contracting parties shall "support local populations to develop and implement remedial action in degraded areas where biological diversity has been reduced." In the absence of a clear idea of what is meant by "support," indigenous peoples should formulate their own guidelines. Both the CBD and *Agenda 21* stress restoration and remedial action in degraded areas. Funding priorities will probably reflect this emphasis and restoration and revitalization projects will proliferate. Indigenous peoples should be prepared to develop their own projects for their own lands and territories, using their own conservation technologies and management models as the basis.

Articles 11, 12, and 13 call for "incentive measures" to finance research, training, public education, and awareness to effect conservation and sustainable use of components of biological diversity. These sections should be interpreted by indigenous peoples to strengthen their own research agendas. Emphasis should be placed on collaborative research and community-controlled research (see Chapter 14), in which indigenous and traditional communities themselves set, guide, and control the research priorities, standards, and guidelines for nonindigenous research partners or contractors. Indigenous peoples should seek support, financial and otherwise, for establishing their own programs for scientific and technical education and training in "measures for the identification, conservation, and sustainable use of biological diversity" (Article 12(a)). Likewise, they should seek support in their own media projects as provided for in Article 13(a).

Article 14 deals with "impact assessment and minimizing adverse impacts." Section 1(a) calls for the parties to

> Introduce appropriate procedures requiring environmental impact assessment of its proposed project that are likely to have significant adverse effects on biological diversity with a view to avoiding or minimizing such effects, and where appropriate, allow for public participation in such procedures.

Effective implementation of this article depends upon local participation in projects that affect indigenous, traditional, or local communities (see Box 10.1).

Article 16 deals with "access to and transfer of technology." Indigenous and traditional technologies have rarely been considered to be "technologies" in international parlance. This pattern is part of the larger trend to downgrade, overlook, and minimize the knowledge, innovations, and practices of indigenous peoples. The CBD, however,

Box 10.1

Environmental impact assessment

Indigenous, traditional, and local communities require the following to make the provisions for environmental impact assessments (EIAs) effective:

- Full participation in all phases of conceptualization, implementation, and analysis;
- Inclusion of their own guidelines, criteria, and mechanisms for assessment;
- Full disclosure of all information relevant to the project, including technical and feasibility studies and assessments;
- Access to information on the results of the EIA (Principle 10 of the preamble);
- Their prior informed consent (see Principle 10, Article 8) before studies are undertaken or implemented in an area;
- National and international mechanisms with legal jurisdiction to handle matters of redress, liability, restoration, and compensation.

specifically elevates these elements to a central concern (see also Articles 8(j) and 18.4) as technologies relevant to the conservation and sustainable use of biological diversity. Thus, it is clear that "indigenous and traditional technologies" are covered under the technologies section of Article 16:

- Article 16.2 provides that access and transfer of technologies "subject to patents and other intellectual property rights" must occur on mutually agreed terms that "recognize and are consistent with the adequate and effective protection of intellectual property rights."

- Article 16.3 calls for contracting parties to take legislative, administrative, or policy measures to provide access to and transfer of technology "including technology protected by patents and other intellectual property rights." This is to be carried out "in accordance with international law."

- Article 16.4 calls on contracting parties to take legislative, administrative, or policy measures to facilitate the private sector's "joint development and transfer of technology."

- Article 16.5 recognizes that "patents and other intellectual property rights may have influence on the implementation" of the CBD, but states are called upon to cooperate to "ensure that such rights are supportive of and do not run counter to" the CBD's objectives.

In some ways, Article 16, together with Articles 8(j) and 18.4, is one of the most important sections for indigenous peoples. The article specifically provides for national and international legislative, administrative, and policy measures to protect IPR to technologies, which must be interpreted to include "indigenous and traditional technologies." Specific mention of the private sector in "joint development and transfer of technology" is subject to mutually agreed terms that require legal recognition and protection of patents and other IPR.

There can be no clearer call for IPR protection for indigenous knowledge, innovations, and practices. Furthermore, international measures are specifically called for, necessitating an international system to regulate IPR, including those for indigenous and traditional technologies (for a discussion of relevant IPR instruments, see Glowka et al. 1994).

Article 18 refers to technical and scientific cooperation. Article 18.2 calls for the promotion of cooperation to develop and strengthen "national capabilities, by means of human resources development and institutional building." Article 18.3 specifically calls for the establishment of a clearing-house mechanism to "promote and facilitate technical and scientific cooperation." This mechanism would be established by a "Conference of the Parties" and could include a central base with many satellites, including community-controlled research and training centres developed in partnership with indigenous peoples (see Box 10.2). In addition to a central clearing-house, additional mechanisms can include databases designed and maintained by indigenous peoples, monitoring, and conservation centres, which should be afforded funding priorities under the financial mechanisms established by the CBD (Articles 20 and 21). Whatever the solution, or combinations of solutions, the concept of a clearing-house implies the establishment of ethical and legal guidelines governing access to and use of information secured through IPR agreements.

Article 23 establishes the Conference of the Parties, which has full authority to establish, review, consider, and adopt measures, acts, subsidiary bodies, protocols, and

Box 10.2

A clearing-house mechanism

To be effective, a clearing-house mechanism should include:
- Indigenous participation in all phases of conceptualization, implementation, and maintenance;
- Establishment of priorities and guidelines developed by communities embodying traditional lifestyles;
- Creation of community-controlled regional clearing-houses;
- Secure IPR agreements to ensure protection and compensation for information transfer.

Article 23 establishes the Conference of the Parties, which has full authority to establish, review, consider, and adopt measures, acts, subsidiary bodies, protocols, and implementing mechanisms. Two particularly interesting possibilities are included:

- Possibility of the establishment of a "special subsidiary body on indigenous and traditional scientific, technical and technological advice." This body would be constituted to advise the Conference of the Parties on all aspects of in situ conservation and sustainable development as it relates to indigenous and traditional technologies, as well as knowledge, innovations, and practices of local communities embodying traditional lifestyles.

- Development of a "special protocol on indigenous and traditional technologies based on knowledge, innovations and practices of local communities embodying traditional lifestyles." This could be used to develop mechanisms for strengthening indigenous, traditional, and local communities. It would have an international legal basis, because it would be subsidiary to the CBD, which is a legally binding international agreement (see Article 25).

Article 24 establishes the CBD Secretariat. To implement the functions of the Secretariat, as defined in sections 1(a–e), indigenous peoples should be among the permanent members and staff of the Secretariat.

Article 25 provides details about the Subsidiary Body on Scientific, Technical and Technological Advice, which is open to participation by all parties and "shall be" (notice the mandatory language) multidisciplinary. The Conference of the Parties is to provide guidelines and establish the authority of the advisory group. The CBD outlines its functions as providing

- "Scientific and technical assessments of the status of biodiversity" (24.2.a);

- Assessments of measures taken in the implementation of the CBD (24.2.b);

- Identification of "innovative, efficient and state-of-the-art technologies and know-how," while "promoting development and/or transferring such technologies" (24.2.c);

- Provision of advice on international cooperation in R&D (24.2.d);

- Response to technical, technological, and methodological questions that arise.

Indigenous peoples should be well represented on the subsidiary body. Because knowledge, innovations, and practices of local communities embodying traditional lifestyles are highlighted elsewhere as relevant to conservation and sustainable use of biological diversity (for example, Articles 8(j) and 18.4), the subsidiary body should give research into and application of traditional technologies the highest priority (see Box 10.3).

Alternatively, a Special Subsidiary Body on Indigenous and Traditional Scientific, Technical and Technological Advice could be established to deal exclusively with these matters (see discussion of Article 23).

Box 10.3

Subsidiary Body on Scientific, Technical and Technological Advice

The Subsidiary Body on Scientific, Technical and Technological Advice, described in Article 25 of the CBD, should:

- Include a fair representation of scientific and technical specialists from indigenous, traditional, and local communities;
- Identify relevant traditional technologies, innovations, and practices;
- Apply and seek wider application of indigenous and traditional knowledge, innovations, and practices;
- Develop methods, techniques, and strategies for use of indigenous criteria for evaluation, assessment, and monitoring;
- Give priority to, and develop guidelines for, collaborative and community-controlled research with indigenous, traditional, and local communities;
- Develop guidelines and proposals for model legislation on IPR and TRR for indigenous, traditional, and local communities;
- Develop guidelines and proposals for model legislation to establish monitoring and enforcement institutions to insure that the CBD is fairly and properly implemented and that indigenous, traditional, and local communities benefit from it.

Article 28 deals with the process of adoption of protocols. Protocols establish a subset of agreements within the framework of a convention. Thus a protocol to the CBD would define specific aspects of items provided for in the convention. Two interesting possibilities exist:

- As previously suggested, a protocol on indigenous and traditional technologies based on knowledge, innovations, and practices of local communities embodying traditional lifestyles could be negotiated (see Box 10.4).

- The well-being of indigenous and traditional communities could be included as a major aspect of a protocol on biosafety. Indigenous and local communities embodying traditional lifestyles are recognized as having knowledge, innovations, and practices relevant to the conservation of biological diversity and the sustainable use of its components (see CBD preamble). Furthermore, these local communities are seen as fundamental to in situ conservation and, indeed, as integral parts of the ecosystems they inhabit (Article 8).

The disadvantage of this strategy is that few states would support the negotiation of such protocols because they would be controversial and of little interest to most contracting parties.

> Box 10.4
>
>
>
> ## Special protocols on indigenous and traditional technologies based on the knowledge, innovations, and practices of local communities embodying traditional lifestyles
>
> Options for such protocols include:
>
> - Define and develop mechanisms for "sharing equitably benefits arising from the use of traditional knowledge, innovations, and practices relevant to the conservation of biological diversity and the sustainable use of its components" (CBD preamble);
> - Define, document, and investigate "knowledge, innovations, and practices of indigenous and local communities embodying traditional lifestyles relevant for the conservation and sustainable use of biological diversity" (Article 8(j));
> - Define and develop effective mechanisms to "promote the wider application" of traditional knowledge, innovations, and practices (Article 8(j));
> - Establish guidelines and mechanisms for training and surveying programs in indigenous and traditional knowledge (Article 17);
> - Develop a clearing-house mechanism for technical and scientific cooperation between and with local communities (Article 18);
> - Develop financial mechanisms to strengthen local communities to preserve and maintain their knowledge, innovations, and practices (Article 20).

There is, however, already a strong international movement to implement a biosafety protocol for the CBD. It should cover the impact of biotechnology and its risks on local communities. This should include guidelines for equitable sharing and IPR protection, because these are the mechanisms that guarantee benefits for local communities and ensure their continued conservation of biological diversity (see Box 10.5).

Article 8(g) calls for the establishment and maintenance of

> Means to regulate, manage or control the risks associated with the use and release of living modified organisms resulting from biotechnology that are likely to have adverse environmental impacts that could affect the conservation and sustainable use of biological diversity, taking also into account the risks to human health.

Indigenous, traditional, and local communities would clearly be among those most affected by these modified organisms.

> Box 10.5
>
> ### Options for a protocol on biosafety and traditional technologies
>
> - Develop criteria and mechanisms to identify and prepare baseline inventories of existing components of biological diversity using local communities and their own criteria.
> - Develop criteria and mechanisms to identify and prepare baseline inventories of knowledge, innovations, and practices of traditional communities that currently maintain and conserve biological diversity.
> - Develop criteria and mechanisms to assess the impact of intended new technologies and genetically modified organisms on traditional lifestyles and the conservation and sustainable use of biological diversity by local communities.
> - Develop criteria and mechanisms to monitor change, including adverse effects of external technologies and genetically modified organisms on traditional lifestyles and the conservation and sustainable use of biological diversity.
> - Develop equitable sharing mechanisms for biotechnology developed, based upon or derived from traditional technologies.

International Covenant on Economic, Social and Cultural Rights and the International Covenant on Civil and Political Rights

The ICESCR and ICCPR are the two main international legal instruments dealing with human rights. Article 1(2) of both these documents states:

> All peoples may, for their own ends, freely dispose of their natural wealth and resources without prejudice to any obligations arising out of international economic cooperation, based upon the principle of mutual benefit, and international law. In no case may a people be deprived of its own means of subsistence.

This is a clear call for the recognition of collective human rights.

Article 15(1c) of the ICESCR states:

> The States Parties to the present Covenant recognize the right of everyone ... (c) To benefit from the protection of the moral and material interests resulting from any scientific, literary or artistic production of which he is the author.

These provisions support the view that international law gives indigenous peoples the right to safeguard their own resources and to benefit from their knowledge and from goods produced or owned by them, regardless of whether they wish to commercialize them. However, these covenants are frequently ignored by many governments that violate them with impunity, although even nondemocratic governments might respond favourably to international pressure from citizens and foreign governments. There is little that communities working alone can do, but tribes, people's organizations, and communities acting together have occasionally succeeded, especially when their campaigns have attracted the support of citizens and even governments around the world. For example, the efforts of the Yanomami of Amazonia to secure legal recognition of their land rights has been reasonably successful because of international support.

The World Heritage Convention

The main instrument of international law concerned with cultural heritage is the 1972 Unesco *Convention Concerning the Protection of the World Cultural and Natural Heritage* (often called the World Heritage Convention). The goal of this convention is to mobilize international cooperation for the protection of the cultural and natural heritage of humankind. According to the convention, cultural heritage includes

- *Monuments*: architectural works, works of monumental sculpture and painting, elements or structures of an archeological nature, inscriptions, cave dwellings and combinations of features that are of outstanding universal value from the point of view of history, art, or science;

- *Groups of buildings*: groups of separate or connected buildings that, because of their architecture, their homogeneity, or their place in the landscape, are of outstanding universal value from the point of view of history, art, or science;

- *Sites*: works of people or the combined works of nature and people and areas, including archaeological sites, that are of outstanding value from the historical, esthetic, ethnological, or anthropological points of view (Article 1).

"Natural heritage" is confined to natural or geologic features of outstanding universal value.

In view of their universal value, state parties are required to draw up an inventory of world cultural and natural heritage properties (Article 11). From their inventories, states can nominate sites that they wish to be included on the World Heritage List. The World Heritage Committee evaluates these nominations and, when accepted by the committee, these are included in the World Heritage List to be protected under the convention with funds provided by the state parties. Such international cooperation is considered necessary because many countries lack the resources to prevent the deterioration and disappearance of their cultural and natural assets.

To be considered by the committee, nominated properties should conform to certain criteria. Thus, each cultural property nominated should (Unesco 1994)

> (v) be an outstanding example of a traditional human settlement or land-use which is representative of a culture (or cultures), especially when it has become vulnerable under the impact of irreversible change; or (vi) be directly or tangibly associated with events or living traditions, with ideas, or with beliefs, with artistic and literary works of outstanding universal significance (the Committee considers that this criterion should justify inclusion in the List only in exceptional circumstances or in conjunction with other criteria).

Of the several hundred listed sites, about 300 were selected for their cultural importance and over 100 for their natural significance. The rest are either joint cultural and natural heritage sites or "cultural landscapes." The so-called cultural landscape has only recently been adopted under the category of "combined work(s) of nature and of man." This category is intended to recognize "the complex interrelationships between man and nature in the construction, formation and evolution of landscapes" (Rossler 1993a, p. 14). It may be quite useful in protecting the cultural heritage of some indigenous peoples.

There are three main types of cultural landscape:

— "Clearly defined landscapes designed and created intentionally by man, such as for example, gardens and parks" (Rossler 1993b);

— "Organically evolved landscape resulting from successive social and economic imperatives and in response to the natural environment" (Rossler 1993b). There are two subcategories: the relict landscape; and the continuing landscape, "which retains an active social role in contemporary society closely associated with the traditional way of life" (Unesco 1994, p. 11);

— Associative cultural landscapes, which have "powerful religious, artistic or cultural associations of the natural element rather than material cultural evidence, which may be insignificant or even absent" (Unesco 1994).

The first cultural landscape to be designated is Tongariro National Park in New Zealand, which was originally nominated as a joint natural and cultural site and was then listed as a natural site. It was selected because of the importance of the area in Maori mythology and the sacred nature of the mountains. According to *World Heritage Newsletter* (Rossler 1993c, p. 15), "The Park was the first in the world to be donated by an indigenous people to a State." At its 17th session, the World Heritage Committee concluded that it was "an outstanding example of an associative cultural landscape tied to the cultural identity of the Maori people."

In addition to Tongariro, there are other important places for indigenous groups on the World Heritage List. One of these is Uluru (Ayers Rock) in Australia, which belongs to the Anangu people and is considered a sacred place by them. However, one cannot assume that as a result, local community's territorial and resource rights are respected. Rights of access of local people to such designated places may still be restricted in some way by governments that do not believe that indigenous peoples are the most effective conservers of them.

If the World Heritage Convention is to prove beneficial to indigenous peoples, the committee and its advisory organizations (such as IUCN) must pay heed to indigenous peoples' interests when considering new nominations and properties already listed under the new criteria. Ultimately, the extent to which the religious and cultural importance of places and objects for ethnic minorities and indigenous peoples is taken into account in the World Heritage List depends on

— Whether governments are willing to consult indigenous peoples;

- Whether national legislation to implement the convention allows for a flexible or broad interpretation of "cultural and national heritage"; and
- Whether the committee is prepared to take the view that cultural and natural properties important to an indigenous people constitute part of the heritage of humankind of sufficient importance to justify the expense of their protection.

The Rome Convention

The concept of "neighbouring rights" arose in response to technological developments that allowed a much broader dissemination of artistic works and made manifest the failure of copyright law to protect the rights of performers, recorders, and other disseminators. These latter groups were responsible for the enormous increase in public exposure, but only the copyright owners of the works were able to benefit from this. In a similar way, some indigenous peoples were becoming aware of an increase in the scope for commercial exploitation of their folkloric expressions but found it hard to benefit commercially or to prevent others from doing so. Because copyright law did not protect "unfixed" works (see Chapter 8), indigenous peoples found it difficult to prevent loss of control over their performing arts. Consequently, others were free to disseminate and profit from recordings of these performances and make changes to their form and content without legal obligations to the original performers.

In 1961, the *International Convention for the Protection of Performers, Producers of Phonograms and Broadcasting Organizations* (the Rome Convention) provided so-called neighbouring rights protection from the following acts carried out without the performer's prior consent:

- Broadcasting or communication to the public of a "live" performance;
- Recording an unfixed performance;
- Reproducing a *fixation* of the performance, provided that the original fixation was made without the consent of the performer or the reproduction is made for purposes not permitted by the convention or the performer (Article 7).

According to Article 12, if a phonogram is made for a commercial purposes and communicated publicly, the user must pay an "equitable remuneration" to the performers or to the producer of the phonogram, or to both. The minimum term of protection is 20 years from the performance, fixation, or broadcast.

According to WIPO, "The Convention is particularly interesting for those countries whose civilization and tradition are oral and where the author is often the performer as well" (WIPO 1988, p. 240). Of the more than 50 countries that have so far enacted legislation related to the Rome Convention, more than half are developing countries. Although neighbouring rights can be a useful legal tool to protect folklore in countries that legally recognize them, protection is limited in time and excludes copying what is not performed, broadcast, or contained in phonograms (WIPO 1988, p. 246).

Convention on the Means of Prohibiting and Preventing the Illicit Import, Export and Transfer of Ownership of Cultural Property

This 1970 Unesco convention is the main international legal instrument to suppress the illegal transfer of, and trade in, cultural property across national boundaries. It requires the issue of export certificates and prohibits the importing of stolen cultural property. The weaknesses of the convention as an instrument to protect indigenous peoples' cultural property are as follows:

- It does not apply to objects stolen before the convention came into force.
- It does not apply to stolen objects that do not cross national boundaries.
- Many of the major importing nations have not ratified the convention.
- Cultural property is defined to include objects valuable for several reasons but not for their direct relevance to the lives of present-day peoples.
- Cultural property as defined by the convention excludes immovable property, such as sacred sites and cultural landscapes.
- Although the geographic origins and location of cultural properties in relation to national boundaries are of great importance, there is no requirement that ethnic origins be taken into account when making or considering restitution claims. Thus, governments may decide that property should be kept in national museums.

The extent to which the convention has succeeded in stemming the flow of cultural property to dealers in ethnic artworks is not clear and may be minimal. However, the return of the sacred weavings to the Aymara people of Coroma, Bolivia, from the United States was certainly helped by the fact that both countries were parties to the convention, but other factors were also essential, especially the efforts of individual people, a law firm, and the indigenous community itself (see Box 10.6).

The success or failure of restitution claims depends on the scope of legislation to implement the convention adopted by the countries in which "stolen" artifacts are held. Despite such reservations, the convention does allow for imaginative interpretations of "cultural property." Article 4, for example, includes property "created by the individual or collective genius of nationals of the State"; and article 1, "rare collections of fauna [and] flora ... [and] objects of ethnological interest," all of which could conceivably include several cultural property categories of interest to indigenous peoples and even folk crop varieties and medicinal plants (Downes et al. 1993, pp. 285–286).

Thus, under the Australian law to implement the convention (*Protection of Movable Cultural Heritage Act*, 1986), the term "movable cultural heritage" can include cultural objects relating to Aboriginal and Torres Strait Islanders that must be important to Australia "for ethnological, archaeological, historical, literary, artistic, scientific or technological reasons." Such criteria could include, as protectable properties, "bark and log coffins, human remains, rock art, cared trees, sacred and secret ritual objects, information about indigenous leaders and activists, original documents, photographs, drawings, sound recordings, film and video recordings and any similar records relating to such objects" (Sutherland 1993).

Box 10.6

The sacred weavings of Coroma, Bolivia

The sacred garments of Coroma in Bolivia have enormous spiritual, historical, and social significance for the local Aymara people. The weavings, which are believed to embody the souls of their ancestors, are regarded as being the property of the whole community; no one can sell them or give them away.

Since the late 1970s, many weavings have fallen into the hands of North American ethnic art and antiquities dealers, either through outright theft by intermediaries or purchase from local people who are violating the laws of their own community.

Tracing the missing weavings began with a piece of good fortune. Professor John Murra, a specialist on the Andean region, received a postcard announcing an ethnic art exhibition organized by a dealer in San Francisco and showing one of the weavings. He contacted the Bolivian embassy and a social scientist (Cristina Bubba Zamora) who had been involved with making an inventory of Coroma weavings. This case attracted the attention of several sympathetic academics, including anthropologists, archeologists, and art historians, as well as native Americans.

In February 1988, in response to a request from the Bolivian embassy and two representatives of the Coroma, US customs authorities confiscated about 1000 objects (mostly weavings) from the dealer.

An international campaign, assisted by a San Francisco law firm, resulted in an agreement by the dealer to give up some, but not all, of the weavings in exchange for immunity from prosecution. In September 1992, the US government handed over the weavings to President Zamora who received them on behalf of the people of Coroma.

According to Professor Murra, the most important factor that led to this successful outcome was not that both countries had signed the Unesco convention but the efforts of Miss Bubba to attract support for the people of Coroma. Nevertheless, the fact that the US government did agree that the weavings constituted "material of ethnological interest" and were, therefore, "cultural property" under the convention was crucial. Awareness among older community members of the cultural significance of the weavings and the involvement of the law firm were also important factors.

An important lesson of this case is that it can be difficult, time-consuming, and expensive to trace stolen objects, identify them, and prove that they were not purchased legally. Indeed, because the US law passed to implement the convention requires proof that objects are obtained fraudulently, it was possible to force the return of only 49 of the weavings; the rest had to be returned to the dealer.

For further information, contact Cristina Bubba Zamora, Responsable del Proyecto Textiles de Coroma, Casilla 12154, La Paz, Bolivia.

The International Labour Organisation's Convention 169

The ILO was the first United Nations organization to deal with indigenous issues. A Committee of Experts on Native Labour was established in 1926 to develop international standards for the protection of native workers. In 1959, the ILO adopted a special convention (number 105) known as the *Convention Concerning the Protection and Integration of Indigenous and Other Tribal and Semi-Tribal Populations in Independent Countries*. It was revised in June 1989 as Convention 169, *Convention Concerning Indigenous Peoples in Independent Countries*, and much of the "integrationist language" of the original was removed.

Its preamble refers to "the distinctive contributions of indigenous and tribal peoples to the cultural diversity and social and ecological harmony of humankind." Article 7 guarantees the right of indigenous peoples to decide their own development priorities and to control their own economic, social, and cultural development. Article 13(1) states that governments "shall respect the special importance of the cultures and spiritual values of the peoples concerned, of their relationship with the lands or territories, or both as applicable, which they occupy or otherwise use, and in particular the collective aspects of this relationship." This recognition of collective rights is a critical aspect of the convention and is important in IPR issues, because collectivity is fundamental to the transmission, use, and protection of traditional knowledge.

ILO 169 offers only limited rights to indigenous peoples for the protection of their knowledge, although it upholds their rights to land, natural resources, and traditional livelihood activities. It also provides for limited recognition of customary law (Article 9) and for consultation with indigenous and tribal peoples when considering "legislative or administrative measures which may affect them directly" (Article 6(1.a)). This makes it possible for indigenous peoples to influence the drafting of new national laws.

Despite many loopholes, ILO 169 does have widely agreed upon terminology that should be exploited in defining the new TRR concept. However, so far only seven countries have accepted the convention as law: Bolivia, Colombia, Costa Rica, Mexico, Norway, Paraguay, and Peru. Other countries that claim not to have indigenous peoples are unlikely to sign, though it can be argued that the convention is relevant to many of these countries, too. This is because indigenous peoples find themselves affected by policies of foreign governments, such as overseas development assistance.

Conclusions

Several international legal instruments contain useful principles and rights that contribute to the TRR concept. Unfortunately, these provisions and principles are often ignored. One of the problems involved in taking legal action against governments is that even if they sign and ratify international laws, they are not obliged to pass national laws to implement them, and often they do not do so.

Furthermore, most governments are dualist (international law cannot be invoked in their national courts) rather than monist (international treaties become part of a country's national law as soon as it has been ratified by that government). This makes it difficult for an indigenous group to turn knowledge of international laws into a strategy to have them implemented in their own country. Nevertheless, campaigns based on alliances of indigenous peoples, people's organizations, NGOs, and even individuals can lead to pressure on governments that can turn international laws into more effective tools to protect their rights and even guide effective national legislation. The Coroma case shows that such efforts can sometimes be successful, although it is an exception rather than the rule.

Chapter 11

How can communities use "soft law" and nonbinding international agreements?

Soft law consists of documents that are not directly enforceable in courts and tribunals but that nonetheless have an impact on international relations and, ultimately, international law. Many such international agreements may prove useful and may serve as the basis of future legally binding agreements, just as ICESCR and ICCPR grew out of the Universal Declaration of Human Rights. This chapter details agreements relevant to the protection of TRR.

What is "soft law" and why is it relevant?

The international community lacks a central law-making authority; thus, the creation of new law must be through consensual processes. Historically, there are two main sources of international law: customary law and treaties. Customary law evolves over time, becoming universally accepted through continuous practice, whereas treaties take the form of documents signed by governments that agree to be bound by their contents.

Soft law is a rapidly developing, though controversial source of international law. The term itself is misleading, as strictly speaking it is not law at all. In practice, soft law refers to a great variety of instruments: declarations of principles, codes of practice, recommendations, guidelines, standards, charters, resolutions, etc. Although all these kinds of documents lack legal status (are not legally binding), there is a strong expectation that their provisions will be respected and followed by the international community. According to Bothe (1980):

> A nonlegal commitment is ... often much easier for a state to accept than a legal one. In all probability, here lies the reason why states do not reject resolutions the terms of which they would by no means accept as a treaty. This presents both an opportunity and a danger. As resolutions also give rise to expectations, they trigger a certain pressure for compliance that is often, as has been shown, effective in the long run. They influence practice, and practice influences law.

One reason why soft law is of interest stems from the very fact that governments undertake moral obligations when they sign such agreements, and some may be influenced by moral suasion. The evolution of customary international law can be accelerated by the inclusion of principles in soft law agreements and in nongovernmental declarations and resolutions (James Cameron, Foundation for International Environmental Law and Development, London, UK, 1995, personal communication). Because of the growing number and influence of such documents, which uphold the rights of indigenous peoples to their knowledge, territories, and resources, it is not inconceivable that such rights could become part of international law in the near future, even if they are not included in conventions (Tobin 1995). In this chapter, we describe several of these soft law instruments and consider how they might be useful.

The Universal Declaration of Human Rights

The 1948 UDHR is a significant nonbinding international agreement. It guarantees fundamental freedoms of personal integrity and action and individual political, social, economic, and cultural rights. With regard to the protection of cultural or traditional resources, a principal problem with the "human rights approach" of the UDHR is that action is directed toward nation states. It does not easily provide a basis for claims against multinational companies or individuals who profit from traditional knowledge.

Article 7 of the UDHR supports equal protection for all under the law, thereby implying that IPR protection should be available to all peoples including indigenous peoples. Article 17 provides for the right to own collective property and not to be arbitrarily deprived of that property. Article 23 guarantees the right to just and favourable remuneration for work, which can be interpreted as work related to traditional knowledge. Finally, Article 27 provides for the right to culture and recognition of interest in scientific production, including the right to the protection of the moral and material interests resulting from any scientific, literary, or artistic production.

The conversion of sacred places to other uses by outsiders and lack of respect of such places by visitors could be compared with the destruction of a church, temple, or mosque, and the infringement of people's religious rights. In these terms, Article 18 of the UDHR becomes relevant. It states in part:

> Everyone has the right to freedom of thought, conscience and religion ... and freedom, either alone or in community with others and in public or private, to manifest his religion or belief in teaching, practice, worship and observance.

Religious freedom is an important concept to indigenous peoples. For example, at a seminar on IPR at the United Nations Human Rights Convention in Vienna, June 1993, Ray Apoaka of the North American Indian Congress suggested that IPR are a matter of religious freedom for indigenous peoples: "Much of what they want to commercialize is sacred to us. We see intellectual property as part of our culture. It cannot be separated into categories as [Western] lawyers would want."

Pauline Tangiora, a Maori leader, agrees: "Indigenous Peoples do not limit their religion to buildings, but rather see the sacred in all life" (Posey 1994). Therefore, laws governing religious freedom may be open to far-reaching interpretations. For example, the patenting of human cell lines may infringe indigenous peoples' religious freedom if it conflicts with religious beliefs.

Many countries that signed the UDHR have violated many of the rights that it enshrines. Nevertheless, it can be argued that the worldwide acceptance of the UDHR means that it is now part of international customary law and is, therefore, legally binding. If so, this is an important example of soft law being "hardened" (Shaw 1994, p. 196).[5] What is indisputable is that a number of other human rights treaties did emerge out of the UDHR, such as the ICESCR and the ICCPR (see Chapter 10), that makes its provisions binding.

ECOSOC and the Working Group on Indigenous Populations

The United Nations Economic and Social Council (ECOSOC) authorized the Commission on Human Rights to form a special subcommission "to conduct a broad study of the problem of discrimination against Indigenous Peoples" (Kahn and Talal 1987, p. 121). The Subcommission on Prevention of Discrimination and Protection of Minorities found that current international instruments were not "wholly adequate for

---

[5] When the UDHR was adopted by the United Nations (without opposition from any country), it was intended that it would become international law soon afterward in the form of a single convention. Instead, a number of human rights conventions were developed and adopted over a much longer period.

the recognition and promotion of the specific rights of indigenous populations as such within the overall societies of the countries in which they now live" (ECOSOC 1986).

In 1982, ECOSOC created a Working Group on Indigenous Populations (WGIP), which has become the most open international forum for indigenous representatives and advocates of indigenous rights. The WGIP has prepared a Declaration on the Rights of Indigenous Peoples (see Appendix 4 for the latest official draft) that should lead to a *Convention on the Rights of Indigenous Peoples*.

In Resolution 1990/27, the Subcommission on Prevention of Discrimination and Protection of Minorities recommended that any UNCED convention should "provide explicitly for the role of indigenous peoples as resource users and managers, and for the protection of indigenous peoples' right to control of their own traditional knowledge of ecosystems." Resolution 1991/31 calls for a study on the applicability of collective rights regarding property, including intellectual property.

In 1991, the subcommission requested that the UN Secretary-General prepare a concise report on the extent to which indigenous peoples can use existing international standards and mechanisms for the protection of their intellectual property, drawing attention to any gaps or obstacles and to possible measures for addressing them. WIPO was also specifically requested to help in "formulating recommendations for the effective protection of the intellectual property of Indigenous Peoples" (ECOSOC 1992a).

In May 1992, the United Nations held a Technical Conference on Indigenous Peoples and the Environment in Santiago, Chile. Participants established some basic principles, including "recognition, protection and respect for indigenous knowledge and practices that are essential contributions to the sustainable management of the environment." It was also recommended that the United Nations system take effective measures to protect the rights of indigenous peoples to their cultural property, genetic resources, biotechnology, and biodiversity (ECOSOC 1992b).

In July 1993, the subcommission produced its *Study on the Protection of the Cultural and Intellectual Property of Indigenous Peoples* (ECOSOC 1993). This document is a survey of issues relating to indigenous heritage, with particular emphasis on cultural heritage, and of international legal instruments — particularly human rights and IPR instruments. One problem with the emphasis on cultural issues is that insufficient attention is given to the protection of biological resources and traditional knowledge.

In these declarations, recommendations, and studies, as in the Draft Declaration on the Rights of Indigenous Peoples, there has been a clear call from the Human Rights Commission for protection of, and just compensation for, the IPR of indigenous and tribal peoples. Because this forum can activate other UN agencies, it may eventually produce important results at the international level.

The Rio Declaration

The *Rio Declaration on Environment and Development* was signed in June 1992 at UNCED and clearly establishes the relevance of indigenous peoples and the central importance of their protection in achieving "sustainable development." Given the reluctance of many nation states to recognize indigenous peoples' rights in the past, the tone of the Rio Declaration is indeed progressive and welcome. Principle 22 states:

> Indigenous people and their communities, and other local communities, have a vital role in environmental management and development because of their knowledge and traditional practices. States should recognize and duly support their identity, culture and interests and enable their effective participation in the achievement of sustainable development.

Agenda 21

Agenda 21 is the program of action for sustainable development agreed to at UNCED. *Agenda 21* has been described as "possibly the most far-reaching and voluminous" example of international soft law "ever to be attempted," and as a text "which has moral if not legal force and which may subsequently serve to underpin both national actions and subsequent, possibly more stringent, international agreements in specific areas" (Johnson 1993).

It emphasizes the conservation and utilization of plant genetic resources in situ as a component of programs to promote sustainable agriculture (ODI 1993). It recognizes the importance of indigenous and local communities, their knowledge and culture, and the contribution they can make to protecting biodiversity, and states that they should be rewarded.

Material relevant to protecting the rights of indigenous farming communities can be found in chapters 14, 15, 16, 26, and 32 of *Agenda 21*. The areas of focus are reinforcing indigenous communities' rights to pursue their traditional way of life and land rights. Also noteworthy are paragraphs regarding the use of indigenous knowledge in training other rural peoples and in working for conservation of crop diversity.

Chapter 32 relates to the role of farmers, calling for a "farmer-centred approach" as the "key" to attaining sustainability. The chapter concentrates on increasing the role of farmers in decision-making through the creation of organizations and decentralization of the process.

Chapter 26 is the key chapter regarding indigenous peoples' rights. It sets out UNCED's specifications for empowering indigenous peoples and their communities. It defines "lands" as including "the environment of the areas which the people concerned traditionally occupy." Clause 4 gives indigenous people an opportunity for greater control over their life and lands "in accordance with national legislation" and the possibility of participating "in the establishment or management of protected areas." This is an extremely important clause because it recommends government action to strengthen the legal position of indigenous peoples nationally and internationally. It is supported by clause 26.5 recommending that governments, United Nations organizations, and other international organizations formally include indigenous people in planning by appointing "a special focal point within each international organization" and holding annual interorganizational coordination meetings.

The FAO International Code of Conduct for Plant Germplasm Collecting and Transfer

The FAO *International Code of Conduct for Plant Germplasm Collecting and Transfer* is part of the FAO's Global System on Plant Genetic Resources, the International Undertaking on Plant Genetic Resources, and its annexes. The code provides a set of general principles that governments may wish to use in developing national regulations or formulating bilateral agreements on the collection of germplasm.

The code of conduct was adopted as Resolution 8/93 by the 27th session of the FAO conference in November 1993. Its first objective is to

> Promote the conservation, collection and use of plant genetic resources from their natural habitats or surroundings in ways that respect the environment and local traditions and cultures.

It aims to involve farmers, scientists, and organizations in conservation programs in countries where collecting is taking place, to promote the "sharing of benefits," and increase recognition of the rights and needs of local communities and farmers so that they may be compensated for their contribution to the conservation and development of plant genetic resources and not have their current benefits undermined by resource transfer.

Among the code's provisions are

- Collectors should respect local customs, traditions, values, and property rights; not deplete local resources; and work with the agreement of and in cooperation with local communities. Duplicate sets of all collections and associated materials are to be deposited with the host country.

- Curators are directed to take practical steps, such as the use of MTAs, to share benefits derived from collected germplasm with the local communities, farmers, and host countries.

- Users should consider some form of compensation to local communities, farmers, and host countries for the benefits derived from the use of germplasm.

Unesco's cultural documents

Unesco has produced a number of nonbinding documents of relevance to indigenous peoples. For example, the 1966 *Declaration on the Principles of International Cultural Cooperation* states:

> Each culture has a dignity and value which must be respected and preserved .... Every people has the right and duty to develop its own culture.

The importance of this statement is that it can be interpreted to uphold collective rights as opposed to individual rights.

Although the Unesco–WIPO model provisions (described in Chapter 9) have not been adopted in full by any country, they did influence the drafters of the 1989 Unesco *Recommendations on the Safeguarding of Traditional Culture and Folklore*, which were adopted unanimously by member states. Folklore is defined as follows (Unesco 1990):

> Folklore (or traditional and popular culture) is the totality of tradition-based creations of a cultural community, expressed by a group or individuals and recognized as reflecting the expectations of a community in so far as they reflect its cultural and social identity; its standards and values are transmitted orally, by imitation or by other means. Its forms are, among others, language, literature, music, dance, games, mythology, rituals, customs, handicrafts, architecture and other arts.

Among the provisions of the recommendations are the following:

> E. *Dissemination of folklore*: The attention of people should be drawn to the importance of folklore as an ingredient of cultural identity. It is essential for the items that make up this cultural heritage to be widely disseminated so that the value of folklore and the need to preserve it can be recognized. However, distortion during dissemination should be avoided so that the integrity of the traditions can be safeguarded. To promote a fair dissemination, Member States should: ... (g) encourage the international scientific community to adopt a code of ethics ensuring a proper approach to and respect for traditional cultures.
>
> F. *Protection of folklore*: In so far as folklore constitutes manifestations of intellectual creativity whether it be individual or collective, it deserves to be protected in a manner inspired by the protection provided for intellectual productions. Such protection of folklore has become indispensable as a means of promoting further development, maintenance and dissemination of those expressions, both within and outside the country, without prejudice to related legitimate interests. Leaving aside the "intellectual property aspects" of the protection of expressions of folklore, there are various categories of rights that are already protected and should continue to enjoy protection in the future in folklore documentation centres and archives. To this end, Member States should: (a) regarding "intellectual property" aspects: call the attention of relevant authorities to the important work of Unesco and WIPO in relation to intellectual property, while recognizing that this work relates to only one aspect of folklore protection and that the need for separate action in a range of areas to safeguard folklore is urgent; (b) regarding the other rights involved: (i) protect the informant as the transmitter of tradition (protection of privacy and confidentiality); (ii) protect the interest of the collector by ensuring that the materials gathered are conserved in archives in good condition and in a methodical manner; (iii) adopt the necessary measures to safeguard the materials gathered against misuse, whether intentional or otherwise; (iv) recognize the responsibility of archives to monitor the use made of the materials gathered.
>
> G. *International cooperation*: In view of the need to intensify cultural cooperation and exchanges, in particular through the pooling of human and material resources, in order to carry out folklore development and revitalization programmes as well as research made by specialists who are the nationals of one Member State on the territory of another Member State, Member States should: (c) cooperate closely so as to ensure internationally that the various interested parties (communities or natural or legal persons) enjoy the economic, moral and so-called neighbouring rights resulting from the investigation, creation, composition, performance, recording and/or dissemination of folklore.

Conclusions

Soft law is important for at least two reasons:

- Even though soft law documents are not legally binding, they establish what are accepted by states as standards of behaviour, and they promote some policies that can benefit traditional communities.
- Soft law documents may ultimately have an impact on international law.

Therefore, although indigenous peoples may feel that attempting to influence international law should be a priority, soft law options should not be neglected. The efforts of the WGIP show that many indigenous peoples are already aware of this.

Chapter 12

Are nongovernmental, nonlegal instruments useful?

Nonlegal instruments can also be helpful. Nongovernmental institutions, including professional organizations, academic associations, indigenous organizations, and NGOs may produce declarations, codes of conduct, codes of ethics, and guidelines. Some of these can raise awareness among people, governments, and other institutions that deal with indigenous peoples, thereby facilitating more equitable relations. In this chapter, we describe nonlegal instruments that may be helpful in building a system of TRR.

Declarations, resolutions, and codes of practice are sometimes drawn up by academic or scientific organizations, intergovernmental agencies, and people's organizations. They often result from international conferences where delegates discover that they share many concerns. The hope is that these documents will raise awareness of such concerns, improve people's behaviour, and sometimes even influence lawmakers. Not only may such documents be considered during the drafting of hard and soft law instruments, but also if they are observed, over time they become customary practices that may achieve legal standing in courts.

Indigenous peoples' declarations

Indigenous peoples' organizations and conferences have produced their own declarations to raise awareness among indigenous peoples and help build international alliances. Some of these are the following:

- *Declaration of Principles of the World Council of Indigenous Peoples,* 1984 (Appendix 3);

- *Kari-Oca Declaration* and the *Indigenous Peoples' Earth Charter* from the Kari-Oca World Indigenous Conference, 1992 (Appendix 5);

- *Charter of the Indigenous–Tribal Peoples of the Tropical Forests* of the International Alliance of Indigenous–Tribal Peoples of the Tropical Forests, 1992 (Appendix 6);

- *The Mataatua Declaration on Cultural and Intellectual Property Rights of Indigenous Peoples* from the First International Conference on the Cultural and Intellectual Property Rights of Indigenous Peoples, 1993 (Appendix 7);

- Recommendations from the congress "Voices of the Earth: Indigenous Peoples, New Partners, the Right to Self-determination in Practice," 1993 (Appendix 8);

- Statements from the Julayinabul Conference on Intellectual and Cultural Property (1993)[6];

- Statement and basic points of agreement from the COICA/UNDP Regional Meeting on Intellectual Property Rights and Biodiversity, 1994 (Appendix 9);

- Final statement from the UNDP Consultation on the Protection and Conservation of Indigenous Knowledge, Sabah, Malaysia, 1995 (Appendix 10);

- Final statement from the UNDP Consultation on Indigenous Peoples' Knowledge and Intellectual Property Rights, Suva, Fiji, 1995 (Appendix 11);

- *Declaration of the Indigenous Peoples of the Western Hemisphere Regarding the Human Genome Diversity Project* (HGDP) (see Appendix 1).

---

[6] For further information, contact Henrietta Fourmile (see Resource Guide, Australia).

Some indigenous groups already have their own policies addressing the need to control access to their territories, to monitor the activities of plant collectors and researchers, and to become beneficiaries of plant collections and research. The experience of the Kuna and the Awa are described in Chapter 14.

Ethical guidelines and declarations

Ethical guidelines (or codes of ethics) are statements that clarify what is ethically acceptable behaviour for scientists when performing their work. Although they are not legally binding, they are often the result of consensus among concerned scientists, and they are expected to be complied with. Declarations, on the other hand, contain more general principles.

In 1988, the ISE established a set of principles for research and work with indigenous and local communities. *The Declaration of Belém* (see Introduction) was the first such statement to call attention to the "inextricable link" between the conservation of biological diversity and the preservation of cultural diversity. It was the first international declaration to call specifically for the protection of and compensation for IPR (IPR are treated as inalienable rights). Principle 4 of the declaration demands that "procedures be developed to compensate native peoples for the utilization of their knowledge and their biological resources."

The following ethical guidelines and declarations of scientific and professional organizations currently exist:

— *The Declaration of Belém* from the International Society for Ethnobiology, 1988;

— *Chiang Mai Declaration for Conservation of Medicinal Plants* by WWF/IUCN/WHO, 1988;

— *Code of Ethics for Foreign Collectors of Biological Samples* developed at the Botany 2000 Herbarium Curation Workshop, 1990 (Cunningham 1993b, p. 20);

— *Code of Ethics on Obligations to Indigenous Peoples* of the World Archaeological Congress, 1990 (Southworth 1994);

— *Professional Ethics in Economic Botany: A Preliminary Draft of Guidelines* of the Society of Economic Botany, 1991 (ECOSOC 1993, pp. 47–48);

— *Conclusions of the Workshop on Drug Development, Biological Diversity and Economic Growth* of the NIH and NCI, 1992 (Schweitzer et al. 1991);

— *The 1992 Global Biodiversity Strategy* of the World Resources Institute/IUCN/United Nations Environment Programme (UNEP), 1992 (World Resources Institute 1992);

— *Williamsburg Declaration* of the American Society of Pharmacognosy, 1992;

— *The Bukittinggi Declaration* at the Unesco Seminar on the Chemistry of Rainforest Plants, 1992;

— *The Manila Declaration*, developed at the Seventh Asian Symposium on Medicinal Plants, Spices and Other Natural Products, 1992

— *Guidelines for Equitable Partnerships in New Natural Products Development* of the People and Plants Initiative of WWF, Unesco, and RBG, 1993 (Cunningham 1993b).

The WWF/Unesco/RBG guidelines are interesting in that they consider the wide range of subjects relevant to equitable relations between institutions, corporations, local communities, and indigenous peoples. While recognizing that governments hold sovereignty over biogenetic resources, the guidelines call upon them to "accept the responsibility for establishing or implementing national policies for the conservation and use of biological diversity" (Section 1.1); collectors are urged to "respect local social values, traditional, and customary law" (Section 5.4). Although encouraging "ethno-directed" screening and collection, the guidelines leave the IPR issue up to national governments who "should be free to decide whether or not to adopt IPR protection for new natural products" (Section 8.3). Unfortunately, there is very little to console, encourage, or even orient local communities in dealing with IPR issues.

The NCI in the United States has also developed a set of general principles to govern its extensive collecting activities across the globe. Compensation for traditional knowledge and biogenetic resources is central, with "compensation" interpreted as including "training, institution building and information transfer" (see Chapter 7). Similar arrangements have been set up by the New York Botanical Garden and the RBG in London, with state governments as beneficiaries.

At its 1994 congress, the ISE agreed to develop a code of ethics, to be completed in 1995. Both the code and the ISE's new constitution are being written in conjunction with indigenous peoples led by a Maori lawyer.

One problem with declarations, ethical guidelines, and codes of practice, of course, is that they are not legally binding. They are often effective only if the government body or NGO is willing to respect them. Because they often do not, documents of this kind have been subject to criticism. Nevertheless, their existence may well make scientists more aware of their moral obligations. Furthermore, they may influence legislators who are drafting national and international laws and even serve as templates for such laws.

Indigenous peoples and developing countries have taken steps on their own to deal with misappropriation and misuse or unauthorized use of traditional knowledge. In 1979, the Organization of African Unity urged that herbal medicine research be carried out in secrecy to prevent multinational companies from developing new drugs and selling them back to developing countries at high prices (Hanlon 1979). In 1988, the Kuna of Panama prepared a 26-page manual to regulate scientific research in their area (see Chapter 14). The Kayapó Indians of Brazil are currently negotiating an IPR code and contract with The Body Shop to regulate commercial activities in their region, especially regarding the development of new products based on traditional knowledge and local biological resources (see Chapter 5).

Conclusions

Local communities might benefit from greater awareness of the existence of official statements produced by indigenous peoples, because they outline common concerns and can point to new strategies that can be fruitful. Furthermore, they can stimulate the growth of international alliances and make it more difficult for governments and corporations to ignore the just claims of indigenous and traditional communities.

It may also be useful to be aware of professional and academic codes of practice because even if they are not legally binding, they are at least morally binding on many scientists with whom community members might interact. They may also influence national and international laws as well as guidelines developed by indigenous and traditional peoples themselves.

Chapter 13

Why are funds and funding guidelines important?

As discussed in Chapter 3, one possible means for compensating communities (apart from IPR mechanisms or contracts) is through funding mechanisms. Indeed, local communities often find that adequate funding of community-controlled initiatives is vital in the protection of their TRR. The Small Grants Programme of the Global Environment Facility (GEF) and the Fund for Farmers' Rights are examples of international funds that are intended to benefit local communities, but other sources exist that are more accessible to communities. Whether the stated objective of funding mechanisms is conservation, community development, or compensation, ideally they should include a range of monetary and nonmonetary benefits. Preferably, they should support community-controlled (not just community-based) projects. This chapter concludes by suggesting ways for indigenous peoples to ensure that their own priorities and criteria for conservation and development projects are taken into account by funding institutions.

Who are the funders?

It may not be a simple task to discover to whom applications for funding should be made; indeed, this is one of the major problems faced by nonprofit organizations. In the United Kingdom, for example, lists of award-giving bodies and their spheres of interest exist, but they are not all-inclusive and searching them is time-consuming. Filling out applications for funding has become a specialized skill. Private and public funding organizations that have been set up with the sole purpose of benefiting humankind (including animal and plant charities where the benefit to humanity may be indirect) exist. However, finding the appropriate ones to apply to and filling a superb application (which may have to be written in a foreign language) may be serious obstacles, especially for local communities that may lack the necessary expertise.

Historically, help for indigenous and traditional people has been available from religious bodies; the merits of such sources aside, there is still a considerable amount of aid available through church societies and a willingness on their part to give time and money.

In recent years, there has also been a significant increase in the number of charitable organizations dedicated to environmental protection, both at national and international levels. One of the best known is the WWF, which began as a charity to save endangered animals (represented by its panda logo) and developed into a body dedicated to protecting nature in all its forms. At the other end of the scale, small charities such as the Rainforest Action Network in the United States provide funding for specific projects (see Box 13.1). Guidelines for project applications supplied by a funder should be examined carefully to ensure that the criteria are adhered to and that sufficient information is provided to allow the funder to assess the proposal.

Many rich people and organizations in the world have committed part of their wealth to a cause they believe in by setting up trusts. Capital is invested and the profits are distributed in the name of the cause (education, health, animal welfare, travel, or anything the benefactor chooses). Well-invested funds maintain their capital value and therefore the level of their disbursements for many years.

Governments dedicate a portion of their budgets to aid, which may be distributed via government departments, agencies, or NGOs. In the United Kingdom, for example, the Overseas Development Administration distributes funds on behalf of the government to programs run by university departments, such as the Forestry Research Programme of the Oxford Forestry Institute. The funding of university programs is complex because many sources may be administered by a department. Links with university programs need not be damaging for a community seeking to protect its knowledge and resources if they are entered into with full prior understanding of the university's goals. The expertise of members of universities in obtaining funds can be used to great advantage by a community that understands its own and the researchers' needs and objectives.

United Nations agencies may be a source of funding for specific projects. For example, the Global Environment Facility (see below) has a Small Grants Programme to which applications may be made. The FAO is the source of a proposed Fund for Farmer's Rights (see below), which is intended to provide compensation to farmers for their "past,

> Box 13.1
>
> ### The Protect-an-Acre Program of the Rainforest Action Network
>
> The purpose of the Protect-an-Acre Program is to maintain the ecological and cultural integrity of tropical rainforests. The program funds projects to help forest inhabitants secure land rights, thus helping to preserve ethnic identity and social autonomy by maintaining their traditional customs and practices. Projects are approved only if they support communities and strengthen the human rights of the original population (for example, the demarcation of indigenous territories) or they contribute toward the creation of extracting reserves, management of natural resources, or preservation of the ecological balance of a forest.
>
> The amount of funding available for any one project is limited, and a project may only receive one grant. Applicants are required to send a proposal, limited to eight pages, with a letter of presentation. The proposal should include an executive summary; information on its general and specific objectives, definition, and importance; history of the organization or group; strategies and methods for evaluating results; estimated budget; and assessment of the sustainability of the project.
>
> Many applications are received for such programs; they are generally evaluated by committee and funds are awarded to projects that most closely fit the charity's criteria.
>
> *Source: Rainforest Action Network*

present and future contributions ... in conserving, improving and making available plant genetic resources particularly those in the centres of origin/diversity" (FAO resolution 5/89).

The Global Environment Facility

The GEF was set up in 1990 to fund projects that provide global environmental benefits with reference to greenhouse gases, biological diversity, international waters, and ozone depletion (UNDP 1993). The GEF's implementing agencies are

— The World Bank, which is trustee for the funds, administrator of projects, and chair of the GEF;

— UNDP, which is responsible for technical assistance and administers the Small Grants Programme, the budget line for NGOs;

— UNEP, which supplies environmental expertise for projects and houses the secretariat of the independent Scientific and Technical Advisory Panel of 21 scientists and researchers.

The countries represented at the Earth Summit agreed to adopt the GEF as an interim mechanism to fund environmental protection projects of global importance in accordance with the provisions of the biodiversity and climate change conventions signed at Rio.

The Small Grants Programme is a pilot project, whose principal objective is to identify and demonstrate effective community-based approaches and strategies that could reduce threats to the global environment in 32 countries in Africa, the Arab States, Asia and the Pacific, Europe, and Latin America and the Caribbean.[7] The program awards grants of up to $50 000 to NGOs and community groups for small-scale activities that "reduce or eliminate environmental problems within the GEF programme areas ... [and] motivate and enable communities and people to maintain the biological diversity of their environment and its productive capacity" (UNDP 1993, p. 2). For example, a project in the Philippines was awarded $6 590 to document the indigenous practices for controlling rice pests of the Holok and forest management systems of the Muyong people (UNDP 1993, p. 29). Awardees are chosen by a National Selection Committee, which is usually made up of representatives of NGOs, the host government, academic and scientific institutions, and community-based organizations. Priority is expected to be given to projects that "involve communities in their design, implementation and planning, respond to the needs of, and involve, women and/or indigenous peoples, include a capacity-building component which may be met by using local resources, and include provision for evaluation" (UNDP 1993, p. 5).

However, the program's record gives cause to wonder if it will be a suitable tool for funding biodiversity conservation. For example, in 1991 (Kothari 1993, p. 17)

> The Indian government asked for a substantial sum (US $10–12 million) from the GEF biodiversity funds for ecodevelopment to divert human pressure away from biodiversity-rich areas. However, the proposal was formulated in an ad hoc manner, without consultations with even major citizen's groups, leave alone local communities .... Fortunately, the GEF funds did not come through, and the Ministry of Environment and Forests now proposes to involve a large number of citizens and community groups in the development of plans. Hopefully, ... future funds ... will be utilized with much greater public participation, transparency and openness.

If a local community wishes to obtain funding for a community-based project, it must produce a detailed funding proposal according to an accepted formula that includes a statement explaining why the project is important and how it accords with the above guidelines. It must also include a budget. When an NGO is awarded a grant for a community-based project, participating communities should be aware that the guidelines do not contain provisions for IPR or prior informed consent. Therefore, they should insist on such provisions as a condition of their agreement to collaborate.

---

[7] For information about the Small Grants Programme, contact UNDP, One United Nations Plaza, rooms 2050–2052, New York, NY 10017, USA (fax: (212) 906-5313).

The Fund for Farmers' Rights

The Fund for Farmers' Rights was originally intended to be an international fund that would be disbursed to national governments on behalf of their farmers. Although there was widespread agreement on the need for such a fund to compensate farmers, the means of dispersing the funds was considered inappropriate and the plan did not proceed. However, the issue has become prominent in international agendas, and upcoming Conferences of the Parties to the CBD may develop a protocol to the CBD that will give farmers' rights a legal status.

Genetic Resources Action International (GRAIN) and RAFI have undertaken to develop a definition of farmers' rights (GRAIN 1995). The GRAIN–RAFI initiative suggests that farming communities have a right

- To receive direct financial support for their past, present, and future contribution to the conservation and development of plant genetic resources for food and agriculture. This support will be provided through an international fund and any other financial mechanisms established at the national levels. Such funding mechanisms shall be substantial and equitable.

- To receive direct financial and other benefits, such as those derived from the commercialization of their knowledge and materials, access to research and technology they deem beneficial to their communities, support for their own development activities, training, and other forms of capacity building.

This type of fund would be an asset if means are found by which farmers and local communities can benefit from it, but there is a danger that there will be few trickle-down benefits to the community level from an intergovernmental fund. Some have suggested that one possible means by which local communities could benefit would be by using their share as a means of financing IPR mechanisms such as patents, or PBR (if applicable) to claim ownership of their own resources. This may be a means by which communities can have the same kind of legal protection as well-funded international seed companies.

Conclusions

There are funding institutions that can provide indigenous peoples and local communities with financial resources for conservation efforts, the application of indigenous and traditional knowledge, and the pursuit of economic options. However, indigenous peoples often lack information on sources of funding and on how to apply. Many of the institutions listed in the resource guide can provide advice.

Unfortunately, funds are often provided for community-based research or development projects without even the permission of the communities involved. To protect IPR and TRR, the following steps should be considered:

- All applications for funding must contain a clause protecting the IPR and TRR of any indigenous groups involved in the project.

- Outside agencies such as government, NGOs, and research bodies should not make any application for funding without including evidence that the application was prepared in collaboration with any indigenous people living in the area concerned.

- Indigenous groups applying for funding for projects involving outside collaboration should ensure that their collaborators agree in writing to respect the IPR and TRR of groups.

Chapter 14

What creative strategies and unique solutions have been developed?

Developing policies, strategies, and laws for protection, compensation, and community empowerment requires a great deal of creativity and tenacity. International law is important, and alliances of people's organizations can have an impact at the international level. However, local communities and indigenous peoples may find that initiatives at the local, regional, and national levels will prove to be more fruitful in the short term. Therefore, it is useful to learn about community-based activities and even national policies in different parts of the world that have attempted to empower communities, conserve environments, and revitalize traditional cultures.

This chapter is a "menu" of a range of interesting strategies, policies, concepts, and laws developed by academics, policymakers, politicians, and local communities, which might be used to empower communities, conserve environments, or protect cultural integrity.

Community-based initiatives

Collaborative and community-controlled research

Collaborative research involves a partnership of equal parties in which local communities are treated as expert collaborators. The conditions necessary for true collaborative research may depend on the ability of an indigenous group to control access to its lands. This is because controlling access helps to create a "level playing field" by making it easier for the group to regulate (or prevent) the activities of researchers, and thereby to negotiate favourable terms for participation. If the land belongs to the state, an individual, or a company, control may be more difficult, but the group can still exercise its right to refuse to participate.

However, if indigenous peoples are to collect, record, and control knowledge useful to themselves, they should ideally initiate research projects rather than be participants in other people's plans. With community-controlled research, the priorities, methodologies, and procedures are decided by the local people. In some cases such research is intended to contribute to a community-controlled conservation or development project. Outside collaboration is often considered desirable, but all research data is the property of community members unless they agree otherwise. In fact, in recent years there have been cases of indigenous people hiring researchers who agree that the community or tribe will hold copyright for results. For example, communities in the Solomon Islands have secured copyright for their ecological knowledge recorded by researchers (Baines 1992).

Some indigenous groups have produced guidelines for researchers who visit their lands to ensure that all scientific research taking place on their territories furthers the interests of these groups by being collaborative or community-controlled.

The Kuna guidelines for research

In 1988, the Proyecto de Estudio para el Manejo de Areas Silvestres de Kuna Yala (PEMASKY) and the Asociación de Empleados Kunas of Panama produced an information manual for researchers entitled *Programa de Investigación: Monitoreo y Cooperación Científica* (research program: scientific monitoring and cooperation). It provides an outline of Kuna objectives with regard to forest management, the conservation of biological and cultural wealth, scientific collaboration, and research priorities, and establishes guidelines for researchers including the nature of benefits to be returned to the Kuna. It reflects a recognition of the need for collaboration between Kuna and Western scientists to improve documentation and management of their cultural and natural resources. Included among research priorities are basic ecological research, botanical and faunal inventories, soil surveys, socioeconomic studies, ethnobotanical studies, and the recording of Kuna traditions and culture. However, all research is geared toward providing the Kuna themselves with the maximum amount of information.

The manual concludes with guidelines for visiting scientists, provisions controlling research activities, and a description of benefits that should be returned to the Kuna. Researchers are required to

- Develop a proposal outlining the timing, extent, and potential environmental and cultural impact of a research program. This must be approved by the Scientific Committee of PEMASKY.

- Provide PEMASKY with written reports of the research, and two copies of any publication, in Spanish.

- Provide PEMASKY with copies of photographs or slides taken during the research program.

- Include in their research program Kuna collaborators, assistants, guides, and informants, and undertake training in relevant scientific techniques.

- Provide descriptions of all species new to science.

- Receive approval for the collection of species from the Scientific Committee of PEMASKY. All collections must be done in a nondestructive manner, may not include any endangered species, and may not be used for commercial purposes. Samples of all collected specimens must be left with PEMASKY (to be added to collections at the University of Panama).

- Undergo an orientation into the culture of the Kuna Yala and respect the norms of the communities in which they work.

The guidelines also forbid the introduction of exotic plant or animal species or the manipulation of genes. Research is restricted to certain areas of the reserve, prohibited in some sites, such as ceremonial or sacred sites, and controlled in other specific sites, such as some forest areas under community management.

The Awa Federation's relations with the New York Botanical Garden

In April 1993, following a 30-year informal relationship, the New York Botanical Garden signed an agreement on academic scientific research with the Awa Federation, who live in the extremely biodiverse province of Cachi in Ecuador. The Awa Federation is a legal institution that administers the land held under communal title by the Awa people and makes collective decisions regarding its use. The Awa have only recently (in 1988) acquired legal recognition as citizens of Ecuador; since then, they have been developing a program to protect their territory, including planting a 50-metre wide border with fruit trees and expelling colonist settlers. The agreement — called the *Reglamentos para la Realización de Estudios Científicos en al Territorio de la Federación Awa* — will be in effect for 2 years. It includes the following regulations:

- All scientists must ask for written permission to carry out studies. The request for permission must include a description of objectives, size and composition of the research party, duration of the research program, species or object of study, and the manner in which this research will benefit the Awa community.

— At least 2 months' notice is required before submitting a request for permission. The widely dispersed communities meet only four times a year for 4 days.

— A research group may consist of no more than five people.

— Local guides and informants must accompany all scientists.

— No object may be removed from Awa territory without the approval of the federation.

— Payments to Awa Federation members for their services should be in accordance with a schedule established by the Federation.

— The Awa Federation must receive acknowledgment in all publications.

The Inuit Tapirisat of Canada

The Inuit Tapirisat produced a background paper, "Negotiating research relationships in the North," containing a useful list of principles based on existing ethical guidelines and the concerns expressed by members of Inuit communities.[8] They may be highly relevant for indigenous peoples in other countries. The principles are as follows:

— Informed consent should be obtained from the community and from any individuals involved in research.

— In seeking informed consent, the researcher should at least explain the purpose of the research, name the sponsors and the person in charge, describe the potential benefits and possible problems associated with the research for people and the environment, outline the research methods, and state whether the research will involve participation of or contact with residents of the community.

— Anonymity and confidentiality must be offered and, if accepted, guaranteed except where this is legally precluded.

— Ongoing communication of research objectives, methods, findings, and interpretation should occur from inception to completion of project.

— If, during the project, the community decides that the research is unacceptable, it should be suspended.

— Serious efforts must be made to include local and traditional knowledge at all stages of research including problem identification.

— Research should be designed to anticipate and provide meaningful training of Aboriginal researchers.

---

[8] For further information about these guidelines, contact the Inuit Tapirisat of Canada (see Resource Guide, Canada).

- Researchers must avoid causing social disruption.
- Research must respect the privacy, dignity, culture, traditions, and rights of Aboriginal people.
- Written information should be available in appropriate language(s).
- The peer-review process must be outlined to the communities and their advice or participation sought.
- Aboriginal people should have access to research data, not just summaries and research reports. The extent of access to data that participants and communities can expect should be clearly stated and agreed upon as part of any approval process.

Putting the principles of collaborative and community-controlled research into practice has in fact been achieved by other indigenous peoples around the world. For example, there was a successful collaborative research project in the Uluru National Park of Australia based on the ecological knowledge of the Anangu people. It appears to have been a success because "the Anangu owned the land on which it [the research] was conducted, there had been two-way information flows, Anangu had decision-making power and had been involved in all stages of the project, gender-specific skills were recognized, Anangu experts were paid expert consulting rates, flexible work arrangements and good working relationships were developed, and the Anangu vetted all information before publication" (Sutherland 1993).

Some professional societies, and even state agencies such as the Canadian Royal Commission on Aboriginal Peoples, have developed ethical codes of conduct for research (see Chapter 12) (Sutherland 1993). This suggests that in some countries at least, institutions and scientists are becoming more sensitive to the ethical dimensions of their research activities that involve indigenous peoples or that are carried out in their territories. Nevertheless, because indigenous peoples often lack their own research and documentation facilities and are therefore most likely to be the "subjects" of other people's research, it is vital for them to negotiate a collaborative research agreement with prospective researchers, rather than assume that voluntary ethical guidelines will be adhered to. The Anangu, Kuna, and Awa cases suggest that this is more likely to be achieved if the indigenous group has legal title to its territories or recognition as a juridical person (see Chapter 6). However, even if a group does not, there are international treaties, and perhaps domestic laws, regulations, and constitutional stipulations that can be used to support the rights of indigenous peoples to require that research activities affecting them should respect their knowledge and be fair and nonexploitive.

Self-demarcation

It is extremely important for traditional communities to secure legal title to their territories. To exercise their development rights (see Chapter 5), they must be able to control access to the lands they occupy and use. Indigenous peoples' impacts on land and use of natural resources may be virtually invisible to an outsider, making it easier for people to justify colonization by claiming that undemarcated land is nothing more than unoccupied and unused "virgin forest." Self-demarcation is one possible strategy to combat this view.

The case of the Ye'kuana of southern Venezuela

The territorial integrity of the 3600 Ye'kuana of southern Venezuela, as for many Amazonian indigenous peoples, is threatened by incursions from outsiders and national and regional governments that seem indifferent, if not hostile, to their land rights. Indeed, the national government has established a national park and a biosphere reserve on their land without consulting them.

In 1993, Simeon Jimenez, a member of a Ye'kuana community, arranged a meeting of several communities to discuss the possibility of taking the initiative and demarcating their lands themselves. Consultation with a lawyer and Otro Futuro, an NGO in Caracas, confirmed that self-demarcation might be the best way to achieve legal recognition of their territorial rights. Otro Futuro, the Assembly of First Nations (AFN), and the Local Earth Observation Project helped the Ye'kuana produce a project proposal.

The project, in which nearly all Ye'kuana communities have agreed to participate, involves creating land boundaries consisting of a series of cleared circles connected by trails and painted signs along physical boundaries like rivers. Each village will be linked to the boundaries by paths. A map will be prepared using satellite imagery and handheld Global Positioning System units will be used to enter the boundaries on the map accurately. This "technical map" will then be presented to the government and members of congress in support of the Ye'kuana land title claim.

Even before implementation, the project gave the Ye'kuana a sense of common purpose and unity that had not been present since before the rubber boom and the time when missionaries became active in the area. However, the main benefits will come when the project is completed and the Ye'kuana can use the law to help them resist invasion of their territory by outsiders.

In the longer term, the Ye'kuana hope that they will be more able to develop self-sufficient and environmentally sound livelihood strategies, based in part on equitable trading relations with non-Ye'kuana people. To secure such a future, they intend to create an "economic and cultural map" that would include fishing and hunting areas, places containing medicinal plants, and other locations important for economic and cultural reasons. It would demonstrate traditional Ye'kuana land use and help them explore new ways to exploit the natural environment on a sustainable basis. It also establishes ownership of biological resources, making misappropriation by bioprospectors more difficult. This case is of great relevance to many indigenous peoples in the Americas. Indeed, the AFN plans to disseminate the results of the project to other peoples as part of a reference file on self-demarcation projects.[9]

---

[9] For further information, contact Nelly Arvelo-Jiménez or Keith Conn, Assembly of First Nations, or Peter Poole (see Resource Guide, Canada).

Networks

The Indigenous Peoples' Biodiversity Network

The IPBN[10] has been set up by indigenous peoples to influence policy development and to exchange information on biodiversity issues. It has established the Indigenous Working Group on Cultural and Intellectual Integrity Issues with IPBN members from the Americas, Asia, and Africa. Its aims are to exchange ideas, search for alternatives, and establish a distinctive voice on the issue. Thus, indigenous peoples themselves are taking the lead in the search for long-term protection of their knowledge, resources, and rights to self-determination.

The IPBN's objectives are as follows:

— To share and distribute key information on biodiversity conservation issues among members and supporters;

— To support indigenous peoples' initiatives on biological diversity conservation and protection of traditional resources and knowledge;

— To catalyze the establishment of joint positions and initiatives among members;

— To establish or improve communications on biodiversity issues and opportunities among indigenous peoples and other sectors such as advocacy groups, science, government, industry, and others;

— To support and facilitate indigenous peoples' participation in intergovernmental meetings regarding the CBD and in other relevant domestic and international biodiversity policymaking processes;

— To foster a new communication alternative, based on the emerging electronic "information highway," through the use of computer networking to enhance biodiversity conservation and cultural survival.

SRISTI and the Honey Bee Newsletter

The Society for Research and Initiatives for Sustainable Technologies and Institutions (SRISTI) is an initiative in India for the diffusion of knowledge by and for farmers. Founded by Professor Anil Gupta of the Indian Institute of Management, SRISTI communicates with over 300 villages in the Indian subcontinent. Its key objectives are to "strengthen the capacity of grassroots innovators and inventors engaged in conserving biodiversity to: protect their intellectual property rights; experiment to add value to their knowledge; evolve entrepreneurial ability to generate returns from this knowledge; and enrich their cultural and institutional basis for dealing with nature."

---

[10] Alejandro Argumedo is interim coordinator at the IPBN General Coordinating Office (see Resource Guide, Canada). IPBN has regional coordinating offices in Bangladesh, Ecuador, Kenya, Panama, Peru, and the United States.

The search for sustainable technologies the world over provides a great opportunity for empowering the poor in hills, forests, and drought- and flood-prone regions. SRISTI intends to support the IPR of rural innovators by lobbying for their rights to genes, herbal medicines, plant protection and veterinary medicine recipes, implements, vegetable dyes, antioxidants, etc. It aims to link knowledge, institutions, technology, and politics in such a manner that control of the future direction of development passes into the hands of those who solve the problems in a sustainable manner (the communities themselves). SRISTI's key tasks are the following:

- To look into the taxonomic basis of indigenous ecological knowledge systems and derive a comparative understanding of local and global categories;
- To survey, document, and disseminate local innovations throughout India and in other collaborating countries;
- To provide training and technical, methodological, and institutional support to Honey Bee Network members;
- To install the software and hardware required to support access to information, data analysis, and electronic communication for researchers and network members;
- To provide legal, technical, and managerial support to local innovators to protect their IPR and ensure their ability to generate returns for their knowledge, inventions, or value-added;
- To provide support in market research, product development, and testing;
- To produce training material supporting the incorporation of insights from indigenous knowledge systems into educational curricula.

SRISTI aims to develop a computer database that can be used through electronic mail to make innovative solutions available to as wide an audience as possible in developing countries. It publishes *The Honey Bee Newsletter* in English, Hindi, Gujarati, Malayalam, Tamil, Oriya, and Zonkha to disseminate information to farmers on innovations. Emphasis is placed on information provided by farmers themselves. To prevent the newsletter from becoming a means by which indigenous knowledge is freely available to commercial interests, Anil Gupta[11] suggests four kinds of compensation mechanisms for the innovators:

- *Material specific:* This would include royalty payment to a particular individual or group and would be appropriate in the case of an innovation that is not widely known.
- *Nonmaterial specific:* This would mean a reward of honour by means of recognition without involving any monetary compensation.

---

[11] Further information about SRISTI may be obtained from Professor Anil Gupta (see Resource Guide, India).

- *Nonspecific material:* This implies monetary investment in an institution that would use the resources for preservation and augmentation through experimentation and value additions in the innovations and even apply for patents in the name of the local people.

- *Nonspecific nonmaterial:* This would mean changes in the basic protocol of dialogue on IPR and also implies improvements in the legal environment regarding the rights of people over resources around which they have developed various innovative strategies of management.

The Working Group on Traditional Resource Rights' GreenNet Conference

The WGTRR, which is based at the Oxford Centre for the Environment, Ethics and Society of Mansfield College, University of Oxford, UK, has opened a conference on GreenNet. The conference will give users the opportunity to take part in an open exchange of views and information relating to the intellectual, scientific, and cultural property rights of indigenous and local communities. WGTRR will operate the conference and provide information on request, including reports on recent and upcoming events, declarations and statements from meetings and conferences, bibliographic information, and details of indigenous organizations and groups working on TRR.

Because the medium allows two-way exchange, it is hoped that users will have input into the conference by keeping the WGTRR[12] informed of news and events of interest so that such information can be passed on. The conference is entitled "IPR, Indigenous Peoples and TRR" (indig.ipr-trr) and can be found under the categories "Human rights" and "Environment, general."

Model laws to implement the Convention on Biological Diversity

National and regional laws to implement the CBD are being drafted in some parts of the world. To be consistent with the convention and to benefit local communities they should include at least the following provisions:

- Overseas collectors should fulfill conditions acceptable to providers of biological resources before access is granted.

- If states assume sovereignty rights to biological resources within national borders, they should still accept the fact that local communities own such resources and have the right to veto commercial exploitation and to share the benefits when communities agree to such commercialization.

---

[12] Mailing address: Working Group on Traditional Resource Rights, Oxford Centre for the Environment, Ethics and Society, Mansfield College, University of Oxford, Oxford OX1 3TF, United Kingdom (phone/fax: 1865 284665; e-mail: wgtrr.ocees@mansfield.ox.ac.uk).

- Benefit sharing with communities must include a share of profits and IPR protection for their knowledge.
- Collectors of samples and knowledge must obtain prior informed consent of local communities as well as governments before permission is granted to collect the samples.
- Collectors must pay governments and local people for the right to collect.

A number of model laws have already been drawn up.

Access to genetic resources of the Andean Pact[13]

The Andean Pact's model law — whose initial drafter was the IUCN's Environmental Law Centre — addresses the conservation and sustainable use of biological material used as genetic resources. It would permit member states to set terms for access to their biological resources. Such terms may include the following:

- Sharing of benefits between receivers of biological resources, members states, and providers, who may be legal entities, individuals, or indigenous or local communities;
- Restrictions on transfer to third parties;
- Reporting obligations on future uses;
- Obligations related to intellectual property;
- Exclusivity and confidentiality;
- Measures to enable indigenous and local communities to enter into access agreements;
- Recognition of the member states or provider in publication of research results.

The model law also provides for funds consisting of royalties contained in access agreements to be administered by the Andean Pact and member states and used for conserving genetic resources.

Many of these provisions are extremely vague. Therefore, it remains to be seen whether the final version of the law will provide firm and unequivocal guarantees to respect the rights of local communities.

Collectors Act

Based on the concept of prior informed consent, this model national law was proposed by the Third World Network (Nijar 1994). It would set out the obligations required of collectors and grant them a licence if they are deemed able to fulfill the requirements made of them. The licence would be given for a prescribed period, subject to conditions.

---

[13] A regional economic union comprising Bolivia, Colombia, Ecuador, Peru, and Venezuela.

The powers of the Act would be strong enough so that contravention of its conditions would be subject to penal sanctions to the extent of making directors and employees of companies contravening the Act liable to imprisonment, in addition to withdrawal of the licence.

The collector would be required to provide the following:

- Plans for prospecting;
- Details of types of material to be collected in terms of species and quantities;
- Details of the evaluation, storage, and use of the collected material, including the uses to which it would be put;
- Explanation of the benefit the host country or community may derive from the collection of germplasm.

Conditions relating to collection and obligations related to post-collection activities would be enumerated, in order that the community or state would receive fair recompense for sharing their resources. Sums of money to be paid include

- A sum payable by the collector, representing not less than a fixed percentage of any income arising from the supply of germplasm extracts to commercial organizations;
- A similar sum for any royalties obtained as a result of the creation or invention of a marketable product from the collected materials.

An endorsement would be required from the collector's country (an accredited representative) agreeing to indemnify the source country for any losses it may sustain should the collector breach the agreement, plus surrender of the results of any report of studies or experimentation made on the collected specimens. The obligation imposed on the collector would read

- "No patent application shall be filed within or outside the country in respect of the collected specimens or any part thereof, its properties or activity or any derivatives that utilize the knowledge of indigenous groups or communities in the commercialization of any product as well as to a more sophisticated process for extracting, isolating, or synthesizing the active chemical in the plant extracts or compositions used by indigenous peoples or if the same represents the intellectual right of the indigenous communities."

Including the requirement for a contract between government and collector will give a country greater scope for enforcing penalties associated with any breach of the agreement. A country's legislation does not apply outside its territory; however, many countries have reciprocal enforcement arrangements that include breach of contract provisions. A contract is also more flexible in that it can be tailored to a particular circumstance, and the existence of one contract does not preclude others, as long as they are not in conflict.

Discoverer's rights

Michael Gollin, a lawyer in the United States, has suggested a new concept called "discoverer's rights," by which exclusive rights to living resources would be awarded to any individual or community that completed a taxonomic description of a species or variety not already in the public domain (Gollin 1993, pp. 180–181). In theory, a community developing a community register (see Chapter 9) could claim discoverer's rights for certain species and varieties in its register. Such a community could then share the benefits of commercial exploitation through an international technology agreement (ITA), material transfer agreement (MTA), or licencing agreement with a company, allowing the company to use the species and the community's knowledge of it in exchange for a licencing fee, royalties, patent-sharing, or other benefits. It should be emphasized that implementing discoverer's rights would be controversial and possibly unrealistic. For one thing, many species unknown to western scientists (who would probably constitute the majority of applicants) are known to indigenous peoples, who have their own taxonomic systems for species. Also, even if a community did apply for discoverer's rights to a plant, it is likely that neighbouring communities would also have the same knowledge of the plant. If this were true, the community would be privatizing a common resource.

If the discoverer's rights concept is developed further, it could be included in national laws to implement the CBD. However, since there may be multiple claims to the same species or variety, many of which could come from foreign citizens, it might be better for an international institution to be established to accept deposits and deal with claims and awards.

Other national laws

The South Korean cultural assets protection system

The South Korean system for protecting its national heritage provides for the preservation and promotion of both tangible and intangible cultural expressions. Its approach is completely different from copyright law and the Unesco–WIPO model provisions (see Chapter 9), yet it has been somewhat effective in maintaining the regional diversity of traditional cultural expressions in a country that is ethnically homogeneous. The system also provides protection for unique and important environments, landscapes, and species (Howard 1989, 1993).

In 1962, the South Korean government passed the *Law for Protection of Cultural Properties* providing for the documentation, preservation, and promotion of tangible and intangible cultural assets for present and future generations, with a very strong emphasis on local folklore rather than "high culture" alone. This makes it a unique system. To carry out the work, which would be continuous, the Cultural Properties Committee was set up as part of the Ministry of Culture.

Once an important cultural asset is selected and approved by the ministry, it is numbered and listed under one of the following designations:

– *Tangible cultural assets:* These are cultural artifacts with great historic value.

- *Intangible cultural assets:* These are cultural expressions with historic or artistic value, such as dramas, music, dances, crafts, and manufacturing techniques. Also included under this category are Bearers of Intangible Cultural Assets (more popularly known as "Living Treasures"). These are people with outstanding technical skills, knowledge, and artistic abilities. The government provides a stipend for them and their apprentices, some of whom may become Future Human Assets, and then Living Treasures themselves, in some cases upon the death of their teacher. In addition to their obligation to pass on knowledge to the next generation, Living Treasures are expected to display their abilities in public on a regular basis. The primary objective is not in fact to honour individual people, but to ensure that traditional knowledge and skills are preserved, perpetuated, and developed further. The designation Living Treasure has the advantage of legitimizing individual influence on an art form or craft, so that it is allowed to evolve rather than remain fixed in time. This is very appropriate for Korean traditional music, because improvisation is such an essential feature and is important if folklore is to remain a part of peoples lives, rather than simply entertainment for the urban middle classes.

- *Important folk cultural assets:* These may be tangible or intangible expressions of traditional culture related to the everyday lives of common people, including religion, work, and annual events.

- *Natural monuments and sites of scenic beauty:* These include plant and animal habitats, breeding and migration sites, and minerals.

There are tensions within the system, for example between those scholars in the committee who have a Western preservationist view of folklore as relics of the past, and the government, which has tended to be concerned first and foremost with finding "icons for national identity." Whereas such scholars are preoccupied with historical "authenticity," the government has shown a preference for allowing the authenticity of performances to be compromised if this increases their appeal to urban Koreans. Such manipulation may result in a performance losing its cultural relevance to local people, and this does appear to have happened with some shamanist rituals. Furthermore, the selection of individuals and artistic genres has sometimes been controversial. For example, the appointment of a shamanistic ritual known as the "ssikkim kut," performed to assist the soul of a dead person on its way to the next world, along with a number of shamans, was considered by some to be a primitive relic of the past that did not merit such an honour.

In recent years, rapid economic development has profoundly affected Korea. In spite of the pervasive influence of Western culture, Koreans still have a deeply ingrained cultural identity based on a long history as a distinct people. This state-sponsored system for upholding the nation's cultural heritage has been successful in stimulating greater interest among many Koreans in some parts of the country, in spite of the preservation versus performance conflict and occasional cases of corruption. For example, a significant number of villagers have been inspired to revive traditional performing arts, and annual folk festivals have become popular, with performers competing for government recognition and prizes. Van Zile (1993, p. 118) remarks that "Whether these dances are actual historical activities or recent constructions of a perhaps romanticized past, they nonetheless contribute to an important contemporary living tradition."

The success of the system has had some unintended consequences. A notable example is the 1980s revival of interest in traditional performing arts among college students, many of whom had embraced a politically more radical brand of anti-Western and anti-Japanese nationalism than that of the government. Many student demonstrations were accompanied by traditional farmers bands, masked dances, and shamanistic rituals "to 'purify' the campus of government sympathizers" (Howard 1989, p. 244).

Adoption of the Korean system by other countries would require long-term financial commitments by governments to set it up and keep it going. Although it does not seem appropriate for more ethnically diverse countries, the system has revived respect for local traditions even among westernized urban populations. It is just conceivable, then, that a similar system could be effective in countries committed to forging a national identity based on tolerance and respect for ethnic minorities and indigenous peoples and their cultures.

The Brazilian Indigenous Societies Act

This proposed law was originally prepared for the Brazilian Congress by the NGO, Nucleus for Indigenous Rights (NDI). In June 1994 it was approved by the Chamber of Deputies (Bill 2057/1991), has since been passed by the Senate, and currently awaits evaluation by a special committee as to its constitutionality before it can finally be enacted. The Act is intended to protect and assure respect for indigenous peoples' social organization, customs, languages, beliefs, traditions, and rights over their territories and possessions. Articles 18 to 29 deal with the intellectual property of indigenous peoples. Among the important provisions of benefit to indigenous peoples are the following:

- The right to maintain the secrecy of traditional knowledge;
- The right to refuse access to traditional knowledge;
- The right to apply for IPR protection, which, in the case of collective knowledge will be granted in the name of the community or society;
- The right of prior informed consent (to be given in writing) for access to, use of, and application of traditional knowledge;
- The right to co-ownership of research data, patents, and products derived from the research;
- The right of communities to nullify patents derived from their knowledge;
- The provision that IPR of indigenous communities are perpetual.

The US religious freedom law

When enshrined in law, religious freedom can be a useful concept, because a great many of the concerns of indigenous peoples can be characterized in terms of the desire to safeguard religious rights. The US *American Indian Religious Freedom Act*, passed in 1978, states:

> Henceforth it shall be the policy of the United States to protect and preserve for American Indians their inherent right to believe, express and exercise the traditional religions of the American Indian, Eskimo, Aleut, and Native Hawaiians, including but not limited to access to sites, use and possession of sacred objects, and the freedom to worship through ceremonials and traditional rites.

Indigenous peoples have intimate ties with the natural world, of which they consider themselves a part. Certain places may have become established as sites of special cultural and spiritual significance over thousands of years. They may be places where the dead are buried, places where important ceremonies are held or material used in these ceremonies is gathered, sources of medicinal plants, or the abodes of deities that no one is allowed to enter. Often they are human-modified environments, produced and maintained over centuries by environmental management practices based on a highly developed system of ecological knowledge. The existence and use of sacred sites and groves is another demonstration that the distinction among cultural, scientific, and intellectual resources is not a genuine one.

However, the fact that they may not be permanently settled can make it more difficult to claim sovereignty over them under the law. Indigenous peoples may not wish to exclude others from visiting these places if they are treated with respect. One additional problem that indigenous groups in the United States southwest have encountered is that a claim of sovereignty over sacred sites requires disclosure of the sacred features of the place, thereby diminishing its sacred nature. This is a very painful dilemma (Pinel and Evans 1994; Ruppert 1994). However, a bill to amend the Act, if passed by Congress, would permit the protection of culturally sensitive information from public disclosure.

Chapter 15

Toward protection, compensation, and community development

This final chapter consists of general guidelines for the protection of, and compensation for, the knowledge and resources of indigenous and local communities.

Guideline 1

If you are working with a company or other outside organization, develop a relationship in which the community is an equal partner. The community may be content simply to supply raw materials, but in many cases this role will not bring the greatest benefit to the community. The community may "add value" by processing plants into extracts, for example, and be compensated for this work. They may also be more actively involved in research and development or marketing of the material. As much as possible, local expertise and should be a part of these relationships. Make sure that what you receive in return for sharing your knowledge reflects the input you are contributing. However, be aware not only of the potential for commercialization of what you are sharing but also of the fact that most traditional knowledge may not generate commercial benefits.

It is also important to understand that nonindigenous peoples, including scientists and corporations, have little experience in dealing with indigenous peoples. This increases the potential for misunderstandings. Also, institutions or corporations tend to be fragmented in their organization and change policies and personnel over time. Therefore, they may not be consistent in their dealings with you. Also, negotiations will be somewhat different for each company.

Consider the implications carefully before entering into relations with brokers and go-betweens, who may approach your community with an interest in commercializing your knowledge and resources. Using these agents might make sense as they have access to legal and market information that communities may not easily acquire on their own. However, look into these relations carefully. Try to find out

— What the brokers are offering that you cannot do for yourselves;

— Whether these are the best people to work with;

— Whether they are nonprofit organizations and, if so, whether they are associated with for-profit organizations;

— What experience other communities have had with them.

Determine precisely how your knowledge and resources are to be used and in what way your community will benefit. Be aware also that some people believe that indigenous peoples are incapable of dealing with the markets or with IPR agreements. It will be necessary to put the exact nature of your collaboration with the company or broker in writing or on tape. Ask for advice and feedback from groups such as those listed in the accompanying guide. There are many good reasons to collaborate with outside commercial and research institutions, but make sure that you have all the information you need and that the relationship is structured to serve the interests of the community.

Before you have any interaction with visitors, exercise your right to prior informed consent and full disclosure by

— Being certain you fully understand who the person is and who he or she represents;

- Obtaining the researcher's signature on a full disclosure statement giving reasons for the visit and stating the intended use of material acquired from you (this may be recorded on audio- or videotape or in writing);

- Asking for proof of identity;

- Asking for letters of affiliation;

- Asking to see documentation, including proof of approval of the relevant authorities (if appropriate) in the official language of the country.

It is important to insist on seeing all proposals and budgets and to insist that agreements are made in writing, or on audio- or videotape.

Reach a mutual understanding about what group or individual will carry out independent monitoring of agreements, including the community criteria that will be used for evaluation.

In dealing with corporations or companies:

- Establish a legal trust fund as part of up-front payments;

- Establish up-front arrangements for immediate financial and nonfinancial benefits. To do this, find out what informants should be paid, the rent that should be paid by visitors for accommodation and food, etc., and be clear about the other benefits in terms of development, health, and education that the community may be able to claim;

- Ensure that you know what the long-term returns will be: nonmonetary (schools or teaching equipment, hospitals, medical services, medicines, transportation, or an airstrip); monetary (royalty agreements, profit sharing); or in compensation in kind (full disclosure of results, return of research results in a form useful to indigenous communities, including translation into the local languages).

Ensure that your autonomy is maintained:

- In the case of conservation, by ensuring that territory is seen as cultural landscape with social significance and treated accordingly;

- In the case of tourism, by ensuring that financial returns from tourism activities in the area are held in the community and do not accrue only to outside organizations;

- In relation to trade, several measures could be adopted by a community to take control of trading, for example, using some of the IPR tools described in Chapter 8 (trademarks, appellations of origin, and labeling); carrying out community inventories in conjunction with self-demarcation for delimiting areas or for appellations of origin; establishing indigenous councils to advise on how to set up markets; issuing guidelines for royalty payments (realistic percentages in profit-sharing arrangements).

Guideline 2

Your community may decide it is better not to collaborate with outside institutions and organizations that want to investigate your knowledge and resources and to discourage such activities on your territories. If so, following the example of the participants of the Consultation on Indigenous Peoples' Knowledge and Intellectual Property Rights in Suva, Fiji (Appendix 11), declare a moratorium on biodiversity prospecting and urge all community members not to cooperate in such activities. If other communities also disapprove of biodiversity prospecting, a joint declaration could be made. This action is easy to implement, requires no legal advice, and can serve to raise awareness among members of indigenous groups and local communities. Although in some cases it may be difficult to enforce, it is an assertion of self-determination and a clear message to outside institutions that they do not have the right to enter indigenous peoples' lands and collect biogenetic resources and traditional knowledge without the prior informed consent of local peoples.

Guideline 3

Control the publication of traditional knowledge and resource management practices. As part of their work, researchers will customarily publish the results of their studies in academic journals, books, or even popular magazines, including information on indigenous cultures, traditional knowledge, and resource management practices. They are motivated by a desire to share their writings but also to improve their reputations in the academic community. Researchers must often be educated about the implications of this practice. Many have never given a thought to the result of placing indigenous knowledge in the public domain and beyond the control of communities. Other researchers may knowingly disregard their responsibilities in this matter.

Professional societies have begun to draft codes of ethics to direct researchers, but communities should be prepared to educate researchers as well and to set terms for their work. Communities should ensure autonomy by engaging in collaborative research, by contracting outside researchers to carry out the required research (community-controlled research), or by establishing guidelines for equitable research contracts, following the example of the Kuna and Awa (see Chapter 14).

Guideline 4

Make sure that researchers supply a detailed description of their funding sources and their obligations to those sources. Funding agencies, whether private, commercial, or governmental, often attach conditions to the research projects they fund. Make sure you are fully informed of these conditions before collaborating with a researcher. For example, government funding of research in the United States requires publication of results, which would place traditional knowledge in the public domain. In a number of countries, government research agencies are required to pass on the results of any research with commercial potential to national industry. Ask for copies of research agreements and contracts and pay attention to IPR arrangements, especially the potential for commercialization of results.

Find out the implicit conditions behind every research program proposed for your community.

Guideline 5

Companies may wish to use photographs and images of indigenous people, homes, and cultural artifacts on their merchandise or in advertising. Indeed, some companies assume that buying raw materials and goods from a community entitles them to use such images. Communities should inform companies of their views on reproduction of their images (any objections they may have and what they regard as exploitative and an invasion of privacy).

Guideline 6

Be aware of processes in the drafting of national laws that may include consultations with members of the public, NGOs, and people's organizations. Insist on being included. One possible avenue for achieving empowerment through national laws is to investigate religious freedom acts to see how they can be further exploited to protect sacred sites, plants, or animals.

Guideline 7

Traditional communities often share many of the same experiences, yet have little access to the fruits of each others' work. Indigenous communities can more effectively support each other if they are organized internationally. Thus, it may be beneficial to broaden alliances between indigenous and other traditional and community groups by

- Establishing TRR centres that could carry out basic research and provide training and education programs;
- Supporting and strengthening information networks;
- Working for the establishment of indigenous funds using existing national, international, or regional organizations.

When planning the structure of an organization to represent you, consider the following:

- The criteria for appointing suitable and effective representatives;
- Gender issues in the context of the organization or community;
- The inadequacy of international mechanisms for enforcement of your rights;
- The inequality of access to national legal systems;
- The possibility that interest in traditional knowledge may fluctuate over time.

It is important to consider carefully the choice of overseas representatives so that unscrupulous individuals or groups do not try to use your image to further their own goals. Use of information networks to share experiences could be a means of preventing exploitation.

Guideline 8

The CBD offers opportunities that indigenous peoples may be able to exploit (see Chapters 10 and 14). However, acceptance of it implies nationalization of resources and a diminishing control over TRR. Indigenous peoples can act to ensure that they are consulted and set the conditions for such consultation in

- National legislation following ratification of the CBD;
- An indigenous peoples' interpretive statement on the CBD;
- Environmental impact assessments;
- National inventories;
- Development of sui generis systems;
- International mechanisms of enforcement;
- National mechanisms of enforcement.

Guideline 9

Consider working with other communities and indigenous groups to develop your own creative strategies, unique solutions, and culturally appropriate sui generis and TRR systems. The declarations and statements of indigenous peoples and local communities that are appended to this book are a useful source of ideas.

Appendix 1

The Human Genome Diversity Project

The Human Genome Organization has taken on the task of overseeing the Human Genome Diversity Project (HGDP) as part of the much larger Human Genome Project. The HGDP involves the collection, preservation, and analysis of human genetic material from ethnic groups around the world and the accumulation and storage of genetic information from such material in databases. Although planners of the project are now reluctant to emphasize the fact, many of the peoples to be investigated are very small indigenous groups chosen in part because of their endangered situation. The demise of indigenous peoples and their cultures used to be viewed as an inevitable outcome of modernization. However, indigenous peoples have rejected this scenario and are resisting assimilation. Thus, to many, the idea that endangered groups should be asked to give samples before they disappear is one that is antithetical, suggestive of outdated attitudes and self-fulfilling pessimism. However, there are other reasons why the Human Genome Diversity Project is highly controversial. Explanations of these follow.

Background

The Human Genome Diversity Project was conceived by Luigi Luca Cavalli-Sforza, a population geneticist at Stanford University, and other scientists in the United States (Cavalli-Sforza et al. 1991). Walter Bodmer, then president of the Human Genome Organization (HUGO) (see Box A1.1), became involved in planning the project. He referred to it as "a cultural obligation of the Human Genome Project" (Lewin 1993, p. 27). The cost was estimated at $23–35 million over 5 years (RAFI 1993, pp. 1–2). Once sufficient funding is secured, the project aims to collect blood, skin, and hair samples from hundreds of ethnic groups around the world and use new techniques to preserve genetic information indefinitely, either by developing cell lines or by isolating and storing DNA segments using polymerase chain reaction (PCR) technology. These techniques will enable scientists to study the samples many years into the future, perhaps after many of the ethnic groups providing them have merged with other populations and ceased to be sufficiently distinct to be deemed of scientific interest. Indeed, the endangered status of many populations is one reason why the planners believe that the project should be implemented with some urgency (Cavalli-Sforza et al. 1991, p. 490):

> The populations that can tell us the most about our evolutionary past are those that have been isolated for some time, are likely to be linguistically and culturally distinct, and are often surrounded by geographic barriers. Isolated human populations contain much more informative genetic records than more recent, urban ones. Such isolated human populations are being rapidly merged with their neighbours, however, destroying irrevocably the information needed to reconstruct our evolutionary history. Population growth, famine, war, and improvements in transportation and communication are encroaching on once stable populations. It would be tragically ironic if, during the same decade that biological tools for understanding our species were created, major opportunities for applying them were squandered.

Box A1.1

The Human Genome Organization (HUGO)

The Human Genome Project is an international undertaking to find the location of every one of the 100 000 or so genes in human chromosomes. It consists of all national programs to map the human genome, most of which are state-funded. Many scientists involved in the project agreed that it was important to coordinate their efforts, keep the project global so that data are not monopolized by any one country or institution, and ensure that new data are freely accessible by way of databases. To further these aims, the scientists established the Human Genome Organization (HUGO) in 1988 with funding from charitable research foundations and with administrative headquarters in Europe, America, and the Pacific. Sir Walter Bodmer became president for a 3-year term. HUGO does not carry out research itself. Instead, it organizes workshops and conferences that bring together scientists from around the world who are doing the research.

Objectives

The project is expected to benefit research into human origins, migratory and mating patterns, adaptation and disease, and forensic anthropology (Lewin 1993).

One of the key questions for anthropologists and archeologists concerns the origins of the human species. Although most scientists are convinced that humans evolved only in Africa, then spread around the globe, some are less willing to discount the possibility that we may have evolved simultaneously in several locations, not only in Africa. It is hoped that the project will finally resolve this issue.

The planners hope to trace the movements of human populations and measure the genealogical relationships between these populations. Specifically, the project is expected to reveal new information on ancient migratory patterns resulting, for example, in the settlement of the Americas and Australia from Asia, as well as important clues about the evolution, dispersal, and current distribution of languages. At the more local level, it is thought that comparing genes of neighbouring populations of indigenous peoples could indicate the extent to which these groups have interbred, and even help scientists to estimate how long ago (or how recently) each of these populations reached the territories that they now inhabit and from where they came. The planners believe that mapping the "geography" of human genes will provide data of value to linguisticians, anthropologists, archaeologists, and historians, not just to population geneticists, and they feel that this is an important reason for the project to be supported (HUGO 1994, p.7). However, for genetics to provide insights for the humanities, there must be, as Cavalli-Sforza believes there is, a close correlation between language and patterns of population dispersal and distribution to the extent that family trees of populations and languages show a marked overlap (Cavalli-Sforza et al. 1994).

This whole approach has been questioned by scientists, some of whom have opposed the project. The main criticism is based on the fact that the units of investigation and analysis are human populations. Such populations are assumed, to some degree at least, to be discrete in terms of genetic, linguistic, and cultural characteristics and to have been so since prehistoric times. This is why linguists and historians will supposedly be able to derive revealing inferences from the genetic data. Critics have argued that this is a doubtful assumption in view of the many thousands of years of contact and intermingling between human populations (Lewin 1993, p. 25; Lock 1994, p. 604; Marks 1995). Furthermore, even though HUGO claims that the project will undermine racism, according to some critics the division of humankind into units that are genetically distinct implicitly revives the discredited notion of racial types (Lewin 1993, p. 25; Marks 1995). Another criticism of this population-based approach is that the lines of demarcation for a specific population can vary considerably depending on whether one is talking to a geneticist, an anthropologist, a linguist, or a member of the population in question (Lock 1994).

According to HGDP scientists, it is important to know all the normal genetic variations for the benefit of future studies of genetically based diseases. So far, 4 000 diseases are known to be caused by single-gene defects. However, many other disorders are to some extent genetically related. A comparison of the differences between populations in terms of physiology and susceptibility to certain diseases like diabetes, sickle cell anemia, and hypertension, whose incidence seems to result from genetic and environmental interactions, would be of great interest to medical researchers. They would particularly like to know if these differences result from adaptation by long-established populations to local conditions or whether they arise from random genetic changes. Also, organ-rejection study, which involves matching the precise genetic makeup of donor and recipient **antibodies** and **antigens,** might benefit from investigation of genetic differences found in a wide variety of populations.

"DNA fingerprinting" refers to techniques that can be used to identify individuals and to determine blood relationships from DNA samples. It is used in criminal investigation and as evidence in some court cases. Proponents of the HGDP believe it will lead to the discovery of a wide range of **DNA markers** existing in different populations, thereby increasing the accuracy of DNA fingerprinting.

The project planning workshops

The project planners organized a series of workshops to decide how to implement the project and develop funding proposals. At the first workshop, at Stanford University in July 1992, it was agreed that sampling should be based on populations rather than individuals. Obtaining samples from 25 individuals from each population was deemed sufficient.

At the second workshop at Pennsylvania State University in October 1992, discussions centred on which groups to select and the criteria for selection. Anthropologists compiled a list of populations "that would be interesting to sample" (H. Greely, Chair of the Ethics Subcommittee of the North American Regional Committee of the project, 1994, personal communication). HUGO now denies that indigenous peoples are the main focus of the survey or that endangered status is one of the main criteria for selection (E. Evans, Secretary of HUGO Europe, 1994, personal communication). However, the list includes several small, geographically isolated groups that were almost certainly chosen because their status as genetically discrete populations (or "integral units" in HGDP terminology) was deemed to be threatened. Some of these groups are very small indeed, numbering fewer than 100 people. Among those included in the draft list are the Yukaghir of Siberia, the Onge and Greater Andamanese (who have only one fertile couple left) of the Andaman Islands, the Dorasque of Panama, the Akuriyo from Amazonia, and the Ona, Yahgan, and Alacaluf from southern Chile and Argentina. Such groups were referred to at the second workshop as "isolates of historic interest ... because they represent groups that should be sampled before they disappear as integral units so that their role in history can be preserved" (RAFI 1993, p. 2).

The third workshop, at the National Institutes of Health (NIH) in February 1993, dealt specifically with ethical and human rights issues. Among the ethical issues discussed were those relating to informed consent, privacy and confidentiality, IPR, access to and use of data, international law, and the morality of "immortalizing" the genes of peoples whose disappearance is expected to be imminent.

At the fourth workshop, in Sardinia in September 1993, discussions, including ethical matters, were continued from the previous workshops, and the relative merits of cell lines and DNA extraction using PCR technology were considered. Cell lines can be used to store and replicate all of the donor's genetic makeup. PCR technology enables scientists to store and replicate only sections of DNA but is much less expensive. For this reason, probably only about 10 percent of the samples will be developed into cell lines (E. Evans, 1994, personal communication). It was agreed that the project should proceed under the auspices of HUGO, which would organize discussions on ethical and social matters as they relate to the project and set up regional ethics committees. Another list of populations was drawn up,[14] but HUGO's summary document of the Sardinia workshop makes no mention of this or any other list. What the document does reveal is that whereas 25 samples per population "may be sufficient ... a norm of 150 samples is generally recommended" (HUGO 1994, p. 16), and that many samples already collected by scientists involved in the project may be included in the database. Furthermore, in the document is the following statement (HUGO 1994, p. 15)

> In previous years, samples from a large number of different populations have been collected by individual researchers. As a result, cell lines as well as DNA samples exist in many laboratories around the world. Consideration should be given to assembling the most relevant of these samples into the central repositories for the HGD Project in order to give researchers access to them.

This statement gives the impression that the project is not yet under way, and that existing samples only may be used for the project. However, in a recent book (Bodmer and McKie 1994), Bodmer appears to contradict HUGO:

> One of the project's many centres is Professor Kidd's [a member of the Human Genome Diversity Project executive] laboratory at Yale University. There huge liquid nitrogen freezers are filled with blood samples taken from races and tribes from around the globe. By the beginning of 1992, Kidd and his colleagues had collected more than 800 specimens obtained by anthropologists from the Baika pygmies of Central Africa, Cambodians, Basques, New Guineans, Samoans, Yemenite Jews, Ethiopian Jews, Malayans, Sardinians and a host of different ethnic populations. Many other laboratories have accumulated equally large genetic repositories.

Quite clearly, sampling has been going on in a systematic manner, and it is hardly conceivable that HUGO will neglect to add the data already gathered to the database. Indeed, this possibility is mentioned in HUGO's 1994 report (pp.15-16).

---

[14] According to Greely (1994, personal communication), "At this point, the Penn State and Sardinia lists are clearly understood to be of little value. Their main value lies as a way to point to the kinds of things that are interesting about groups ... those comprise characteristics of unusual linguistic, cultural, or historical interest; proximity (geographical, linguistic, or cultural) to such an interesting group; and linguistic, geographical, or cultural 'coverage.' The apparent existing speed of assimilation, or, in a few rare cases, actual physical death, remains one factor, but it is only one among many. Geographical isolation is never a positive factor and may be a negative one."

Implications of the project

Ethics, the law and human rights are all legitimate areas of concern that the project planners have considered, especially at the NIH and Sardinia workshops. To what extent have the planners addressed these matters in a satisfactory manner? So far no representatives of the peoples who may be asked to give samples have been invited to attend any of the workshops. However, this is not to say that those participating in the workshops are unaware of the need to involve indigenous peoples more directly. Greely, who chaired the NIH workshop, recommended that the project should have an ethics committee, including members of the ethnic groups to be sampled and a representative from an indigenous peoples' advocacy group. He has had discussions with indigenous peoples' organizations himself.[15] Since then, the North American Regional Committee of the HGDP has set up an ethics subcommittee, with Professor Greely as the chair. It remains to be seen whether indigenous people will be invited to join the subcommittee.

Informed consent

According to US government regulations for research conducted by government agencies, the "legally effective informed consent of the subject or the subject's legally authorized representative" if the subject is the donor of a blood sample is a legal requirement (*Code of Federal Regulations*, Title 45, Protection of Human Subjects). Specifically, researchers should provide full information to the subjects regarding the following:

- The purposes of the research;
- Any benefits for the subjects and the sponsors of the research;
- Possible alternative procedures or treatments;
- Any reasonably foreseeable risks entailed by the research; and
- Discoveries made in the course of research that might affect the willingness of the subjects to permit the research to continue.

Therefore, US institutions like the NIH or the National Science Foundation that agree to fund the project will presumably have to abide by these legal requirements in research that involves the extraction of human material. The regulations can be interpreted to imply that the subjects should be informed of the possible commercial exploitation of their samples at some future time. Also, because a sample may be the subject of multiple research activities in the distant future, the donors must have the option of requesting the cancellation of any and all research at any time in the future and asking for their DNA to be returned. Project researchers or their assistants should also be prepared to explain the legal rights of research subjects and their own legal obligations at the time the samples are being requested.

---

[15] For example, Greely attended the General Assembly of the World Council of Indigenous Peoples in Quezaltenango, Guatemala, in December 1993.

Box A1.2

Hoffmann-La Roche, the NIH, and the Aeta

It was reported recently that the Hoffmann-La Roche company was collaborating with the NIH in supposedly nonprofit research funded by the NIH. As part of this research, the company's Department of Human Genetics became interested in obtaining samples of cells from the oral cavities of members of the Aeta people of the Philippines. The Aeta are an isolated indigenous group of hunters and gatherers who may have been the first people to populate the Philippines 30 000 years ago. Nowadays they suffer from discrimination, poverty, and disease. Therefore, the Aeta are likely to be one of the populations that HGDP scientists would find interesting to sample.

The company is interested in the Aeta because they appear to be resistant to malaria. Two attempts were made to obtain samples under the cover of medical aid missions. Both were unsuccessful: the first, because the mission did not go to the area after all; the second, because a member of the company's research team used offers of money and the chance to contribute to important medical breakthroughs in the future to induce Dr Camara of the Makati Medical Center to assist them. He refused on the grounds that only a governmental institution should carry out such a project to ensure that benefits are shared equitably.

In view of the NIH's status as a government institution, it appears that the "success" of this project would have been illegal on the grounds of failure to follow government regulations regarding informed consent.

Source: Keller (1994)

Many scientists need to be educated about their responsibilities and must also be accountable to the organizations that fund their work, especially when such organizations have their own guidelines or are obliged to obey legally binding regulations (see Box A1.2).

Kenneth Weiss, who is a member of the NIH Human Genome Diversity Committee, suggested at the NIH workshop that explaining the goals of the HGDP to indigenous peoples living in isolated regions would be very difficult and should be done by people who are familiar with the populations concerned (HUGO 1993). Explanations to make the idea of informed consent meaningful would be difficult to translate and might cause anger, confusion, and distress. Possible problems could arise, for example, when telling an indigenous group that blood samples are needed to find out about their origins, and when explaining the fact that cell lines will outlive the donors. According to the draft report of the second workshop, "the establishment of permanent cell lines needs to be explained in terms that are understandable, but that do not mislead subjects in any population. English terms such as 'immortalization' of cell lines can be badly misunderstood" (RAFI 1993, p. 2). It is not difficult to imagine that members of a small group being told that samples are needed because they are endangered would be deeply offended, and it is unlikely that they would take much comfort from being told that they are making an important contribution to the advancement of scientific knowledge about the human body. They may well opt to exercise their right not to assist the project.

According to Greely (1994, personal communication):

> What had been clear, I think, to some even at the Penn State meeting was this time [at the Sardinia workshop] clear to all — the populations that were sampled would be the populations that chose to participate. No one could select populations in advance; the populations that get sampled will be sampled because of their own interest in participating, the interest of scientists who have worked with them in sampling them, and, perhaps, some modest degree of scientific interest in that population compared to others.

Consent may be oral or written. Weiss suggested that the former is more practical because many indigenous peoples are suspicious of the whole idea of signing legal documents, often through bitter experience (HUGO 1993, p. 6). Cavalli-Sforza, who has already collected blood samples from many peoples around the world, took the view that it would be difficult to obtain informed consent to a standard that would be acceptable in the United States, but concluded that this should not impede the project (HUGO 1993, p. 10).

One matter that has not been considered at the planning workshop is obtaining the informed consent of donors of samples that have already been collected. It is to be hoped that HUGO will undertake to inform past donors of the purposes and full implications of the project and ask their permission before including information generated from their samples in the database.

Confidentiality and privacy

HUGO has stipulated that all samples must be handled anonymously at the level of individuals (E. Evans, 1994, personal communication). The possibility of depositing DNA samples with national or regional governments has been discussed. This may satisfy the governments but will be of little consolation to indigenous groups, who may be concerned that others will possess fragments of, and insights into, their bodies. However unlikely it may be that unscrupulous scientists will find ways to exploit a people's genetic vulnerabilities exposed by their research, indigenous peoples often believe that those with the power to cure also have the power to poison.[16] The disclosure that a certain disease is particularly prevalent in a population may be beneficial or harmful to a group. It might result in medical treatment that would otherwise not have been available, but in the case of a high-profile infectious disease like HIV, the information could lead to violation of the group's right to privacy. Note: If examination of an anonymously donated sample reveals that the donor is carrying a serious disease, it is standard practice in medical research to make no attempt to locate or inform the donor if nothing can be done to improve his or her quality of life (E. Evans, 1994, personal communication).

---

[16] This does not seem so unreasonable when it is understood that indigenous peoples have already been victims of biological warfare. For example, it appears that the Indonesian government knowingly introduced pigs to West Papua that are indigenous to Bali and known to be carriers of a tapeworm. Now, 25 percent of the Ekari people have cysticercosis, a dangerous disease caused by eating the meat of pigs infected with this tapeworm (Anti-Slavery Society 1990, pp. 44–45).

Intellectual property rights

The HGDP is not a commercial venture as such; its sponsors may decide to adopt a policy of not applying for patents at all. However, the commercial potential of the DNA and genetic information that will be collected may be enormous (see Box A1.3). At least one of the US governmental public health agencies that may fund the project (the NIH) has applied for patents for human genetic material (see Chapter 2), and there is no doubt that some companies will be very interested in looking at the project's database and samples.

Box A1.3

IPR and human genetic material

In the United States, plants, animals, collections of cells, and even human genetic material considered to have been substantially modified as a result of human inventiveness have been patented. All of the following have been patented in the United States (some also in other countries):

- Transgenic organisms: Plants, bacteria and animals containing a foreign gene inserted by scientists can be patented. The first and only patented transgenic animal so far is the oncomouse, patented in the USA and the UK. This was a mouse containing a human gene that increased its susceptibility to cancer. The patent covered **all** animals into which this gene could be inserted, not just mice.
- Cell lines (see Chapter 2).
- **Hybridomas:** Cells are created in a laboratory by fusing a blood plasma tumor cell with a type of white blood cell.
- Proteins: A purified isolated protein may be deemed "novel" and patentable together with the **cDNA** gene responsible for its production. The patent could also include the organism into which the gene is inserted (Kevles and Hood 1992, p. 313).
- **Cloned** genes: Genes or DNA fragments may be extracted from an organism and inserted into a cell using recombinant DNA technology (genetic engineering). If the cell is a bacterium, as it divides it will produce ever-increasing quantities of the protein that is coded by the gene. This technique can, for example, be used to produce human insulin for diabetics. cDNA fragments alone would probably be the subject of product and use patents if there were an industrial application.

Understanding the extent of patentable matter in the United States is important because many other countries are likely to extend coverage of patentability in the same direction and accept similar interpretations of novelty, usefulness, and nonobviousness. In addition, the geographic location of the source of the genetic material has no bearing on the decision to accept or reject a patent application in the United States. In most other countries, patenting life is not yet possible, although many countries will probably allow this in the next few years.

The HGDP is committed to the principle of open access to the DNA, the cell lines, and the database. Although a company could not simply patent information from a database, it might find interesting data, in which case it could either examine the cell line or obtain its own samples directly from the donor community. Indigenous communities should be aware of this possibility.

The possibility of a patent application from any one sample is slim, but if the subjects are left unaware of this and a patent application is subsequently filed without the donor being notified (assuming he or she can be identified), accusations of exploitation would be fully justified. Regardless of whether group members are given the opportunity to refuse to allow their cells to be the subject of commercial research and patent applications, if such research is considered sacrilegious it would constitute an infringement of their human rights. In some countries it may also be illegal. For example, in France donors of DNA for a gene bank must be informed that a company can use it for commercial purposes (Patel 1994, p. 9).

At the NIH workshop, the possibility of MTAs was discussed. The purpose of such contracts would not be to prevent access to cell lines, but to provide access subject to conditions, such as confidentiality, a guarantee that there would be no patent applications, or provision for a royalty payment if genetic material were commercialized. Quite possibly a similar agreement could be made between communities and researchers. However, communities would benefit from legal advice to negotiate a favourable contract.

Access to and use of data

As stated earlier, data from the samples will be made available in the form of databases. There is understandable concern that some information will be used either to deny people's human rights or to justify human rights violations already taking place. Probably, sampling would confirm that most conflicts around the world are between neighbouring groups that are genetically similar. Nevertheless, it is possible to challenge the scepticism of at least one person involved in the project (Walter Bodmer, 1994, personal communication) that the results would be of any use to politicians.

For example, if sampling took place in the former Yugoslavia and the conclusion was drawn that Bosnian Muslims are genetically closer to Turks than to other southern Slavs, it is all too likely that this disclosure would be exploited to justify further oppression of these people. Although sampling in Cyprus has indicated that the people are genetically closer to each other than to either Greeks or Turks, it does not follow that such a discovery will lead to peace and harmony. Without a genetic foundation on which to justify discrimination and oppression, nationalist politicians can always exploit cultural and religious differences, which are usually the basis for racism anyway.

Politics being what they are, there is a disquieting possibility that genetic evidence will be used to further discrimination. For example, evidence that an indigenous group entered the region it occupies more recently than other inhabitants could be used as a pretext to deny group members their land rights. It may even be "proved" that a population is not actually indigenous at all, but is a mix of traditional inhabitants and settlers. This could be used to deny them the rights that may be due to them as indigenous peoples. In fact, some Canadian geneticists have already started to use DNA fingerprinting techniques as a way to distinguish between Caucasian Americans and Native Americans (Vines 1995, p. 37).

Scientists in industrial countries tend to believe that discoveries they make in their quest for knowledge are the responsibility of governments and society at large and that it is not up to scientists to tell people what to do with the discoveries. However, governments and others may misuse scientific knowledge. Indigenous peoples should, therefore, be aware that information uncovered by the HGDP could be used for malign purposes.

The CBD, GATT, Unesco, and the HGDP

Any possibility that the CBD could be interpreted to include human genes as genetic resources was eliminated at the Second Conference of the Parties, in November 1995, which decided that "human genetic resources are not included within the framework of the Convention" (UNEP 1995). As regards GATT, Article 27, Section 3, of the TRIPs agreement states:

> Members may [also] exclude from patentability: (a) diagnostic, therapeutic and surgical methods for the treatment of humans or animals; (b) plants and animals other than microorganisms, and essentially biological processes for the production of plants or animals other than nonbiological and microbiological processes.

GATT appears to neither oblige nor forbid countries to enact legislation allowing patents for human genetic material. Even though traditional peoples may see the whole idea as a violation of the sanctity of life, this is irrelevant if their national governments do not share their view.

The International Bioethics Committee of Unesco was invited by HUGO to support the project. Although the committee agreed that the project's scientific goals were valid, it decided not to endorse the project. The committee shared many of the concerns expressed by indigenous peoples and criticized the project on both ethical and human rights grounds (see Unesco 1995).[17]

Indigenous peoples' reactions

The Canadian NGO, RAFI, informed indigenous groups about the project in the absence of any initial dialogue between indigenous peoples and HUGO. Among indigenous organizations the reaction was almost universally condemnatory. The World Council of Indigenous Peoples (WCIP) in Canada and the Cordillera Peoples Alliance (CPA) in the Philippines took the opportunity to express their opposition to the project at the World

---

[17] The International Bioethics Committee is currently developing a Declaration on the Human Genome, which will address ethical, legal, and social issues relating to human genome research.

Conference on Human Rights in June 1993 in Vienna and at the first session of the Commission on Sustainable Development. Victoria Tauli-Corpuz of the CPA made the following points in her statement:

> After being subjected to ethnocide and genocide for 500 years, which is why we are endangered, the alternative is for our DNA to be collected and stored. This is just a more sophisticated version of how the remains of our ancestors are collected and stored in museums and scientific institutions .... Why don't they address the causes of our being endangered instead of spending $20 million for 5 years to collect and store us in cold laboratories. If this money will be used instead to provide us basic social services and promote our rights as Indigenous Peoples, then our biodiversity will be protected.

The *Mataatua Declaration on Cultural and Intellectual Property Rights* called for an immediate halt to the project until all of its implications had been discussed, understood and approved by indigenous peoples (see Appendix 7). Elsewhere, opposition has come from the European Greens and the Pan-American Health Organization, which produced a resolution at its 1993 workshop that was highly critical of the project. The WCIP (1993) has also expressed strong views:

> The research will supposedly help preserve indigenous gene cultures for generations to come. The real agenda is the future development of pharmaceuticals that will generate huge corporate profits, long after indigenous people have been left to disappear.
>
> The assumption that indigenous peoples are doomed adds insult to the indignity of being used as human guinea pigs. The millions of dollars to be spent on the HGDP could fund healing and community development for those indigenous peoples that are considered at risk.
>
> The HGDP has already begun dehumanizing us by labelling us as "Isolates of Historic Interest" (IHI). Once human beings are depersonalized, it is easier to go about destroying them or allowing them to be destroyed.

The WCIP produced a statement based on Article 18 of its 1984 Declaration of Principles. It demands

— Establishment of an enforceable, international code of ethics to regulate all forms of human genetic research;

— Suspension of all patent applications until the issue of human ownership of human tissue can be examined;

— Full documentation and disclosure of all human genetic research projects; and

— Meaningful participation of representatives of indigenous peoples' organizations in any committees overseeing human genetic research.[18]

---

[18] This states: "Indigenous Peoples and their designated authorities have the right to be consulted and to authorize the implementation of technological and scientific research conducted within their territories and the right to be informed about the result of such activities."

The WCIP also drafted a memorandum for indigenous organizations and NGOs, which states in part:

> The danger in this project, acknowledged even by its proponents, is that the information gathered will, under the best of circumstances, be used to satisfy scientific curiosity, "even after the disappearance of these tribes". Here exists a basic ethical problem: human beings will only count as objects of research and not as beneficiaries of scientific development.

The *Declaration of Indigenous Peoples of the Western Hemisphere Regarding the Human Genome Diversity Project*, proclaimed by 18 indigenous peoples' organizations from the Americas in February 1995, opposed the HGDP and the patenting of genetic material. It states:

> We demand the Human Genome Diversity Project and any other such scientific project cease any attempts to seduce or coerce participation in their projects through promises of benefits and financial gain in order to obtain consent and participation of Indigenous Peoples.
>
> We demand an immediate moratorium on collections and/or patenting of genetic materials from Indigenous persons and communities by any scientific project, health organization, governments, independent agencies, and individual researchers.

At the *Consultation on Indigenous Peoples' Knowledge and Intellectual Property Rights*, held in Suva, Fiji, in April 1995, and attended by indigenous peoples from the Pacific region, participants agreed to propose and seek support for a plan of action to

> Initiate the establishment of a treaty declaring the Pacific Region to be a life forms patent-free zone ... [including] in the treaty protocols governing bioprospecting, human genetic research, in situ conservation by indigenous peoples, ex situ collections and relevant international instruments. [1.1]

Quite clearly indigenous peoples see little, if any, benefit for themselves from participating in the HGDP, and until their fears are allayed they will continue to oppose the project.

Conclusions

The HGDP claims to be at the planning stage, but collections have been taking place for a number of years. Therefore, in a sense it is already in progress. There are many reasons why indigenous peoples should be concerned about it. The best means of ensuring that indigenous peoples do not suffer and are not exploited as a result of the project may well be to

- Disseminate correct information about the project as widely as possible with accurate assessments of all the potential negative and positive implications so that indigenous peoples likely to be asked to participate can make a real choice; and

- Monitor the project closely to ensure that HUGO is fully accountable to all peoples.

Sources of further information

- Professor Henry Greely, Stanford Law School, Crown Quadrangle, Stanford University, Stanford CA, USA 94305-8610
- Darryl Macer, Institute of Biological Sciences, University of Tsukuba, Ibaraki 305, Japan
- RAFI (see Resource Guide, Canada)
- Swissaid (see Resource Guide, Switzerland)
- World Council of Indigenous Peoples (see Resource Guide, Canada)

Appendix 2

The Covenant on Intellectual, Cultural, and Scientific Resources

Prologue

Indigenous peoples are unanimous in identifying their primary concern as being self-determination, which subsumes such basic rights as recognition of and respect for their cultures, societies, and languages, as well as ownership over their own lands and territories, and control over the resources that are associated with those lands and territories. Intellectual, cultural and scientific property rights are seen as a starting point to defining a more useful category of traditional values, knowledge, and resources that have often been used and misused without authorization, recognition of origin, or just compensation.

This Covenant should in no way be construed as being a call for commoditization–commercialization of culture, biogenetic resources, or knowledge; nor is it a justification for bringing indigenous peoples unwillingly into commercial relationships with other societies. The Covenant recognizes that trade relationships have been generally harmful to local communities in the past. It is exactly for this reason, together with the fact that an increasing number of indigenous and traditional communities are opting for or are being forced into dangerous trade relationships, that a Covenant is necessary. This is an attempt to provide a basic code of ethics and conduct that will hopefully form the basis for equitable partnerships that lead to economic independence for local communities, while providing for the conservation of natural resources.

Practically, the Covenant is proposed as a model that can be tried in many parts of the world by many partners. There will undoubtedly be failures, but hopefully there will be many successes. The accumulation of these experiences will produce a new category that will replace IPR with a more powerful and decisive concept that, ideally, will catalyze the replacement of markets for temporary gain with trade based upon long term commitments that result in mutual advantages — turning businesses from being vanguards of destruction into equitable partners with local communities in the conservation of biological and cultural diversity.

Implementation of the Covenant will be a long-term process that will require nurturing, patience, and tolerance. The process can only work successfully if both parties come to understand and appreciate the other, and if both see the relationship as a means to improving not just their own lots, but the whole of the Earth.

Spirit of the Covenant

This Covenant is celebrated in order to:

Support indigenous and traditional peoples in their fight against genocide and for their land, territory, and control over their own resources, while strengthening the culture and local community through recognition and support of the groups' own goals, values, and objectives, by helping to find ways of responsibly utilizing, while conserving the biological, ecological, and cultural richness of the region, through equitable and responsible trade, sourcing, research and development, thereby establishing a long term relationship built through joint decision-making based upon the principles of equality of relationships and protection of traditional values, knowledge and culture; if these basic elements are not respected, then the Covenant is endangered, and along with it, the spirit of trust and partnership between responsible businesses, scientists, and institutions and local communities that is essential for the future well-being of the planet.

What is being protected

Although the essence of this Covenant is about the development of responsible research and equitable trade, any Intellectual Property Rights agreement must inevitably deal with protection. The first concern of indigenous peoples is their right not to sell, commoditize or have expropriated from them certain domains of knowledge and certain sacred places, plants, animals and objects. All other elements of the Covenant are preconditioned by this basic right, which is considerd a fundamental element of self-determination.

Thus, the first category for protection is

1. Sacred property (images, sounds, knowledge, material, culture or anything that is deemed sacred and, thereby, not commoditizable).

The following categories are recognized as providing the basis for protection and just compensation if, and only if, authorized by the community, society and cultural group.

2. Knowledge of current use, previous use, and/or potential use of plant and animal species, as well as soils and minerals;

3. Knowledge of preparation, processing, or storage of useful species;

4. Knowledge of formulations involving more than one ingredient;

5. Knowledge of individual species (planting methods, care for, selection criteria, etc.);

6. Knowledge of ecosystem conservation (methods of protecting or preserving a resource that may be found to have commercial value, although not specifically used for that purpose or other practical purposes by the local community or the culture);

7. Biogenetic resources that originate (or originated) on indigenous lands and territories;

8. Cultural property (images, sounds, crafts, arts and performances);

9. Classificatory systems of knowledge, such as traditional plant taxonomies.

All of these are protected as part of the larger need to protect land, territory and resources and to stimulate self-determination for indigenous, traditional peoples.

Basic principles to be exercised by all Partners

I. Equity of partners, including profit sharing, joint planning, and goal setting, informed consent and full disclosure in all aspects of the project, including results;

II. Working to insure that compensation is equitably shared within and among groups, and that compensation is in a form that strengthens the community and ethnic group;

III. Nonexclusivity of relationships, meaning that both parties are free to enter into agreements with other parties; priority for exchange will obviously be between partners;

IV. Confidentiality of information and resources, meaning that information imparted by the indigenous group to the partner cannot be passed on to others without the consent of the giver;

V. Continual dialogue and mutual review, supported by independent monitoring and, if necessary, mediation by a third party (as agreed by partners); mandatory review is required if there is a change of status of either party or in the law;

VI. Diversification of the economic base through diversification of collecting, ingredients and products based upon traditional knowledge, cultural practice, and local resources, as well as diversification of markets;

VII. Cooperation with local (indigenous and nonindigenous) educational, health, research, and nongovernmental institutions;

VIII. Insuring ecological and cultural sensitivity in all phases of any project, including collecting, screening, sourcing, production, and manufacture;

IX. Encouragement of community autonomy and control over all aspects of the projects as early as possible.

Additional principles to be observed by the company, scientist or institution

X. Responsibility to be informed about local, regional and national laws, customs, and cultures.

XI. Judicial recognition and registration of this agreement, followed by appropriate legal protection to enable the indigenous group to protect its knowledge and bio-genetic resources.

Additional principles to be observed by the indigenous group

XII. Establishment of a consensus on representation, group participation, ethnic boundaries, and "legal personality(ies) of partner(s)";

XIII. Commitment to work toward assuming legal, economic, and financial independence.

Additional principles for independent monitors

XIV. Must have no conflict of interests and be able to act as arbitrators or mediators for all parties.

XV. Must have the professional qualifications and relevant experiences to represent all parties equitably.

XVI. Must practice full information disclosure and provide a public statement of working procedures and principles.

XVII. Must serve as the guardian of the Covenant, providing audits when requested by either party, but at least once annually, on actual practice in all areas of the agreement.

Appendix 3

Declaration of Principles of the World Council of Indigenous Peoples

1. All human rights of Indigenous Peoples must be respected. No form of discrimination against Indigenous Peoples shall be allowed.

2. All Indigenous Peoples have the right to self-determination. By virtue of this right they can freely determine their political, economic, social, religious, and cultural development in agreement with the principles stated in this declaration.

3. Every nation-state within which Indigenous Peoples live shall recognize the population, territory, and institutions belonging to said peoples.

4. The culture of Indigenous Peoples is part of mankind's cultural patrimony.

5. The customs and usages of the Indigenous Peoples must be respected by the nation-states and recognized as a legitimate source of rights.

6. Indigenous Peoples have the right to determine which person(s) or group(s) is (are) included in its population.

7. Indigenous Peoples have the right to determine the form, structure, and jurisdiction of their own institutions.

8. The institutions of Indigenous Peoples, like those of a nation-state, must conform to internationally recognized human rights, both individual and collective.

9. Indigenous Peoples and their individual members have the right to participate in the political life of the nation-state in which they are located.

10. Indigenous Peoples have inalienable rights over their traditional lands and over the use of their natural resources which have been usurped, or taken away without the free and knowledgeable consent of indian peoples, shall be restored to them.

11. The rights of the Indigenous Peoples to their lands includes: the soil, the subsoil, coastal territorial waters in the interior, and coastal economic zones all within the limits specified by international legislation.

12. All Indigenous Peoples have the right to freely use their natural wealth and resources in order to satisfy their needs and in agreement with principles 10 and 11.

13. No action or process shall be implemented which directly and/or indirectly would result in the destruction of land, air, water, glaciers, animal life, environment, or natural resources, without the free and well-informed consent of the affected Indigenous Peoples.

14. Indigenous Peoples will reassume original rights over their material culture, including archaeological zones, artifacts, designs, and other artistic expressions.

15. All Indigenous Peoples have the rights to be educated in their own language and to establish their own educational institutions. Indigenous Peoples' languages shall be respected by nation-states in all dealings between them on the basis of equality and nondiscrimination.

16. All treaties reached through agreement between Indigenous Peoples and representatives of the nation-states will have total validity before national and internatioal law.

17. Indigenous Peoples have the rights, by virtue of their traditions, to freely travel across international boundaries, to conduct traditional activities, and to maintain family links.

18. Indigenous Peoples and their designated authorities have the right to be consulted and to authorize the implementation of technological and scientific research conducted within their territories and the right to be informed about the results of such activities.

19. The aforementioned principles constitute the minimal rights to which Indigenous Peoples are entitled and must be complemented by all nation-states.

Ratified by the IV General Assembly of the World Council of Indigenous Peoples.

Appendix 4

UN Draft Declaration on the Rights of Indigenous Peoples

Affirming that indigenous peoples are equal in dignity and rights to all other peoples, while recognizing the right of all peoples to be different, to consider themselves different, and to be respected as such,

Affirming also that all peoples contribute to the diversity and richness of civilizations and cultures, which constitute the common heritage of humankind,

Affirming further that all doctrines, policies, and practices based on or advocating superiority of peoples or individuals on the basis of national origin, racial, religious, ethnic, or cultural differences are racist, scientifically false, legally invalid, morally condemnable, and socially unjust,

Reaffirming also that indigenous peoples, in the exercise of their rights, should be free from discrimination of any kind,

Concerned that indigenous peoples have been deprived of their human rights and fundamental freedoms, resulting, inter alia, in their colonization and dispossession of their lands, territories, and resources, thus preventing them from exercising, in particular, their right to development in accordance with their own needs and interests,

Recognizing the urgent need to respect and promote the inherent rights and characteristics of indigenous peoples, especially their rights to their lands, territories, and resources, which derive from their political, economic, and social structures, and from their cultures, spiritual traditions, histories, and philosophies,

Welcoming the fact that indigenous peoples are organizing themselves for political, economic, social, and cultural enhancement and in order to bring an end to all forms of discrimination and oppression wherever they occur,

Convinced that control by indigenous peoples over developments affecting them and their lands, territories, and resources will enable them to maintain and strengthen their institutions, cultures and traditions, and to promote their development in accordance with their institutions, cultures, and traditions, and to promote their development in accordance with their aspirations and needs,

Recognizing also that respect for indigenous knowledge, cultures, and traditional practices contributes to sustainable and equitable development and proper management of the environment,

Emphasizing the need for demilitarization of the lands and territories of indigenous peoples, which will contribute to peace, economic, and social progress and development, understanding, and friendly relations among the nations and peoples of the world,

Recognizing in particular the right of indigenous families and communities to retain shared responsibility for the upbringing, training, education, and well-being of their children,

Recognizing also that indigenous peoples have the right freely to determine their relationships with States in a spirit of coexistence, mutual benefit, and full respect,

Considering that treaties, agreements, and other arrangements between States and indigenous peoples are properly matters of international concern and responsibility,

Acknowledging that the Charter of the United Nations, the International Covenant on Economic, Social and Cultural Rights, and the International Covenant on Civil and Political Rights affirm the fundamental importance of the right of self-determination of all peoples, by virtue of which they freely determine their political status and freely pursue their economic, social, and cultural development,

Bearing in mind that nothing in this Declaration may be used to deny any peoples their right of self-determination,

Encouraging States to comply with and effectively implement all international instruments, in particular those related to human rights, as they apply to indigenous peoples, in consultation and cooperation with the peoples concerned,

Emphasizing that the United Nations has an important and continuing role to play in promoting and protecting the rights of indigenous peoples,

Believing that this Declaration is a further important step forward for the recognition, promotion, and protection of the rights and freedoms of indigenous peoples and in the development of relevant activities of the United Nations system in this field,

Solemnly proclaims the following United Nations Declaration on the Rights of Indigenous Peoples:

Articles

Part I

1. Indigenous peoples have the right to the full and effective enjoyment of all human rights and fundamental freedoms recognized in the Charter of the United Nations, the Universal Declaration of Human Rights, and international human rights law.

2. Indigenous individuals and peoples are free and equal to other individuals and peoples in dignity and rights, and have the right to be free from any kind of adverse discrimination, in partiular that based on their indigenous origin or identity.

3. Indigenous peoples have the right of self-determination. By virtue of that right they freely determine their political status and freely pursue their economic, social, and cultural development.

4. Indigenous peoples have the right to maintain and strengthen their distinct political, economic, social, and cultural characteristics, as well as their legal systems, while retaining their rights to participate fully, if they so choose, in the political, economic, social, and cultural life of the State.

5. Every indigenous individual has the right to a nationality.

Part II

6. Indigenous peoples have the collective right to live in freedom, peace, and security as distinct peoples and to full guarantees against genocide or any other act of violence, including the removal of indigenous children from their families and communities under any pretext. In addition, they have the individual rights to life, physical and mental integrity, liberty and security of person.

7. Indigenous peoples have the collective and individual right not to be subjected to ethnocide and cultural genocide, including prevention of and redress for:
    (a) Any action which has the aim or effect of depriving them of their integrity as distinct peoples, or of their cultural values or ethnic identities;
    (b) Any action which has the aim or effect of dispossessing them of their lands, territories, or resources;
    (c) Any form of population transfer which has the aim or effect of violating or undermining any of their rights;
    (d) Any form of assimilation or integration by other cultures or ways of life imposed on them by legislative, administrative or other measures;
    (e) Any form of propaganda directed against them.

8. Indigenous peoples have the collective and individual right to maintain and develop their distinctive identities and characteristics, including the right to identify themselves as indigenous and to be recognized as such.

9. Indigenous peoples and individuals have the right to belong to an indigenous community or nation, in accordance with the traditions and customs of the community or nation concerned. No disadvantage of any kind may arise from the exercise of such a right.

10. Indigenous peoples shall not be forcibly removed from their lands or territories. No relocation shall take place without the free and informed consent of the indigenous peoples concerned and after agreement on just and fair compensation and, where possible, with the option of return.

11. Indigenous peoples have the right to special protection and security in periods of armed conflict. States shall observe international standards, in particular the Fourth Geneva Convention of 1949, for the protection of civilian populations in circumstances of emergency and armed conflict, and shall not:
    (a) Recruit indigenous individuals against their will into the armed forces and, in particular, for use against other indigenous peoples;
    (b) Recruit indigenous children into the armed forces under any circumstances;

(c) Force indigenous individuals to abandon their lands, territories or means of subsistence, or relocate them in special centres for military purposes;

(d) Force indigenous individuals to work for military purposes under any discriminatory purposes.

Part III

12. Indigenous peoples have the right to practice and revitalize their cultural traditions and customs. This includes the right to maintain, protect, and develop the past, present, and future manifestations of their cultures, such as archaeological and historical sites, artifacts, designs, ceremonies, technologies, and visual and performing arts and literature, as well as the right to the restitution of cultural, intellectual, religious, and spiritual property taken without their free and informed consent or in violation of their laws, traditions, and customs.

13. Indigenous peoples have the right to manifest, practice, develop, and teach their spiritual and religious traditions, customs, and ceremonies; the right to maintain, protect, and have access in privacy to their religious and cultural sites; the right to the use and control of ceremonial objects; and the right to the repatriation of human remains. States shall take effective measures, in conjunction with the indigenous peoples concerned, to ensure that indigenous sacred places, including burial sites, be preserved, respected, and protected.

14. Indigenous peoples have the right to revitalize, use, develop, and transmit to future generations their histories, languages, oral traditions, philosophies, writing systems, and literatures, and to designate and retain their own names for communities, places and persons. States shall take effective measures, whenever any right of indigenous peoples may be threatened, to ensure this right is protected and also to ensure that they can understand and be understood in political, legal, and administrative proceedings, where necessary through the provision of interpretation or by any other appropriate means.

Part IV

15. Indigenous children have the right to all levels and forms of education of the State. All indigenous peoples also have this right and the right to establish and control their educational systems and institutions providing education in their own languages, in a manner appropriate to their cultural methods of teaching and learning. Indigenous children living outside their communities have the right to be provided access to education in their own culture and language. States shall take effective measures to provide appropriate resources for these puposes.

16. Indigenous peoples have the right to have the dignity and diversity of their cultures, traditions, histories, and aspirations appropriately reflected in all forms of education and public information. States shall take effective measure, in consultation with the indigenous peoples concerned, to eliminate prejudice and discrimination and to promote tolerance, understanding, and good relations among indigenous peoples and all segments of society.

17. Indigenous peoples have the right to establish their own media in their own languages. They also have the right to equal access to all forms of nonindigenous media. States shall take effective measures to ensure that State-owned media duly reflect indigenous cultural diversity.

18. Indigenous peoples have the right to enjoy fully all rights established under international labour law and national labour legislation. Indigenous peoples have the right not to be subjected to any discriminatory conditions of labour, employment, or salary.

Part V

19. Indigenous peoples have the right to participate fully, if they so choose, at all levels of decision-making in matters which may affect their rights, lives, and destinies through representatives chosen by themselves in accordance with their own procedures, as well as to maintain and develop their own indigenous decision-making institutions.

20. Indigenous peoples have the right to participate fully, if they so choose, through procedures determined by them, in devising legislative or administrative measures that may affect them. States shall obtain the free and informed consent of the peoples concerned before adopting and implementing such measures.

21. Indigenous peoples have the right to maintain and develop their political, economic, and social systems, to be secure in the enjoyment of their own means of subsistence and development, and to engage freely in all their traditional and other economic activities. Indigenous peoples who have been deprived of their means of subsistence and development are entitled to just and fair compensation.

22. Indigenous peoples have the right to special measures for the immediate, effective, and continuing improvement of their economic and social conditions, including in the areas of employment, vocational training and retraining, housing, sanitation, health, and social security. Particular attention shall be paid to the rights and special needs of indigenous elders, women, youth, children, and disabled persons.

23. Indigenous peoples have the right to determine and develop priorities and strategies for exercising their right to development. In particular, indigenous peoples have the right to determine and develop all health, housing, and other economic and social programs affecting them and, as far as possible, to administer such programs through their own institutions.

24. Indigenous peoples have the right to their traditional medicines and health practices, including the right to the protection of vital medicinal plants, animals and minerals. They also have the right to access, without any discrimination, to all medical institutions, health services, and medical care.

Part VI

25. Indigenous peoples have the right to maintain and strengthen their distinctive spiritual and material relationships with the lands, territories, waters, and coastal seas and other resources which they have traditionally owned or otherwise occupied or used, and to uphold their responsibilities to future generations in this regard.

26. Indigenous peoples have the right to own, develop, control, and use the lands and territories, including the total environment of the lands, air, waters, coastal seas, sea-ice, flora and fauna, and other resources which they have traditionally owned or otherwise occupied or used. This includes the right to the full recognition of their laws, traditions and customs, land-tenure systems, and institutions for the development and management of resources, and the right to effective measures by States to prevent any interference with, alienation of, or encroachment upon these rights.

27. Indigenous peoples have the right to the restitution of the lands, territories, and resources which they have traditionally owned or otherwise occupied or used; and which have been confiscated, occupied, used, or damaged without their free and informed consent. Where this is not possible, they have the right to just and fair compensation. Unless otherwise freely agreed upon by the peoples concerned, compensation shall take the form of lands, territories, and resources equal in quality, size, and legal status.

28. Indigenous peoples have the right to the conservation, restoration, and protection of the total environment and the productive capacity of their lands, territories, and resources, as well as to assistance for this purpose from States and through international cooperation. Military activities shall not take place in the lands and territories of indigenous peoples, unless otherwise freely agreed upon by the peoples concerned. States shall take effective measures to ensure that no storage of hazardous materials shall take place in the lands and territories of indigenous peoples. States shall also take effective measures to ensure, as needed, that programs for monitoring, maintaining, and restoring the health of indigenous peoples, as developed and implemented by the peoples affected by such materials, are duly implemented.

29. Indigenous peoples are entitled to the recognition of the full ownership, control, and protection of their cultural and intellectual property. They have the right to special measures to control, develop, and protect their sciences, technologies, and cultural manifestations, including human and other genetic resources, seeds, medicines, knowledge of the properties of fauna and flora, oral traditions, literatures, designs, and visual and performing arts.

30. Indigenous peoples have the right to determine and develop priorities and strategies for the development or use of their lands, territories, and other resources, including the right to require that States obtain their free and informed consent prior to the approval of any project affecting their lands, territories, and other resources, particularly in connection with the development, utilization, or exploitation of mineral, water, or other resources. Pursuant to agreement with the indigenous peoples concerned, just and fair compensation shall be provided for

any such activities and measures taken to mitigate adverse environmental, economic, social, cultural, or spiritual impact.

Part VII

31. Indigenous peoples, as a specific form of exercising their right to self-determination, have the right to autonomy or self-government in matters relating to their internal and local affairs, including culture, religion, education, information, media, health, housing, employment, social welfare, economic activities, land and resources managment, environment, and entry by nonmembers, as well as ways and means for financing these autonomous functions.

32. Indigenous peoples have the collective right to determine their own citizenship in accordance with their customs and traditions. Indigenous citizenship does not impair the right of indigenous individuals to obtain citizenship of the States in which they live. Indigenous peoples have the right to determine the structures and to select the membership of their institutions in accordance with their own procedures.

33. Indigenous peoples have the right to promote, develop, and maintain their institutional structures and their distinctive juridical customs, traditions, procedures, and practices, in accordance with internationally recognized human rights standards.

34. Indigenous peoples have the collective right to determine the responsibilities of individuals to their communities.

35. Indigenous peoples, in particular those divided by international borders, have the right to maintain and develop contacts, relations, and cooperation, including activities for spiritual, cultural, political, economic, and social purposes, with other peoples across borders. States shall take effective measures to ensure the exercise and implementation of this right.

36. Indigenous peoples have the right to the recognition, observance, and enforcement of treaties, agreements, and other constructive arrangements concluded with States or their successors, according to their original spirit and intent, and to have States honour and respect such treaties, agreements, and other constructive arrangements. Conflicts and disputes which cannot otherwise be settled should be submitted to competent international bodies agreed to by all parties concerned.

Part VIII

37. States shall take effective and appropriate measures, in consultation with the indigenous peoples concerned, to give full effect to the provisions of this Declaration. The rights recognized herein shall be adopted and included in national legislation in such a manner that indigenous peoples can avail themselves of such rights in practice.

38. Indigenous peoples have the right to have access to adequate financial and technical assistance, from States and through international cooperation, to pursue freely their political, economic, social, cultural, and spiritual development and for the enjoyment of the rights and freedoms recognized in this Declaration.

39. Indigenous peoples have the right to have access to and prompt decision through mutually acceptable and fair procedures for the resolution of conflicts and disputes with States, as well as to effective remedies for all infringements of their individual and collective rights. Such a decision shall take into consideration the customs, traditions, rules, and legal systems of the indigenous peoples concerned.

40. The organs and specialized agencies of the United Nations system and other intergovernmental organizations shall contribute to the full realization of the provisions of this Declaration through the mobilization, inter alia, of financial cooperation and technical assistance. Ways and means of ensuring participation of indigenous peoples on issues affecting them shall be established.

41. The United Nations shall take the necessary steps to ensure the implementation of this Declaration including the creation of a body at the highest level with special competence in this field and with the direct participation of indigenous peoples. All United Nations bodies shall promote respect for and full application of the provisions of this Declaration.

Part IX

42. The rights recognized herein constitute the minimum standards for the survival, dignity, and well-being of the indigenous peoples of the world.

43. All the rights and freedoms recognized herein are equally guaranteed to male and female indigenous individuals.

44. Nothing in this Declaration may be construed as diminishing or extinguishing existing or future rights indigenous peoples may have or acquire.

45. Nothing in this Declaration may be interpreted as implying for any State, group, or person any right to engage in any activity or to perform any act contrary to the Charter of the United Nations.

As agreed upon by members of the Working Group on Indigenous Populations at its 11th session, 1993.

Appendix 5

Kari-Oca Declaration and the Indigenous Peoples' Earth Charter

Kari-Oca Declaration

Preamble

The World Conference of Indigenous Peoples on Territory, Environment and Development (25–30 May 1992).

The Indigenous Peoples of the Americas, Asia, Africa, Australia, Europe, and the Pacific, united in one voice at Kari-Oca Villages, express our collective gratitude to the indigenous peoples of Brazil. Inspired by this historical meeting, we celebrate the spiritual unity of the indigenous peoples with the land and ourselves. We continue building and formulating our united commitment to save our Mother the Earth. We, the indigenous peoples, endorse the following declaration as our collective responsibility to carry our indigenous minds and voices into the future.

Declaration

We, the Indigenous Peoples, walk to the future in the footprints of our ancestors.

From the smallest to the largest living being, from the four directions, from the air, the land, and the mountains, the Creator has placed us, the Indigenous Peoples, upon our Mother the Earth.

The footprints of our ancestors are permanently etched upon the land of our peoples.

We, the Indigenous Peoples, maintain our inherent rights to self-determination.

We have always had the right to decide our own forms of government, to use our own laws to raise and educate our children, to our own cultural identity without interference.

We continue to maintain our rights as peoples despite centuries of deprivation, assimilation, and genocide.

We maintain our inalienable rights to our lands and territories, to all our resources — above and below — and to our waters. We assert our ongoing responsibility to pass these on to the future generations.

We cannot be removed from our lands. We, the Indigenous Peoples, are connected by the circle of life to our land and environments.

We, the Indigenous Peoples, walk to the future in the footprints of our ancestors.

Signed at Kari-Oca, Brazil, on the 30th day of May, 1992

Indigenous Peoples' Earth Charter[19]

Human rights and international law

1. We demand the right to life.

2. International law must deal with the collective human rights of indigenous peoples.

3. There are many international instruments which deal with the rights of individuals, but there are no declarations to recognize collective human rights. Therefore, we urge governments to support the United Nations Working Group on Indigenous Peoples' (UNWGIP) Universal Declaration of Indigenous Rights, which is presently in draft form.

4. There exist many examples of genocide against indigenous peoples. Therefore, the convention against genocide must be changed to include the genocide of indigenous peoples.

5. The United Nations should be able to send indigenous peoples' representatives, in a peace-keeping capacity, into indigenous territories where conflicts arise. This would be done at the request and consent of the indigenous peoples concerned.

6. The concept of Terra Nullius must be eliminated from international law usage. Many state governments have used internal domestic laws to deny us ownership of our own lands. These illegal acts should be condemned by the world.

7. Where small numbers of indigenous peoples are residing within state boundaries, so-called democratic countries have denied indigenous peoples the right of consent about their future, using the notion of majority rules to decide the future of indigenous peoples. Indigenous peoples' right of consent to projects in their areas must be recognized.

8. We must promote the term "indigenous peoples" at all fora. The use of the term "indigenous peoples" must be without qualifications.

9. We urge governments to ratify International Labour Organisation (ILO) Convention 169 to guarantee an international legal instrument for indigenous peoples (Group 2 only).

---

[19] Please note, for the purposes of the Declaration, and this statement, any use of the term "indigenous peoples" also includes tribal peoples.

10. Indigenous peoples' distinct and separate rights within their own territories must be recognised.

11. We assert our rights to free passage through state-imposed political boundaries dividing our traditional territories. Adequate mechanisms must be established to secure this right.

12. The colonial systems have tried to dominate and assimilate our peoples. However, our peoples remain distinct despite these pressures.

13. Our indigenous governments and legal systems must be recognized by the United Nations, state governments, and international legal instruments.

14. Our right to self-determination must be recognized.

15. We must be free from population transfer.

16. We maintain our right to our traditional way of life.

17. We maintain our right to our spiritual way of life.

18. We maintain the right to be free from pressures from multinational (transnational) corporations upon lives and lands. All multinational (transnational) corporations which are encroaching upon indigenous lands should be reported to the United Nations Transnational Office.

19. We must be free from racism.

20. We maintain the right to decide the direction of our communities.

21. The United Nations should have a special procedure to deal with issues arising from violations of indigenous treaties.

22. Treaties signed between indigenous peoples and nonindigenous peoples must be accepted as treaties under international law.

23. The United Nations must exercise the right to impose sanctions against governments that violate the rights of indigenous peoples.

24. We urge the United Nations to include the issue of indigenous peoples in the agenda of the World Conference of Human Rights to be held in 1993. The work done so far by the United Nations Inter-American Commission of Human Rights and the Inter-American Institute of Human Rights should be taken into consideration.

25. Indigenous peoples should have the right to their own knowledge, language, and culturally appropriate education, including bicultural and bilingual education. Through recognizing both formal and informal ways, the participation of family and community is guaranteed.

26. Our health rights must include the recognition and respect of traditional knowledge held by indigenous healers. This knowledge, including our traditional medicines and their preventive and spiritual healing power, must be recognized and protected against exploitation.

27. The World Court must extend its powers to include complaints by indigenous peoples.

28. There must be a monitoring system from this conference to oversee the return of delegates to their territories. The delegates should be free to attend and participate in international indigenous conferences.

29. Indigenous women's rights must be respected. Women must be included in all local, national, regional, and international organizations.

30. The above-mentioned historical rights of indigenous peoples must be guaranteed in national legislation.

Land and territories

31. Indigenous peoples were placed upon our Mother the Earth by the Creator. We belong to the land. We cannot be separated from our lands and territories.

32. Our territories are living totalities in permanent vital relation between human beings and nature. Their possession produces the development of our culture. Our territorial property should be inalienable, unceasable, and not denied title. Legal, economic, and technical back-up are needed to guarantee this.

33. Indigenous peoples' inalienable rights to land and resources confirm that we have always had ownership and stewardship over our traditional territories. We demand that these be respected.

34. We assert our rights to demarcate our traditional territories. The definition of territory includes space (air), land, and sea. We must promote a traditional analysis of traditional land rights in all our territories.

35. Where indigenous territories have been degraded, resources must be made available to restore them. The recuperation of those affected territories is the duty of the respective jurisdiction in all nation states, which cannot be delayed. Within this process of recuperation the compensation for the historical ecological debt must be taken into account. Nation states must revise in depth the agrarian, mining, and forestry policies.

36. Indigenous peoples reject the assertion of nonindigenous laws onto our lands; states cannot unilaterally extend their jurisdiction over our lands and territories. The concept of Terra Nullius should be forever erased from the law books of states.

37. We, as indigenous peoples, must never alienate our lands. We must always maintain control over the land for future generations.

38. If a nonindigenous government, individual, or corporation wants to use our lands, then there must be a formal agreement which sets out the terms and conditions. Indigenous peoples maintain the right to be compensated for the use of their lands and resources.

39. Traditional indigenous territorial boundaries, including the waters, must be respected.

40. There must be some control placed upon environmental groups who are lobbying to protect our territories and the species within those territories. In many instances, environmental groups are more concerned about animals than human beings. We call for indigenous peoples to determine guidelines prior to allowing environmental groups into their territories.

41. Parks must not be created at the expense of indigenous peoples. There is no way to separate indigenous peoples from their lands.

42. Indigenous peoples must not be removed from their lands in order to make it available to settlers or other forms of economic activity on their lands.

43. In many instances, the numbers of indigenous peoples have been decreasing because of encroachment by nonindigenous peoples.

44. Indigenous peoples should encourage their peoples to cultivate their own traditional forms of products rather than to use imported exotic crops which do not benefit local peoples.

45. Toxic wastes must not be deposited in our areas. Indigenous peoples must realize that chemicals, pesticides, and hazardous wastes do not benefit the peoples.

46. Traditional areas must be protected against present and future forms of environmental degradation.

47. There must be a cessation of all uses of nuclear material.

48. Mining of products for nuclear production must cease.

49. Indigenous lands must not be used for the testing or dumping of nuclear products.

50. Population transfer policies by state governments in our territories are causing hardship. Traditional lands are lost and traditional livelihoods are being destroyed.

51. Our lands are being used by state governments to obtain funds from the World Bank, the International Monetary Fund, the Asian Pacific Development Bank, and other institutions, which has led to a loss of our lands and territories.

52. In many countries, our lands are being used for military purposes. This is an unacceptable use of the lands.

53. The colonizer governments have changed the names of our traditional and sacred areas. Our children learn these foreign names and start to lose their identity. In addition, the changing of the name of a place diminishes respect for the spirits which reside in those areas.

54. Our forests are not being used for their intended purposes. The forests are being used to make money.

55. Traditional activities, such as making pottery, are being destroyed by the importation of industrial goods. This impoverishes the local peoples.

Biodiversity and conservation

56. The Vital Circles are in a continuous interrelation in such a way that the change of one of its elements affects the whole.

57. Climatic changes affect indigenous peoples and all humanity. In addition, ecological systems and their rhythms are affected, which contributes to the deterioration of our quality of life and increases our dependency.

58. The forests are being destroyed in the name of development and economic gains without considering the destruction of ecological balance. These activities do not benefit human beings, animals, birds, and fish. The logging concessions and incentives to the timber, cattle, and mining industries affecting the ecosystems and the natural resources should be cancelled.

59. We value the efforts of protection of the Biodiversity but we reject being included as part of an inert diversity which pretends to be maintained for scientific and folkloric purposes.

60. The indigenous peoples' strategies should be kept in a reference framework for the formulation and application of national policies on environment and biodiversity.

Development strategies

61. Indigenous peoples must consent to all projects in our territories. Prior to consent being obtained the peoples must be fully and entirely involved in any decisions. They must be given all the information about the project and its effects. Failure to do so should be considered a crime against the indigenous peoples. The person or persons who violate this should be tried in a world tribunal within the control of indigenous peoples set for such a purpose. This could be similar to the trials held after World War II.

62. We have the right to our own development strategies based on our cultural practices and with a transparent, efficient, and viable management and with economical and ecological viability.

63. Our development and life strategies are obstructed by the interests of the government and big companies and by the neoliberal policies. Our strategies have, as a fundamental condition, the existence of international relationships based on justice, equity, and solidarity between the human beings and the nations.

64. Any development strategy should prioritize the elimination of poverty, the climatic guarantee, the sustainable manageability of natural resources, the continuity of democratic societies, and the respect of cultural differences.

65. The Global Environmental Facility should assign at best 20 percent for indigenous peoples' strategies and programs of environmental emergency, improvement of life quality, protection of natural resources, and rehabilitation of ecosystems. This proposal in the case of South America and the Caribbean should be concrete in the

indigenous development fund as a pilot experience in order to be extended to the indigenous peoples of other regions and continents.

66. The concept of development has meant the destruction of our lands. We reject the current definition of development as being useful to our peoples. Our cultures are not static and we keep our identity through a permanent recreation of our life conditions; but all of this is obstructed in the name of so-called developments.

67. Recognizing indigenous peoples' harmonious relationship with Nature, indigenous sustainable development strategies and cultural values must be respected as distinct and vital sources of knowledge.

68. Indigenous peoples have been here since the time before time began. We have come directly from the Creator. We have lived and kept the Earth as it was on the First Day. Peoples who do not belong to the land must go out from the lands because those things (so called "development" on the land) are against the laws of the Creator.

69. (a) In order for indigenous peoples to assume control, management and administration of their resources and territories, development projects must be based on the principles of self-determination and self-management.
    (b) Indigenous peoples must be self-reliant.

70. If we are going to grow crops, we must feed the peoples. It is not appropriate that the lands be used to grow crops which do not benefit the local peoples.
    (a) Regarding indigenous policies, state government must cease attempts of assimilation and integration.
    (b) Indigenous peoples must consent to all projects in their territories. Prior to consent being obtained, the peoples must be fully and entirely involved in any decisions. They must be given all the information about the project and its effects. Failure to do so should be considered a crime against indigenous peoples. The person or persons responsible should be tried before a world tribunal, with a balance of indigenous peoples set up for such a purpose. This could be similar to the trials held after the World War II.

71. We must never use the term "land claims." It is the nonindigenous peoples which do not have any land. All the land is our land. It is nonindigenous peoples who are making claims to our lands. We are not making claims to our lands.

72. There should be a monitoring body within the United Nations to monitor all the land disputes around the world prior to development.

73. There should be a United Nations conference on the topic of "Indigenous Lands and Development."

74. Nonindigenous peoples have come to our lands for the purpose of exploiting these lands and resources to benefit themselves, and to the impoverishment of our peoples. Indigenous peoples are victims of development. In many cases, indigenous peoples are exterminated in the name of a development program. There are numerous examples of such occurrences.

75. Development that occurs on indigenous lands, without the consent of indigenous peoples, must be stopped.

76. Development which is occurring on indigenous lands is usually decided without local consultation by those who are unfamiliar with local conditions and needs.

77. The Eurocentric notion of ownership is destroying our peoples. We must return to our own view of the world, of the land, and of development. The issue cannot be separated from indigenous peoples' rights.

78. There are many different types of so-called development: road construction, communication facilities such as electricity, telephones. These allow developers easier access to the areas, but the effects of such industrialization destroy the lands.

79. There is a world-wide move to remove indigenous peoples from their lands and place them in villages. The relocation from the traditional territories is done to facilitate development.

80. It is not appropriate for governments or agencies to move into our territories and to tell our peoples what is needed.

81. In many instances, the state governments have created artificial entities such as "district council" in the name of the state government in order to deceive the international community. These artificial entities then are consulted about development in the area. The state government, then, claims that indigenous peoples were consulted about the project. These lies must be exposed to the international community.

82. There must be an effective network to disseminate material and information between indigenous peoples. This is necessary in order to keep informed about the problems of other indigenous peoples.

83. Indigenous peoples should form and direct their own environmental network.

Culture, science, and intellectual property

84. We feel the Earth as if we are within our mother. When the Earth is sick and polluted, human health is impossible. To heal ourselves, we must heal the Planet, and to heal the Planet, we must heal ourselves.

85. We must begin to heal from the grassroots level and work towards the international level.

86. The destruction of the culture has always been considered an internal, domestic problem within national states. The United Nation must set up a tribunal to review the cultural destruction of the indigenous peoples.

87. We need to have foreign observers come into our indigenous territories to oversee national state elections to prevent corruption.

88. The human remains and artifacts of indigenous peoples must be returned to their original peoples.

89. Our sacred and ceremonial sites should be protected and considered as the patrimony of indigenous peoples and humanity. The establishment of a set of legal and operational instruments at both national and international levels would guarantee this.

90. The use of existing indigenous languages is our right. These languages must be protected.

91. States that have outlawed indigenous languages and their alphabets should be censored by United Nations.

92. We must not allow tourism to be used to diminish our culture. Tourists come into the communities and view the people as if indigenous peoples were part of a zoo. Indigenous peoples have the right to allow or to disallow tourism within their areas.

93. Indigenous peoples must have the necessary resources and control over their own education systems.

94. Elders must be recognized and respected as teachers of the young people.

95. Indigenous wisdom must be recognized and encouraged.

96. The traditional knowledge of herbs and plants must be protected and passed onto future generations.

97. Traditions cannot be separated from land, territory, or science.

98. Traditional knowledge has enabled indigenous peoples to survive.

99. The usurping of traditional medicines and knowledge from indigenous peoples should be considered a crime against peoples.

100. Material culture is being used by the nonindigenous to gain access to our lands and resources, thus destroying our cultures.

101. Most of the media at this conference were only interested in the pictures which will be sold for profit. This is another case of exploitation of indigenous peoples. This does not advance the cause of indigenous peoples.

102. As creators and carriers of civilizations which have given and continue to share knowledge, experience, and values with humanity, we require that our right to intellectual and cultural properties be guaranteed and that the mechanism for each implementation be in favour of our peoples and studied in depth and implemented. This respect must include the right over genetic resources, genebanks, biotechnology, and knowledge of biodiversity programs.

103. We should list the suspect museums and institutions that have misused our cultural and intellectual properties.

104. The protection, norms, and mechanisms of artistic and artisan creation of our peoples must be established and implemented in order to avoid plunder, plagiarism, undue exposure, and use.

105. When indigenous peoples leave their communities, they should make every effort to return to the community.

106. In many instances, our songs, dances, and ceremonies have been viewed as the only aspects of our lives. In some instances, we have been asked to change a ceremony or a song to suit the occasion. This is racism.

107. At local, national, and international levels, governments must commit funds to new and existing resources to education and training for indigenous peoples, to achieve their sustainable development, to contribute and to participate in sustainable and equitable development at all levels. Particular attention should be given to indigenous women, children, and youth.

108. All kinds of folkloric discrimination must be stopped and forbidden.

109. The United Nations should promote research into indigenous knowledge and develop a network of indigenous sciences.

Appendix 6

Charter of the Indigenous–Tribal Peoples of the Tropical Forests

Article 1: We, the indigenous–tribal peoples of the tropical forests, present this charter as a response to hundreds of years of continual encroachment and colonization of our territories and the undermining of our lives, livelihoods, and cultures caused by the destruction of the forests that our survival depends on.

Article 2: We declare that we are the original peoples, the rightful owners, and the cultures that defend the tropical forests of the world.

Article 3: Our territories and forests are to us more than an economic resource. For us, they are life itself and have an integral and spiritual value for our communities. They are fundamental to our social, cultural, spiritual, economic, and political survival as distinct peoples.

Article 4: The unity of people and territory is vital and must be recognized.

Article 5: All policies towards the forests must be based on a respect for cultural diversity, for a promotion of indigenous models of living, and an understanding that our peoples have developed ways of life closely attuned to our environment.

Therefore, we declare the following principles, goals, and demands:

Respect for our rights

Article 6: Respect for our human, political, social, economic, and cultural rights, respect for our right to self-determination, and to pursue our own ways of life.

Article 7: Respect for our autonomous forms of self-government, as differentiated political systems at the community, regional, and other levels. This includes our right to control all economic activities in our territories.

Article 8: Respect for our customary laws and that they be incorporated in national and international law.

Article 9: Where the peoples so demand, nation states must comply with the different treaties, agreements, covenants, awards, and other forms of legal recognition that have been signed with us indigenous peoples in the past, both in the colonial period and since independence, regarding our rights.

Article 10: An end to violence, slavery, debt–peonage, and land grabbing; the disbanding of all private armies and militias and their replacement by the rule of law and social justice; the means to use the law in our own defence, including the training of our people in the law.

Article 11: The approval and application of the Universal Declaration of Indigenous Peoples, which must affirm and guarantee our right to self-determination, being developed by the United Nations, and the setting up of an effective international mechanism and tribunal to protect us against the violation of our rights and guarantee the application of the principles set out in this charter.

Article 12: There can be no rational or sustainable development of the forests and of our peoples until our fundamental rights as peoples are respected.

Territory

Article 13: Secure control of our territories, by which we mean a whole living system of continuous and vital connection between man and nature; expressed as our right to the unity and continuity of our ancestral domains; including the parts that have been usurped, those being reclaimed and those that we use; the soil, subsoil, air, and water required for our self-reliance, cultural development, and future generations.

Article 14: The recognition, definition, and demarcation of our territories in accordance with our local and customary systems of ownership and use.

Article 15: The form of land tenure will be decided by the people themselves, and the territory should be held communally, unless the people decide otherwise.

Article 16: The right to the exclusive use and ownership of the territories which we occupy. Such territories should be inalienable, not subject to distraint and not negotiable.

Article 17: The right to demarcate our territories ourselves and that these areas be officially recognized and documented.

Article 18: The right to legalize the ownership of lands used by nonindigenous peoples who live within and on the forests' margins in the areas that are available once title has been guaranteed to the indigenous peoples.

Article 19: Land reforms and changes in land tenure to secure the livelihoods of those who live outside the forests and indigenous territories, because we recognize that landlessness outside the forests puts heavy pressure on our territories and forests.

Decision-making

Article 20: Control of our territories and the resources that we depend on: all development in our areas should only go ahead with the free and informed consent of the indigenous people involved or affected.

Article 21: Recognition of the legal personality of our representative institutions and organizations that defend our rights, and through them the right to collectively negotiate our future.

Article 22: The right to our own forms of social organization; the right to elect and revoke the authorities and government functionaries who oversee the territorial areas within our jurisdiction.

Development policy

Article 23: The right to be informed, consulted, and, above all, to participate in the making of decisions on legislation or policies, and in the formulation, implementation or evaluation of any development project, be it at local, national or international levels, whether private or of the state, that may affect our futures directly or indirectly.

Article 24: All major development initiatives should be preceded by social, cultural, and environmental impact assessments, after consultation with local communities and indigenous peoples. All such studies and projects should be open to public scrutiny and debate, especially the indigenous peoples affected.

Article 25: National or international agencies considering funding development projects which may affect us must set up tripartite commissions — including the funding agency, government representatives and our own communities as represented through our representative organizations — to carry through the planning, implementation, monitoring, and evaluation of the projects.

Article 26: The cancellation of all mining concessions in our territories imposed without the consent of our representative organizations. Mining policies must prioritize, and be carried out under, our control, to guarantee rational management and a balance with the environment. In the case of the extraction of strategic minerals (oil and radioactive minerals) in our territories, we must participate in making decisions during planning and implementation.

Article 27: An end to imposed development schemes and fiscal incentives or subsidies that threaten the integrity of our forests.

Article 28: A halt to all imposed programs aimed at resettling our peoples away from their homelands.

Article 29: A redirection of the development process away from large-scale projects towards the promotion of small-scale initiatives controlled by our peoples. The priority for such initiatives is to secure our control over our territories and resources on which our survival depends. Such projects should be the cornerstone of all future development in the forests.

Article 30: The problems caused in our territories by international criminal syndicates trafficking in products from plants like poppy and coca must be confronted by effective policies which involve our peoples in decision-making.

Article 31: Promotion of the health systems of the indigenous peoples, including the revalidation of traditional medicine, and the promotion of programs of modern medicine and primary health care. Such programs should allow us to have control over them, providing suitable training to allow us to manage them ourselves.

Article 32: Establishment of systems of bilingual and intercultural education. These must revalidate our beliefs, religious traditions, customs, and knowledge, allowing our control over these programs by the provision of suitable training, in accordance with our cultures, in order to achieve technical and scientific advances for our peoples, in tune with our own cosmo-visions, and as a contribution to the world community.

Article 33: Promotion of alternative financial policies that permit us to develop our community economies and develop mechanisms to establish fair prices for the products of our forests.

Article 34: Our policy of development is based, first, on guaranteeing our self-sufficiency and material welfare, as well as that of our neighbours; a full social and cultural development based on the values of equity, justice, solidarity, and reciprocity, and a balance with nature. Thereafter, the generation of a surplus for the market must come from a rational and creative use of natural resources and through developing our own traditional technologies and selecting appropriate new ones.

Forest policy

Article 35: Halt all new logging concessions and suspend existing ones that affect our territories. The destruction of forests must be considered a crime against humanity and a halt must be made to the various antisocial consequences, such as roads across indigenous cultivations, cemeteries, and hunting zones; the destruction of areas used for medicinal plants and crafts; the erosion and compression of soil; the pollution of our environment; the corruption and enclave economy generated by the industry; the increase of invasions and settlement in our territories.

Article 36: Logging concessions on lands adjacent to our territories, or which have an impact on our environment, must comply with operating conditions — ecological, social, of labour, transport, health, and others — laid down by the indigenous peoples, who should participate in ensuring that these are complied with. Commercial timber extraction should be prohibited in strategic and seriously degraded forests.

Article 37: The protection of existing natural forests should take priority over reforestation.

Article 38: Reforestation programs should be prioritized on degraded lands, giving priority to the regeneration of native forests, including the recovery of all the functions of tropical forests, and not being restricted only to timber values.

Article 39: Reforestation programs on our territories should be developed under the control of our communities. Species should be selected by us in accordance with our needs.

Biodiversity and conservation

Article 40: Programs related to biodiversity must respect the collective rights of our peoples to cultural and intellectual property, genetic resources, gene banks, biotechnology, and knowledge of biological diversity; this should include our participation in the management of any such project in our territories, as well as control of any benefits that derive from them.

Article 41: Conservation programs must respect our rights to the use and ownership of the territories we depend on. No programs to conserve biodiversity should be promoted on our territories without our free and informed consent as expressed through our representative organizations.

Article 42: The best guarantee of the conservation of biodiversity is that those who promote it should uphold our rights to the use, administration, management, and control of our territories. We assert that guardianship of the different ecosystems should be entrusted to us, indigenous peoples, given that we have inhabited them for thousands of years and our very survival depends on them.

Article 43: Environmental policies and legislation should recognize indigenous territories as effective "protected areas," and give priority to their legal establishment as indigenous territories.

Intellectual property

Article 44: Since we highly value our traditional technologies and believe that our biotechnologies can make important contributions to humanity, including "developed" countries, we demand guaranteed rights to our intellectual property, and control over the development and manipulation of this knowledge.

Research

Article 45: All investigations in our territories should be carried out with our consent and under joint control and guidance according to mutual agreement, including the provision for training, publication and support for indigenous institutions necessary to achieve such control.

Institutions

Article 46: The international community, particularly the United Nations, must recognize us indigenous peoples as peoples, as distinct from other organized social movements, nongovernmental organizations and independent sectors, and respect our right to participate directly and on the basis of equality, as indigenous peoples, in all fora, mechanisms, processes, and funding bodies so as to promote and safeguard the future of the tropical forests.

Education

Article 47: The development of programs to educate the general public about our rights as indigenous peoples and about the principles, goals, and demands in this charter. For this we call on the international community for the necessary recognition and support.

Article 48: We indigenous peoples will use this charter as a basis for promoting our own local strategies for action.

Penang, Malaysia, 15 February 1992

Appendix 7

The Mataatua Declaration on Cultural and Intellectual Property Rights of Indigenous Peoples

In recognition that 1993 is the United Nations International Year for the World's Indigenous Peoples, the Nine Tribes of Mataatua, in the Bay of Plenty Region of Aotearoa New Zealand, convened the First International Conference on the Cultural and Intellectual Property Rights of Indigenous Peoples (12–18 June 1993, Whakatane).

Over 150 delegates from 14 countries attended, including indigenous representatives from Ainu (Japan), Australia, Cook Islands, Fiji, India, Panama, Peru, the Philippines, Surinam, USA, and Aotearoa.

The Conference met over 6 days to consider a range of significant issues, including the value of indigenous knowledge, biodiversity and biotechnology, customary environmental management, arts, music, language, and other physical and spiritual cultural forms. On the final day, the following Declaration was passed by the Plenary.

Preamble

Recognizing that 1993 is the United Nations International Year for the World's Indigenous Peoples;

Reaffirming the undertaking of United Nations Member States to:

"Adopt or strengthen appropriate policies and/or legal instruments that will protect indigenous intellectual and cultural property and the right to preserve customary and administrative systems and practices." — *Agenda 21*, United Nations Conference on Environment and Development (UNCED), (26.4b);

Noting the Working principles that emerged from the United Nations Technical Conference on Indigenous Peoples and the Environment in Santiago, Chile, 18–22 May 1992 (E/CN.4/Sub.2/1992/31); and

Endorsing the recommendations on Culture and Science from the World Conference of Indigenous Peoples on Territory, Environment, and Development, Kari-Oca, Brazil, 25–30 May 1992;

We

Declare that Indigenous Peoples of the world have the right to self determination, and in exercising that right must be recognized as the exclusive owners of their cultural and intellectual property;

Acknowledge that Indigenous Peoples have a commonality of experiences relating to the exploitation of their cultural and intellectual property;

Affirm that the knowledge of the Indigenous Peoples of the world is of benefit to all humanity;

Recognize that Indigenous Peoples are capable of managing their traditional knowledge themselves, but are willing to offer it to all humanity provided their fundamental rights to define and control this knowledge are protected by the international community;

Insist that the first beneficiaries of indigenous knowledge (cultural and intellectual property rights) must be the direct indigenous descendants of such knowledge; and

Declare that all forms of discrimination and exploitation of Indigenous Peoples, indigenous knowledge, and indigenous cultural and intellectual property rights must cease.

1. Recommendations to Indigenous Peoples

In the development of policies and practices, Indigenous Peoples should:

1.1 Define for themselves their own intellectual and cultural property.

1.2 Note that existing protection mechanisms are insufficient for the protection of Indigenous Peoples' intellectual and cultural property rights.

1.3 Develop a code of ethics which external users must observe when recording (visual, audio, written) their traditional and customary knowledge.

1.4 Prioritize the establishment of indigenous education, research, and training centres to promote their knowledge of customary environmental and cultural practices.

1.5 Reacquire traditional indigenous lands for the purpose of promoting customary agricultural production.

1.6 Develop and maintain their traditional practices and sanctions for the protection, preservation, and revitalization of their traditional intellectual and cultural properties.

1.7 Assess existing legislation with respect to the protection of antiquities.

1.8 Establish an appropriate body with appropriate mechanisms to:
   (a) Preserve and monitor the commercialism or otherwise of indigenous cultural properties in the public domain;
   (b) Generally advise and encourage Indigenous Peoples to take steps to protect their cultural heritage; and
   (c) Allow a mandatory consultative process with respect to any new legislation affecting Indigenous Peoples' cultural and intellectual property rights.

1.9 Establish international indigenous information centres and networks.

1.10 Convene a Second International Conference (Hui) on the Cultural and Intellectual Property Rights of Indigenous Peoples to be hosted by the Coordinating Body for the Indigenous Peoples Organizations of the Amazon Basin (COICA).

2. Recommendations to states, and national and international agencies

In the development of policies and practices, states, and national and international agencies must:

2.1   Recognize that Indigenous Peoples are the guardians of their customary knowledge and have the right to protect and control dissemination of that knowledge.

2.2   Recognize that Indigenous Peoples also have the right to create new knowledge based on cultural traditions.

2.3   Note that existing protection mechanisms are insufficient for the protection of Indigenous Peoples cultural and intellectual property rights.

2.4   Accept that the cultural and intellectual property rights of Indigenous Peoples are vested with those who created them.

2.5   Develop in full cooperation with Indigenous Peoples an additional cultural and intellectual property rights regime incorporating the following:
   (a)   Collective (as well as individual) ownership and origin-retroactive coverage of historical as well as contemporary works;
   (b)   Protection against debasement of culturally significant items;
   (c)   Cooperative rather than competitive framework;
   (d)   First beneficiaries to be the direct descendants of the traditional guardians of that knowledge; and
   (e)   Multigenerational coverage span.

Biodiversity and customary environmental management

2.6   Indigenous flora and fauna are inextricably bound to the territories of indigenous communities and any property right claims must recognize their traditional guardianship.

2.7   Commercialization of any traditional plants and medicines of Indigenous Peoples, must be managed by the Indigenous Peoples who have inherited such knowledge.

2.8   A moratorium on any further commercialization of indigenous medicinal plants and human genetic materials must be declared until indigenous communities have developed appropriate protection mechanisms.

2.9   Companies and institutions, both governmental and private, must not undertake experiments or commercialization of any biogenetic resources without the consent of the appropriate Indigenous Peoples.

2.10   Prioritize settlement of any outstanding land and natural resources claims of Indigenous Peoples for the purpose of promoting customary, agricultural, and marine production.

2.11   Ensure current scientific environmental research is strengthened by increasing the involvement of indigenous communities and of customary environmental knowledge.

Cultural objects

2.12 All human remains and burial objects of Indigenous Peoples held by museums and other institutions must be returned to their traditional areas in a culturally appropriate manner.

2.13 Museums and other institutions must provide, to the country and Indigenous Peoples concerned, an inventory of any indigenous cultural objects still held in their possession.

2.14 Indigenous cultural objects held in museums and other institutions must be offered back to their traditional owners.

3. Recommendations to the United Nations

In respect for the rights of Indigenous Peoples, the United Nations should:

3.1 Ensure that the process of participation of Indigenous Peoples in United Nations fora is strengthened so their views are fairly represented.

3.2 Incorporate the Mataatua Declaration in its entirety in the United Nations Study on Cultural and Intellectual Property of Indigenous Peoples.

3.3 Monitor and take action against any states whose persistent policies and activities damage the cultural and intellectual property rights of Indigenous Peoples.

3.4 Ensure that Indigenous Peoples actively contribute to the way in which indigenous cultures are incorporated into the 1995 United Nations International Year of Culture.

3.5 Call for an immediate halt to the ongoing Human Genome Diversity Project (HUGO) until its moral, ethical, socioeconomic, physical, and political implications have been thoroughly discussed, understood, and approved by Indigenous Peoples.

4. Conclusion

The United Nations, international and national agencies, and states must provide additional funding to indigenous communities in order to implement these recommendations.

June 1993

Appendix 8

Recommendations from the Voices of the Earth Congress

Preamble

We, the indigenous peoples assembled at the congress "Voices of the Earth: Indigenous Peoples, New Partners, the Right to Self-Determination in Practice," hereby declare the results of our deliberations as an important contribution and milestone in our struggle for promotion, protection, and recognition of our inherent rights.

We, the indigenous participants, consider the outcome of our meeting as a continuation of all indigenous conferences during this important United Nations Year of the World's Indigenous Peoples.

We, the indigenous peoples, express our deep gratitude to the moral and political support of those who have contributed to this congress.

As we continue to walk to the future in the footprints of our ancestors, we spoke in Amsterdam on November 10 and 11, 1993.

Recommendations

Political rights

1. The right of indigenous peoples to self-determination as stated in the Preamble of the Kari-Oca Declaration and Indigenous Peoples Earth Charter and in article 3 of the UN Draft Declaration on the Rights of Indigenous Peoples must be fully recognized.

2. Indigenous peoples are clearly to be distinguished from minorities. Therefore the protection of their rights cannot be adequately considered under article 27 of the Covenant on Civil and Political Rights.

3. Procedures should be developed for indigenous peoples to bring conflicts with national government concerning political self-determination and other questions before an independent international body such as the International Court of Justice. The European Community, the Dutch government, and all other governments should take the initiative to work toward the establishment of those procedures.

4. Indigenous peoples should be provided with legal and technical assistance, at their request, to effectively defend their rights.

5. The European Community, the Dutch government, and all other governments should fully support the UN Draft Declaration on the Rights of Indigenous Peoples (UN doc.E/CN.4/Sub.2/1993/29) that will be for adoption by the UN Working Group on Indigenous Populations at its 1994 session.

6. The European Community, the Dutch government, and all other governments should work toward facilitating open access and full participation for indigenous peoples in the entire process of debate concerning the adoption of the UN Declaration and in all other forums discussing indigenous issues.

7. The European Community, the Dutch government, and all other governments should support the designation of an International Decade of Indigenous Peoples by the UN General Assembly. This Decade should start in 1995 with a preparatory year in 1994.

8. The European Community, the Dutch government, and all other governments should take the initiative for the implementation of the recommendation of the Vienna World Conference on Human Rights that a permanent forum be established in the United Nations for the rights of indigenous peoples, in cooperation with the representatives of indigenous peoples.

9. The European Community should also recognize the full right to self-determination of the indigenous peoples presently living on European Community territory (New Caledonia, French Polynesia, and French Guyana).

Economic rights

The effective enjoyment of the economic rights of indigenous peoples depends on a recognition of their right to self-determination.

1. *Territories* — Indigenous peoples' rights to their territories, meaning full ownership of their lands and natural resources above and below the earth and waters, must be fully recognized.

2. *Control* — Indigenous peoples' rights to control the use of resources in their territories must be fully recognized.

3. *Trade offs* — These rights are nonnegotiable and cannot be traded off in the name of development of the nation state or other sectors. However, indigenous peoples may choose to promote the use of their resources in ways that benefit others; they need to be assured that they enter such discussions from a position of power.

4. *Private sector*
    (i) The private sector must assume responsibility for its activities. A wider notion of profit should be a condition of investment practice, giving emphasis to the quality of life, not just the quantity of money.

(ii) NGOs monitoring transnational corporations should focus more on indigenous peoples and share information widely with them.
(iii) In developing Codes of Conduct, companies must engage in dialogue with indigenous peoples and create mechanisms that allow public scrutiny of their adherence to these codes.
(iv) An organization parallel to the International Centre for the Settlement of Investment Disputes must be established to resolve conflicts between transnational corporations and indigenous peoples.

5. *Role of the state* — States should provide adequate assistance to indigenous peoples to enable them to develop their own economic base and power. Control over the process must be vested with the indigenous peoples concerned to avoid the creation of dependency.

6. *Environment* — Bearing in mind the two major international human rights covenants of December 1966, according to which (Part 1, Article 1, in both covenants) no peoples may under any circumstances be deprived of its own means of subsistence;

Conscious that the 1992 Rio Summit recognized the valuable role of indigenous peoples in maintaining a sustainable use of natural resources, and underlined in Principle 22, the pressing need for indigenous peoples' active participation in environmental management;

Acknowledging the Brundtland Commission report's recommendation of 1987 about the empowerment of vulnerable groups;

Aware that the World Conservation Strategy of 1991, *Caring for the Earth*, supports a special role for indigenous peoples in global efforts for a sound environment;

Mindful that the World Conservation Union (IUCN) at its 18th General Assembly unanimously adopted two resolutions supporting the indigenous peoples' cause, including their right to use nature's resources wisely;

Conscious of the Biodiversity Convention and ILO Convention 169, both of which lend support to indigenous peoples and their role in sustainable development; and

Pointing to the fact that as a general rule, ecosystems that appear as the most sound are also those which are under indigenous control;

Now, therefore, the "Voices of the Earth" Congress, assembled in Amsterdam, calls on governments;
(i) To heed the concerns of indigenous peoples worldwide;
(ii) To give effect in their respective national policies to the above cited international instruments to which they have given their assent;
(iii) To properly protect the market access for indigenous peoples' products derived from a sustainable and wise use of nature; and
(iv) To give financial support to the UN's decade for indigenous peoples.

7. *International legislation* — States should recognize the Declaration on the Rights of Indigenous Peoples as presently drafted. It was suggested that an ombudsman be nominated to oversee the adherence of states to this Declaration. An independent tribunal might also review adherence to the Declaration.

8. *Demilitarization* — There should be a demilitarization of indigenous territories. In this respect it is the special responsibility of the Dutch government to immediately stop the low-level flying activities of the Royal Dutch Air Force above the territories of the Innu people in Canada. Compulsory military service for indigenous people must be abolished.

9. *Dutch government's responsibilities* — In addition to observing the above recommendations, the Dutch government is urged to press for an enhanced allocation to indigenous peoples of the resources of the UN agencies and other multilateral bodies.

Cultural, scientific, and intellectual property

1. All relevant agencies and programs of the Dutch government, European Community, and the United Nations (such as the World Bank, WIPO, UPOV UNCTAD, UNEP, UNDP, the Centre for Human Rights, ILO, GATT, etc.) should develop a common policy, based on dialogue with and consent of indigenous peoples, on how protection of and compensation for indigenous intellectual, scientific, and cultural property can be established and effected.

2. A "Council on Indigenous Intellectual, Cultural, and Scientific Property Rights," composed of indigenous people, should be established, funded, and given special international status in order to:

    (a) Develop educational materials on intellectual, cultural, and scientific property rights;
    (b) Develop mechanisms for protection and compensation;
    (c) Advise indigenous and traditional communities on legal and political actions;
    (d) Monitor unethical activities by individuals, institutions, and governments that are misusing intellectual, scientific, and cultural property;
    (e) Develop mechanisms for enforcement of rules, regulations, and laws for protection and compensation, including legal advice and counsel; and
    (f) Establish a network to exchange information about successful and unsuccessful attempts by local communities to secure their rights.

3. Governmental and nongovernmental organizations, as well as scientific and professional groups, should develop Codes of Ethics and Conduct regarding respect for indigenous peoples and their intellectual, cultural, and scientific property. Funding agencies should require that effective measures for protection and compensation for intellectual, cultural, and scientific property be an integral part of all projects and such measures be a requirement for funding.

4. Rights of indigenous peoples to their traditional properties supersede the rights of anyone, including the rights of museums to possess these properties. No international or national agencies may infringe on the right of indigenous peoples to refuse to share their intellectual, cultural, and scientific properties.

   Museums all over the world should cooperate fully with indigenous peoples to reidentify their cultural heritage and recognize their right to repossess it.

5. All governments, international institutions, nongovernmental organizations, and indigenous peoples are called upon to establish the "University of the Earth" which shall incorporate the values and the knowledge of both indigenous and non-indigenous peoples. This University need not have a specific location but would take the form of a global network of journalists, farmers, foresters, engineers, shaman, hunters, scientists, artists, and others who will exchange information through journals, television, films, videos, conferences and other forms of mass media. The mission of this "University of the Earth" will be to enhance all peoples' respect for and knowledge of the Earth. The European Community and the Dutch government are called upon to strengthen indigenous peoples' newspapers and other forms of information dissemination.

Right to self-development

1. Effective enjoyment of indigenous peoples' right to self-development depends on the recognition of the right of indigenous peoples to self-determination.

2. International institutions and funding agencies should adapt their requirements, structures, and policies to the cultures, needs, and aspirations of indigenous peoples.

3. Indigenous peoples must have full control over the planning, implementation, monitoring, evaluation, and follow-up of projects affecting them.

4. Indigenous peoples' knowledge and culture should be fully taken into consideration before entering into development relations with indigenous peoples.

5. Results of studies, carried out with the full participation of indigenous peoples, concerning the impacts of development projects on indigenous peoples should be carefully taken into account before implementing a proposed project.

6. The European Community, the Dutch government and all other governments should respect the indigenous peoples' social and political organizations, and assist them to give these institutions an impulse by institution building for the sake of sustainable, "grassroots" development.

7. A code of conduct for international institutions such as the World Bank, the IMF, the EC Development Fund, and the UNDP, must be established in collaboration with indigenous peoples to ensure that funding for development activities does not infringe on the territorial and environmental integrity of indigenous peoples.

8. The European Community, the Dutch government, and all other governments should take into consideration the actual situation of indigenous peoples in developed countries. Indigenous peoples in developed countries should not be overlooked or discriminated against by funding institutions because they may be in circumstances similar to those in developing countries.

9. The European Community, the Dutch government, and all other governments, international institutions, and funding agencies should take into consideration the specific interests of indigenous women and children in planning and implementation of development projects.

Amsterdam, Netherlands, 10–11 November 1993

Appendix 9

COICA/UNDP Regional Meeting on Intellectual Property Rights and Biodiversity

Basic points of agreement

1. Emphasis is placed on the significance of the use of intellectual property systems as a new formula for regulating North–South economic relations in pursuit of colonialist interests.

2. For indigenous peoples, the intellectual property system means legitimation of the misappropriation of our peoples' knowledge and resources for commercial purposes.

3. All aspects of the issue of intellectual property (determination of access to national resources, control of the knowledge or cultural heritage of peoples, control of the use of their resources, and regulation of the terms of exploitation) are aspects of self-determination. For indigenous peoples, accordingly, the ultimate decision on this issue is dependent on self-determination. Positions adopted under a trusteeship regime will be of a short-term nature.

4. Biodiversity and a people's knowledge are concepts inherent in the idea of indigenous territoriality. Issues relating to access to resources have to be viewed from this standpoint.

5. Integral indigenous territoriality, its recognition (or restoration), and its reconstitution are prerequisites for enabling the creative and inventive genius of each indigenous people to flourish and for it to be meaningful to speak of protecting such peoples. The protection, reconstitution, and development of indigenous knowledge systems call for additional commitments to the effort to have them reappraised by the outside world.

6. Biodiversity and the culture and intellectual property of a people are concepts that mean indigenous territoriality. Issues relating to access to resources and others have to be viewed from this standpoint.

7. For members of indigenous peoples, knowledge, and determination of the use of resources are collective and intergenerational. No indigenous population, whether of individuals or communities, nor the government, can sell or transfer ownership of resources which are the property of the people and which each generation has an obligation to safeguard for the next.

8. Prevailing intellectual property systems reflect a conception and practice that is:
   - Colonialist, in that the instruments of the developed countries are imposed in order to appropriate the resources of indigenous peoples;
   - Racist, in that it belittles and minimizes the value of our knowledge systems; and
   - Usurpatory, in that it is essentially a practice of theft.

9. Adjusting indigenous systems to the prevailing intellectual property systems (as a world-wide concept and practice) changes the indigenous regulatory systems themselves.

10. Patents and other intellectual property rights to forms of life are unacceptable to indigenous peoples.

11. It is important to prevent conflicts that may arise between communities from the transformation of intellectual property into a means of dividing indigenous unity.

12. There are some formulas that could be used to enhance the value of our products (brand names, appellations of origin), but on the understanding that these are only marketing possibilities, not entailing monopolies of the product or of collective knowledge. There are also some proposals for modifying prevailing intellectual property systems, such as the use of certificates of origin to prevent use of our resources without our prior consent.

13. The prevailing intellectual property systems must be prevented from robbing us, through monopoly rights, of resources and knowledge in order to enrich themselves and build up power opposed to our own.

14. Work must be conducted on the design of a protection and recognition system which is in accordance with the defence of our own conception, and mechanisms must be developed in the short and medium term which will prevent appropriation of our resources and knowledge.

15. A system of protection and recognition of our resources and knowledge must be designed which is in conformity with our world view and contains formulas that, in the short and medium term, will prevent appropriation of our resources by the countries of the North and others.

16. There must be appropriate mechanisms for maintaining and ensuring rights of indigenous peoples to deny indiscriminate access to the resources of our communities or peoples and making it possible to contest patents or other exclusive rights to what is essentially indigenous.

17. There is a need to maintain the possibility of denying access to indigenous resources and contesting patents or other exclusive rights to what is essentially indigenous.

18. Discussions regarding intellectual property should take placewithout distracting from priorities such as the struggle for the right to territories and self-determination, bearing in mind that the indigenous population and the land form an indivisible unity.

Short-term recommendations

1. Identify, analyse, and systematically evaluate from the standpoint of the indigenous world view different components of the formal intellectual property systems, including mechanisms, instruments, and forums, among which we have:

    - *Intellectual property mechanisms* — Patents; Trademarks; Authors' rights; Rights of developers of new plant varieties; Commercial secrets; Industrial designs; Labels of origin

    - *Intellectual property instruments* — The Agreement on Trade-Related Aspects of Intellectual Property Rights (TRIPS) of the General Agreement on Tariffs and Trade (GATT); the Convention on Biological Diversity, with special emphasis on the following aspects: environmental impact assessments, subsidiary scientific body, technological council, monitoring, national studies and protocols, as well as on rights of farmers and ex situ control of germplasm, which are not covered under the Convention.

    - *Intellectual property forums* — Define mechanisms for consultation and exchange of information between the indigenous organizational universe and international forums such as: the Treaty for Amazonian Cooperation; the Andean Pact; the General Agreement on Tariffs and Trade; the European Patent Convention; the United Nations Commission on Sustainable Development; the Union for the Protection of New Varieties of Plants; the World Intellectual Property Organization (WIPO); the International Labour Organisation (ILO); the United Nations Commission on Human Rights.

2. Evaluate the possibilities offered by the international instruments embodying cultural, political, environmental, and other rights that could be incorporated into a sui generis legal framework for the protection of indigenous resources and knowledge.

3. Define the content of consultation with such forums.

4. Define the feasibility of using some mechanisms of the prevailing intellectual property systems in relation to: Protection of biological–genetic resources; Marketing of resources.

5. Study the feasibility of alternative systems and mechanisms for protecting indigenous interests in their resources and knowledge.

    - *Sui generis systems for protection of intellectual property* — Inventors' certificates; Model legislation on folklore; New deposit standards for material entering germplasm banks; Commissioner for intellectual property rights; Tribunals; Bilateral and multilateral contracts or conventions; Material transfer agreements; Biological prospecting; Defensive publication; Certificates of origin.

6. Seek to make alternative systems operational within the short term, by establishing a minimal regulatory framework (for example, bilateral contracts).

7. Systematically study, or expand studies already conducted of, the dynamics of indigenous peoples, with emphasis on:
   - Basis of sustainability (territories, culture, economy);
   - Use of knowledge and resources (collective ownership systems, community use of resources); and
   - Community, national, regional, and international organizational bases.

   That will make it possible to create mechanisms within and outside indigenous peoples capable of assigning the same value to indigenous knowledge, arts, and crafts as to western science.

8. Establish regional and local indigenous advisory bodies on intellectual property and biodiversity with functions involving legal advice, monitoring, production, and dissemination of information and production of materials.

9. Identify national intellectual property organizations, especially in areas of biodiversity.

10. Identify and draw up a timetable of forums for discussion and exchange of information on intellectual property and/or biodiversity. Seek support for sending indigenous delegates to participate in such forums. An effort will be made to obtain information with a view to the eventual establishment of an Information, Training, and Dissemination Centre on Indigenous Property and Ethical Guidelines on contract negotiation and model contracts.

Medium-term strategies

1. Plan, program, and establish timetables, and seek financing for the establishment of an indigenous program for the collective use and protection of biological resources and knowledge. This program will be developed in phases in conformity with areas of geographical coverage.

2. Plan, draw up timetables for, and hold seminars and workshops at the comunity, national, and regional levels on biodiversity and prevailing intellectual property systems and alternatives.

3. Establish a standing consultative mechanism to link community workers and indigenous leaders, as well as an information network.

4. Train indigenous leaders in aspects of intellectual property and biodiversity.

5. Draw up a Legal Protocol of Indigenous Law on the use and community knowledge of biological resources.

6. Develop a strategy for dissemination of this Legal Protocol at the national and international levels.

Santa Cruz de la Sierra, Bolivia, 28–30 September 1994

Appendix 10

UNDP Consultation on the Protection and Conservation of Indigenous Knowledge

Basic points of agreement on the issues faced by the indigenous peoples of Asia

From the deliberations it is clear that self-determination is most important to the indigenous people. The definition of self-determination is different in different countries, ranging from land rights, autonomy, self rule without secession, and autonomy under federal system, to independence. Indigenous peoples' struggle and right to self-determination are being threatened by repressive governments (such as in Myanmar); development policies and projects such as large dams (such as in North Thailand and Sarawak in East Malaysia); unjust land laws (such as with the Hill Tribes of Thailand, Malaysia, and Viet Nam); genocide (such as with the Chittagong Hill Tribes of Bangladesh); religion and the dominant culture.

Land, in particular native customary or ancestral land, is significant to indigenous peoples because it is the source of their livelihood and the base of their indigenous knowledge, spiritual, and cultural traditions.

The indigenous peoples' struggle for self-determination is a very strong counterforce to the intellectual property rights system vis-à-vis indigenous knowledge, wisdom, and culture. Therefore, the struggle for self-determination cannot be separated from the campaign against intellectual property rights systems, particularly their applications on life forms and indigenous knowledge.

Specific points raised on indigenous knowledge and intellectual property rights (IPR)

For the indigenous peoples of Asia, the intellectual property rights system is not only a very new concept but it is also very western. However, it is recognized that the threats posed by the intellectual property rights systems are as grave as the other problems faced by the indigenous peoples at present. When in the past, indigenous peoples' right to land has been eroded through the imposition of exploitative laws imposed by outsiders; with intellectual property rights, alien laws will also be devised to exploit the indigenous knowledge and resources of the indigenous peoples.

The prevailing intellectual property rights system is seen as a new form of colonization and a tactic by the industrialized countries of the North to confuse and to divert the struggle of indigenous peoples from their rights to land and resources on, above, and under it.

The intellectual property rights system and the (mis)appropriation of indigenous knowledge without the prior knowledge and consent of indigenous peoples evoke feelings of anger, of being cheated, and of helplessness in knowing nothing about intellectual property rights and indigenous knowledge piracy. This is akin to robbing indigenous peoples of their resources and knowledge through monopoly rights.

Indigenous peoples are not benefiting from the intellectual property rights system. Indigenous knowledge and resources are being eroded, exploited, or appropriated by outsiders in the likes of transnational corporations (TNCs), institutions, researchers, and scientists who are after the profits and benefits gained through monopoly control.

The technological method of piracy is too sophisticated for indigenous peoples to understand, especially when indigenous communities are unaware of how the system operates and who are behind it.

For indigenous peoples, life is a common property which cannot be owned, commercialized, and monopolized by individuals. Based on this worldview, indigenous peoples find it difficult to relate intellectual property rights issues to their daily lives. Accordingly, the patenting of any life forms and processes is unacceptable to indigenous peoples.

The intellectual property rights system is in favour of the industrialized countries of the North who have the resources to claim patent and copyright, resulting in the continuous exploitation and appropriation of genetic resources, indigenous knowledge, and culture of the indigenous peoples for commercial purposes. The intellectual property rights system totally ignores the contribution of indigenous peoples and the peoples of the South in the conservation and protection of genetic resources through millennia.

The intellectual property rights system totally ignores the close interrelationship between indigenous peoples, their knowledge, genetic resources and their environment. The proponents of intellectual property rights are only concerned with the benefits that they will gain from the commercial exploitation of these resources.

The indigenous peoples of Asia strongly condemn the patenting and commercialization of their cell lines or body parts, as being promoted by the scientists and institutions behind the Human Genome Diversity Project (HGDP).

Plan of actions proposed by the Asian consultation workshop

The Consultation recognizes that the struggle for self-determination is closely connected to retaining rights over ancestral lands and the entire way of life of the indigenous peoples. The threats that indigenous peoples have been facing in this regard are very clear, and they have their own plans of action to address these concerns.

The Consultation also recognizes that indigenous knowledge is closely linked to land which can be taken away from indigenous peoples. Thus, the need to protect and conserve indigenous knowledge is just as important as the struggle for self-determination.

In a broad sense, therefore, the indigenous peoples of Asia have one common aspiration — to reclaim their right to self-determination and to their indigenous knowledge.

The question of sovereignty is traditionally understood as one of land, but now it also encompasses indigenous knowledge since the two are very closely linked.

Towards this end, the Consultation has suggested the following course of actions and strategies:

A. Plan of actions at the local level

Noting the different experiences, prevailing realities in the political environment and varied situations that the indigenous peoples of Asia currently find themselves in, the methods for achieving their aspirations may again differ, or be in different stages of expression at the local or national level. In such circumstances, it was generally felt that the general plan of action be disseminated to indigenous peoples organizations for them to implement them in their own ways, based on their specific realities.

However, it became clear during the Consultation that there is a need to emphasize the following aspects in the activities related to indigenous knowledge at the local level:

— Strengthen the indigenous peoples' organizations and communities to be able to collectively address local concerns related to indigenous knowledge and intellectual property rights.

— Continue the indigenous peoples' struggle for self-determination since this can be a strong counter force against the threats posed by intellectual property rights systems on indigenous knowledge and genetic resources.

— Raise the awareness of indigenous peoples' organizations and communities on the global trends and developments in intellectual property rights systems, especially as they apply to life forms and indigenous knowledge.

B. General plan of action

Immediate, short-term strategies

— Issue a statement to the European Parliament calling for the rejection of the patenting of life forms in the European Union, in time for its voting on the issue on 1 March 1995.

— Disseminate information pertaining to the Asian Consultation Workshop to the local mass media for publication and wider mass awareness.

— Organize follow-up workshops at the community level to raise awareness of local farmers and indigenous peoples on the prevailing intellectual property systems.

— Organize local or national conferences on customary laws to explore indigenous mechanisms and systems of effectively protecting and conserving indigenous knowledge.

— Plan regional meetings for follow-up discussion and exchange of information on indigenous self-determination and related issues such as indigenous knowledge, intellectual property rights systems and the patenting of life forms. At the outset, the Alliance of Taiwan Aborigines (ATA) has expressed its plan to initiate a regional meeting on these issues in Taiwan in 1996. The ATA will look for funding sources and will welcome financial support from the United Nations Development Programme (UNDP).

Medium-term strategies

- Intensify advocacy and campaign works against intellectual property systems and the Human Genome Diversity Project (HGDP) at national and international levels.

- Provide updates on the HGDP and patenting, to be disseminated to indigenous peoples, indigenous organizations, and nongovernmental organizations sympathetic to the cause of indigenous peoples. The Rural Advancement Foundation International (RAFI) has been requested to collaborate with local and Asia-based regional organizations to produce and disseminate materials in popular forms, written in the local languages and based on the local context. The Southeast Asia Regional Institute for Community Education (SEARICE) will also distribute their monographs on the impact of global developments on the indigenous peoples, and will assist in information dissemination.

- Develop the capacity of the Asian Indigenous Peoples Pact (AIPP), a forum for indigenous peoples movements in Asia. In this respect, national indigenous peoples organizations will contribute human and material resources, as well as identify members for short to medium-term internship programmes.

- AIPP to coordinate and monitor activities and developments related to the plans formulated for the region.

- Build alliances and network with groups within Asia and outside, such as the AIPP, RAFI, SEARICE, and the Indigenous Peoples' Biodiversity Network (IPBN).

- Indigenous peoples to design their own educational curriculum that will help promote their culture and indigenous knowledge. Such educational curriculum will instill a deep awareness and pride among indigenous peoples, especially children, on the importance of their indigenous knowledge, culture, and resources.

Sabah, East Malaysia, 24–27 February 1995

Appendix 11

UNDP Consultation on Indigenous Peoples' Knowledge and Intellectual Property Rights

We, the participants at the Regional Consultation on Indigenous Peoples' Knowledge and Intellectual Property Rights, held in April 1995 in Suva, Fiji, from independent countries and from nonautonomous colonized territories hereby:

- Recognize that the Pacific Region holds a significant proportion of the world's indigenous cultures, languages, and biological diversity;
- Support the initiatives of the Mataatua Declaration (1993), the Kari-Oca Declaration (1992), Julayabinul Statement (1993), and the South American and Asian Consultation Meetings;
- Declare the right of indigenous peoples of the Pacific to self-governance and independence and ownership of our lands, territories, and resources as the basis for the preservation of indigenous peoples' knowledge;
- Recognize that indigenous peoples of the Pacific exist as unique and distinct peoples irrespective of their political status;
- Acknowledge that the most effective means to fulfill our responsibilities to our descendants is through the customary transmission and enhancement of our knowledge;
- Reaffirm that imperialism is perpetuated through intellectual property rights systems, science, and modern technology to control and exploit the lands, territories, and resources of indigenous peoples;
- Declare that indigenous peoples are willing to share our knowledge with humanity provided we determine when, where, and how it is used. At present, the international system does not recognize or respect our past, present, and potential contributions;
- Assert our inherent right to define who we are. We do not approve of any other definition;
- Condemn attempts to undervalue indigenous peoples' traditional science and knowledge;
- Condemn those who use our biological diversity for commercial and other purposes without our full knowledge and consent; and

— Propose and seek support for the following plan of action:

1. Initiate the establishment of a treaty declaring the Pacific Region to be a life forms patent-free zone.
    1.1 Include in the treaty protocols governing bioprospecting, human genetic research, in situ conservation by indigenous peoples, ex situ collections, and relevant international instruments.
    1.2 Issue a statement announcing the treaty and seeking endorsement by the South Pacific Forum and other appropriate regional and international fora.
    1.3 Urge Pacific governments to sign and implement the treaty.
    1.4 Implement an educational awareness strategy about the treaty's objectives.

2. Call for a moratorium on bioprospecting in the Pacific and urge indigenous peoples not to cooperate in bioprospecting activities until appropriate protection mechanisms are in place.
    2.1 Bioprospecting as a term needs to be clearly defined to exclude indigenous peoples' customary harvesting practices.
    2.2 Assert that in situ conservation by indigenous peoples is the best method to conserve and protect biological diversity and indigenous knowledge, and encourage its implementation by indigenous communities and all relevant bodies.
    2.3 Encourage indigenous peoples to maintain and expand our knowledge of local biological resources.

3. Commit ourselves to raising public awareness of the dangers of expropriation of indigenous knowledge and resources.
    3.1 Encourage chiefs, elders, and community leaders to play a leadership role in the protection of indigenous peoples' knowledge and resources.

4. Recognize the urgent need to identify the extent of expropriation that has already occurred and is continuing in the Pacific.
    4.1 Seek repatriation of indigenous peoples' resources already held in external collections, and seek compensation and royalties from commercial developments resulting from these resources.

5. Urge governments who have not signed the General Agreement on Tariffs and Trade (GATT) to refuse to do so, and encourage those governments who have already signed to protest against any provisions which facilitate the expropriation of indigenous peoples' knowledge and resources and the patenting of life forms.
    5.1 Incorporate the concerns of indigenous peoples to protect their knowledge and resources into legislation by including "Prior Informed Consent or No Informed Consent" (PICNIC) procedures and exclude the patenting of life forms.

6. Encourage the South Pacific Forum to amend its rules of procedure to enable accreditation of indigenous peoples and NGOs as observers to future Forum officials meetings.

7. Strengthen indigenous networks. Encourage the United Nations Development Programme (UNDP) and regional donors to continue to support discussions on indigenous peoples' knowledge and intellectual property rights.

8. Strengthen the capacities of indigenous peoples to maintain their oral traditions, and encourage initiatives by indigenous peoples to record their knowledge in a permanent form according to their customary access procedures.

9. Urge universities, churches, governments, nongovernmental organizations, and other institutions to reconsider their roles in the expropriation of indigenous peoples' knowledge and resources and to assist in their return to their rightful owners.

10. Call on the governments and corporate bodies responsible for the destruction of Pacific biodiversity to stop their destructive practices and to compensate the affected communities and rehabilitate the affected environment.
    10.1 Call on France to stop definitively its nuclear testing in the Pacific and repair the damaged biodiversity.

Suva, April 1995

Glossary

Antibody
> Protein, produced by the body, that plays an important role in the immune system.

Antigen
> A substance that stimulates the production of antibodies when it enters the body.

Biodiversity
> The variety of life in all its forms, levels, and combinations (also known as "biological diversity"). It encompasses genetic diversity, species diversity, and ecosystem diversity.

Biodiversity prospecting
> The search for and collection of biological material for commercial purposes. The areas where prospecting takes place are usually species-rich environments, such as tropical forests and coral reefs. The practice is also sometimes called chemical prospecting.

Biogenetic resources
> Biological and genetic resources. Biogenetic resources may include plant material, animals, microorganisms, cells, and genes.

Biotechnology
> "Any technique that uses living organisms (or parts of organisms) to make or modify products, to improve plants or animals, or to develop microorganisms for specific uses" (OTA 1984).

Broker
> A person or organization that acts as an intermediary between a buyer and a seller. Brokers may benefit financially from facilitating agreements made between suppliers or producers of goods and purchasers.

cDNA
> Also called "copy" or "complementary" DNA. For cells to build protein molecules, the genetic sequence of the gene that codes for the protein is transcribed onto messenger RNA (mRNA). The mRNA carries the information to the area of the cell where the protein molecules are produced. Scientists can apply an enzyme (called reverse transcriptase) to make DNA copies (cDNA) of the mRNA that are identical to the naturally occurring DNA, but without the sequences that do not code for the protein (see "Gene").

Cell line
> A collection of cells that grows and multiplies in a laboratory, providing the full genetic code of the donor organism for an indefinite period if it is stored at low temperature (for example, in liquid nitrogen). One method of developing a cell

line is by infecting B-lymphocytes (a type of white blood cell) with the Epstein-Barr virus.

Clones
Organisms containing exactly the same genetic information as the host from which they are derived. Scientists can clone a gene by inserting it into a bacterium, which, as it divides, will produce increasing quantities of the protein coded by the gene. For example, insulin is manufactured in the laboratory by cloned bacteria containing the gene that codes for insulin.

Collaborative research
Scientific research in which local communities are treated as expert collaborators. True collaborative research is nonexploitive and addresses issues of IPR, privacy, confidentiality, and prior informed consent.

Community-controlled research
Scientific research with or without the involvement of outsiders. Where involved, their work is supervised by community members, and all data are the property of the community. Information enters the public domain only at the discretion of the community.

Community register
A register or inventory carried out by a community, perhaps with outside assistance, of all plant and other species that are known to the community. It should include details of uses of these species, including information on how to prepare them for use. The register could be in written form or in a database, perhaps held in conjunction with a herbarium.

Conservation
"The management of human use of the biosphere so that it may yield the greatest sustainable benefit to present generations while maintaining its potential to meet the needs and aspirations of future generations. Thus conservation is positive, embracing preservation, maintenance, sustainable utilization, restoration, and enhancement of the natural environment" (IUCN 1980). However, conservation means different things to different people, and advocates of conservation, whether of landscapes or of species (in situ), vary in their attitudes to local people. Although some believe that local communities, their knowledge, and their traditional life-styles must have an important role in conservation, others believe that conservation requires the tight restriction of human activities (and sometimes even human presence) in the targeted area.

Contract
A legally binding agreement between two or more parties containing obligations that are to be fulfilled by all sides. It may have a fixed time limit, or its duration may depend upon completion of all obligations or mutual agreement to terminate it. Contracts are used to establish and define certain relationships legally, such as those between employer and employee, or between a drug company and a supplier of biological samples. Know-how and confidentiality agreements, for

example, are contracts (or clauses of contracts) made by parties, one of which may be a patent owner, who seek to exploit an invention or inventive process through exchange of information. Contracts are usually in the form of written documents that are signed by all the parties.

Customary law

"Customs, usages, and practices deserve the name of customary law when they are sufficiently fixed and settled over a substantial area, known and recognized and deemed obligatory, as much as are systems of law based on written formulations of rules" (Walker 1980). In international law, customary law refers to rules and practices that are recognized and accepted internationally, usually over a long period.

DNA

Deoxyribonucleic acid, the long chains of molecules in most cells that carry the genetic hereditary message and control all cellular functions in most forms of life.

DNA marker

A short length of DNA at a known location on a chromosome that can be used by scientists as a "landmark" to locate genes close to it, helping scientists build up a map of the organism's genome.

Ecosystem

A system of plants, animals, and other organisms together with the nonliving components of their environment.

Eminent domain

"A doctrine giving the government the right to take private property for public purpose. In international law, the state is regarded as not only having a power of disposition over the whole of the national territory, but also as being the representative owner of both the national teritoiry and all other property found within its limits" (Rutherford and Bone 1993, p. 128).

Expressions of folklore

Productions consisting of characteristic elements of the traditional artistic heritage developed by a community or by individuals reflecting the traditional artistic expectations of such a community (see WIPO 1985, section 2).

Fixation

Expressing and recording an intellectual work in a physical form that can be reproduced. For example, a song can be written down in the form of musical notation or recorded on audio tape, and a performance of the song can be recorded on a videotape.

Foreign exchange leakage

The reverse or outward flow of financial benefits from a project or economic activity (such as tourism) that is undesirable from the point of view of local people and national governments hoping to capture all the available economic benefits generated by the activity.

Gene
: The linear unit of heredity transmitted from generation to generation during sexual or asexual reproduction. More generally, the term "gene" may be used in relation to the transmission and inheritance of particular identifiable traits (IDRC 1985). Genes are involved in the production of proteins.

Genetic engineering
: Techniques used by scientists to transfer genes from one organism to another. One such method is using recombinant DNA.

Genome
: The entire hereditary message of an organism contained in all of its genes, which are present in nearly all of the organism's cells.

Germplasm
: Often synonymous with "genetic material," when applied to plants it is the name given to seed or other material from which plants are propagated (IDRC 1985).

Hybridomas
: Cells created in a laboratory by fusing a blood plasma tumor cell with a type of white blood cell. They are used to produce antibodies that help to diagnose certain diseases.

Inalienable
: Incapable of being surrendered or transferred (such as rights to land, knowledge, or resources).

Indigenous peoples
: "The existing descendants of the people who inhabited the present territory of a country wholly or partially at the time when persons of a different culture or ethnic origin arrived there from other parts of the world, overcame them and, by conquest, settlement, or other means reduced them to a nondominant or colonial situation; who today live more in conformity with their particular social, economic, and cultural customs and traditions than with the institutions of the country of which they now form a part, under state structure, which incorporates mainly the national, social, and cultural characteristics of other segments of the population which are predominant" (working definition adopted by the UN Working Group on Indigenous Populations).

Intellectual property rights
: Legal rights can attach to information emanating from the mind of a person if it can be applied to making a product that is made distinctive and useful by that information. Legal rights prevent others from copying, selling, and importing the product without authorization from the holder of the property right.

Inventive step
: See "Nonobviousness."

Juridical (or juristic) person

"Those groups of natural persons or things which a particular legal system endows with legal personality and treats as being, in law, kinds of persons and, accordingly, being able to sustain legal rights and duties" (Walker 1980).

Know-how

Certain practical knowledge or expertise known only to a few people needed to manufacture a product. A licence agreement between a patent owner and a manufacturer may include know-how and demonstrations or instructions that transfer this knowledge to the manufacturer.

Landrace

"Landraces are varieties that were developed over many plant generations, sometimes encompassing thousands of years, by farmers selecting plants with desired characteristics. Usually landraces are more genetically diverse than modern farm varieties and often are adapted to specific local environments. Sometimes called 'peasant varieties,' they are valuable because of the genetic traits allowing them to survive" (OTA 1987, p. 170). Landraces are also known as folk varieties.

Letter of intent

A type of nonbinding agreement that contains commitments that may later be formalized through the drawing up of a contract (see "Memorandum of understanding").

Licence

A type of contract between an intellectual property owner and another allowing the latter to use, manufacture, or market the invention in exchange for a royalty, a fee, or an immediate payment. The subject of the licence might be patented information, a trade secret, a copyright protected work, etc.

Material transfer agreement

A type of contract or agreement involving the provision of material (such as biogenetic resources) in exchange for monetary or nonmonetary benefits.

Memorandum of understanding

A type of nonbinding agreement that outlines the preliminary understanding between parties who usually intend to enter into a contract (see "Letter of intent").

Moral rights

In the copyright laws of some countries, authors are protected by one or both of two moral rights: the right of paternity and the right of integrity. The former means that they have the right to be identified as the author of the copyrighted work. The latter means that the authors can prevent distortion of the work that would have a negative effect on their reputation.

Natural resources

Naturally occurring living and nonliving substances that are useful or potentially useful to peoples.

Nonobviousness
: In patent law, nonobvious implies that a technician could copy a product or process, but would not be capable of doing so without prior knowledge of the patented information. This is due to the fact that the invention involved a certain amount of individual creativity (an "inventive step") beyond what was already known. In actual cases, the terms may be subject to conflicting interpretation.

The North
: The industrialized countries, which are mostly in the northern hemisphere: the United States, Canada, and the countries of western Europe and Japan, but also Australia and New Zealand.

Orthodox seed
: Orthodox seeds have low water content. They retain their ability to germinate for a considerable time and can therefore be stored by drying or freezing until needed.

Passing off
: In common-law countries (the UK, the United States, and other ex-British colonies), passing off is an actionable offence in which consumers are deliberately or accidentally deceived by a trader into believing that a product is that of another business, when in fact it is not.

Plant genetic resources
: In agriculture, the reproductive or vegetative propagating material of varieties cultivated in the present or past, wild and weedy species, and special genetic stocks (including elite and current breeders' lines and mutants) (*International Undertaking on Plant Genetic Resources*, Article 2.1a).

Polymerase chain reaction
: A technology that enables scientists to renew DNA from collected samples indefinitely in the laboratory without using recombinant DNA technology.

Prior art
: Knowledge already in the public domain that disqualifies a patent application on the grounds that the invention is not novel. Patent offices must search for prior art before awarding a patent.

Prior informed consent
: Consent to an activity, given after receiving full disclosure regarding the reasons for the activity, the specific procedures the activity would entail, the potential risks involved, and the full implications that can be realistically foreseen.

Property
: Property implies ownership by natural persons or legal persons (corporations, etc.) of anything limited in supply. This could be moveable objects, static objects on or under land, an area of the land surface itself, or information (intellectual property). The fact of ownership places limitations as established by custom or law on use of that property by nonowners. Ownership rights are normally accompanied by certain obligations.

Public domain
: Everything that is known in the world that is not protected as intellectual property.

Recalcitrant seed
: Recalcitrant seeds have a high water content and cannot at present be saved for later use by drying or freezing.

Recombinant DNA
: A strand of DNA synthesized in the laboratory by splicing together selected parts of DNA strands from different organic species, or by adding a selected part of an existing DNA strand (see IDRC 1985). It is a method of genetic engineering.

Registry of invention
: A system proposed by the Third World Network as a state institution, where communities could register their innovations, thus placing them in the public domain.

Resource
: Anything that is used directly by people. A renewable resource is one that can quite quickly renew itself; a nonrenewable resource is one whose consumption results in its depletion.

Reverse engineering
: Close inspection of a product including its component parts to ascertain their source and methods of assembly.

Royalty
: A payment, usually a fixed percentage per unit sold or per performance or broadcast, to an intellectual property owner established by contract or other agreement. Royalties may also be payable, if stipulated in a contract, by a drug company to a supplier of biological matter if it contains a biochemical useful in developing a new drug product. Royalties may also be payable by the extractor of minerals to a landowner or owner of the mineral rights. The owner could be the state, a private landowner, or the occupiers if they have legal title that extends to the subsoil.

Self-determination
: "The claim of a group of people, having some degree of national consciousness, to form their own state and govern themselves" (Walker 1980). It also implies also a claim to certain territory.

The South
: The developing (or "less-developed") countries, which are technologically poor, but often rich in terms of biological diversity. The South includes countries in Africa, Latin America, the Middle East, and most of Asia.

Species
: "A species is a population whose members are able to interbreed freely under natural conditions" (Wilson 1992, p. 38).

Sui generis
: Of its own kind; constituting a class alone; unique; peculiar.

Sustainable development
: "Development that meets the needs of the present without compromising the ability of future generations to meet their own needs" (WCED 1987). "Improving the quality of human life whilst living within the carrying capacity of supporting ecosystems" (IUCN 1991).

Traditional peoples
: As described in the *Convention on Biological Diversity*, traditional peoples are "indigenous and local comunities embodying traditional lifestyles."

Trust fund
: A fund set up by two parties that could be used to enable a person or juridical person to obtain independent legal advice before entering into a contractual agreement.

Value added
: The increase in the price a product gathers between its point of origin (the raw material) and its point of sale. The price increase may be justified by refinement or purification processes or by packaging.

Virus
: The smallest known type of organism. Viruses cannot reproduce alone but must first infect a living cell and usurp its synthetic and reproductive facilities (see IDRC 1985).

Acronyms and abbreviations

AFN	Assembly of First Nations
AIPP	Asian Indigenous Peoples Pact
ATA	Alliance of Taiwan Aborigines
ATCC	American Type Culture Collection
BGCI	Botanic Gardens Conservation International
CAH	Consejo Aguaruna/Huambisa
CAMPFIRE	Communal Areas Management Programme
CBD	Convention on Biological Diversity
CDC	Centers for Disease Control
CGIAR	Consultative Group on International Agricultural Research
CIKARD	Center for Indigenous Knowledge for Agriculture and Rural Development
CIR	community intellectual rights
CIRAN	Centre for International Research and Advisory Networks
COICA	Coordinadora de Organizaciones Indigenas de la Cuenca Amazónica (Coordinating Body for the Indigenous Organizations of the Amazon Basin)
CPA	Cordillera Peoples Alliance
DNA	deoxyribonucleic acid
ECOSOC	United Nations Economic and Social Council
EIA	environmental impact assessment
FAO	Food and Agriculture Organization of the United Nations
FENAMAD	Native Federation of the River Madre de Dios and Affluents
FSC	Forest Stewardship Council
GATT	General Agreement on Tariffs and Trade
GEF	Global Environment Facility
GRAIN	Genetic Resources Action International
HGDP	Human Genome Diversity Project
HTLV	human T-cell lymphotrophic virus
HUGO	Human Genome Organization
HYVs	high-yielding varieties
IARC	international agriculture research centre
ICCPR	International Covenant on Civil and Political Rights
ICDP	integrated conservation–development project
ICESCR	International Covenant on Economic, Social and Cultural Rights
IDRC	International Development Research Centre
ILO	International Labour Organisation
IMF	International Monetary Fund
INBio	National Biodiversity Institute of Costa Rica
IPBN	Indigenous Peoples Biodiversity Network
IPGRI	International Plant Genetic Resources Institute
IPR	intellectual property rights
ISCA	Institute of Social and Cultural Anthropology
ISE	International Society for Ethnobiology

ITA	international technology agreement
IUCN	International Union for the Conservation of Nature (or World Conservation Union; a conservation organization based in Switzerland)
IUPGR	International Undertaking on Plant Genetic Resources
LEAD	Leiden Ethnosystems and Development Programme
LOC	letter of collection
MTA	material transfer agreement
NCI	National Cancer Institute (part of the US National Institutes of Health)
NDI	Nucleus for Indigenous Rights
NGO	nongovernmental organization
NIH	National Institutes of Health
NTFP	nontimber forest product
Nuffic	Netherlands Organization for International Cooperation in Higher Education
PBR	plant breeders' rights
PCR	polymerase chain reaction
PCT	Patent Cooperation Treaty
PEMASKY	Proyecto de Estudio para el Manejo de Areas Silvestres de Kuna Yala
PIC	prior informed consent
PICNIC	prior informed consent or no informed consent
PROCOMITH	Programa de Colaboración sobre Medicina Tradicional y Herbolaria
R&D	research and development
RAFI	Rural Advancement Foundation International
RBG	Royal Botanic Gardens
SEARICE	Southeast Asia Regional Institute for Community Education
SRISTI	Society for Research and Initiatives for Sustainable Technologies and Institutions
TEA	Toledo Ecotourism Association
TRIPs	Trade-Related Aspects of Intellectual Property Rights
TRRs	traditional resource rights
UDHR	Universal Declaration of Human Rights
UNCED	United Nations Conference on Environment and Development (the Earth Summit)
UNCTAD	United Nations Conference on Trade and Development
UNDP	United Nations Development Programme
UNEP	United Nations Environment Programme
Unesco	United Nations Educational, Scientific and Cultural Organisation
UPOV	Union for the Protection of New Varieties of Plants
WCIP	World Council of Indigenous Peoples
WGIP	United Nations Working Group on Indigenous Populations
WGTRR	Working Group on Traditional Resource Rights
WHO	World Health Organization
WIPO	World Intellectual Property Organization
WTO	World Trade Organization
WWF	World Wide Fund for Nature (called the World Wildlife Fund in the United States)

References

Acosta, G.I. 1994. The Guaymi patent claim. *In* van der Vlist, L., ed., Voices of the earth: indigenous peoples, new partners and the right to self-determination in practice. Netherlands Centre for Indigenous Peoples, Amsterdam, Netherlands. pp. 44–51.

Adams, K.M. 1990. Cultural commoditization in Tana Toraja, Indonesia. Cultural Survival Quarterly, 14(1), 31–34.

Allott, A.N. 1987. Introduction. *In* Cotran, E., ed., Casebook on Kenya customary law. Professional Books Ltd and Nairobi University Press, Nairobi, Kenya.

Anti-Slavery Society. 1990. West Papua: plunder in paradise. Anti-Slavery Society, London, UK. Indigenous People and Development Series Report No. 6.

Axt, J.R.; Corn, M.L.; Lee, M.; Ackerman, D.M. 1993. Biotechnology, indigenous peoples, and intellectual property rights. Congressional Research Service, Library of Congress, Washington, DC, USA. April 16.

Ayad, W.G. 1994. The CGIAR and the Convention on Biological Diversity. *In* Krattiger, A.F.; McNeely, J.A.; Lesser, W.H.; Miller, K.R.; St Hill, Y.; Senanyake, R., ed., Widening perspectives on biodiversity. International Union for the Conservation of Nature, Gland, and International Academy of the Environment, Geneva, Switzerland. pp. 243–254.

Baines, G. 1992. Traditional environmental knowledge from the Marovo area of the Solomon Islands. *In* Johnson, M., ed., Lore: capturing traditional environmental knowledge. International Development Research Centre, Ottawa, ON, Canada. pp. 91–110.

Bangs, P. 1993/94. Controversy over patents on genes from indigenous peoples leads to NIH retreat. Diversity, 9(4)/10(1), 55–57.

Bérard, L.; Marchenay, P. 1993. Tradition, regulation and intellectual property: local agricultural products and foodstuffs in France. Presented at the Workshop on Intellectual Property Rights and Indigenous Knowledge, 5–10 October 1993, Granlibakken, Lake Tahoe, CA, USA. National Science Foundation, Society for Applied Anthropology and American Association for the Advancement of Science, Washington, DC, USA.

Berlin, E.A. 1993. Use and conservation of natural and cultural resources: issues of IPR and sustainable economic development. Presented at the Workshop on Intellectual Property Rights and Indigenous Knowledge, 5–10 October 1993, Granlibakken, Lake Tahoe, CA, USA. National Science Foundation, Society for Applied Anthropology, and American Association for the Advancement of Science, Washington, DC, USA.

Blundell, V. 1993. Aboriginal empowerment and souvenir trade in Canada. Annals of Tourism Research, 20, 64–87.

Bodmer, W.; McKie, R. 1994. The book of man: the quest to discover our genetic heritage. Little, Brown and Co. Ltd, London, UK.

Bothe, M. 1980. Legal and nonlegal norms: a meaningful distinction in international relations? Netherlands Yearbook of International Law, 11, 65–95.

Brown, M.; Wyckoff-Baird, B. 1992. Designing integrated conservation and development projects. Biodiversity Support Program, Washington, DC, USA.

Burnie, D. 1994. Ecotourists to paradise. New Scientist, 16 April, 23–27.

Cavalli-Sforza, L.L.; Wilson, A.C.; Cantor, C.R.; Cook-Deegan, R.M.; King, M.C. 1991. Call for a worldwide survey of human genetic diversity: a vanishing opportunity for the Human Genome Project. Genomics, 11, 490–491.

Cavalli-Sforza, L.L.; Menozzi, P.; Piazza, A. 1994. The history and geography of human genes. Princeton University Press, Princeton, NJ, USA.

CGIAR (Consultative Group on International Agricultural Research). 1995. CGIAR Directory/ Research Centers. http://www.worldbank.org/html/cgiar/centers.html. October.

Clay, J. 1992. Building and supplying markets for nonwood tropical forest products. In The rainforest harvest: sustainable strategies for saving the tropical forests? Friends of the Earth, London, UK. pp. 250–255.

COICA (Coordinadora de Organizaciones Indígenas de la Cuenca Amazónica). 1990. Primer encuentro cumbre entre pueblos indígenas y ambientalistas. Manifesto público. COICA, Iquitos, Peru.

Corry, S. 1992. Letter. New Statesman and Society, 23 October, 27–28.

Corry, S. 1993. Harvest moonshine taking you for a ride. Survival International, London, UK.

Cunningham, A.B. 1993a. Conservation, knowledge and new natural products development: partnership or privacy? Presented at the Workshop on Intellectual Property Rights and Indigenous Knowledge, 5–10 October 1993, Granlibakken, Lake Tahoe, CA, USA. National Science Foundation, Society for Applied Anthropology, and American Association for the Advancement of Science, Washington, DC, USA.

———— 1993b. Ethics, ethnobiological research, and biodiversity. World Wide Fund for Nature International, Gland, Switzerland.

Crucible Group. 1994. People, plants, and patents: the impact of intellectual property on trade, plant biodiversity, and rural society. International Development Research Centre, Ottawa, ON, Canada.

Davis, S.H. 1993. Pathways to economic development through intellectual property rights. Presented at the First International Conference on the Cultural and Intellectual Property Rights of Indigenous Peoples, June 1993, Whakatane, New Zealand. [available from S.H. Davis, World Bank, Washington, DC, USA]

Diversity. 1994. Managing global genetic resources: agricultural crop issues and policies (special report). Diversity, 10(2), 19.

Downes, D.; Laird, S.A.; Klein, C.; Carney, B.K. 1993. Biodiversity prospecting contract. In Reid, W.V.; Laird, S.A.; Meyer, C.A.; Gamez, R.; Sittenfeld, A.; Janzen, D.H.; Gollin, M.A.; Juma, C., ed., Biodiversity prospecting: using genetic resources for sustainable development. World Resources Institute, Washington, DC, USA. pp. 255–287.

ECOSOC (United Nations Economic and Social Council). 1986. Study of the problem of discrimination against indigenous populations. ECOSOC, Geneva, Switzerland. E/CN.4/sub.2/1986/7. Addendum 4, paragraph 625.

———— 1992a. Intellectual property of indigenous peoples: a concise report of the secretary-general. ECOSOC, Geneva, Switzerland. E/CN.4/sub.2/1992/30.

———— 1992b. Report of the UN technical conference on practical experience in the realization of sustainable and environmentally sound self-development of indigenous peoples. ECOSOC, Geneva, Switzerland. E/CN.4/sub.2/1992/31.

ECOSOC (United Nations Economic and Social Council), Working Group on Indigenous Populations. 1993. Discrimination against indigenous peoples: study on the protection of the cultural and intellectual property of indigenous peoples. ECOSOC, Geneva, Switzerland. E/CN.4/sub.2/1993/28.

Elisabetsky, E.; Posey, D.A. 1994. Ethnopharmacological search for antiviral compounds: treatment of gastrointestinal disorders by Kayapó medical specialists. In Ethnobotany and the search for new drugs. John Wiley and Sons, Chichester, UK. Symposium 185, pp. 77–94.

Farnsworth, N.R. 1988. Screening plants for new medicines. In Wilson, E.O., ed., Biodiversity. National Academy Press, Washington, DC, USA. pp. 83–97.

Freedman, P. 1994. Boundaries of good taste. Geographical, 66(4), 12–14.

Glowka, L.; Burhenne-Guilmin, F.; Synge, H.; McNeely, J.A.; Gundling, L. 1994. A guide to the Convention on Biological Diversity. International Union for the Conservation of Nature, Gland, Switzerland. Environmental Policy and Law Paper No. 30.

Gollin, M.A. 1993. An intellectual property rights framework for biodiversity prospecting. In Reid, W.V.; Laird, S.A.; Meyer, C.A.; Gamez, R.; Sittenfeld, A.; Janzen, D.H.; Gollin, M.A.; Juma, C., ed., Biodiversity prospecting: using genetic resources for sustainable development. World Resources Institute, Washington, DC, USA. pp. 159–197.

Golvan, C. 1992. Aboriginal art and the protection of indigenous cultural rights. European Intellectual Property Law Review, 7, 227–232.

Gradwohl, J.; Greenberg, R. 1988. Saving the tropical forests. Island Press, Washington, DC, USA.

GRAIN (Genetic Resources Action International). 1995. Framework for a full articulation of farmers' rights. GRAIN, Barcelona, Spain. Discussion paper.

Gray, A. 1994. Territorial defence as the basis for indigenous self-development. Indigenous Affairs, 4, 2–3.

Greaves, T., ed. 1993. Intellectual property rights for indigenous peoples: a sourcebook. Society for Applied Anthropology, Oklahoma City, OK, USA.

Hanlon, J. 1979. When the scientist meets the medicine man. Nature, 279, 284–285.

Howard, K. 1989. Bands, songs and shamanistic rituals: fold music in Korean society. Royal Asiatic Society, Korea Branch, Seoul, Korea.

———— 1993. Use and abuse in the preservation of a Korean shaman ritual. Quaderni dell'Accademia Chigiana, 45, 169–188.

HUGO (Human Genome Organization). 1993. Human Genome Diversity Workshop: summary of planning workshop 3B. HUGO, London, UK.

———— 1994. The Human Genome Diversity Project: summary document. HUGO, London, UK.

IDRC (International Development Research Centre). 1985. Biotechnology: opportunities and constraints (Appendix XII). IDRC, Ottawa, Canada. IDRC-MR110e.

IUCN (International Union for the Conservation of Nature). 1980. World conservation strategy: living resource conservation for sustainable development. IUCN, Gland, Switzerland.

———— 1991. Caring for the earth: a strategy for sustainable living. IUCN, United Nations Environment Programme, and World Wide Fund for Nature, Gland, Switzerland.

———— 1994. Guidelines for protected area management categories. IUCN Commission of National Parks and Protected Areas, Gland, Switzerland; with the assistance of the World Conservation Monitoring Centre, Cambridge, UK.

Jacobs, J.W.; Petroski, C.; Friedman, P.A.; Simpson, E. 1990. Characterization of the anticoagulant activities from a Brazilian arrow poison. Thrombosis and Haemostasis, 63(1), 31–35.

Johnson, S.P. 1993. The Earth Summit, UNCED (introduction and commentary). Graham and Trotman/Nijhoff, London, UK. International Environmental Law and Policy Series.

Juma, C. 1989. The gene hunters: biotechnology and the scramble for seeds. Princeton University Press, Princeton, NJ, USA.

Kahn, S.; Talal, H. 1987. Indigenous peoples: a global quest for justice (report for the Independent Commission on International Humanitarian Issues). Zed Books, London, UK.

Keller, C. 1994. Gen-Jäger und Sammler [Gene hunters and gatherers]. Philippinen Forum, 38, 39–41.

Kennedy, K.J.; Zerner, C. 1994. Equity in biodiversity prospecting: a comparative analysis on institutional approaches for the return of benefits. Rainforest Alliance, New York, NY, USA.

Kevles, D.J.; Hood, L. 1992. The code of codes: scientific and social issues of the Human Genome Project. Harvard University Press, Cambridge, MA, USA.

King, S. 1994. Establishing reciprocity: biodiversity, conservation and new models for cooperation between forest-dwelling peoples and the pharmaceutical industry. In Greaves, T., ed.,

Intellectual property rights for indigenous peoples: a sourcebook. Society for Applied Anthropology, Oklahama City, OK, USA. pp. 69–82.

Kloppenburg, J.R. 1988a. First the seed: the political economy of plant biotechnology, 1492–2000. Cambridge University Press, Cambridge, UK.

——— ed. 1988b. Seeds and sovereignty. Duke University Press, Durham, NC, USA.

Kloppenburg, J.; Gonzales, T. 1994. Between state and capital: NGOs as allies of indigenous peoples. In Greaves, T., ed., Intellectual property rights for indigenous peoples: a sourcebook. Society for Applied Anthropology, Oklahama City, OK, USA. pp. 163–177.

Kothari, A. 1993. Beyond the biodiversity convention: a view from India. African Centre for Technology Studies, Maastricht, Netherlands. Biopolicy International Series 13.

Laird, S.A. 1993. Contracts for biodiversity prospecting. In Reid, W.V.; Laird, S.A.; Meyer, C.A.; Gamez, R.; Sittenfeld, A.; Janzen, D.H.; Gollin, M.A.; Juma, C., ed., Biodiversity prospecting: using genetic resources for sustainable development. World Resources Institute, Washington, DC, USA. pp. 99–130.

Lerner, S. 1992. Beyond the Earth Summit: conversations with advocates of sustainable development. Commonweal, Bolinas, CA, USA.

Lesser, W. 1991. Equitable patent protection in the developing world: issues and approaches. Eubios Ethics Institute, Christchurch, New Zealand.

Lewin, R. 1993. Genes from a disappearing world. New Scientist, 29 May, 26–29.

Lock, M. 1994. Interrogating the human diversity genome project. Social Science and Medicine, 39(5), 603-606.

Loita Naimina Enkiyio Conservation Trust Company. 1994. Forest of the lost child. Loita Naimina Enkiyio Conservation Trust Company, Narok, Kenya.

Lynch, O.J.; Alcorn, J.B. 1993. Tenurial rights and community based conservation. Presented at the Workshop on Community-Based Conservation, October 1993. Liz Claiborne and Art Ortenberg Foundation, Airlie, VA, USA. [A copy may be obtained from Dr Janis Alcorn, Biodiversity Support Program, c/o WWF, 1250 24th Street NW, Washington, DC 20037, USA.]

Marks, J. 1995. Human biodiversity: genes, race, and history. Walter de Gruyter, New York, NY, USA.

McIntyre, L. 1989. Last days of Eden. National Geographic, 174(6), 800–817.

Mead, A.T.P. 1993. Delivering good services to the public without compromising the cultural and intellectual property rights of indigenous peoples: the economics of customary knowledge. New Zealand Institute of Public Administration Research Papers, 10(3), 31–36.

Megarry, V.C. 1977. *Tito v Waddell* (no. 2) (1977) 3 all E.R. 129. [Decision of the English Chancery Division Court]

Moran, A.G., ed. 1994. IPR sourcebook Philippines: with emphasis on intellectual property rights in agriculture and food. Los Baños College of Agriculture and Management, University of the Philippines, and Organizational Development for Empowerment, Los Baños, Philippines.

Moran, W. 1993. Rural space as intellectual property. Political Geography, 12(3), 263–277.

Myers, N. 1993. Biodiversity and the precautionary principle. Ambio, 22(2–3), 74–79.

National Geographic. 1994. From museums, Indian remains go home. National Geographic, 185, 1.

Nijar, G.S. 1994. Towards a legal framework for protecting biological diversity and community intellectual rights — a Third World perspective. Presented at the second session of the International Committee for the Convention on Biological Diversity, 20 June to 1 July 1994, Nairobi, Kenya. Third World Network, Penang, Malaysia.

Nuttall, M. 1994. Greenland: emergence of an Inuit homeland. In Minority Rights Group, ed., Polar peoples: self-determination and development. Minority Rights Publications, London, UK.

ODI (Overseas Development Institute). 1993. Patenting plants: the implications for developing countries. ODI, London, UK. Briefing paper.

Okoth-Ogendo, H.W.O. 1989. Some issues of theory in the study of tenure relations in African agriculture. Africa, 59(1), 6–17.

OTA (Office of Technology Assessment). 1984. Commercial biotechnology: an international analysis. US Government Printing Office, Washington, DC, USA.

―――― 1987. Technologies to maintain biological diversity. OTA, Washington, DC, USA. OTA-F-330.

Patel, S. 1994. Patients could lose out in tussle over gene bank. New Scientist, 26 March.

Petersen, T.S. 1994. The home rule situation in Greenland. In van der Vlist, L., ed., Voices of the earth: indigenous peoples, new partners and the right to self-determination in practice. Netherlands Centre for Indigenous Peoples, Amsterdam, Netherlands. pp. 113–123.

Pinel, S.L.; Evans, M.J. 1994. Tribal sovereignty and the control of knowledge. In Greaves, T., ed., Intellectual property rights for indigenous peoples: a sourcebook. Society for Applied Anthropology, Oklahoma City, OK, USA. pp. 41–55.

Posey, D.A. 1990. Intellectual property rights and just compensation for indigenous knowledge. Anthropology Today, 6(4), 13–16.

―――― 1994. International agreements and intellectual property right protection for indigenous peoples. In Greaves, T., ed., Intellectual property rights for indigenous peoples: a sourcebook. Society for Applied Anthropology, Oklahoma City, OK, USA. pp. 223–251.

Posey, D.A.; Argumedo, A.; da Costa e Silva, E.; Dutfield, G.; Plenderleith, K. 1995. Indigenous peoples, traditional technologies and equitable sharing: international instruments for the protection of community intellectual property and traditional resource rights. International Union for the Conservation of Nature, Gland, Switzerland.

Principe, P.P. 1989. Valuing the biodiversity of medicinal plants. In Akerele, O.; Heywood, V.; Synge, H., ed., The conservation of medicinal plants. Cambridge University, Cambridge, UK.

RAFI (Rural Advancement Foundation International). 1993. Patents, indigenous peoples, and human genetic diversity. RAFI, Ottawa, Canada. Communiqué, May.

Richardson, B.J.; Craig, D.; Boer, B. 1994. Aboriginal participation and control in environmental planning and management: review of Canadian regional agreements and their potential planning application to Australia. North Australian Research Unit, Australian National University, Darwin, Australia.

Roddick, G. 1992. Letter. New Statesman and Society, 23 October, 28–29.

Ross, H.; Young, E.; Liddle, L. 1994. An inspiration for Australian land management. Australian Journal of Land Management, 1(1).

Rossler, M. 1993a. Conserving outstanding cultural landscapes. World Heritage Newsletter, 2, 14–15.

―――― 1993b. The integration of cultural landscapes into the world heritage. World Heritage Newsletter, 1, 15.

―――― 1993c. Tongariro: first cultural landscape on the World Heritage List. World Heritage Newsletter, 4.

Ruppert, D. 1994. Buying secrets: federal government procurement of intellectual cultural property. In Greaves, T., ed., Intellectual property rights for indigenous peoples: a sourcebook. Society for Applied Anthropology, Oklahoma City, OK, USA. pp. 111–128.

Rutherford, L.; Bone, S., ed. 1993. Osborn's concise law dictionary (8th ed.). Sweet and Maxwell, London, UK.

Sasson, D. 1989. Considering the perspective of the victim: the antiquities of Nepal. *In* Messenger, P.M., ed., The ethics of collecting cultural property: whose culture? whose property? University of New Mexico Press, Albuquerque, NM, USA. pp. 61–72.

Schweitzer, J.F.; Gray Handley, F.; Edwards, J.; Harris, W.F.; Grever, M.; Schepartz, S.; Cragg, G.; Snader, K.; Bhat, A. 1991. Summary of the workshop on drug development, biological diversity, and economic growth. Journal of the National Cancer Institute, 83, 1294–1298.

Seedling. 1990. New Delhi Declaration. Seedling, 7(2), 4–5.

——— 1994. Special issue on international agricultural research. Seedling, 11(2).

Shand, H. 1993. Biodiversity, patents and indigenous peoples. Presented at a panel discussion, Indigenous Peoples: Human Rights and Sustainable Development, at the World Conference on Human Rights, 18 June 1993, Vienna. The author may be contacted at RAFI-USA, PO Box 655, Pittsboro, NC 27312, USA.

Shaw, M.N. 1994. International law (3rd ed.). Cambridge University Press, Cambridge, UK.

Shiva, V. 1994a. Freedom for seed. Resurgence, March/April, 36–39.

——— 1994b. The need for sui generis rights. Seedling, 12(1), 11–15.

Snead, B. 1992. Forest conservation helps Amazon peoples. Front Lines, June, 5–6.

Sorenson, C. 1993. Controls and sanctions over the use of forest products in the Kafue River basin of Zambia. Overseas Development Institute, Rural Development Forestry Network, London, UK. Paper 15a.

Southworth, E. 1994. A special concern. Museums Journal, July, 23–25.

Stephenson, D.J. 1994. A legal paradigm for protecting traditional knowledge. *In* Greaves, T., ed., Intellectual property rights for indigenous peoples: a sourcebook. Society for Applied Anthropology, Oklahoma City, OK, USA. pp. 179–189.

Sutherland, J. 1993. National overview of policies, protocols and legislation dealing with indigenous Australians' intellectual and cultural property. Presented at a workshop of the Rainforest Aboriginal Network and Wet Tropics Management Authority, 25–27 November 1993 (unpublished). The author may be reached at Australian National University, Department of International Relations, GPO Box 4, Canberra, ACT 2601, Australia.

Swain, M.B. 1989. Developing ethnic tourism in Yunnan, China. Tourism Recreation Research, 14(1), 33–39.

Tobin, B. 1995. Putting the commercial cart before the cultural horse: a study of the international cooperative biodiversity group (ICBG) program in Peru (unpublished). The author may be reached at Sociedad Peruana de Derecho Ambiental, Plaza Arrospide No. SPDA 9, San Isidro, Lima 27, Peru.

UNDP (United Nations Development Programme). 1993. The GEF Small Grants Programme: progress report no.3. UNDP, New York, NY, USA.

UNEP 1995. Report of the Second Meeting of the Conference of the Parties to the Convention on Biological Diversity (UNEP/CBD/COP/2/19). UNEP, Geneva.

Unesco (United Nations Education, Scientific and Cultural Organization). 1990. Recommendations on the safeguarding of traditional culture and folklore adopted by the Geneva Conference of Unesco at its 25th session. Copyright Bulletin, 24(1), 8–12.

——— 1994. Operational guidelines for the implementation of the World Heritage Convention. Intergovernmental Committee for the Protection of the World Cultural and Natural Heritage, Unesco, Paris, France.

——— 1995. Report of the IBC Working Group on Population Genetics: bioethics and human population genetics research. Unesco, Paris, France.

Valentine, P.S. 1993. Ecotourism and nature conservation: a definition with some recent developments in Micronesia. Tourism Management, April, 107–115.

van Wijk, J.; Cohen, J.I.; Komen, J. 1993. Intellectual property rights for agricultural biotechnology: options and implications for developing countries. International Service for National Agricultural Research, The Hague, Netherland. Research Report 3.

Van Zile, J. 1993. The many faces of Korean dance. In Korea briefing: festival of Korea. Westview Press, Boulder, CO, USA. pp. 99–119.

Vines, G. 1995. Genes in black and white. New Scientist, 8 July, 34-37.

Walgate, R. 1990. Miracle or menace? Biotechnology and the Third World. Panos Institute, London, UK.

Walker, D.M. 1980. The Oxford companion to law. Oxford University Press, Oxford, UK.

Warren, D.M. 1990. Indigenous knowledge and development. Agriculture Department, World Bank, Washington, DC, USA. Seminar series on sociology and natural resource management.

WCED (World Commission on Environment and Development). 1987. Our common future. Oxford University Press, New York, NY, USA.

WCIP (World Council of Indigenous Peoples). 1993. Presumed dead ... but still useful as a human by-product. WCIP, Ottawa, Canada.

Wells, M. 1992. Biodiversity conservation, affluence and poverty: mismatched costs and benefits and efforts to remedy them. Ambio, 21(3), 237–243.

Wells, M.P.; Brandon, K.E. 1993. The principles and practice of buffer zones and local participation in biodiversity conservation. Ambio, 22(3), 157–162.

Wheat, S. 1994. Taming tourism. Geographical, 66(4), 16–19.

Wilson, E.O. 1992. The diversity of life. Belknap Press, Cambridge, MA, USA.

WIPO (World Intellectual Property Organization). 1985. Model provisions for national laws on the protection of expressions of folklore against illicit exploitation and other prejudicial actions. WIPO and Unesco, Geneva, Switzerland.

―――― 1988. Background reading material on intellectual property. WIPO, Geneva, Switzerland.

―――― 1989. Protection of expressions of folklore (lecture). International Bureau, WIPO, Geneva, Switzerland.

Worede, M.; Mekbib, H. 1993. Linking genetic resource conservation to farmers in Ethiopia. In de Boef, W.; Amanor, K.; Wellard, K.; Bebbington, A., ed., Cultivating knowledge: genetic diversity, farmer experimentation and crop research. Intermediate Technology Publications, London, UK.

Working Group on Intellectual Property Rights. 1993. Report presented at the Conference on Intellectual Property Rights and Indigenous Knowledge, 5–11 October 1993, Granlibakken, Lake Tahoe, CA, USA. National Science Foundation, Society for Applied Anthropology, and American Association for the Advancement of Science, Washington, DC, USA.

World Resources Institute. 1992. Global biodiversity strategy: guidelines for action to save, study and use Earth's biotic wealth sustainably and equitably. World Resources Institute, International Union for the Conservation of Nature, United Nations Environment Programme, Washington, DC, USA.

Young, E. 1995. Third World in the First: development and indigenous peoples. Routledge, London, UK.

Zurick, D.N. 1992. Adventure travel and sustainable tourism in the peripheral economy of Nepal. Annals of the Association of American Geographers, 82(4), 606–628.

Resource guide

This resource guide includes lists of indigenous and nonindigenous peoples' organizations, institutions, and individuals who are interested in intellectual property rights (IPR), traditional resource rights (TRR), and related issues. Many of these people and organizations are referred to in this book. The mailing list is organized by continent and country; within each country institutions are arranged alphabetically with unaffiliated individuals at the end.

For organizations with access to the World Wide Web, the list of electronic conferences dealing with environmental sustainability, social and economic justice, universal human rights, and peace will be useful. Also included are home-page addresses of some key organizations.

The final section of the resource guide contains an annotated bibliography — an extensive list of relevant publications on the issues covered in *Beyond Intellectual Property*. It represents the most comprehensive list of material on IPR and TRR to date, and is indexed by major subject.

People and organizations

Africa

Cameroon

Sarah Laird
Limbe Botanic Garden and Herbarium
BP 437
Limbe
Sud-Ouest, Cameroon

Ada Ndeso-Atanga
**Private Voluntary Organization–
Non-Governmental Organization/
Natural Resources Management Project**
Radio House, SNAC Building
BP 422
Yaoundé, Cameroon

Ethiopia

Regassa Feyissa
Biodiversity Institute
PO Box 30726
Addis Ababa, Ethiopia

Getachew Mengistie
Ethiopian Science and Technology Commission
PO Box 2490
Addis Ababa, Ethiopia
Tel: +251 1 51 13 44
Fax: +251 1 51 88 29

Tsedeke Abate
Institute of Agricultural Research
PO Box 2003
Addis Ababa, Ethiopia
Tel: +251 1 612633/41
Fax: +251 1 611222

J. Hanson
International Livestock Centre for Africa (ILCA)
PO Box 5689
Addis Ababa, Ethiopia
Tel: +251 1 61-32-15, ext. 224
Fax: +251 1 61-18-92
E-mail: j.hanson@cgnet.com

Kenya

African Centre for Technology Studies
PO Box 45917
Nairobi, Kenya
Tel: +254 2 741651
Fax: +254 2 743 995
E-mail: acts@elci.gn.apc.org

Agnes Ndungi
Coffee Research Foundation
PO Box 4
Ruiru, Kenya

Indigenous Peoples of East Africa Foundation
PO Box 59516
Nairobi, Kenya
Tel: +254 2 723002/3/4

Kennedy Wanyonyi Barasa
Institute of Diplomacy and International Studies
University of Nairobi
PO Box 30197
Nairobi, Kenya
Tel: +254 2 334244
Fax: +254 2 339014

William Overholtz
International Centre for Insect Physiology
 and Ecology
PO Box 30772
Nairobi, Kenya

Douglas John Boland or
Hannah Jaenicke
International Centre for Research in Agroforestry
 (ICRAF)
PO Box 30677
Nairobi, Kenya
Tel: +254 2 521 450
Fax: +254 2 521 001
E-mail: icraf@cgnet.com

G.N. Kibata
Kenya Agricultural Research Institute
PO Box 14733
Nairobi, Kenya

Ian Gordon
Kipepeo Project
PO Box 57
Kilifi, Kenya

MAA Development and Welfare Association
PO Box 231
Nairobi, Kenya
Tel: +254 2 335457
Fax: +254 2 219022

E.M. Mbogo or
Ibrahim Ngozi
Department of Kiswahili
Maseno University College
Private Bag
Maseno, Kenya

E. Kipruto Maru or
Inyani K. Simala
School of Social, Cultural and Development Studies
Moi University
PO Box 3900
Eldoret, Kenya
Tel: +254 321 43620/43001-8
Fax: +254 321 43047

Christine H.S. Kabuye or
Esther N. Kioko
National Museums of Kenya
PO Box 40658
Nairobi, Kenya
Tel: +254 2 742 161/4 or 742 131/4
Fax: +254 2 741 424
E-mail: biodiver@elci.gn.apc.org (Biodiversity Centre)

Patrick N. Muthoka
Plant Propagation Unit
National Museums of Kenya
PO Box 40658
Nairobi, Kenya

Pauline Ngunjiri
Trans World Radio
PO Box 21514
Nairobi, Kenya
Tel: +254 2 560 552/560 572/560 574
Fax: +254 2 560 599

Cyriaque Sendashonga
United Nations Environment Programme (UNEP)
PO Box 30552
Nairobi, Kenya
Tel: +254 2 621 234
Fax: +254 2 219 270/226 886/226 890

Peter Ngunjiri
World Vision Kenya
PO Box 12515
Nairobi, Kenya

Nigeria

Hilaire C.I. Adibe
**Enugu/Nigeria Working Group, Traditional
 Resource Rights**
PO Box 71
Enugu, Nigeria

Ethnic Minority Rights Organization of Africa
PO Box 696
Surulere
Lagos, Nigeria
Tel: +23 41 832218
Fax: +23 41 832218

M.A. Azuine or
K. Gamaniel or
C.O.N. Wambebe
**National Institute for Pharmaceutical Research
 and Development**
Idu Industrial Area, PMB 21, Garki PO
Abuja, Nigeria
Tel: +234 9 523 1602
Fax: +234 9 523 1043

Miriam Isoun
Niger Delta Wetlands Foundation
PO Box 7390
Port Harcourt, Nigeria
Tel: +234 84 334 042

Clement O. Adewunmi
Drug Research and Production Unit *or*
A.A. Elujoba *or*
Abayomi Sofowora
Faculty of Pharmacy
Obafemi Awolowo University
Ile-Ife, Nigeria
Tel: +234 36 230 368
Fax: +234 22 417 715

C.O.C. Agwu *or*
Nwofia Godson Emeka
Department of Botany *or*
P.C. Onokala
Department of Geography
University of Nigeria
Nsukka, Nigeria

Rwanda

Association pour la Promotion des Batwa
PO Box 2472
Kigali, Rwanda
Tel: +250 75416
Fax: +250 74671

South Africa

Susan Higgins-Opitz
Centre for Indigenous Plant Use Research
Department of Biology
University of Natal (Durban)
Private Bag X10
Dalbridge 4014, KwaZulu-Natal
South Africa
Tel: +27 31 260 1337
Fax: +27 31 260 2029

Anthony B. Cunningham
People and Plants Programme
World Wide Fund for Nature/Unesco/Kew
PO Box 42
Bettys Bay 7141, South Africa

Tanzania

Director
Institute of Resource Assessment
University of Dar-es-Salaam
PO Box 35097
Dar es Salaam, Tanzania

Korongoro Integrated Peoples Oriented to Conservation
PO Box 94
Loliondo
Ngorongoro District, Tanzania
Fax: +255 51 46607

Director
National Plant Genetic Resources Centre, TPRI
PO Box 3024
Arusha, Tanzania

Sabina Mnaliwa
Traditional Medicine Unit
Ministry of Health
PO Box 9083
Dar-es-Salaam, Tanzania

Uganda

J.M.A. Opio-Odongo
United Nations Development Programme
15B Clement Hill Road
PO Box 7184
Kampala, Uganda
Tel: +256 41 233 440/1/2/5
Fax: +256 41 244 801

Zambia

Godfrey Lieto Wamulwange
Barotse Royal Establishment
PO Box 910033
Mongu, Zambia

Director
Nayuma Museum
PO Box 910284
Mongu, Zambia

Zimbabwe

Gama Mutemeri
Development Dialogue
4 Mansfield Road, Marlborough
Harare, Zimbabwe
Tel: +263 4 300 509
Fax: +263 4 728 376
E-mail: mutemeri@mango.apc.org

India Musokatwane
Regional Office for Southern Africa
International Union for the Conservation of Nature and Natural Resources (IUCN)
PO Box 745
Harare, Zimbabwe
Tel: 263 472 8266
Fax: 263 472 0738

Asia

Bangladesh

Chittagong Hills Tracts Peoples Council
PO Box 86
Klong Chan PO
Bangkok 10240, Thailand
Tel: +66 2 3750478
Fax: +66 2 3185447

World Chakma Organization
3 Sambhu Das Lane
Bowbazar
Calcutta 12, India
Tel: +91 33 269658
Fax: +91 33 269658

Bhutan

Dennis F. **Desmond**
United Nations Volunteers, Forestry
 Extension Specialist
c/o Terence Jones, UNDP Resident Representative
GPO Box 103
Thimphu, Bhutan

India

A.K. Ramesh
Bank Workers Forum
c/o PB 86
Kozhikode 673001, South India

P.K. Hajra
Director
Botanical Survey of India
P-8 Brabourne Road
Calcutta 700001, India
Tel: +91 33 242 4922
Fax: +91 33 242 9330

A.N. Henry
Botanical Survey of India
Tamil Nadu Agricultural University
PO Lawley Road
Coimbatore, India

V. Mudgal
Botanical Survey of India
Pharmacognosy Section
PO Botanic Garden
Howrah 711103, India

D.C. Pal
Botanical Survey of India
Economic Botany Section
PO Botanic Garden
Howrah 711103, India

Winin Pereira
Centre for Holistic Studies
79 Carter Road
Bandra
Bombay 40050, India

Vijaylakshmi
Centre for Indigenous Knowledge Systems
2, 25th East Street
Tiruvanmiyur
Madras 60041, India

Anil Agarwal
Centre for Science and Environment
41 Tughlakabad Institutional Area
(Near Batra Hospital)
New Delhi 110 062, India
Tel: +91 11 6981110
Fax: +91 11 6985879
E-mail: cse@unv.ernet.in

Dalit Youth Movement
161 T.T.K. Road
Alwarpet
Madras 600018, India
Tel: +91 44 453757
Fax: +91 44 453757

Ashok Khosla
Development Alternatives
B-32 Tara Crescent, Qutab Institutional Area
New Delhi 110016, India
Tel: +91 11 66 5370/65 7938
Fax: +91 11 686 6301

Darshan Shankar
**Foundation for the Revitalisation of
 Local Health Traditions**
50 MSH Layout, 2nd Stage, 3rd Main
Anandnagar
Bangalore 560024, India
Tel: +91 80 336909
Fax: +91 80 334167

Director
Girijan Corporation
Ministry of Tribal Welfare/Social Welfare
Government of Andhra Pradesh
Andra Pradesh, India

Indian Council of Indigenous and Tribal Peoples
14 Jangpura-B
Mathura Road
New Delhi 110014, India
Tel: +91 11 4619821
Fax: +91 11 4623681

Ashish Kothari
Indian Institute of Public Administration (IIPA)
IP Estate
New Delhi 110002, India
Tel: +91 11 331 730, ext. 292
E-mail: ashish%iipa@isidev.nic.in

Madhav Gadgil
Centre for Ecological Sciences
Indian Institute of Science
Bangalore 560012, India
Tel: +91 80 334 0985
Fax: +91 80 334 1683
E-mail: madhav@ces.iisc.ernet.in

M.S. Swaminathan
M.S. Swaminathan Foundation
3rd Cross Street
Taramani Institutional Area
Madras 600085
Tamil Nadu, India
Tel: +91 44 235 1319
Fax: +91 44 235 1698
E-mail: mssrf.madras@sm8.sprintrpg.sprint.com

Naga Peoples Movement for Human Rights
CEC Office
F 20 Ground Floor, Jankpura Extension
New Delhi 110014, India
Tel: +91 11 4624874
Fax: +91 11 4624874

Naga Students' Federation
Kohima 797001, India
Tel: +91 3862 525526

Visier Sanyu
Department of History
Nagaland University
Kohima 797001, India

S.K. Jain
National Botanical Research Institute
Rana Pratap Marg
Lucknow 226001
Uttar Pradesh, India
Tel: +91 522 236 431
Fax: +91 522 244 330

National Socialist Council of Nagaland
PO Box 1731
Bangkok 10501, Thailand
Tel: +66 2 3189034
Fax: +66 2 3189034

Vandana Shiva
Research Foundation for Science, Technology and Natural Resource Policy — Navdanya
A-60, 2nd floor, Hauz Khas
New Delhi 110016, India
Tel: +91 11 665 003
Fax: +91 11 685 6795
E-mail: twn@unv.ernet.in

Surendra Patel
Sardar Patel Institute of Economic and Social Research
Thaltej Road
Ahmedabad 380054, India
Tel: +91 272 429 598

Anil K. Gupta
Society for Research and Initiatives for Sustainable Technologies and Institutions (SRISTI)
Indian Institute of Management
Ahmedabad 380015, India
Tel: +91 272 407241
Fax: +91 272 427896
E-mail: anilg@iimahd.ernet.in

G. Melchias
Environment Science Unit
St Joseph's College
Tiruchirapalli 620002
Tamil Nadu, India

Amrita N. Achanta
Tata Energy Research Institute
Darbari Seth Block (3rd floor)
India Habitat Centre
Lodi Road
New Delhi 110003, India
Tel: +91 11 463 8058/460 1920/460 1921

Tropical Botanic Garden and Research Institute
Pacha Palode
Thiruvananthapuram
Kerala, India

A.K. Ghosh
Director
Zoological Survey of India
M Block, New Alipur
Calcutta 700053, India
Tel/fax: +91 33 478 6893

K. Ravi **Srinivas**
Pushpak
Malligai Street, Bank Colony
Madurai 625014, India

Indonesia

Setjati Sastrapradja
Center for Research in Biotechnology
PO Box 323
Bogor, Indonesia

Director
International NGO Forum on Indonesian Development (INFID)
Jalan Penjernihan I Komp, Kenangan No. 10
Pejompongan
Jakarta 10210, Indonesia

Hadi Alileodra
Ministry of the Environment
Jakarta, Indonesia

Republik Maluku
PO Box 9841
1006 AM Amsterdam, The Netherlands
Tel: +31 83 3475388
Fax: +31 83 3475388

West Papua Peoples Front
PO Box 75916
1007 AX Amsterdam, The Netherlands
Tel: +31 15 566071

Japan

Ainu Association of Hokkaido
The Ainu Center
Kita 2, Nishi 7
Chuo-ku, Sapporo
Hokkaido 060, Japan
Tel: +81 11 2210462
Fax: +81 112210672

Eugenio da Costa e Silva
Institute of Advanced Studies
United Nations University
53-67 Jingumae, 5-Chome
Shibuya Ku
Tokyo 150
Tel: +81 3 5467 2323
Fax: +81 3 5467 2324
E-mail: dacosta@ias.unu.edu

Malaysia

Center for Orang Asli Concerns
23 Jalan SS 25/29
47301 Petaling Jaya, Malaysia
Tel: +03 7042814
Fax: +03 7042863

K'ntah People
Orang Asli Village
KG Tawai
Grik
Perah, Malaysia

Partners of Community Organizations (PACOS)
WDT 136
88866 Kota Kinabalu
Sabah, Malaysia
Tel: +60 88 718669
Fax: +60 88 238000

Martin Khor
Third World Network
87 Cantonment Road
10250 Penang, Malaysia
Tel: +60 4 226 6159
E-mail: twn@igc.apc.org

World Rainforest Movement
87 Cantonment Road
10250 Penang, Malaysia
E-mail: wrmpen@peg.apc.org

Gurdial **Nijar**
8 Jalan Padi 2
Bandar Baru Uda
81200 Johor Baru
Johor, Malaysia

Nepal

National Committee for the International Year for the World's Indigenous People Nepal
PO Box 822
Kathmandu, Nepal
Tel: +977 1 471179
Fax: +977 1 220082

Nepal Indigenous People Movement and Information Service Centre
PO Box 4282
Bagbazar
Kathmandu, Nepal

Pakistan

Aban Kabraji
International Union for the Conservation of Nature and Natural Resources (IUCN-Pakistan)
1 Bath Island Road
Karachi 755309, Pakistan
Tel: +92 21 578 067
Fax: +92 21 587 0287

Philippines

Tunay na Alyansa ng Bayan sa Katutubo (TABAK)
Alliance of Advocates for Indigenous Peoples' Rights
1 B Guijo Street
Project 3
Quezon City 1101, Philippines
Fax: +63 2 922003

Director
Center for Development and Programs in the Cordillera
Room 304, Hamada Building
Upper Mabini Street
Baguio City, Philippines

Ponciano L. Bennagen
Sentro Para sa Ganap na Pamayanan Inc.
Center for Holistic Community Development
Room 100-D, Philippine Social Science Center
Commonwealth Avenue
Diliman
Quezon City 1101, Philippines
Tel: +63 922 9621340
Fax: +63 2 952197

Minnie M. Degawan
Cordillera Peoples Alliance
PO Box 975
Baguio City 2600, Philippines
Tel: +63 74 442 7008
Fax: +63 74 442 5347
E-mail: cwerc@phil.gn.apc.org

Cordillera Resource Center for Indigenous Peoples' Rights
PO Box 7691
Airmail Distribution Center
NAIA 1300
Pasay City, Philippines
Tel: +63 74 4424175

Cordillera Women's Education and Resource Center, Inc.
PO Box 7691
GARCOM Baguio (752)
DAPO 1300
Domestic Road
Pasay City, Philippines
Tel: +63 74 4425347
Fax: +63 74 4425347

José Empeso
Department of Foreign Affairs
2330 Roxas Blvd
Pasay City, Philippines

Kalipunan Ng Mga Katutubong Mamamayan Ng Pilipinas
Federation of Indigenous Peoples Organizations of the Philippines
PO Box 10125
Quezon City Main, Philippines
Tel: +63 2 7120951, ext. 14
Fax: +63 2 9220033

First Asian Indigenous Women's Network
PO Box 7691
GARCOM Baguia (752)
DAPO 1300
Domestic Road
Pasay City, Philippines
Tel: +63 74 4425347
Fax: +63 74 4425347

Director
Kinaiyahan Foundation Inc.
c/o Yap Compound, Room 5 JP Laurel Avenue
Bajada 8000
Davao City, Philippines
Tel: +63 82 72654

Lumad Mindanaw Peoples' Federation
PO Box 332
Davao City 8000, Philippines
Tel: +63 82 79947

Director
Montanosa Research and Development Center
Sagada
Mountain Province, Philippines

Director
Peasant Update Philippines
Rm 210 Kaimo Building
Quezon City 1101, Philippines

Pinaltakan Tribal Council Association
Palayan City
Nueva Ecija
c/o Gregoria A. Santos
37-G Antonio Luna Street
Project 4
Quezon City, Philippines
Tel: +63 2 9210580

Corazon Catibog-Sinha
Director
Protected Areas and Wildlife Bureau
Department of Environment and Natural Resources
Quezon Avenue
Diliman
Quezon City, Philippines
Tel: +63 924 6031/2/3/4/5
Fax: +63 924 0109

Elenita C. Daño or
Rene Salazar
Southeast Asia Regional Institute for Community Education
Unit 332, Eagle Court Condominium
26 Matalino Street
Diliman
Quezon City, Philippines
Tel: +63 2 921 5432/921 7544
Fax: +63 2 921 5432
E-mail: searice@phil.gn.apc.org

Tribal Filipino Center for Development, Inc.
De Mazenod Center
303 Quezon Boulevard
Kidapawan
Cotabato 9400, Philippines

Director
Ugnayang Pang-Aghamtao Inc.
Room 208 Philippines Social Science Center
Commonwealth Avenue
Diliman
Quezon City 1101, Philippines
Tel: +63 92 29621 340

Levita Duhay Lungsod
Department of Agricultural Education and Rural Studies
University of Philippines at Los Banos
Laguna 4031, Philippines

Oscar Zamora
Department of Agronomy
University of the Philippines at Los Banos
Laguna 4031, Philippines
Tel: +63-94-2466 / 2568 / 2217
Fax c/o SEARCA: +63 2 817 0598
E-mail: pgf@mudspring.uplb.edu.ph

Sri Lanka

T.A. Dharmaratne
Agrarian Research and Training Institute
MFP Division, 119 Wijerama Mawatha
PO Box 1522
Colombo 07, Sri Lanka
Tel: +94 1 696981
Fax: +94 1 692423

Sri Lanka Resource Centre for Indigenous Knowledge
University of Sri Jayewardenepura
Nugegoda, Sri Lanka

Gallege Punyawardena
Swarna Hansa Foundation
09 Windsor Avenue
Vandervette Place
Dehiwala, Sri Lanka
Tel: +94 1 712 566
Fax: +94 1 723 649

Premarathna Alokabandara
Swarna Hansa Regional Centre
Sanhinda
Nikaweratiya, Sri Lanka

Suriya **Gunasekara**
458/1 Pitakotte Road
Kotte, Sri Lanka

P. **Ukwatta**
Station Master
Anuradhapura, Sri Lanka

Taiwan

Alliance of Taiwan Aborigines
175 Chung-Cheng Road
Jih Yeh Village
Sun Moon Lake
Nan Tou County, Taiwan
Tel: +886 49 850187

Indigenous Work Committee of the Presbyterian Church in Taiwan
Lane 269, No. 3
Roosevelt Road section 3
Taipei, Taiwan
Tel: +886 2 3625282
Fax: +886 2 3628096

Thailand

Arakenese Movement
PO Box 1076
Silom PO
Bangkok 10504, Thailand

Asia Indigenous Peoples Pact
PO Box 26
Bungthonglong PO
Bangkok 10240, Thailand
Tel: +66 2 3189034
Fax: +66 2 3189034

Committee of Human Rights Action for Indigenous Peoples (Burma)
PO Box 227
Bangkok 10501, Thailand
Tel: +66 2 3325062
Fax: +66 2 2531571

Hill Area Development Foundation
PO Box 11
Mae Chan
Chang Rai 57110, Thailand
Tel: +66 53 715696
Fax: +66 53 715696

Human Rights Committee for Non-Burman Nationalities
PO Box 118
Chiang Mai 50000, Thailand

Karen National Union
PO Box 792
Phrakhanong PO
Bangkok 10110, Thailand
Tel: +66 2 3327554
Fax: +66 2 3321924

Mon National Relief Committee
PO Box 1983
Bangkok 10501, Thailand

Viet Nam

Mai Van Tri
Institute of Natural Products Chemistry
Centre for Natural Sciences and Technology of Viet Nam
Nghia Do, Tu Liem
Hanoi, Viet Nam
Tel: +84 345390
Fax: +84 352483

Central America

Bahamas

P.A. Mailus
Bahamas National Trust
PO Box N.4014
Wassan, Bahamas

Donald Cooper
Ministry of Health and Environment
Nassau, Bahamas

Belize

Caribbean Organization of Indigenous Peoples
PO Box 229
Belize City, Belize
Tel: +501 2 44100
Fax: +501 2 32136

Joseph Palacio
National Garifuna Council
PO Box 229
Belize City, Belize

Costa Rica

Ulises Hernandez Nersis
Asociación Cultural Sejekto
La Voz del Indio
AP 1293-2150, Moravia
San José, Costa Rica
Tel/fax: +506 234 7115

Asociación de Desarrollo Indígena "Cabecar"
AP 170-2070
Sabanilla, Costa Rica
Tel: +506 243570
Fax: +506 537524

Asociación Indígena de Costa Rica
AP 6979
San José 1000, Costa Rica

Coordinadora Regional de Pueblos Indígenas de Centro America, Mexico y Panama
AP 6979
San José 1000, Costa Rica
Tel: +506 259573

J.A. Cabrera
Medaglia Fundación AMBIO
Avenida 10 Y Bis, Calle 23, Apartado 14
87-1002 San José, Costa Rica
Tel: +506 248 782
Fax: +506 249 169

El Salvador

Asociación Nacional Indígena Salvadoreña
Calle Obispo Marroquín
Antigua Aduana
Sonsonate, El Salvador
Tel: +503 510742/256746
Fax: +503 266903

Guatemala

500 Años de Resistencia Indígena, Negra y Popular
Secretaria Operativa
AP 7-B, Sucursal El Trebol
Guatemala, Guatemala
Tel: +502 2 28932
Fax: +502 2 28932

Asociación de Escritores Mayances de Guatemala
Calle 14054, Zona 3
AP 168
Quezaltenango, Guatemala
Tel: +502 9 614645
Fax: +502 9 614219

Comité de Unidad Campesina
AP 7-B, Sucursal El Trebol 01903
Guatemala, Guatemala
Tel: +502 2 28932
Fax: +502 2 28932

Comité Organizador Indígena Kaqchiquel
Cantón Sur
Colonia San José
Patzún
Chimaltenango, Guatemala

Consejo de Mujeres Mayas de Guatemala
25 Avenida 0-73, Zona 3
Quezaltenango, Guatemala
Tel: +502 9 614219
Fax: +502 9 614219

Consejo de Organizaciones Mayas de Guatemala
1a Calle 4-20, Zona 3
Chimaltenango, Guatemala
Tel: +502 9 391031
Fax: +502 9 571018

Consejo Nacional de Desplazados de Guatemala
7a Avenida 8-56, Zona 1
Edificio del Centro
7 nivel-oficina 7-12
Guatemala, Guatemala
Tel: +502 5 32853

Coordinadora Nacional de Viudas de Guatemala
8a Avenida 2-29, Zona 1
Guatemala 01001, Guatemala
Tel: +502 2 537914
Fax: +502 2 25642

Honduras

Comité Pro-Desarollo Integral de la Moskitia
Residencial Las Counas
Bloque P, Casa No. 396
Tegucigalpa, Honduras

Confederación de Pueblos Autóctonos de Honduras
AP 20598
Tegucigalpa, Honduras
Tel: +504 344925
Fax: +504 344925

Osvaldo **Munguia**
Executive Director
Mopawi
AP 2175
Tegucigalpa, Honduras
Tel/fax: +504 37 2864

Mexico

Agencia Internacional de Prensa India
Madero 67-611
Colonia Centro
Mexico DF 06000, Mexico
Tel: +52 5 1031151
Fax: +52 5 7618573

Alianza de Profesionales Indígenas Bilingues
Grupo Purhepecha
Dr Verduzco 424
Paracho 60250, Mexico

Asamblea de Autoridades Mixes de Mexico
AP 1089
Oaxaca 68000, Mexico

Centro Cultural Driki
Chicahuaxtla
Oaxaca 71010, Mexico
Tel: +52 955 20057

Comité de Solidaridad Triqui
63, Avenido Centenario
San Antonio Zomeyucan
Naucalpan 53570, Mexico
Tel: +91 5 5503372
Fax: +91 5 5503372

Consejo de Pueblos Nahuas del Alto Balsas
AP 134
Iguala Guerrero, Mexico
Tel: +52 733 5611321

Consejo Nacional de Médicos Indígenas
Avenida Revolución 1227 PB
Colonia Alpes
Mexico DF 01010, Mexico
Tel: +52 5 5933870
Fax: +52 5 6515194

Ignacio H. Chapela
Estudios Rurales y Asesoria
Oxaca, Mexico
Tel: +1 202 337 6294 (in USA)

Frente Independiente de Pueblos Indios
AP 28-145, Col. Centro, Del.
Mexico DF 06080, Mexico
Tel: +52 5 5252545
Fax: +52 5 2083044

Andres Fabrigas *or*
Jacinto Arias
Instituto Chiapaneco de Cultura
Tuxtla, Gutierrez
Chiapas, Mexico

Arturo Argueta
Instituto Nacional Indigenista
Avenida Revolución 1279, Col. Alpes
Mexico DF 01010, Mexico

Oficina de Rigoberta Menchú
Heriberto Frías 339
Colonia Narvarte
Mexico DF 03020, Mexico
Tel: +52 5 6391492/+52 5 6393091
Fax: +52 5 6380439

Organizaciones Azachis Zapoteca
AP 1137
Oaxaca 68000, Mexico

Programa de Colaboración sobre Medicina Tradicional y Herbolaria (PROCOMITH)
AP 267
29290 San Cristobal de Las Casas
Chiapas, Mexico
Tel: +52 967 83083
Fax: +52 967 82322

Union de Comuneros "Emiliano Zapata" de Michoacán
Carretera Morelia
Mexico no. 3, 725
Poblado Ocolusen
Morelia
Michoacan, Mexico

Robert A. Bye, Jr
Jardin Botanico
Instituto de Biologia
Universidad Nacional Autónoma de México
AP 70-614 Coyoacan
Mexico DF 04510, Mexico

Victor Manuel Toledo
Universidad Nacional Autónoma de México
Instituto de Biologia
AP 41 H
Santa Maria Guido
Morelia
Michoacan 58090, Mexico

Zapotec Nation
Melchor Ocampo 111
Quinta
Sección Guichitán
Oaxaca, Mexico

Nicaragua

Parlamento Indígena de America
Asamblea Nacional
Managua, Nicaragua
Tel: +505 2 673038/+505 2 781029
Fax: +505 2 22370

Sonia Lagos-Witte
Traditional Medicine in the Islands (TRAMIL)
   for Central America and Panama
Enda-Caribe
PO Box 64
Managua, Nicaragua
Tel: +505 2-651 410
Fax: +505 2-667 039

Panama

Asociación Kunas Unidos por Nabguana
AP 536
Via Espana, "Brasilia" Piso 1
Oficina 9-A
Panama 1, Panama
Tel: +507 638879
Fax: +507 693514

Atencio Lopez Martinez
Asociación Napguana
PO Box 536
Panama 1, Panama
Tel/fax: +507 638879

Centro de Desarrollo Indígena
Calle U
Parque Lefevre, No. 75-35
Panama, Panama

Comarca Kuna Yala
AP 2012
Paraiso-Ancon, Panama

Congreso de Organizaciones Indias de Centro América, México y Panamá
AP 536
Panama 1, Panama

Congreso General Guaymi
AP 3-189
Panama 3, Panama
Tel: +507 274917

Congreso General Kuna
AP 87-1610
Panama 7, Panama
Fax: +507 418805

Movimiento de la Juventud Kuna
AP 536
Panama 1, Panama
Tel: +507 228965

George R. Angehr
Smithsonian Tropical Research Institute
AP 2072
Balboa, Panama
Tel: +507 27 6022
Fax: +507 32 5978

Union Nacional de Mujeres Kunas
AP E, Zona S
Panama, Panama
Tel: +507 253911

Europe

Austria

Peter Schwarzbauer
Association of Endangered Peoples, Austria
Mariahilferstrausse 105/11/13
A-1060 Vienna, Austria
Tel: +43 1 597 1176
Fax: +43 1 597 3743
E-mail: h440t4@mail.boku.ac.at

Manfred Schneider
Federal Environmental Agency
Spittelauerlande 5
A-1090 Vienna, Austria
Tel: +43 1 31304, ext. 548
Fax: +43 1 31304, ext. 400
E-mail: schneider@dev01.ubavie.gv.at

Christian Weiner
Morogoro Environmental Charter and Consulting Agency
Apollogasse 14/2/11
A-1070 Vienna, Austria

Herbert Berger *or*
Hildegard Steger-Mauerhofer
Renner Institut
Khleslplatz 12
A-1125 Vienna, Austria

Abdulqawi A. Yusuf
United Nations Industrial Development Organization
Vienna International Centre
PO Box 300
A-1400 Vienna, Austria
Tel: +43 1 211 310
Fax: +43 1 232 156
E-mail: ayusuf@unido.org

Rene Kuppe *or*
Richard Potz
Working Group on Legal Anthropology
Law School
University of Vienna
Freyung 6/Stg 2
A-1010 Vienna, Austria
Tel: +43 1 533 9861
Fax: +43 1 535 1019

Belgium

Geertrui Van Overwalle
Centrum voor intellectuele rechten
Rechtsfaculteit K.U. Leuven
Tiensestraat 41
B-3000 Leuven, Belgium

Frederic Hendrickx
Claes and Partners
Regentlaan 58
B-1000 Brussels, Belgium
Tel: +32 2 502 6262
Fax: +32 2 502 3921

M. Jorgensen
European Commission, Directorate General XI
Office TRMF 1/89
Rue de la Loi 200
B-1049 Brussels, Belgium
Tel: +32 2 296 8753
Fax: +32 2 296 9557

Angela Liberatore
European Commission, Directorate General XII — Science, Research and Development
Rue de la Loi 200
B-1049 Brussels, Belgium
Tel: +32 2 295 2229
Fax: +32 2 296 3024

Johan Bosman *or*
Nathalie Weemaels
KWIA Flemish Support Group for Indigenous Peoples
Breughelstraat 31
B-2018 Antwerp, Belgium
Tel: +32 3 218 8488
Fax: +32 3 230 4540

Thierry Verhelst
South–North Network Cultures and Development
174, rue Joseph II
B-1040 Brussels, Belgium

Luc van Puyvelde
Department of Organic Chemistry
University of Gent
Coupure Links 653
B-9000 Gent, Belgium
Tel: +32 9 264 5959
Fax: +32 9 264 6243
E-mail: luc.vanpuyvelde@rug.ac.be

Linda Bullard
Working Group on Genetic Engineering Policy of the Greens in the European Parliament
MON-316 European Parliament
rue Belliard
B-1047 Brussels, Belgium

Bulgaria

Roman **Ratscov**
5 Poltava strasse, v. 6, ap. 19
Veljco Tarnovo 5000, Bulgaria

Denmark

R.J. Pistorius
Centre for Development Studies
Gammel Kongevej 5
Copenhagen, Denmark
Tel: +31 20 525 4587
Fax: +31 20 525 2086

International Work Group for Indigenous Affairs (IWGIA)
Fiolstraede 10
DK-1171 Copenhagen K, Denmark
Tel: +45 3312 4724
Fax: +45 3314 7749

Veit Koester
National Forest and Nature Agency
Danish Ministry for the Environment
Haraldsgade 53
DK-2100 Copenhagen O, Denmark

Finn **Lynge**
Consultant in Greenland Affairs
Asiatisk Plads 2
DK-1448 Copenhagen K, Denmark
Tel: +45 3392 0441
Fax: +45 3392 1585

Finland

Jukka-Pekka Jappinen
National Board of Waters and the Environment
Nature Conservation Research Unit
PO Box 250
FIN-00101 Helsinki, Finland
Tel: +358 0 6951 711
Fax: +358 0 6951 733

Nordic Sami Council
99980 Utsjoki, Finland
Tel: +358 697 71351/52
Fax: +358 697 71353

Elina Helander
Nordic Sami Institute
PL 31
99980 Utsjoki, Finland
Tel/fax: +358 697 71200

Sami Parliament
99870 Utsjoki, Finland
Tel: +358 697 51181/51182

France

Jean-Pierre Ribaut
Head
Environment Conservation and Management Division
Council of Europe
67075 Strasbourg, France
Tel: +33 88 412 256
Fax: +33 88 412 751

Director
International Commission for the Rights of Aboriginal Peoples (ICRA)
236 Avenue Victor Hugo
94120 Fontenay sous Bois, France

Claudine Friedberg
Musée National d'Histoire Naturelle
Laboratoire d'Ethnobiologie-Biogéographie
57 rue Cuvier
75231 Paris, Cedex 05, France
Tel: +33 1 4079 3425

Survie Touaregue Temoust (Mali, Niger)
252 bis rue Paul Bert
69003 Lyon, France
Tel: +33 72 335187
Fax: +33 72 335187

Gary J. Martin
People and Plants Initiative
Division of Ecological Sciences
Man and the Biosphere Programme
Unesco
7 Place de Fontenoy
75732 Paris, Cedex 07 SP, France
Fax: +33 1 4065 9897

Patrick Bernard
World Foundation for the Safeguard of Indigenous Cultures (WOFIC/FMCA)
236 Avenue Victor Hugo
94120 Fontenay sous Bois, France
Tel: +33 1 43 94 92 88
Fax: +33 1 43 94 02 45

P.J. O'Keefe
6-6 bis. Villa des Entrepreneurs
75015 Paris, France
Tel: +33 1 4578 6005
Fax: +33 1 4575 4118

Germany

Horst Korn
Federal Agency for Nature Conservation
Ina Insel Vilm
D-18581 Lauterbach, Germany
Tel: +49 38301 86130
Fax: +49 38301 86150

Gronka Schneider-Ludorff
Forestcampaign, Greenpeace e.V
20450 Hamburg, Germany
Tel: +49 40 311 86 186/86 199
Fax: +49 40 311 84 141

Manfred Nitsch
Institute of Latin American Studies
Free University of Berlin
Ruedesheimer Strasse 54-56
D-14197 Berlin, Germany
Tel: +49 30 838 3072/838 5588
Fax: +49 30 838 5464

F. Seithel
Institute for Ecology and Action Anthropology
Gaussstrasse 15
D-22765 Hamburg, Germany
Tel: +49 40 390 4455

Lyle Glowka
International Union for the Conservation of Nature and Natural Resources (IUCN)
International Law Centre
Adenauer Allee 214
53113 Bonn, Germany
Tel: +49 228 2692 231
Fax: +49 228 2692 250

Peter E. Stuben
Okozid-Redaktion
Hauweg 62
41066 Monchengladbach, Germany
Tel: +49 2161 631583
Fax: +49 2161 630189

Manfred Niekisch *or*
Martin Schlunder
Oro Verde
Bodenstedt Strasse 4
60594 Frankfurt, Germany
Tel: +49 69 619 039
Fax: +49 69 620 979

Crescentia Freudling
Pesticide Action Network
Simonstrasse 11
90763 Furth, Germany
Tel: +49 911 741 9542
Fax: +49 911 741 9745

Albrecht Gotz von Olenhusen
Rechtsanwalt am Land- und Oberlandesgericht
Lehrbeauftragter an der Hochschule fur
 Film u. Fernsehen
Potsdam, D-79100 Freiburg i. Br.
Lessingstrasse 2, Germany
Tel: +49 331 761 75066/75067/73157
Fax: +49 331 761 72843

Bernd Neugebauer
Trees for People
Institut fur okologische Landnutzung in
 entwicklungsgebieten GmbH
Graf-Durckheim-Weg 7
D 79682 Todtmoos-Rutte, Germany
Tel: +49 7674 8806
Fax: +49 7674 8807

Michael Casimir *or*
Aparna Rao
Institut fur Volkerkundt
Universitat zu Koln
Albertus-Magnus Platz
50923 Koln, Germany

Rudolf **Buntzel**
Hohebuch
74638 Waldenburg, Germany

H. **Eilers**
Loehberg 80
D-45468 Muelheim/Ruhr, Germany
Tel/fax: +49 208 477186

Gudrun **Henne**
Yorckstrasse 75
10965 Berlin, Germany
Tel: +49 30 785 6427
Fax: +49 30 838 5142
E-mail: zedat.fu-berlin.de

Greenland

Arnat Peqatigiit Kattuffiat (Women's Association of Greenland)
PO Box 239
DK-3900 Nuuk, Greenland
Tel: +299 2 2835/2333
Fax: +299 2 2042

Inuit Circumpolar Conference (Greenland)
PO Box 204
DK-3900 Nuuk, Greenland
Tel: +299 2 3632
Fax: +299 2 3001

Greenland Home Rule Government
PO Box 909
3900 Nuuk, Greenland
Tel: +299 2 3000
Fax: +299 2 4693

KNAPK (Hunters and Fishermen's Association)
PO Box 386
DK-3900 Nuuk, Greenland
Tel: +299 2 2422/+299 2 1300
Fax: +299 2 5715

Sorlak (Umbrella organization for youth
  organizations)
PO Box 505
DK-3900 Nuuk, Greenland
Tel: +299 2 4880
Fax: +299 2 4835

Ireland

C. Spillane
Department of Genetics
Trinity College Dublin
Dublin 2, Ireland
Tel: +353 1 702 1347

Italy

Antonio Onorati *or*
Andrea Gaifami
Centro Internazionale Crocevia
Via Ferraironi 88/G
00172 Rome, Italy
Tel: +39 6 241 3976
Fax: +39 6 242 4177

Massimo Pieri
Cooperativa Tecnico Scientifica de Base
  (COBASE)
23 Via Vitorchiano
00189 Rome, Italy
Tel: +39 6 333 8552
Fax: +39 6 333 0081

Leena M. Kirjavainen
Room B-560 *or*
David Cooper *or*
Cary Fowler
Food and Agriculture Organization
Viale delle Terme di Caracalla
00100 Rome, Italy
Tel: +39 6 52 25 33 51
Fax: +39 6 52 25 31 52

Pablo Eyzaguirre *or*
Toby Hodgkin
International Plant Genetics Resources Institute
  (IPGRI)
Via delle Sette Chiese 142
00145 Rome, Italy
Tel: +39 6 518 921
Fax: +39 6 575 0309
E-mail: ipgri@cgnet.com

Netherlands

Jeroen Breekveldt
Biotechnologie Archief NoGen
Burgstraat 3
NL-6701 Da Wageningen, Netherlands

Gustaaf von Liebenstein
**Centre for International Research and Advisory
  Networks** (CIRAN/Nuffic)
Kortenaerkade 11
PO Box 29777
2502 LT The Hague, Netherlands
Tel: +31 70 426 0321
Fax: +31 70 426 0329
E-mail: lieb@nufficcs.nl

Walter de Boef
**Centre for Plant Breeding and Reproduction
  Research** (CPRO-DLO)
Centre for Genetic Resources
PO Box 16
6700 AA Wageningen, Netherlands
Tel: +31 8370 77076
Fax: +31 8370 18094
E-mail: w.de.boef@cpro.agro.nl

Bertus Haverkort
**Comparing and Supporting Indigenous
  Agricultural Systems** (COMPAS)
Kastanjelaan 5
PO Box 64
3830 AB Leusden, Netherlands
Tel: +31 33 943 086
Fax: +31 33 940 791
E-mail: etc@antenna.nl

Leo van der Vlist
Dutch Centre for Indigenous Peoples (NCIV)
2e Oosterparkstr 274
1009 AB Amsterdam, Netherlands
Tel: +31 20 693 8625
Fax: +31 20 665 2818
E-mail: nciv@antenna.nl

**Information Centre for Low-External-Input and
  Sustainable Agriculture** (ILEIA)
PO Box 64
3830 AB Leusden, Netherlands
Tel: +31 33 943 086
Fax: +31 33 940 791
E-mail: ileia@antenna.nl

Netherlands Committee
**International Union for the Conservation of
  Nature and Natural Resources** (IUCN)
Plantage Middenlaan 2
1018 Amsterdam, Netherlands
Tel: +31 20 626 1732
Fax: +31 29 627 9349
E-mail: iucnnethcomm@gn.apc.org

Akke W. Tick
**Netherlands Organization for International
  Cooperation in Higher Education** (NUFFIC)
Kortenaerkade 11
PO Box 29777
2502 LT The Hague, Netherlands
Tel: +31 70 426 02 60
Fax: +31 70 426 03 99

Arnoud P. van Seters
Rainforest Medical Foundation
Einthovenlaan 8
2105 TJ Heemstede, Netherlands
Tel/fax: +31 23 528 0081
E-mail: rainforest@rulfsw.leidenuniv.nl

**Stichting Papua Volken/Papua Peoples'
   Foundation**
PO Box 237
2600 AE Delft, Netherlands
Tel: +31 15 612023
Fax: +31 15 626646

Inger van der Werf *or*
Paul Wolvekamp
Tropical Forests Department of Both Ends
Damrak 28-30
1012 LJ Amsterdam, Netherlands
Tel: +31 20 623 0823
Fax: +31 20 620 8049

L. Jan Slikkerveer
Leiden Ethnosystems and Development Programme
   (LEAD)
Institute of Cultural and Social Studies
University of Leiden
PO Box 9555
2300 RB Leiden, Netherlands
Tel: +31 71 273 469/273 472
Fax: +31 71 273 619
E-mail: decherin@rulfsw.leidenuniv.nl

Cyprian F. Fisiy
Department of Agrarian Law
University of Wageningen
Hollandsweg 1
6706 KN Wageningen, Netherlands
Tel: +31 8370 84436

**Unrepresented Nations and Peoples Organization
   (UNPO)**
PO Box 85878
2508 CN The Hague, Netherlands
Tel: +31 70 360 3318
Fax: +31 70 360 3346
E-mail: unponl@antenna.nl

Jenne **de Beer**
Prinsenpracht 834E
1017 JM Amsterdam, Netherlands
Tel/fax: +31 26 44 55 101

R.J. **Pistorius**
O.Z. Achterburgwal 237
1012 DL Amsterdam, Netherlands
Tel: +31 20 525 4587
Fax: +31 20 525 2086

Norway

Oystein B. Thommessen
Green Globe Yearbook
Fridtjof Nansen Institute
PO Box 326
N-1324 Lysaker, Norway
Tel: +47 67 538 912
Fax: +47 67 125 047
E-mail: iliseter@ulrik.uio.no

Nordic Sami Institute
Guovdageanidnu
9520 Kautokeino, Norway
Tel: +47 7848 5000
Fax: +47 7848 6866

**Norske Reindriftsamers Landsforbund/
   Norwegian Sami Reindeer Herders' Association**
PO Box 508
9001 Tromso, Norway
Tel: +47 7765 8599
Fax: +47 7765 8719

**Norske Samers Riksforbund/Norwegian Sami
   National Association**
PO Box 173
9520 Kautokeino, Norway
Tel: +47 7848 6955
Fax: +47 7848 6975

**Samenes Landsforbund/Sami National
   Association**
PO Box 173
9845 Tana, Norway
Tel: +47 7892 8450
Fax: +47 7892 8559

Sami Parliament
PO Box 144
9730 Karasjok, Norway
Tel: +47 7846 7100
Fax: +47 7846 66949

Hanne Svarstad
SUM
University of Oslo
PO Box 1106 Blindern
0317 Oslo, Norway
E-mail: Hanne.svarstad@sum.uio.no

Russian Federation

**Association of the Indigenous Peoples of the
   North of Russia, Siberia and Far East of
   the Russian Federation**
PO Box 121248
Moscow, Russian Federation
Tel: +7 95 2434159
Fax: +7 95 2434158

Inuit Circumpolar Conference
(Russian Federation)
Lavrentia
Chukotka 686940, Russian Federation
Tel: Chukotka 22437
Fax: Chukotka 42460

Spain

Nelson Alvarez *or*
Henk Hobbelink
Genetic Resources Action International (GRAIN)
Girona 25, pral.
E-08010 Barcelona, Spain
Tel: +34 3 301 1381
Fax: +34 3 301 1627
E-mail: grain@gn.apc.org

Manuel Illescas
Spanish Patent and Trade Marks Office
1 Panama Street
28071 Madrid, Spain
Tel: +34 1 349 5310
Fax: +34 1 457 2586

WATU/Acción Indígena
c/o Villalar 4 Bajo
28001 Madrid, Spain
Tel/fax: +34 1 431 3116
E-mail: watu@mad.servicom.es

Sweden

Gun Rudquist
Naturskydds Foreningen
PO Box 4625
Stockholm 116 91, Sweden
Tel: +46 8 702 6506
Fax: +46 8 702 0855

Jakob von Uexkull
Right Livelihood Award Foundation
Box 15072
S-104 65 Stockholm, Sweden
Tel: +46 8 702 0340
Fax: +46 8 702 0338

Same Atnam
Stationsgatan 2
933 00 Arvidsjaur, Sweden
Tel: +46 960 11500/11540/11553
Fax: +46 960 10150

Sami Parliament
Geologgatan 4
98131 Kiruna, Sweden
Tel: +46 980 82702
Fax: +46 980 83541

Arno Rosemarin
Stockholm Environment Institute
Box 2142
S-103 14 Stockholm, Sweden
Tel: +46 8 723 0260
Fax: +46 8 723 0348
E-mail: seihq@nordnet.se

**Svensker Samernas Riksforbund/
Swedish Sami National Association**
Brogatan 5
90325 Umea, Sweden
Tel: +46 90 141180
Fax: +46 90 124564

Daphne Thuvesson
Forests, Trees and People Programme
International Rural Development Strategy
Swedish University of Agricultural Sciences
PO Box 7005
S-75007 Uppsala, Sweden
Tel: +46 18 672 371
Fax: +46 18 671 209
E-mail: ftpp.network@irdc.slu.se

Switzerland

Bruno Manser
Bruno-Manser-Foundation Switzerland
Heuberg 25
CH-4051 Basel, Switzerland
Tel: +41 61 261 9474
Fax: +41 61 261 9473

**Centre for Applied Studies in International
Negotiations** (CASIN)
11a Aveue de la Paix
1202 Geneva, Switzerland
Tel: +41 22 734 8950
Fax: +41 22 733 6444

Julian Burger
UN Working Group on Indigenous Populations
Centre for Human Rights
Palais des Nations, Room D-413
1211 Geneva 10, Switzerland
Tel: +41 22 917 3413
Fax: +41 22 917 0213

Heinrich H. Peter
Biotechnology Research
Ciba-Geigy Ltd
K-681.2.42
CH-4002 Basel, Switzerland
Tel: +41 61 696 4654
Fax: +41 61 696 4069

Michel Pimbert
Genetic Resources Action International (GRAIN)
Chemin en Purian 3
CH-1197 Prangins, Switzerland
Tel: +41 22 362 6389
Fax: +41 22 361 6349

Brigitte Vonasch
Incomindios Switzerland
Schitzenmattstrasse 37
4051 Basel, Switzerland
Tel: +41 61 272 7249
Fax: +41 61 272 7181

Indigenous Peoples' Centre for Documentation,
Research and Information (DOCIP)
14 Avenue de Trembley
CH-1209 Geneva, Switzerland
Tel: +41 22 740 3433
Fax: +41 22 740 3454

International Academy of the Environment
Chemin de Conches 4
CH-1231 Conches
Geneva, Switzerland
Tel: +41 22 789 1311
Fax: +41 22 789 2538

Lee Swepston
Coordinator for Human Rights Questions
International Labour Organization
4 route des Morillons
CH-1211 Geneva 22, Switzerland

Miges Baumann
Swissaid
Jubilaumsstrasse 60
3000 Bern 6, Switzerland
Tel: +41 31 351 3311
Fax: +41 31 351 2783
E-mail: swissaid@igc.apc.org

Jeffrey A. McNeely
World Conservation Union
International Union for the Conservation of
   Nature and Natural Resources
Rue du Mauverney 28
CH 1196 Gland, Switzerland
Tel: +41 22 999 0001
Fax: +41 22 999 0015
E-mail: ccm@hq.iucn.ch

Benta-Giselda Fernandes
2 Avenue des Amazones
CH 1224 Chene-Bougeries
Geneva, Switzerland
Tel/fax: +41 22 349 1442

United Kingdom

Joji Carino
Alliance of the Indigenous-Tribal Peoples of
   the Tropical Forests
23 Bevenden Street
London N1 6BH, UK
Tel: +44 171 251 5893
Fax: +44 171 251 5914
E-mail: morbed@gn.apc.org

Anti-Slavery International
Unit 4 Stableyard
Broomgrove Road
London SW9 9TL, UK
Tel: +44 171 924 9555
Fax: +44 171 738 4110

Barbara Kirsop
Bioline Publications
Stainfield House
Stainfield, Bourne
Lincs PE10 0RS, UK
Tel: +44 1778 570 618
Fax: +44 1778 570 175
E-mail: bio@biostrat.demon.co.uk

T. Gordon Roddick
The Body Shop International
Watersmead
Littlehampton
West Sussex BN17 6LS, UK

Robert C.J. Carling
Chapman and Hall
2-6 Boundary Row
London SE1 8HN, UK
Tel: +44 171 865 0066
Fax: +44 171 522 9624/3
E-mail: bcarling@chall.co.uk

Martin Hyndman
Derwent Information Ltd
14 Great Queen Street
London WC2B 5DF, UK
Tel: +44 171 344 2800
Fax: +44 171 344 2911
E-mail: mhyndman@derwent.co.uk

Earth Love Fund
Belsyre Court
57 Woodstock Road, 1st floor
Oxford OX2 6HU, UK
Tel: +44 1865 511297
Fax: +44 1865 311383

Nicholas Hildyard
The Ecologist
Agriculture House
Bath Road
Sturminster Newton
Dorset DT10 1DU, UK
Tel: +44 01258 473 476
Fax: +44 01258 473 748
E-mail: ecologist@gn.apc.org

Farhana Yamin
Foundation for International Environmental Law
   and Development (FIELD)
School for Oriental and African Studies
University of London
46-47 Russell Square
London WC1B 4JP, UK
Tel: +44 171 637 7950
Fax: +44 171 637 7951
E-mail: field@gn.apc.org

Ed Posey
The Gaia Foundation
18 Well Walk
Hampstead
London NW3 1LD, UK
Tel: +44 171 435-5000
Fax: +44 171 431-0551
E-mail: gaiafund@gn.apc.org

Julie Sheppard
The Genetics Forum
3rd floor, 5-11 Worship Street
London EC2A 2BH, UK
Tel: +44 171 638 0606
Fax: +44 171 628 0817
E-mail: geneticforum@gn.apc.org

Gerry Bodeker
GIFTS of Health
Department of Dermatology
The Churchill
Headington
Oxford OX3 7LJ, UK
Tel: +44 1865 228274
Fax: +44 1865 228260

George Simon
Guyanese Organisation of Indigenous Peoples
Basement Flat
19 Highbury Hill
London N5 1FU, UK
Tel: +44 171 359 5931

Hugh Synge
Plant Talk
49 Kelvedon Close
Kingston upon Thames
Surrey KT2 5LF, UK
Fax: +44 181 974 5127

Catherine Cotton
Department of Biological Sciences
Whitelands College
Roehampton Institute of Higher Education
West Hill
London SW15 3SN, UK
Tel: +44 181 392 3534
Fax: +44 181 392 3531

Alison Hoare
Centre for Economic Botany
Royal Botanic Gardens Kew
Richmond
Surrey TW9 3AB, UK
Tel: +44 181 332 5771
Fax: +44 181 332 5278
E-mail: a.hoare@rbgkew.org.uk

Stephen Corry
Survival International
11-15 Emerald Street
London WC1N 3QL, UK
Tel: +44 171 2421441

Hector L. MacQueen
University of Edinburgh
Department of Private Law, Old College
South Bridge
Edinburgh EH8 9YL, UK
Tel: +44 131 650 2060
Fax: +44 131 662 0724
E-mail: eusl07@srv0.law.ed.ac.uk

Roy F. Ellen
Eliot College
University of Kent
Canterbury CT2 7NS, UK
Tel: +44 1227 764 000
Fax: +44 1227 475 471
E-mail: rfe@ukc.ac.uk

Brian Morris
Goldsmiths College
University of London
Lewisham Way, New Cross
London SE14 6NW, UK
Tel: +44 181 692 7171

Jeremy Harrison
Manager, Protected Areas
World Conservation Monitoring Centre
219 Huntingdon Road
Cambridge CB3 0DL, UK
Tel: +44 1223 277314
Fax: +44 1223 277136
E-mail: jerryh@wcmc.org.uk

Marcus Colchester
World Rainforest Movement
8 Chapel Row
Chadlington
Oxford OX7 3NA, UK
Tel: +44 1608 676691
Fax: +44 1608 676743
E-mail: wrm@gn.apc.org

Alan Hamilton
World Wide Fund for Nature — UK
Panda House
Catteshall Lane
Godalming
Surrey GU7 1XR, UK
Tel: +44 1483 426444
Fax: +44 1483 426409

John A. Burton
World Wide Land Conservation Trust
Old Mission Hall
Sibton Green
Saxmundham
Suffolk, UK
Tel: +44 1728 668 501
Fax: +44 1728 668 680

Andrew **Gray**
15 St Anne's Road
Headington
Oxford OX3 8NN, UK
Tel: +44 1865 750455
Fax: +44 1865 741118

George **Monbiot**
82 Percy Street
Oxford OX4 3AD, UK
Tel: +44 1865 724 360

Peter **Parkes**
27 Lincoln Road
Oxford OX1 4TB, UK
Tel: +44 1865 722 292
Fax: +44 1865 694 1140

North America
Canada

Apamuwek Institute
Eskasoni NS, Canada B0A 1J0
Tel: +1 902 379 2631
Fax: +1 902 379 2361

Keith Conn
Assembly of First Nations
55 Murray Street, 5th floor
Ottawa ON, Canada K1N 5M3
Tel: +1 613 236 0673
Fax: +1 613 238 5780

Assembly of Manitoba Chiefs
400-286 Smith Street
Winnepeg MN, Canada R3C 1K4
Tel: +1 204 956 0610
Fax: +1 204 956 2109

Baffin Region Inuit Association
PO Box 219
Iqaluit NT, Canada X0A 0H0
Tel: +1 819 979 5391
Fax: +1 819 979 4325

Timothy Johns
Centre for Nutrition and the Environment of Indigenous Peoples (CINE)
McGill University, Macdonald Campus
21,111 Lakeshore
Sainte Anne-de-Bellevue PQ, Canada H0X 3V9
E-mail: johns@agradm.lan.mcgill.ca

Julian T. Inglis
Centre for Traditional Knowledge
135 Hawthorne Avenue
Ottawa ON, Canada K1S 0B2
Tel: +1 613 232 0452
E-mail: jtinglis@magi.com

Confederacy of Treaty Six First Nations
10621 - 100 Avenue, Suite 350
Edmonton AB, Canada T5J 0B3
Tel: +1 403 944 0334
Fax: +1 403 944 0346

Council for Yukon Indians
22 Nisutlin Drive
Whitehorse YT, Canada Y1A 3S5
Tel: +1 403 667 7631
Fax: +1 403 668 6577

Cultural Survival Canada
200 Isabella, Suite 304
Ottawa ON, Canada K1S 1V7
Tel: +1 613 237 5361
Fax: +1 613 237 1547
E-mail: csc@web.apc.org

Tara Cullis
The David Suzuki Foundation
West 4th Avenue
Vancouver BC, Canada V6K 4S2
Tel: +1 604 732 4228
Fax: +1 604 732 0752

Dene Cultural Institute
PO Box 570
Hay River NT, Canada X0E 0R0
Tel: +1 403 874 8480
Fax: +1 403 874 3867
E-mail: denecul@internorth.com

Dene Nation
PO Box 2338
Yellowknife NT, Canada X1A 2P7
Tel: +1 403 873 4081
Fax: +1 403 920 2254

Mary Simon
Ambassador for Circumpolar Affairs
Department of Foreign Affairs
125 Sussex Drive, Tower B-4
Ottawa ON, Canada
Fax: +1 613 944 1852

The Eastern Door
PO Box 326
Kahnawake PQ, Canada J0L 1B0
Tel: +1 514 635 3050
Fax: +1 514 635 8479

Federation of Newfoundland Indians
General Delivery
Benoit's Cove NF, Canada A0L 1A0
Tel: +1 709 789 2797

Federation of Saskatchewan Indian Nations
109 Hodsman Road
Regina SK, Canada S4N 5W5
Tel: +1 306 721 2822
Fax: +1 306 721 2707

Four Directions Council
Eskasoni Indian Reserve
Eskasoni NS, Canada B0A 1J0
Tel: +1 902 379 2361
Fax: +1 902 379 2361

Four Nations Administration
PO Box 279
Hobbema AB, Canada T0C 1N0
Tel: +1 403 585 3840
Fax: +1 403 585 2282

Helena Laraque *or*
Cindy Gilday
Department of Renewable Resources
Government of the Northwest Territories
600, 5102 - 50th Avenue
Yellowknife NT, Canada X1A 3S8
Tel: +1 403 873 7080
Fax: +1 403 873 0221

Grand Council of the Crees
24 Bayswater Avenue
Ottawa ON, Canada K1Y 2E4
Tel: +1 613 761 1655
Fax: +1 613 761 1388

Grand Council of the Micmacs
38 Micmac Crescent
PO Box 1320
Sydney NS, Canada B2N 2P4
Tel: +1 902 539 5116

Indian Association of Alberta
PO Box 516
Stony Plain Reserve
Winterburn AB, Canada T0E 2N0
Tel: +1 403 470 5751
Fax: +1 403 470 3077

Indian Governments of Saskatchewan
109 Hodsman Road
Regina SK, Canada S4N 5W5
Tel: +1 306 721 2822
Fax: +1 306 721 2707

Alejandro Argumedo
Indigenous Peoples Biodiversity Network (IPBN)
Cultural Survival Canada
200 Isabella Street, Suite 304,
Ottawa ON, Canada K1S 1V7
Tel: +1 613 237 5361
Fax: +1 613 237 1547
E-mail: ipbn@web.apc.org (IPBN) *or*
csc@web.apc.org (Cultural Survival)

Indigenous Survival International
Department for Natural Resources
Yellow Knife NY, Canada
Tel: +1 403 920 3391
Fax: +1 403 873 0114

Indigenous Women's Network
PO Box 358
Moose Factory ON, Canada P0L 1W0
Tel: +1 705 658 4731
Fax: +1 705 658 4487

Information Network of Indigenous Peoples of the Americas
54 Lochearne Street
Hamilton ON, Canada L8R 1W1
Tel: +1 416 523 7356
Fax: +1 416 523 7356

Innu Tipatshimun Mashineikantsiuap
Sheshatshit
Nitassinan LB, Canada A0P 1M0
Tel: +1 709 497 8794
Fax: +1 709 497 8396

International Organization of Indigenous Resource Development
PO Box 370
Hobbema AB, Canada T0C 1N0
Tel: +1 403 585 3038
Fax: +1 403 585 2025

Inuit Broadcasting Corporation
251 Laurier Avenue W, Suite 703
Ottawa ON, Canada K1P 5J6
Tel: +1 613 235 1892
Fax: +1 613 230 8824

Inuit Circumpolar Conference (Canada)
170 Laurier Avenue W, Suite 504
Ottawa ON, Canada K1P 5V5
Tel: +1 613 563 2642
Fax: +1 613 565 3089

Inuit Tapirisat of Canada
170 Laurier Avenue W, Suite 510
Ottawa ON, Canada K1P 5V5
Tel: +1 613 238 8181
Fax: +1 613 238 1991

Inuit Womens' Association
200 Elgin Street, Suite 804
Ottawa ON, Canada K2P 1L5
Tel: +1 613 238 3977
Fax: +1 613 238 1787

Inuvialuit Regional Corporation
PO Box 2120
Inuvik NT, Canada X0E 0T0
Tel: +1 403 979 2419
Fax: +1 403 979 3256

Labrador Inuit Association
PO Box 70
Nain
Labrador, Canada A0P 1L0
Tel: +1 709 922 2942
Fax: +1 709 922 2931

Mikmaq Research Centre
University College of Cape Breton
PO Box 5300
Sydney NS, Canada B1P 6L2
Tel: +1 902 539 5300/567 1520
Fax: +1 902 539 0119

Native Council of Canada
200-384 Bank Street
Ottawa ON, Canada K2P 1Y4
Tel: +1 613 238 3511
Fax: +1 613 230 6273

Native News Network
University of Western Ontario
Social Science Centre, 3rd floor, #3254
London ON, Canada N6A 5C2
Tel: +1 519 661 2111

Native Women's Association of Canada
600-251 Laurier Avenue West
Ottawa ON, Canada K1P 5J6
Tel: +1 613 236 6057
Fax: +1 613 235 4957

Rural Advancement Foundation International
  (RAFI)
71 Bank Street, Suite 504
Ottawa ON, Canada K1P 5N2
Tel: +1 613 567 6880
Fax: +1 613 567 6884
E-mail: rafican@web.apc.org

Tungavik Incorporated
130 Slater Street, Suite 800
Ottawa ON, Canada K1P 6E2
Tel: +1 613 238 1096
Fax: +1 613 238 4131

Union of British Columbia Chiefs
200-73 Water Street
Vancouver BC, Canada V6B 1A1
Tel: +1 604 684 0231
Fax: +1 604 684 5726

Union of New Brunswick Indians
35 Dedam Street
Fredericton NB, Canada E3A 2V2
Tel: +1 506 458 9444
Fax: +1 506 458 2850

Union of Nova Scotia Indians
PO Box 400
Shubenacadie NS, Canada B0N 2H0
Tel: +1 902 758 2346

Union of Ontario Indians
PO Box 711
North Bay ON, Canada P1B 8J8
Tel: +1 705 497 9127
Fax: +1 705 497 9135

Russel Barsh
Native American Studies
University of Lethbridge
Lethbridge AB, Canada T1K 3M4
E-mail: barsh@hg.uleth.ca

World Council of Indigenous Peoples
100 Argyle Avenue, 2nd floor
Ottawa ON, Canada K2P 1B6
Tel: +1 613 230 9030
Fax: +1 613 230 9340

World Indigenous Women's Science Network
Centre on Indigenous Economy
Department of Sociology and Anthropology
Carleton University
Loeb Building, Room C768
Ottawa ON, Canada K1S 5B6
Tel: +1 403 220 6928
Fax: +1 403 282 7269

Lorraine F. **Brooke**
417 St Pierre Street, Suite 503
Montreal PQ, Canada H2Y 2M4
Tel: +1 514 845 7539
Fax: +1 514 845 7446

Petr **Cizek**
292 Miron Drive
Hay River NT, Canada X0E OR2
Tel: +1 403 874 6194
Fax: +1 403 874 2166

Peter **Poole**
4491 Harriet Street
Vancouver BC, Canada K1N 5M3

United States of America

Akwesasne Notes
Mohawk Nation
PO Box 196
Rooseveltown NY, USA 13683
Tel: +1 518 858 9531
Fax: +1 518 575 2064

Alaska Federation of Natives, Inc.
1577 "C" Street, Suite 100
Anchorage AK, USA 99501
Tel: +1 907 274 3611
Fax: +1 907 276 7989

Alaska Native Coalition
PO Box 104024
Anchorage AK, USA 99510-4024
Tel: +1 907 276 0680

Alaska Native Human Resource
  Development Program
707 "A" Street, Suite 205
Anchorage AK, USA 99501
Tel/fax: +1 907 272 9531

Aleutian/Pribilof Islands Association, Inc.
401 E. Fireweed Lane, Suite 201
Anchorage AK, USA 99503-2111
Tel: +1 907 276 2700

American Indian Anti-Defamation League
PO Box 2029
Chinle AZ, USA 86503

American Indian Law Alliance
488 7th Avenue, Room SK
New York NY, USA 10018
Tel: +1 212 268 1347
Fax: +1 212 268 2071

American Indian Movement
PO Box 5672
Berkeley CA, USA 94117
Tel: +1 510 566 0251

Robert F. Barnes
American Society of Agronomy
677 South Segoe Road
Madison WI, USA 53711
E-mail: rbarnes@facstaff.wisc.edu

Edgar J. Asebey
Andes Pharmaceuticals Inc.
PO Box 30420
Bethesda MD, USA 20842

Apache Survival Coalition
PO Box 11814
Tucson AZ, USA 85734
Tel: + 1 602 475 2361

Arctic Village Traditional Council
PO Box 51
Arctic Village AK, USA 99720

Association on American Indian Affairs
245 Fifth Avenue, Suite 1801
New York NY, USA 10016
Tel: +1 212 689 8720
Fax: +1 212 685 4692

Janis B. Alcorn
Biodiversity Support Program, WWF
24th Street NW
Washington DC, USA 20037
Tel: +1 202 293 4800
Fax: +1 202 293 9211
E-mail: alcorn+r%wwfus@micmail.com

Black Hills Teton Sioux Nation
PO Box 383
Pine Ridge SD, USA 57770

George N. Appell
Borneo Research Council
Phillips ME, USA 04966

Margie Macauly
Bristol Bay Native Corporation
PO Box 100220
Anchorage AK, USA 99510

Tom Greaves
Department of Sociology and Anthropology
Bucknell University
Lewisburg PA, USA 17837
Tel: +1 717 524 3406
Fax: +1 717 524 3760
E-mail: greaves@bucknell.edu

Howard R. Berman
California Western School of Law
Cedar Street
San Diego CA, USA 92101

D. Michael Warren
Center for Indigenous Knowledge for Agriculture and Rural Development (CIKARD)
Curtiss Hall
Iowa State University
Ames IA, USA 50011
Tel: +1 515 294 0938
Fax: +1 515 294 6058
E-mail: dmwarren@iastate.edu *or*
s2.dmw@isumvs.bitnet

David Downes
Center for International Environmental Law (CIEL)
1621 Connecticut Avenue NW, Suite 200
Washington DC, USA 20009-1052
Tel: +1 202 332 4840
Fax: +1 202 332 4865
E-mail: ddownes@igc.apc.org

Center for International Indigenous Rights and Development
PO Box 95560
Seattle WA, USA 98145
Tel: +1 206 368 0981
Fax: +1 206 543 9285

Liliana Obregon
Center for Justice and Environmental Law (CEJIL)
1522 K Street NW, Suite 910
Washington DC, USA 20005-1202

David Cleveland *or*
Daniela Soleri
Center for People, Food and Environment
344 South Third Avenue
Tucson AZ, USA 85701
Tel/fax: +1 602 624 5379

Barbara Rose Johnston
Center for Political Ecology
1115 Lennon Way
San José CA, USA 95125
Tel: +1 408 723 8073
Fax: +1 408 978 1660
E-mail: bjohnston@igc.apc.org

Cheryl Eldemar
Central Council Tlingit-Haldi Indian Tribes
Willoughby Avenue, Suite 300
Juneau AK, USA 99801

Marie-Pierre Astier
Companions of Arts and Nature
PO Box 399
Red Hook NY, USA 12571

Steve Rubin
Conservation International
1015 18th Street NW, Suite 1000
Washington DC, USA 20036
Tel: +1 202 429 5660
Fax: +1 202 887 0193
E-mail: lobregon@igc.apc.org

Cook Inlet Tribal Council, Inc.
670 W. Fireweed Lane, Suite 200
Anchorage AK, USA 99503
Tel: +1 907 272 7529
Fax: +1 907 277 9071

Council of Athabascan Tribal Governments
PO Box 126
Fort Yukon AK, USA 99740
Tel: +1 907 662 2587/662 2581

Caroline Wheal
Cousteau Society
Greenbrier Circle, Suite 402
Chesapeake VA, USA 23320-2641

Janet McGowan or
Ted McDonald
Cultural Survival
46 Brattle Street
Cambridge MA, USA 02138
Tel: +1 617 621 3818
Fax: +1 617 621 3814
E-mail: survival@husc.harvard.edu.

Carol J. Piscoya
Department of Community and Regional Affairs
PO Box 1068
Nome AK, USA 99762

Benedict W. Kingsbury
Duke University School of Law
PO Box 90360
Durham NC, USA 27708-0360
Tel: +1 919 613 7059
Fax: +1 919 613 7231
E-mail: kingsbury@faculty.law.duke.edu

Deborah G. Strauss
Diversity
Genetic Resources Communications Systems, Inc.
4905 Del Ray Avenue, Suite 401
Bethesda MD, USA 20814
Tel: +1 301 907 9350
Fax: +1 301 907 9328
E-mail: diversitymag@igc.apc.org

Peter T. Hazlewood
Small Grants Programme
Global Environment Fund
United Nations Development Programme
One United Nations Plaza
New York NY, USA 10017
E-mail: peter.hazlewood@nygate.undp.org

Gwich'in Steering Committee
PO Box 202768
Anchorage AK, USA 99520
Tel: +1 907 258 6814
Fax: +1 907 274 4145

Professor Richard Evans Schultes
Harvard Botanical Museum
Oxford Street
Cambridge MA, USA

Haudenosaunee Land Rights Commission
PO Box 235
Nedrow NY, USA 13120

Katy Moran
The Healing Forest Conservancy
East Coast Office
3521 S Street NW
Washington DC, USA 20007

Dean Suagee
Hobbs, Straus, Dean and Walker
1819 H Street SW, Suite 800
Washington DC, USA 20006

The Hopi Tribe
PO Box 123
Kykotsmovi AZ, USA 86039
Tel: +1 602 734 2441

Melvin Ember
President
Human Relations Area Files
755 Prospect Street
New Haven CT, USA 06511
Tel: +1 203 777 2334
Fax: +1 203 777 2337

Robert T. Coulter
Indian Law Resource Center
508 Stuart Street
Helena MT, USA 59601
Tel: +1 406 449 2006
Fax: +1 406 449 2031

Steven M. Tullberg
Indian Law Resource Center
601 E Street SE
Washington DC, USA 20003
Tel: +1 202 547 2800
Fax: +1 202 547 2803

Indigenous Women's Network
National Office
PO Box 174
Lake Elmo MN, USA 55042
Tel: +1 512 258 3880

Indigenous World Association/Asociación
   Mundo Indigena
275 Grand View Avenue, No. 204
San Francisco CA, USA 94114
Tel: +1 415 647 1966

Kristin Dawkins
Institute for Agriculture and Trade Policy (IATP)
5th Street SE, Suite 303
Minneapolis MN, USA 55414-1546
E-mail: iatp@igc.apc.org

Melody Smith
Institute for Global Ethics
PO Box 563
21 Elm Street
Camden ME, USA 04843

Anthony Arturo
Institute for Public Affairs and Policy Studies
University of Charleston
Charleston SC, USA 29424
Fax: +1 803 953 8140

Wilbur Hoff
International Child Resource Institute
1810 Hopkins Street
Berkeley CA, USA 94707
Tel: +1 510 644 1000
Fax: +1 510 525 4106
E-mail: icri@igc.org

Antonio G. Gonzales
International Indian Treaty Council
123 Townsend Street, Suite 575
San Francisco CA, USA 94107-1907
Tel: +1 415 512 1501
Fax: +1 415 512 1507

William H. Lesser
International Service for the Acquisition of Agri-Biotech Applications (ISAAA)
Department of Plant Breeding and Biometry
260 Emerson Hall
Cornell University
Ithaca NY, USA 14853-1902
Tel: +1 607 255 1724
Fax: +1 607 255 1215

Inuit Circumpolar Conference
3201 "C" Street, Suite 608
Anchorage AK, USA 99503-3934
Tel: +1 907 563 6917
Fax: +1 907 562 0880

K'aayelli Group
PO Box 198
Montezuma Creek UT, USA 85434
Tel: +1 801 587 3225
Fax: +1 801 587 2425

Alexandra Lindgren
Keepers of the Treasures
PO Box 3596
Soldotna AK, USA 99669

Barbara Svarny Carlson
Keepers of the Treasures
PO Box 212646
Anchorage AK, USA 99521-2646

Miranda Wright
Keepers of the Treasures
PO Box 60515
Fairbanks AK, USA 99706

Kodiak Area Native Association
402 Center Avenue
Kodiak AK, USA 99615
Tel: +1 907 486 5725
Fax: +1 907 486 2763

Lakota Sovereignty Organizing Committee
PO Box 5686
Rapid City SD, USA

Robert L. Merriam, Jr
Micro Development Corp.
High Street
Brattleboro VT, USA 05301
Tel: +1 802 254 8569
Fax: +1 802 254 9117

Brian A. Meilleur
Missouri Botanical Garden
Center for Plant Conservation
PO Box 299
St Louis MO, USA 63166-0299
Tel: +1 314 577 9450
Fax: +1 314 577 9465
E-mail: meilleur@mobot.org

Gordon M. Cragg
National Cancer Institute-FCRDC
Fairview Center, Suite 206
PO Box B
Frederick MD, USA 21702-1201
Tel: +1 301 846 5387
E-mail: cragg@dtpvx2.ncifcrf.gov

National Chicano Human Rights Council
4322 West 32nd Avenue
Denver CO, USA 80212
Tel: +1 303 455 8104
Fax: +1 303 936 0438

National Congress of American Indians
900 Pennsylvania Avenue, SE
Washington DC, USA 20003
Tel: +1 202 546 9404
Fax: +1 202 546 3741

National Indian Youth Council, Inc.
318 Elm Street, SE
Albuquerque NM, USA 87102
Tel: +1 505 247 2251
Fax: +1 505 247 4251

Native American Journalists Association
University of Colorado
Campus Box 287
Boulder CO, USA 80309
Tel: +1 303 492 7397
Fax: +1 303 492 0585

Native American Public Broadcasting Consortium
PO Box 83111
Lincoln NE, USA 68501
Tel: +1 402 472 3522
Fax: +1 402 472 1785

Native Lands Research and Policy Institute
809 Copper NW, Suite 200
Albuquerque NM, USA 87102
Tel: +1 505 842 6123
Fax: +1 505 842 6124

Navajo-Hopi Land Commission
PO Box 2549
Window Rock AZ, USA 86515
Tel: +1 602 871 6441
Fax: +1 602 871 7297

Navajo Nation
PO Box 308
Window Rock AZ, USA 86515
Tel: +1 602 871 4941

Brian M. Boom
New York Botanical Garden
Bronx NY, USA 10458
E-mail: bboom@nybg.org

Thomas D. Mays
Office of Technology Development
National Institutes of Health
9000 Rockville Pike, Building 31/Room 4A51
Bethesda MD, USA 20892
Tel: +1 301 496 0477
Fax: +1 301 402 2117
E-mail: mayst%nihcotd1.bitnet@cu.nih.gov

Sarah Lloyd
Siberian Forests Protection Program
Pacific Environment and Resources Center
1055 Fort Cronkhite
Sausalito CA, USA 94965
Tel: +1 415 332 8200
Fax: +1 415 332 8167
E-mail: perc@igc.apc.org

Michael Brown
**Private Voluntary Organization–
Nongovernmental Organization/
Natural Resources Management Project**
c/o World Wide Fund for Nature
1250 24th Street NW
Washington DC, USA 20037
E-mail: browntr%wwfus@mcimail.com

Rainforest Action Network
450 Sansome, Suite 700
San Francisco CA, USA 94111
Tel: +1 415 398-4404
Fax: +1 415 398-2732
E-mail: rainforest@igc.apc.org

Charles Zerner
Rainforest Alliance
65 Bleecker Street
New York NY, USA 10012
Tel: +1 212 677 1900
Fax: +1 212 677 2187

Jason Clay
Rights and Resources
2253 North Upton Street
Arlington VA, USA 22207
Tel/fax: +1 703 524 0092

Hope Shand *or*
Edward Hammond
Rural Advancement Foundation International–USA
PO Box 655
Pittsboro NC, USA 27312
Tel: +1 919 542 1396
Fax: +1 919 542 0069
E-mail: rafiusa@igc.apc.org

Seeds of Change
PO Box 15700
Santa Fe NM, USA 87506-5700

Thomas Carlson *or*
Steven King
Shaman Pharmaceuticals
213 East Grand Avenue
South San Francisco CA, USA 94080-4812
Tel: +1 415 952 7070
Fax: +1 415 873 8367

Adriana Fabra *or*
Neil A.F. Popovic
Sierra Club Legal Defense Fund, Inc.
180 Mongomery Street
San Francisco CA, USA 94104
Tel: +1 415 627 6700
E-mail: san.francisco.scldf@sierraclub.org

**South and Meso American Indian
 Information Center** (SAIIC)
PO Box 28703
Oakland CA, USA 94604
Tel: +1 207 834 4263
Fax: +1 207 834 4264

Southwestern Association on Indian Affairs, Inc.
320 Galisteo St ZY600
Santa Fe NM, USA 87501
Tel: +1 505 983 7647
Fax: +1 505 983 7647

Sovereignty Network of Alaska Native Peoples
HC04 Box 9880
Palmer AK, USA 99645
Tel: +1 907 745 0505
Fax: +1 907 745 6051

June Starr
Department of Anthropology
State University of New York, Stony Brook
Stony Brook NY, USA 11790
Tel: +1 516 751 7707
Fax: +1 516 751 3622

Tlingit and Haida Tribes of Alaska
Andrew P. Hope Building
320 West Willoughby Avenue, Suite 300
Juneau AK, USA 99801-9983
Tel: +1 907 586 1432
Fax: +1 907 586 8970

Tonantzin Land Institute
PO Box 40182
Albuquerque NM, USA 87196-0182
Tel: +1 505 766 9930
Fax: +1 505 766 9931

Traditional Elders Circle
Onondaga Nation
PO Box 200
New York NY, USA 13120

William L. Balee
Department of Anthropology
Tulane University
New Orleans LA, USA 70118
Tel: +1 504 865 5336
Fax: +1 504 865 5338
E-mail: wbalee@mailhost.tcs.tulane.edu

United National Indian Tribal Youth, Inc.
4010 Lincoln Blvd, Suite 202
Oklahoma City OK, USA 73125
Tel: +1 405 424 3010
Fax: +1 405 424 3018

Marcel Viergever
United Nations Development Programme (UNDP)
One United Nations Plaza
New York NY, USA 10017
E-mail: marcelv@undp.org

Gordon L. Pullar
Alaska Native Human Resource Development
  Program
College of Rural Alaska,
University of Alaska
707 A Street, Suite 205
Anchorage AK, USA 99501
Tel: +1 907 272 9531
Fax: +1 907 272 5625
E-mail: anglp1@acadz.alaska.edu

Stephen B. Brush
Department of Applied Behavioural Sciences
University of California, Davis
Davis CA, USA 95616
Tel: +1 916 752 4368
Fax: +1 916 752 5660
E-mail: sbbrush@ucdavis.edu

Susanna Hecht
Graduate School of Public Policy
University of California
Los Angeles CA, USA 90625

Calvin Qualset
Genetic Resource Conservation Program
University of California
Davis CA, USA 95616

Stefano Varese
Native American Studies
University of California
Davis CA, USA 95616
Tel: +1 916 752 0357
Fax: +1 916 752 7097
E-mail: svarese@ucdavis.edu

Elois Ann *or*
Brent Berlin
Department of Anthropology
University of Georgia
Baldwin Hall
Athens GA, USA 30602-1619

Laura C. Merrick
Sustainable Agriculture Program
Department of Applied Ecology and
  Environmental Sciences
University of Maine
5722 Deering Hall
Orono ME, USA 04469-5722
Tel: +1 207 581 2950
Fax: +1 207 581 2999
E-mail: merrick@maine.maine.edu

Tirso Gonzales
Department of Rural Sociology
College of Agricultural and Life Sciences
350 Agriculture Hall
1450 Linden Drive
University of Wisconsin
Madison WI, USA 53706
Tel: +1 608 262 1510
Fax: +1 608 262 6022
E-mail: gonzales@macc.wisc.edu

Jack Kloppenburg
Department of Rural Sociology
College of Agricultural and Life Sciences
340A Agricultural Hall
University of Wisconsin
Madison WI, USA 53076
Tel: +1 608 262 6867
Fax: +1 608 262 6022
E-mail: jrkloppe@facstaff.wisc.edu

Mary N. Layoun
Department of Comparative literature
938 Van Hise Hall
University of Wisconsin
Madison WI, USA 53706-1558
Tel: +1 608 262 9767
Fax: +1 608 262 8570
E-mail: layoun@macc.wisc.edu

James Boyle
Washington College of Law
American University
4801 Massachusetts Ave NW
Washington DC, USA 20016
Tel: +1 202 274 4204
Fax: +1 202 274 4130
E-mail: boyle@postoffice.wcl.american.edu

Walter H. Lewis
Department of Biology
Washington University
PO Box 1137
St Louis MO, USA 63130
E-mail: lewis@biodpt.wustl.edu

Western Shoshone National Council
PO Box 140068
Duckwater NV, USA 89314-0068
Tel: +1 702 863 0227
Fax: +1 702 863 0301

Shelton H. Davis
Social Policy and Resettlement Division,
    Environment Department *or*
Robert Goodland
Environmental Assessment Unit
World Bank
1818 H Street NW
Washington DC, USA 20433
Tel: +1 202 473 3203
Fax: +1 202 477 0565
E-mail: rgoodland@worldbank.org

Walter V. Reid
World Resources Institute
1709 New York Avenue NW
Washington DC, USA 20006
Tel: +1 202 638 6300
Fax: +1 202 638 0036
E-mail: wreid@wri.org

Lori Ann Thrupp
Center for International Development
    and Environment
World Resources Institute
1709 New York Avenue NW
Washington DC, USA 20006

Nancy Lee Peluso
Yale School of Forestry and Environmental Studies
205 Prospect Street,
New Haven CT, USA 06511
Tel: +1 203 432 8930
Fax: +1 203 432 5942

Patricia J. **Cummings**
Bayhills Drive
San Rafael CA, USA 94903
Tel: +1 415 491 1948
Fax: +1 415 491 1240
E-mail: pcummings@ipc.org

Donald N. **Duvick**
PO Box 446
6837 NW Beaver Drive
Johnston IA, USA 50131
Tel: +1 515 278 0861
Fax: +1 515 253 2125
E-mail: duvick@phibred.com

Louise Rosenblatt **Goines**
1479 Harvard Street NW
Washington DC, USA 20009
Tel: +1 202 462 8142

Ellen Hope **Hayes**
Tribal Cultural Resources Consultant
Agate Pt Road NE
Bainbridge Island WA, USA 98110

Carole **Hill**
1197 The By Way NE
Atlanta GA, USA 30306
Tel: +1 404 373 5850
Fax: +1 404 651 1718

Michael F. **Lane**
Consultant
1620 Bolton Street, No. 2
Baltimore MD, USA 21217
Tel/fax: +1 410 462 3053
E-mail: barrenador@nothingness.org

Daniel M. **Putterman**
Biotechnology Consultant
2801 Quebec Street, NW
PO Box 519
Washington DC, USA 20008-1244
E-mail: dputterman@igc.apc.org

Elisabet **Sahtouris**
Massachusetts Avenue NW, No. 543
Washington DC, USA

David J. **Stephenson**
108 South Dexter Street
Denver CO, USA 80222-1053
Tel: +1 303 329 6090
E-mail: DavidS23@aol.com

Mililani B. **Trask**
PO Box 4964
Hilo HI, USA 96720
Tel: +1 808 935 8854
Fax: +1 808 961 2888

Oceania

Australia

Aboriginal and Torres Strait Islander Commission
PO Box 17
Woden
ACT, Australia 2606
Tel: +61 6 2891222
Fax: +61 6 2810772

Aboriginal and Torres Strait Islander Commission News
PO Box 17
Woden
ACT, Australia 2606
Tel: +61 6 2893011
Fax: +61 6 2822854

Aboriginal Hostels Ltd
PO Box 30
Woden
ACT, Australia 2606
Tel: +61 6 2891222
Fax: +61 6 2893874

Aboriginal Reconciliation Council
Locked Bag 14
Queen Victoria Terrace
Parkets
ACT, Australia 2600
Tel: +61 6 2715120
Fax: +61 6 2715168

Helen Ross
Centre for Resource and Environmental Studies
Australian National University
PO Box 4
ACT, Australia 2601
Tel: +61 6 249 2159
Fax: +61 6 249 0757
E-mail: hross@cres.anu.edu.au

Johanna Sutherland
Department of International Relations
Australian National University
PO Box 4
ACT, Australia 2601
Tel: +61 6 249 5111
E-mail: johanna@coombs.anu.edu.au

Alastair Graham
Biodiversity Coalition
c/o PO Cygnet
Tasmania, Australia 7112
Tel: +61 02 951 745
Fax: +61 02 951 964

Central Australian Aboriginal Congress
PO Box 1604
Alice Springs
NT, Australia 5750
Tel: +61 89 523377
Fax: +61 89 530350

Central Australian Aboriginal Media Association
PO Box 2924
Alice Springs
NT, Australia 0871
Tel: +61 089 523744
Fax: +61 089 555219

Central Land Council
PO Box 3321
Alice Springs
NT, Australia 0871
Tel: +61 89 516211
Fax: +61 89 534343

B.O. Rose
Central Land Council
Cross Cultural Land Management Project
PO Box 3321
Alice Springs
NT, Australia 0871
Tel: +61 089 516 255
Fax: +61 089 521 590
E-mail: clcasphbas@peg.apc.org

Iina Torres Strait Islanders Corporation
PO Box 386
South Brisbane
Queensland, Australia 4101
Tel: +61 7 8442140
Fax: +61 7 8449526

Institute for Aboriginal Development
3 South Terrace
PO Box 2531
Alice Springs
NT, Australia 0871
Tel: +61 089 522688
Fax: +61 089 531884

Henrietta Fourmile
Centre for Aboriginal and Torres Strait Islander
 Participation
Research and Development
James Cook University
Cairns Campus
Queensland, Australia
Fax: +61 70 509409

National Aboriginal and Islander Legal Service Secretariat
PO Box 143
Chippendale
NSW, Australia 2008
Tel: +61 76 543352
Fax: +61 76 543182

National Aboriginal Community Controlled Health
PO Box 1174
Strawberry Hills
NSW, Australia 2016
Tel: +61 2 3195823 or 70 515088
Fax: +61 2 3193345 or 70 521482

National Coalition of Aboriginal Organizations
13 Mansfield Street
Glebe
NSW, Australia 2037
Tel: +61 2 6603444
Fax: +61 2 6601924

National Federation of Land Councils
Purnum PO
Victoria, Australia 3278
Tel: +61 55 671003
Fax: +61 55 671298

Ros Sultan
Northern Land Council
9 Rowling St
PO Box 42921
Casuarina
NT, Australia 0811
Tel: +61 89 205 100
Fax: +61 89 452 633

Vratislav Richard Bejsak
Pan Australian Research and Datacollecting Entomological Laboratory (PRDEL)
PO Box 619
Bondi Junction
NSW, Australia 2022
Tel: +61 2 365 5253
Fax: +61 2 369 3962
E-mail: 76711,1261@compuserve.com

John Cordell
Community Resource Management Program
Anthropology-Sociology Department
University of Queensland
Queensland, Australia 4072

David Hyndman
Department of Sociology
University of Queensland
Queensland, Australia 4072
Tel: +61 7 365 3286
Fax: +61 7 365 1544

Donna **Craig**
Level 38
Governor Philip Tower
1 Farrer Place
Sydney
NSW, Australia 2000
Tel: +61 2 241 2122
Fax: +61 2 241 2554

Fiji

Clark Peteru
Pacific Concerns Resource Centre, Inc.
83 Amy Street
Toorak, Private Mail Bag
Suva, Fiji
Tel: +679 304 649
Fax: +679 304 755

Ruth E. Lechte
World YWCA
Box 9874
Nadi Airport PO
Fiji

Hawaii

Ka Lahui Hawai'i (The Sovereign Nations of Hawaii)
PO Box 4964
Hilo HI, USA 96720
Tel: +1 808 961 2888 or 969 7617
Fax: +1 808 935 8854

Pacific Asia Council of Indigenous Peoples
86-649 Puuhulu Road
Wai'anae HI, USA 96792-2723
Tel: +1 808 696 5157 or +1 808 696 7774

Pro-Hawaiian Sovereignty Working Group
3333 Ka'ohinani Drive
Honolulu HI, USA 96817
Tel: +1 808 595 6691
Fax: +1 808 526 2027

Mililani B. **Trask**
PO Box 4964,
Hilo HA, USA 96720

New Caledonia

Front de Libération Nationale Kanak Socialiste
PO Box 288
Commune du Mont-Dore, New Caledonia
Tel: +867 273129
Fax: +687 277016

New Zealand

Federation of Maori Authorities
PO Box 10758
Wellington, Aotearoa New Zealand
Tel: +64 4 4728080
Fax: +64 4 4733276

Maori Congress
PO Box 5079
Wellington, Aotearoa New Zealand
Tel: +64 4 4884602
Fax: +64 4 4994608

Aroha Te Pareake Mead
Deputy Convenor
Maori Congress
PO Box 13-177
Johnsonville
Wellington, Aotearoa New Zealand
E-mail: aroham@nzonline.ac.nz

Maori Women's Welfare League
24 Burnell Avenue
Wellington, Aotearoa New Zealand
Tel: +64 4 4736451
Fax: +64 4 4996802

Diane Crengle
Ministry for the Environment
84 Boulcott Street
PO Box 10362
Wellington, Aotearoa New Zealand
Tel: +64 4 473 4090
Fax: +64 4 471 0195

Moana Jackson
Nga Kaiwhakamarama I Nga Ture
110 Cuba Street
PO Box 6528
Wellington, Aotearoa New Zealand
Tel: +64 4 828 843

Pauline Tangiora
Rongomaiwahine Tribe
PO Box 33 Mahia
Hawkes Bay, Aotearoa New Zealand
Tel: +64 6 837 5816

Wellington Maori Legal Service
139-141 Featherstone Street
PO Box 1268
Wellington, Aotearoa New Zealand
Tel: +64 4 473 1249
Fax: +64 4 473 1781

Donna **Hall**
PO Box 10-205
Wellington, Aotearoa New Zealand
Tel: +64 4 499 1195
Fax: +64 4 499 2008

Maui **Solomon**
Molesworth Chambers
34 Molesworth Street
PO Box 3458
Wellington, Aotearoa New Zealand
Tel: +64 4 472 6744
Fax: +64 4 499 6172

Papua-New Guinea

Bougainville Interim Government
34 Darvall Road
Eastwood 2122
Melbourne, Australia
Tel: +61 2 8047602

Republic of Bougainville
Mount Hamilton
Hamilton Avenue
Bowral
NSW, Australia 2576
Tel: +61 48 621001
Fax: +61 48 621001

Tahiti

Ligue Polynesienne Indépendante des Droits de l'Homme
PO Box 4611
Papeete, Tahiti
Tel: +689 521371
Fax: +689 572880

South America

Argentina

Amerindia por los Derechos de los Pueblos Indios
Avenido Independencia 2287
1225 Buenos Aires, Argentina
Tel: +54 1 9427626/+54 1 5036244
Fax: +54 1 9515226

Asociación de Comunidades del Pueblo Guaraní
Casilla de Correo No. 2
3332 Capioví
Provincia de Misiones, Argentina
Tel: +54 75238280
Fax: +54 75236578

Asociación Indígena de la República de Argentina
Balbastro 1790
1406 Buenos Aires, Argentina

Centro Kolla
Casilla de Correo 305, Sucursal 3-B
1403 Buenos Aires, Argentina
Tel: +54 1 362 8303

Centro Mocoví "Ialek Lav'a"
Casilla de Correo 36
2728 Melincué
Santa Fe, Argentina
Tel: +54 42 215584
Fax: +54 42 661119

Comisión Interamericana de Juristas Indígenas
(Cordinación en Argentina)
Viamonte 1481, 7 "A"
1055 Buenos Aires, Argentina
Tel: +54 1 406147
Fax: +54 1 9411311

Instituto Qheshwa Jujuymanta
Alvear 966, local 6
4600 San Salvador de Jujuy, Argentina
Tel: +54 51 803 431

Organización de las Comunidades Indígenas del Valle Calchaqui
c/o Comunidad de Amaicha del Valle
Ruta 307 - Kilometro 118
4137 Amaicha del Valle
Tucumán, Argentina
Tel: +54 8 922 1076
Fax: +54 8 922 1076

Bolivia

Asociación Nacional de Radialistas y Comunicadores en Idiomas Nativos de Bolivia
Casilla 2116
La Paz, Bolivia
Tel: +591 2 353048
Fax: +591 2 391365

Central de Cabildos Indígenas Moxeños
Casilla 58
Trinidad
Beni, Bolivia

Centro Cultural de Jóvenes Aymaras
Provincia Larecaja
Casilla no. 14358
La Paz, Bolivia

Centro de Difusión Ideológica de la Mujer Aymara
Nicasio Cardoso no. 450
Zona Central Mezzanine
La Paz, Bolivia
Tel: +591 2 354874
Fax: +591 2 354874

Centro Unión Achiri
Urbanización Unión Achiri
El Alto
Casilla 12043
La Paz, Bolivia

Comité de Pueblos y Comunidades Indígenas
Casilla 4213
Santa Cruz, Bolivia

Confederación Indígena del Oriente Chaco y
    Amazonía de Bolivia Villa 10 de Mayo
Casilla 4213
Santa Cruz de la Sierra, Bolivia
Tel: +591 3 469714/460714

Coordinadora Nacional de Pueblos Indígenas
    de Bolivia
Casilla 14358
La Paz, Bolivia
Tel: +591 2 871715

Federación Especial de Trabajadores Campesinos
    del Trópico de Cochabamba
Bolivar E-0862
Cochabamba, Bolivia
Tel: +591 4 24560
Fax: +591 4 24560

Movimiento Indio Tupaj Katari Mitka-I
Calle 3 esq.
Jorge Carrasco no. 2112
Zona 12 de Octubre
El Alto
La Paz, Bolivia
Tel: +591 2 924790

Movimiento Revolucionario Tupaj Katari de
    Liberación de Bolivia
Casilla 9133
La Paz, Bolivia
Tel: +591 2 783612

Organización de Mujeres Aymaras del Kollasuyo
Casilla 13195
La Paz, Bolivia
Tel: +591 20 6938625
Fax: +591 20 6652818

Partido Indio de Liberación
Calle Ingavi
Casilla 1426
La Paz, Bolivia

Taller de Historia Oral Andina
Casilla 9628
939, Avenido Baptista
Zona Garita
La Paz, Bolivia
Tel: +591 2 373021

Brazil

Associaçao Indigena Terena da Cachoeirinha
Posta Restante - Miranda
Aldeia Cachoeirinha
Mato Grosso do Sul 79112-270, Brazil

Director
Associaçao Matarela — Povo Surui
Linha 11, zona rural, Riozinho
Cacoal/RO, CEP 78960, Brazil

Director
Associaçao Xavante de Pimentel Barbosa
CP 77
Nova Xavantina/Mato Grosso CEP 78690-000,
Brazil

Director
MAGUTA
Centro de Documentaçao Pesquisa do
    Alto Solimoes
Rua Gen. Carrumbet, 221
Benjamim Constant/AM CEP 69630, Brazil

Director
Centro de Trabalho Indigenista (CTI)
Rua Fidalga 584
Sao Paulo 054232, Brazil

Comissiao pela Criaçao do Parque Yanomami
Rua Manoel da Nóbrega 111/32
Sao Paulo 04001, Brazil
Tel: +55 11 2891200
Fax: +55 11 2846997

Marcos Terena
Comité Intertribal Memoria e Ciencia (ITC)
Sqn 215, Bloco F, Apto 506
Brasilia 70.874.060, Brazil
Tel/fax: +55 61 347 1337

Conselho Indígena de Roraima
Rua Sebastiao Diniz, No. 1672 W
Boa Vista R R 69300, Brazil
Tel: +55 95 2245761

Coordenaçao Organizaçoes Indígenas de
    Amazonia Brasileira
Avenido Ayrao 235
Matinha
Manaus AM 69025-290, Brazil
Tel: +55 92 2330548
Fax: +55 92 2330209

Director
Federacao das Organizaçoes Indígenas do
    Rio Negro (FOIRN)
Av. Alvaro Maia, 69
CP 31
Sao Gabriel da Cachoeira AM, CEP 69750, Brazil

Alexandre Harkaly
Instituto Biodinamro
CP 321
Botacatu SP 18603-970, Brazil
Tel: +55 14 975 9011/14 922 5066
Fax: +55 14 975 9011/14 922 3648

Luis Carlos Quaresma Lemos
Instituto Ideia
Rua Guajajaras 910, Sala 1814
Belo Horizonte MG 30180-100, Brazil
Fax: +55 31 271 2401/226 3974

Rogerio Konzen
Instituto Verde Vida
Rua Nossa Senhora Da Paz S/N
Colombo-Curitiba-PR, Brazil
Fax: +55 41 223 8490

Ailton Krenak
Nucleo de Cultura Indígena (NCI)
CP 25945
Sao Paulo CEP 05599-970, Brazil
Tel: +55 11 813 1754
Fax: +55 11 211 9996

Nucleo de Direitos Indígenas
SQS-106, Bloco A
AP 102
Brasilia DF 70345, Brazil
Tel: +55 61 2434814

Potiguara Indigenous Council
Potiguara Indigenous Park
Aldeia do Forte do Tamba
Município da Baia da Traiçao
Paraíba 58295, Brazil
Tel: +55 83 2961009
Fax: +55 83 2922765

Uniao das Naçoes Indígenas
Praca Ennio Barbata
s/n-Caxingui
Sao Paulo SP 05517, Brazil
Tel/fax: +55 11 211 9996

Afranio Aragao Craveiro or
Maria Iracema L. Machado or
F.J.A Matos
Laboratorio de Produtos Naturais
Universidade Federal do Ceara
CP 12200
Fortaleza-Ceara, Brazil
Tel: +55 85 243 7721
Fax: +55 85 223 0872

Elaine Elisabetsky
Universidade Federal do Rio Grande do Sul
CP 5072
Porto Alegre 90041-970, Brazil
Tel: +55 51 226 7191
Fax: +55 51 226 7191
E-mail: elisabetsky@ugrgs.br

Director
Vitae Civilis
CP 11260
Sao Paulo SP 05422-970, Brazil
Tel: +55 11 815 8524
Fax: +55 11 815 8524

Chile

Aukin Wallmapu Ngulam: Consejo de Todas las Tierras
Miraflores 1326
Casilla 148
Temuco
Novena Región, Chile
Tel: +56 45 234542

Comite Exterior Mapuche
6 Lodge Street
Bristol, United Kingdom BS1 SLR
Tel: +44 272 279391/732126

Comunidad Cultural Aymara para el Desarollo Andino "Pachu-Aru"
Casilla 1422
Los Piñones 2041
Arica, Chile

Congreso Nacional de Pueblos Indígenas
Claro Solar 394
Temuco
Novena Región, Chile
Tel: +56 45 238798

Director
Consejo de todas las tienes
Miraflores 1326
Casilla 448
Temuco, Chile

Consejo Nacional de Pueblos Indígenas de Chile
Teatinos 371, Oficina 405
Casilla 53499
Correo Central
Santiago, Chile
Tel: +56 2 6958052

Delegación Mapuche Huilliche
Pedro Montt 1040
Osorno
Decima Region, Chile

Carmen Artigas
Division of Natural Resources and Energy
Economic Commission for Latin America and the Caribbean (ECLAC)
Casilla 179
D-Santiago, Chile
Tel: +56 2 208 5051/206 1519
Fax: +56 2 208 1946/208 0252

Federación Unión "Aymar-Marka"
Patricio Lynch 1496
Iquique Región 1, Chile
Tel: +56 57 428900
Fax: +56 57 428900

Organización Mapuche "AD-MAPU"
Cantin 1635, Casilla 1676
Temuco
Novena Región, Chile

Sociedad Mapuche Newën
Carrera 87, Casilla 1429
Temuco
Novena Región, Chile
Tel: +56 45 238519

Florinda **Cheuquepan Arzola**
V. Mackenna, 260, 3er piso
Oficina 5, Camilla 260
Temuco, Chile
Fax: +56 45 210 210

Camila **Montecinos**
Casilla 16557
Correo 9
Santiago, Chile
E-mail: gcu@biodiv.mic.cl

Colombia

Centro de Cooperación Indígena
Calle 20 1-26, Apartado 502, Blocque A
Bogota, Colombia
Tel: +57 1 2819202
Fax: +57 1 2447015

Consejo Regional Indígena Del Cauca
AP 516
Popayan
Cauca, Colombia
Tel: +57 1413

Juan Mayr Maldonado *or*
Rosario Ortiz *or*
Pilar Barrera
Fundación Pro-Sierra Nevada de Santa Marta
Calle 74, No. 2-86, Piso 2
Bogota, Colombia
Tel/fax: +57 1 217 3487
E-mail: snevada@cdcdnet.uniandes.edu.co

Movimiento de Autoridades Indígenas de Colombia
AP 11328
Cali, Colombia
Tel: +57 923 838639

Organización Indígena de Antioquía
Carrera 49, no. 63-85
Prado Centro-Medellín
AP 53433
Medellín, Colombia
Tel: +57 4 2548130/2844845
Fax: +57 4 2844013

Organización Nacional Indígena de Colombia
Calle 13, no. 4-38
AP 32395
Santafe de Bogotá, Colombia
Tel: +57 1 342305 /2846815/2842168
Fax: +57 1 28481

Ecuador

Acción Ecologica
Casilla 17-15-246C
Quito, Ecuador
Tel: +593 2 526 994
Fax: +593 2 547 516
E-mail: verde@acecol.ec

Centro de Comunicación para la Educación Popular
Quijano y Ordonez Apartado 392
Latacunga Cotopaxi, Ecuador

Confederación de Nacionalidades Indígenas de la Amazonía Ecuatoriana
Avenida 6 de Diciembre 159 Pazmiño
Edificio Parlamento, Oficina 408
Quito, Ecuador
Tel: +593 2 543973
Fax: +593 2 548668

Confederación de Nacionalidades Indígenas del Ecuador
CP 17-150092-C, Sucursal 15
Quito, Ecuador
Tel: +593 2 248930
Fax: +593 2 442271

Valerio Grefa
Coordinadora de Organizaciones Indigenas de la Cuenca Amazónica (COICA)
Calle Alemania 832 y Mariana de Jesus
Quito, Ecuador

Federación de Centros Shuar-Achuar
Sucúa
Domingo Comín 17-38
Morona Santiago
Región Amazónica, Ecuador
Fax: +593 7 740108

Federación Nacional de Organizaciones Campesinas Indígenas
Versalles 1008 J. Carrión, Piso 4
Quito, Ecuador
Tel: +593 2 526906
Fax: +593 2 236690

Guyana

Asociación de Pueblos Amerindios de Guyana
c/o 27 Brickdam
PO Box 10720
Georgetown, Guyana
Tel: +592 2 61789
Fax: +592 2 61789

A. Khemraj
Sustainable Development and Intellectual Property
Ministry of Foreign Affairs: Environment
Takuba Lodge, Sout Road
Georgetown, Guyana
Tel: +592 2 61607/09
Fax: +592 2 59192

Amerindian Research Unit
University of Guyana
PO Box 101110
Georgetown, Guyana
Tel: +592 2 54841

Paraguay

Asociación de Parcialidades Indígenas
Calle Don Bosco 745
Casilla de Correos 3151
Asunción, Paraguay
Tel: +595 21 493737

Pueblo Nivakle
25 de Mayo 1618
Casilla Correo 1380
Asunción, Paraguay
Tel: +595 21 24427
Fax: +595 21 550451

Peru

Asociación Cultural de Estudiantes Yaneshas (ACDEY)
AP 1763
Lima 1, Peru
Tel: +51 14 232757

Asociación Interétnica de Desarrollo de la Selva Peruana
Avenida San Eugenio 981
Santa Catalina
La Victoria
Lima 13, Peru
Tel: +51 14 724605/726621
Fax: +51 14 724605

Centro De Culturas Indias — Chirapaq
Avenida Horacio Urteaga no. 534
Dpto 203 Jesus Maria
Lima, Peru
Tel: +51 14 232757
Fax: +51 14 333470

Ali Golmirzaie
Genetic Resources Department
Centro Internacional de la Papa (CIP)
AP 1558
Lima 100, Peru
Tel: +51 14 366 920/354 354
Fax: +51 14 351 570

Chirapaq Centro de Culturas Indias del Perú
Jirón Horacio Ortega no. 534, 203
Casilla Postal 11-0504
Lima 11, Peru
Tel: +51 14 232757
Fax: +51 14 326694

Comision Juridíca de los Pueblos de Integración Tawantinsuyana
Urbanización Dolores G-20
Paucarpata
AP 230
Arequipa, Peru
Tel: +51 21 238383/233800
Fax: +51 21 215732/233803

Confederación de Nacionalidades Amazónicas del Peru
Jirón Brigadier Pumacahua 974
Jesús Maria
Lima 11, Peru
Tel: +51 14 238391

Coordinadora de Organizaciones Indigenas de la Cuenca Amazónica
Jiron Larco Herrera 1057
Magdalena del Mar
Lima 17, Peru
Tel: +51 14 619228
Fax: +51 14 619228

Indian Council of South America/Consejo Indio de Sud América
AP 2054, Correo Central
Lima 100, Peru
Tel: +51 14 236955
Fax: +51 14 236955

Maria Luisa del Rio Mispireta
Instituto Nacional de Recursos Naturales (INRENA)
355 Lima 27, Peru

Sociedad Peruana de Derecho Ambiental
Plaza Arrospide No. 9
San Isidro
Lima 27, Peru
Tel: +51 14 40 0549
Fax: +51 14 42 4365

Suriname

Organization of Indigenous Peoples of Suriname
Nepveustraat 85
Paramaribo, Suriname
Tel: +597 421380
Fax: +597 479480

Uruguay

Asociación Indigenista de Uruguay
Minas 1381
Montevideo, Uruguay
Tel: +598 2 406396
Fax: +598 2 923496

Roberto Bissio
Instituto Tercer Mundo
Jackson 1136
Montevideo 11200, Uruguay
Tel: +598 496 192
Fax: +598 2 419222
E-mail: rbissio@chasque.apc.org

Venezuela

Asociación Civil Indígena del Pueblo Yucpa
AP 006
Machiques
Perija Estado Zulia, Venezuela
Tel: +58 63 72049

Consejo Nacional Indio de Venezuela
Residencia Parque Central
Edificio Tacagua
Apartamento 12 L
Avenida Lecuna
Caracas, Venezuela
Tel: +58 2 5733252
Fax: +58 2 5753279

Federación de Indígenos del Estado Bolivar
5th Avenida Bolivar
Quinta
Devis numero 62
Al lado del Laga City Hotel
Bolivar, Venezuela
Fax: +58 85 40756

Nelly Arvelo-Jimenez
Departamento de Antropologia
Instituto Venezolano de Investigaciones Scientificas
AP 21827
Caracas 1020A, Venezuela
Fax: +58 2 501 1085

E-mail links

Several electronic networks and conferences exchange information on IPR, TRR, biodiversity, and related issues.

The Association of Progressive Communications (APC) is a worldwide partnership of member networks dedicated to providing low-cost and advanced computer communications services to improve networking and information-sharing among organizations and individuals working for environmental sustainability, social and economic justice, universal human rights, and peace. For advice and further information contact

    APC International Secretariat
    IBASE Rua Vicente de Souza 29
    22251-070 Rio de Janeiro, Brazil
    Tel: +55 21 286 4467
    Fax: +55 21 286 0541
    E-mail: apcadmin@apc.org

GreenNet is a member network of APC dealing with environment, peace, human rights, and development. It can be reached at

    GreenNet
    393-395 City Road, 4th floor
    London EC1V 1NE, UK
    Tel: +44 171 713 1941
    Fax: +44 171 833 1169
    E-mail: wwwadmin@gn.apc.org

The following is a list of some of the electronic conferences available on GreenNet.

ai.general
General conference for Amnesty International.

ai.uan
Amnesty International's "urgent action alerts" on human rights.

cries.resumen
Esta conferencia contendra los resumenes de cada edición mensual en espanol de la revista Pensamiento Propio, editada por CRIES.

dh.amiatina
Una conferencia abierta para la red APC que sera alimentada por las instituciones CRIES, ALAI, IBASE e Instituto Tercer Mundo con informaciones relevantes sobro el proceso de preparación de la Conferencia Mundial de Derechos Humanos.

env.letters
Sample letters to politicians, corporations, bureaucracies, the World Bank, etc., on environmental and indigenous issues.

gain.justice
This social and economic conference has legislative and background information along with action suggestions pertaining to areas of environmental concern that have an impact on and relate to social and economic justice.

gen.nativeam
Discussion of native American issues.

gen.nativenet
Discussion of issues related to indigenous peoples of the world.

gen.racism
Discussion of racism and other forms of colour-based discrimination.

gn.tribalsurvi
Issues pertaining to the survival of indigenous peoples.

hr.indigenous
Provides a wide variety of materials on the issue of indigenous peoples and human rights.

hrnet.indigen
Human rights conference concerning the rights of indigenous peoples (contact debra@oln.comlink.apc.org).

indig.rights.o
Australian aboriginal rights issues and discussion.

indig.survival
Issues pertaining to the survival of indigenous peoples.

iprwg
Working Group on Traditional Resource Rights. Issues relating to indigenous peoples knowledge, property rights, and traditional resource rights.

kwia
KWIA, Flemish support group for indigenous peoples.

learn.fp
Dedicated to the study of the cultures, histories, and current issues facing the First Peoples from around the World. Open to all l'EARN participants; others may request access from [peg:bcoppinger].[igc:gates]

mideast.gulf
Events and issues related to countries and peoples in the Persian Gulf region.

mideast.levant
Events and issues related to countries and peoples of the Levant — namely Israel/Palestine, Jordan, Syria, Lebanon.

mnl.meet
Reports and workings from conferences held in Manila, Philippines, and the region, starting with the first regional Asian indigenous women's conference 24–30 January 1993. Originates from the E-mail Centre, Philippines.

native.edu
Native education mailing list conference.

native.lang
Discussion of traditional languages of indigenous peoples.

reg.easttimor
News, views, and resources for an independent East Timor.

reg.indonesia
News and information on Indonesia.

taiga.news
Information from Taiga Rescue Network on conservation and sustainable use of the boreal forests of the world.

unpo.news
The Unrepresented Nations and Peoples Organization's conference on human rights.

web.native
Native Canadian issues.

wrm.rainforest
Information on the threats to forests and their peoples and about the official solutions and NGO responses to them.

The United Nations Non-Governmental Liaison Service has published a practical handbook for NGOs in the South who are using electronic mail. The book, @t ease with e-mail, can be obtained from

United Nations Non-Governmental
 Liaison Service (NGLS)
Palais des Nations
CH-1211 Geneva 10, Switzerland

or

Room 6015
866 UN Plaza
New York NY, USA 10017

The following are useful additions to the e-mail addresses that appear in the mailing list given earlier.

bionet@igc.apc.org
Biodiversity Action Network

cultsurv@igc.org
Cultural Survival

biodiver@elci.gn.apc.org
Environmental Liaison Centre International

tick@nufficcs.nl
Indigenous Knowledge and Development Monitor

listserve@uwvam.u.washington.edu
Indknow: a forum for discussing issues associated with indigenous knowledge systems and traditional ecological knowledge

iirr@phil.gn.apc.org
Regional Program for the Promotion of Indigenous Knowledge in Asia

wgtrr.ocees@mansfield.oxford.ac.uk
Working Group on Traditional Resource Rights (WGTRR)

World Wide Web addresses

http://www.bloorstreet.com/home.htm
Aboriginal Resources Network

http://www.abc.hu/
Agricultural Biotechnology Center

http://www.inform.umd.edu:8080/EdRes/Topic/AgrEnv/Biotech/
The Biotechnology Information Center (BIC) of the United States Department of Agriculture

http://www.physics.iastate.edu/cikard/cikard.html
Centre for Indigenous Knowledge for Agriculture and Rural Development

http://www.halcyon.com/FWDP/un.html
Fourth World Documentation Project of the Center for World Indigenous Studies

http://web.icppgr.fao.org/
FAO Plant Genetic Resources Department

http://www.worldbank.org/html/gef/geffiles/gef.html
Global Environment Facility

http://www.gn.apc.org/gn/links/index.html
GreenNet related links

http://www.nuffics.nl/ciran/ikdm/
Indigenous Knowledge and Development Monitor

http://www.igc.org/iatp/
Institute for Agriculture and Trade Policy

http://www.idrc.ca/
International Development Research Centre

http://hawaii-nation.org/nation/iitc/
International Indian Treaty Council

http://www.iisd.ca/linkages/journal/
/linkages/journal/ of the International Institute for Sustainable Development

http://www.charm.net/~rafi/rafihome.html
Rural Advancement Foundation International

http://www.unep.ch/biodiv.html
Secretariat of the Convention on Biological Diversity

http://www.igc.apc.org/saiic/saiic.html
South and Meso American Indian Rights Center

http://www.survival.org.uk/
Survival International

http://www.un.org/dpcsd/
United Nations Department for Policy Coordination and Sustainable Development

http://www.unicc.org:80/
United Nations home page

Annotated bibliography

1. Acosta G.I. 1994. The Guaymi patent claim. *In* van der Vlist, L., ed., Voices of the earth. Netherlands Centre for Indigenous Peoples and International Books, Amsterdam, Netherlands. pp. 44–51.
   – Describes the Human Genome Diversity Project and explains the circumstances behind an application for a patent on a cell line derived from a blood sample acquired from a Guaymi woman.

2. Alcorn, J.B. 1993. Indigenous peoples and conservation. Conservation Biology, 7(2), 424–426.
   – Author argues that partnerships with indigenous peoples offer the best option for achieving conservation. This requires recognition of indigenous peoples as equals in negotiations.

3. Alexander, D. 1993. Some themes in intellectual property and the environment. Review of European Community and International Environmental Law, 2(2), 113–120.
   – The relation between intellectual property and environmental protection is a complex one. The author calls on lawyers to cooperate to ensure that IPR support the objectives of environmental protection.

4. Appell, G.N. 1996. Our vision of human rights is too small! Anthropological perspective on fundamental human rights. *In* Morris, C.P.; Hitchcock, R.K., ed., International human rights and indigenous peoples. University of Nebraska Press, Lincoln, NB, USA.
   – Human rights declarations fail to address adequately the fundamental paradox: how we can help indigenous peoples preserve their cultures while denying them the benefits of modernity. Also, the economic benefits to national states of violating indigenous peoples' rights militates against serious attention being given to meeting their legitimate demands for fair treatment. The author advocates a wider view of human rights and suggests that anthropological knowledge about human behaviour can play a more important role in the development of such a view than can liberal humanism.

5. Australia, Attorney-General's Department. 1994. Stopping the rip-offs: intellectual property protection for Aboriginal and Torres Strait Islander peoples (issues paper). Commonwealth of Australia, Barton, Australia.
   – Overview of IPR law and its limitations for protecting Aboriginal art and culture. Options are provided for addressing these limitations.

6. Axt, J.R.; Corn, M.L.; Lee, M.; Ackerman, D.M. 1993. Biotechnology, indigenous peoples and intellectual property rights. Congressional Research Service, Library of Congress, Washington, DC, USA.
   – The world may be experiencing mass extinction of species. There is now an increase in biodiversity prospecting, but concerns are being expressed that indigenous peoples should be involved in the selection of species for collection. Some such arrangements have been implemented by the Instituto Nacional de Biodiversidad of Costa Rica, the National Cancer Institute, and Shaman Pharmaceuticals, but a debate is emerging over indigenous peoples' rights and their possible entitlement to protection of their knowledge under IPR laws. The authors suggest that the most promising avenues for compensating indigenous peoples while promoting biodiversity conservation are not through IPR, but through contracts between such peoples and companies and research organizations.

7. Ayad, W.G. 1994. The CGIAR and the Convention on Biological Diversity. *In* Krattiger, A.F.; McNeely, J.A.; Lesser, W.H.; Miller, K.R.; St Hill, Y.; Senanayake, R., ed., Widening perspectives on biodiversity. International Union for the Conservation of Nature and Natural Resources, Gland, and International Academy of the Environment, Geneva, Switzerland. pp. 243–254.
   – Paper developed in consultation with the members of the Consultative Group on International Agricultural Research (CGIAR) explains the willingness of CGIAR to provide its expertise for the further definition and elaboration of the Convention on Biological Diversity and to assist in its implementation.

8. Bainbridge, D.I. 1994. Intellectual property (2nd ed.). Pitman Publishing, London, UK.
   – Text on IPR, with detailed sections on copyright, breach of confidence, patent law, design law, and business goodwill and reputation.

9. Balick, M.J.; Mendelson, R. 1992. Assessing the economic value of traditional medicines from tropical rainforests. Conservation Biology, 6(1), 128–130.
   – Authors quantify the economic value of the tropical forests for their medicinal products using data from Belize. They estimate that the net revenue — market value of plants sold to healers and pharmacists less labour costs — compares favourably with that from agriculture.

10. Barsh, R.L. 1986. Indigenous peoples: an emerging object of international law. American Journal of International Law, 80, 369–385.
    – Reviews the recent evolution of international law and United Nations activities concerned with the rights of indigenous peoples. In spite of differences over matters like assimilation and ways of defining indigenous peoples, nation

states are more willing to discuss the rights of indigenous peoples as groups distinct from other minority populations and to allow advocacy groups to express their views at international forums.

11. Barton, J.H. 1991. Patenting life. Scientific American, 264(3), 40–46.
– Entrepreneurs can now legally protect any novel plant, animal, or micro-organism they "invent." However, the courts have not yet settled many questions about the reach of biotechnology patents.

12. Barton, J.H. 1994. Ethnobotany and intellectual property rights. In Chadwick, D.J.; Marsh, J., ed., Ethnobotany and the search for new drugs. John Wiley and Sons, Chichester, UK. pp. 214–221.
– Reviews intellectual property and related legal principles that apply to folk knowledge of a specific medicinal plant and a marketable drug based on that plant. International law recognizes national sovereignty over genetic resources. The combination of trade secrets and patents is the basis of a plausible agreement pattern, but there are gaps. The best approach is to work informally and to explore approaches to protecting indigenous peoples in a model agreement developed by NGOs.

13. Bellagio Declaration: cultural agency/cultural authority, politics and poetics of intellectual property in the post-colonial era (Appendix 1). In Boyle, J. 1996. Shamans, software and spleens: law and the social construction of the information economy. Harvard University Press, Cambridge, MA, USA.
– The concept of IPR is based on individual authorship. Dependence on such a narrow construct denies similar rights to many other creative sources, such as the scientific and artistic contributions of nonwestern cultures. Thus, traditional knowledge, folklore, genetic material, and native medical knowledge flow out of their countries of origin unprotected by IPR. The IPR system undervalues the importance of the public domain, thereby stifling innovation. As an alternative, neighbouring rights or related rights are advocated for protection of folklore, cultural heritage, and ecological know-how.

14. Berkes, F., ed. 1989. Common property resources: ecology and community-based sustainable development. Belhaven Press, London, UK.
– A wide-ranging survey of the role and importance of natural resources held in common ownership and the issues raised by their conservation as a key element of sustainable economic development. Theoretical problems are discussed and case studies are presented.

15. Bilderbeek, S., ed. 1992. Biodiversity and international law: the effectiveness of international environmental law. IOS Press, Oxford, UK.
– Deals with various legal issues concerning biodiversity: international environmental law and the preservation of biodiversity; the effectiveness of international environmental law; institutional change and the effectiveness of international law; and the role of NGOs.

16. Blundell, V. 1993. Aboriginal empowerment and souvenir trade in Canada. Annals of Tourism Research, 20, 64–87.
– Reviews claims that the production and sale of "native type" souvenirs in Canada violate consumer and intellectual property laws and that the government has responded to these claims with development policies that conflict with policies promoting cultural tourism. It is argued that the debate over souvenirs is related to broader struggles by indigenous peoples to sustain their cultures and transform their relations with the state.

17. Bodeker, G. 1995. Traditional health systems: policy, biodiversity, and global interdependence. Journal of Alternative and Complementary Medicine, 1(3), 231–243.
– There is a resurgence of interest in traditional health care. At the same time, the world's medicinal plant stocks are endangered by deforestation and overharvesting. This situation requires an integrated and comprehensive policy framework to ensure sustainability in natural health care for future generations. This article seeks to develop such a framework.

18. Boyle, J. 1996. Shamans, software and spleens: law and the social construction of the information economy. Harvard University Press, Cambridge, MA, USA.
– This author uses his legal background to construct a social theory of the information society. Central to the analysis is a critique of the notion of authorship upon which Western IPR are founded. This notion is blamed for the restriction of information and stifling of innovation under existing IPR regimes.

19. Breckenridge, L.P. 1992. Protection of biological and cultural diversity: emerging recognition of local community rights in ecosystems under international environmental law. Tennessee Law Review, 59(4), 735–785.
– Examines the alliance between the themes of biological and cultural diversity in the provisions of the Earth Summit documents that relate to biological resources. Explores separately environmental and human rights perspectives on rights to biological resources, shows how the notion of sustainability has become inextricably linked to local community empowerment, and concludes that the alliance of global environmental goals and local community rights has important implications for the management and use of biological resources.

20. Brown, M.; Wyckoff-Baird, B. 1992. Designing integrated conservation-development projects. Biodiversity Support Program, Washington, DC, USA.
— Integrated conservation-development projects are intended to achieve effective conservation while benefiting local communities. This paper explains how such projects should be designed and implemented. Several examples from around the world are presented.

21. Brush, S.B. 1993. Indigenous knowledge of biological resources and intellectual property rights: the role of anthropology. American Anthropologist, 95(3), 653–686.
— IPR for ethnobiological knowledge have been proposed as a way to compensate indigenous peoples. Four obstacles are critical: whether general and collective knowledge can be protected; whether certain indigenous groups can claim exclusive control over knowledge and resources; the uncertain status of indigenous people; and the lack of a well-developed market for biological resources or traditional knowledge. Anthropologists can play a critical role in the debate by providing analysis and ethnobiological information.

22. Brush, S.B. 1994. A non-market approach to protecting biological resources. In Greaves, T., ed., Intellectual property rights for indigenous peoples: a sourcebook. Society for Applied Anthropology, Oklahoma City, OK, USA. pp. 131–143.
— Argues that IPR are not a promising avenue for protecting indigenous rights and advocates instead the concept of farmers' rights.

23. Brush, S.B.; Stabinsky, D., ed. 1996. Valuing local knowledge: indigenous peoples and intellectual property rights. Island Press, Covelo, CA, USA.
— Proceedings of the 1993 conference on IPR and indigenous knowledge, which took place at Lake Tahoe, California. Includes sections on equity and indigenous rights, conservation, knowledge and property, and policy options and alternatives.

24. Byrne, N. 1993. Plant breeding and the UPOV. Review of European Community and International Environmental Law, 2(2), 136–140.
— Contests the view that breeders' rights confer a licence to "pillage" resources of Third World countries and denies that the Union for the Protection of New Varieties of Plants' (UPOV) system is to blame for erosion of genetic diversity of crop plants.

25. Cameron, J.; Makuch, Z. 1995. The UN biodiversity convention and the WTO TRIPs agreement: recommendations to avoid conflict and promote sustainable development. World Wide Fund for Nature, Gland, Switzerland.
— Negotiation of the CBD took place with little discussion of linkages to GATT's section on Trade-Related Aspects of Intellectual Property Rights (TRIPs). The authors analyze the relationship and potential conflicts between these two agreements and make recommendations to defuse any such conflicts and ensure that the objectives of the CBD are not undermined by TRIPs.

26. Canal-Forgues, E. 1993. Code of Conduct for Plant Germplasm Collecting and Transfer. Review of European Community and International Environmental Law, 2(2), 167–171.
— The author, a lawyer with the Food and Agriculture Organization (FAO), describes the FAO's global system, the Commission on Plant Genetic Resources' Code of Conduct for Plant Germplasm Collecting and Transfer, and the relation of the code to the CBD.

27. Carew-Reid, J.; Prescott-Allen, R.; Bass, S.; Dalal-Clayton, B. 1994. Strategies for national sustainable development: a handbook for their planning and implementation. Earthscan, London, in association with the International Union for the Conservation of Nature and Natural Resources, Gland, Switzerland, and International Institute of Environment and Development, London, UK.
— At the United Nations Conference on Environment and Development, the governments of the world agreed to plan for a sustainable future. National sustainable development strategies should be based on participation, building on good existing plans and processes, with clear attention to environment and development priorities. This book contains principles and practical ideas for national strategies.

28. Cavalli-Sforza, L.L.; Wilson, A.C.; Cantor, C.R.; Cook-Deegan, R.M.; King, M.C. 1991. Call for a worldwide survey of human genetic diversity: a vanishing opportunity for the Human Genome Project. Genomics, 11, 490–491.
— Authors call for a coordinated international effort — with the participation of US government agencies, international organizations, and the Human Genome Organization — to obtain and store samples from diverse populations. This research will enable us to find out our evolutionary past, especially if we study isolated populations.

29. Chadwick, D.J.; Marsh, J., ed. 1994. Ethnobotany and the search for new drugs. John Wiley and Sons, Chichester, UK.
— Contains papers and discussions from a symposium during which studies of traditional medicine around the world were presented, and ways to encourage conservation of natural habitats and cultivation of medicinal plants were described. IPR are considered, including the application of patent laws and methods of compensation for the local communities.

30. Chapin, M. 1991. How the Kuna keep scientists in line. Cultural Survival Quarterly, 15(3), 17.
    – Describes a project of the Kuna people of Panama, the purpose of which is to manage a forest reserve. The Kuna have found it necessary to control the activities of visiting researchers and have produced their own regulations for researchers.

31. Chapman, A.R. 1994. Human rights implications of indigenous peoples' intellectual property rights. In Greaves, T., ed., Intellectual property rights for indigenous peoples: a sourcebook. Society for Applied Anthropology, Oklahoma City, OK, USA. pp. 209–222.
    – Reviews existing human rights agreements and suggests strategies by which progress toward the protection of indigenous IPR might be made.

32. Clarkson, L.; Morrissette, V.; Regallet, G. 1992. Our responsibility to the seventh generation: indigenous peoples and sustainable development. International Institute for Sustainable Development, Winnipeg, MN, Canada.
    – Compares the indigenous and nonindigenous world views. It is argued that indigenous societies are the last sustainable societies. Therefore, all humans depend on their continuing existence. Unfortunately, colonial policies and attitudes continue to undermine these societies. The authors conclude with a call for action to guide policy changes in support of indigenous peoples and sustainable development.

33. Clay, J.W. 1991. Cultural survival and conservation: lessons from the past twenty years. In Oldfield, M.L.; Alcorn, J.B., ed., Biodiversity: culture, conservation and ecodevelopment. Westview Press, Boulder, CO, USA. pp. 248–273.
    – Indigenous organizations have found that land rights and development of sustainable systems of resource management are their top priorities. Several case studies are presented to demonstrate this reality.

34. Clay, J.W. 1994. Resource wars: nation and state conflicts of the twentieth century. In Johnston, B.R., ed., Who pays the price? The sociocultural context of environmental crisis. Island Press, Covelo, CA, USA. pp. 17–38.
    – Nations of peoples are challenging the notion that states are the building blocks for global peace and environmental security. At stake is not the existence or even the legitimacy of states but rather the survival of nations. However, no single issue affects the survival of nation peoples as much as state appropriation of resources that indigenous nations require if they are to survive as societies.

35. Clinton, R.N. 1990. The rights of indigenous peoples as collective group rights. Arizona Law Review, 32(4), 739–747.
    – The movement for international and domestic legal protection of the rights of indigenous peoples has refocused attention on the fundamental nature of our conception of human rights. The United Nations' Draft Declaration on the Rights of Indigenous Peoples, which emphasizes group rights, supports the view that collective rights are just as important to human dignity as individual rights.

36. Coghlan, A. 1995. Licensed to sell the stuff of life. New Scientist, 11 February, 12–13.
    – Human gene patents are being questioned increasingly on practical and moral grounds. Criticisms come from within the biotechnology industry as well as outside. A group of lawyers at Glasgow University is working to develop a system that would replace patents arising from the Human Genome Project.

37. Colchester, M. 1994. Salvaging nature: indigenous peoples, protected areas and biodiversity conservation. United Nations Research Institute for Social Development, World Rainforest Movement, Penang, Malaysia, and World Wide Fund for Nature, Geneva, Switzerland. Discussion Paper 55.
    – Conservation increasingly seeks to limit human activities in biodiversity-rich areas. Conflicts between indigenous peoples and conservation agencies have resulted, making protected areas unmanageable and inoperative. Conservation agencies must be more accountable to indigenous peoples.

38. Colchester, M.; Lohmann, L., ed. 1993. The struggle for land and the fate of the forests. World Rainforest Movement, The Ecologist, and Zed Books, Penang, Malaysia.
    – Deforestation is a result of structural inequalities in tropical countries and in their relations with the industrial North. Case studies demonstrate that land concentration, land speculation, and landlessness are the main causes of improvident land use.

39. Cooper, D. 1993. The International Undertaking on Plant Genetic Resources. Review of European Community and International Environmental Law, 2(2), 158–166.
    – Discussion of the International Undertaking on Plant Genetic Resources (IUPGR) as it has developed since 1983. It is suggested that the IUPGR facilitated the negotiations that led to the CBD, but that a new legal instrument is needed to address the conservation and use of plant genetic resources.

40. Corry, S. 1993. "Harvest moonshine" taking you for a ride. Survival International, London, UK.
    – Critique of the rainforest harvest theory and practice with particular reference to Cultural Survival and The Body Shop. It is argued that these organizations make exaggerated claims about their trading practices with indigenous

peoples and deflect concern from other basic rights to which indigenous peoples are entitled.

41. Counsell, S.; Rice, T., ed. 1990. The rainforest harvest: sustainable strategies for saving the tropical forests? Friends of the Earth, Royal Geographic Society, London, UK.
— Proceedings of a conference during which the links between tropical forest conservation and the trade in forest products were the subject of debate.

42. Cox, P.A.; Elmqvist, T. 1991. Indigenous control of tropical rainforest reserves: an alternative strategy for conservation. Ambio, 20(7), 317–321.
— In areas where indigenous peoples have a strong conservation ethic, the creation of reserves under partial or complete aboriginal control represents a viable alternative to the more traditional forms of land acquisition. This proposition is tested by analysis of reserves in Samoa.

43. Cox, P.A.; Elmqvist, T. 1993. Ecocolonialism and indigenous knowledge systems: village controlled rainforest preserves in Samoa. Pacific Conservation Biology, 1(1), 6–13.
— Ecocolonialism, the imposition of European conservation paradigms and power structures on indigenous villagers, is incompatible with the principles of indigenous control of local rainforest preserves. The authors consider this proposition in the context of Samoa and offer suggestions for the establishment of future village-controlled preserves in other areas of the South Pacific.

44. Cragg, G.M.; Boyd, M.R.; Grever, M.R.; Schepartz, S.A. 1994. Policies for international collaboration and compensation in drug discovery and development at the United States National Cancer Institute: the NCI letter of collection. In Greaves, T., ed., Intellectual property rights for indigenous peoples: a sourcebook. Society for Applied Anthropology, Oklahoma City, OK, USA. pp. 83–98.
— The National Cancer Institute has been involved for many years in plant screening and has drawn up a letter of collection to compensate source governments and communities. The authors, who are NCI employers, present the letter in this article.

45. Crucible Group. 1994. People, plants and patents: the impact of intellectual property on trade, plant biodiversity, and rural society. International Development Research Centre, Ottawa, Canada.
— The Crucible Group, which represents a wide cross-section of sociopolitical perspectives, met to discuss IPR and local communities. The group has identified and examined the major issues and the range of policy alternatives including consensus positions and the various conflicting viewpoints.

46. Cunningham, A.B. 1993. Ethics, ethnobiological research and biodiversity. World Wide Fund for Nature, Gland, Switzerland.
— Deals with the ethical problems associated with ethnobiological and biochemical prospecting. To prevent loss of biodiversity, it is necessary to formulate guidelines for equitable partnerships in research and development on natural products. Several existing ethical guidelines are reviewed. The paper concludes with new recommendations for a code of practice developed by the author.

47. da Costa e Silva, E. 1995. The protection of intellectual property for local and indigenous communities. European Intellectual Property Review, 17(11), 546–549.
— Presents and analyzes recent legislative processes in Latin America relevant to the IPR of indigenous peoples. These processes are concerned with national and regional implementation of GATT's section on Trade-Related Aspects of Intellectual Property Rights in conformity with the requirements of the CBD vis-à-vis indigenous peoples.

48. Davis, S.H.; Ebbe, K. (ed.) 1995. Traditional knowledge and sustainable development. World Bank, Washington, DC, USA. Environmentally Sustainable Development Proceedings Series, 4.
— Proceedings of a conference that brought together indigenous peoples, NGOs, and United Nations agencies to discuss the relationship of traditional knowledge with sustainable development.

49. de Klemm, C.; Shine, C. 1993. Biological diversity conservation and the law: legal mechanisms for conserving species and ecosystems. International Union for the Conservation of Nature and Natural Resources, Gland, Switzerland.
— Review of international law and conservation strategies relating to species and ecosystems. The book is intended to guide national implementation of international agreements such as the CBD.

50. Downes, D.; Laird, S.A.; Klein, C.; Carney, B.K. 1993. Biodiversity prospecting contract. In Reid, W.V.; Laird, S.A.; Meyer, C.A.; Gamez, R.; Sittenfeld, A.; Janzen, D.H.; Gollin, M.A.; Juma, C., ed., Biodiversity prospecting: using genetic resources for sustainable development. World Resources Institute, Washington, DC, USA; Instituto Nacional de Biodiversidad, San José, Costa Rica; Rainforest Alliance, New York, NY, USA; African Centre for Technology Studies, Nairobi, Kenya. pp. 255–287.
— This contract is meant to be used as a model in the negotiation of contracts for the collection of biological samples. The parties are pharmaceutical companies and collectors. The draft contract includes requirements for local

participation and benefits, environmental assessment, and prior informed consent.

51. Durning, A.T. 1992. Guardians of the land: indigenous peoples and the health of the earth. Worldwatch Institute, Washington, DC, USA. Worldwatch Paper, 112.
– Explains why indigenous peoples have an important role to play in managing fragile ecosystems. In spite of this, they are still victims of severe abuse of their basic rights.

52. Economic and Social Council of the United Nations (ECOSOC), Working Group on Indigenous Populations. 1993. Discrimination against indigenous peoples: study on the protection of the cultural and intellectual property of indigenous peoples. ECOSOC, Geneva, Switzerland. E/CN.4/sub.2/1993/28.
– Study requested by the UN Commission on Human Rights to consider ways to strengthen respect by the international community for the intellectual and cultural property rights of indigenous peoples. Argues that it would be more appropriate to refer to the collective "heritage" of a people than to intellectual and cultural property. Concludes with recommendations for action by the international community.

53. Elisabetsky, E. 1991. Sociopolitical, economical and ethical issues in medicinal plant research. Journal of Ethnopharmacology, 3(2), 235–239.
– Medicinal plant research usually starts with collection of indigenous medical knowledge, but indigenous groups tend not to benefit. Many of these groups as well as governments perceiving scientific imperialism are becoming reluctant to permit such research. Unless equity issues are discussed and resolved, medicinal plant researchers will find themselves unable to carry out their research or, if allowed, they may be serving ethically dubious purposes.

54. Esquinas-Alcazar, J. 1993. The global system on plant genetic resources. Review of European Community and International Environmental Law, 2(2), 151–157.
– The Secretary of the Food and Agricultural Organization's (FAO) Commission on Plant Genetic Resources describes the development of the FAO Global System for Plant Genetic Resources and the implications of the CBD for the system.

55. Falk, R. 1988. The rights of peoples, in particular indigenous peoples. In Crawford, J., ed., The rights of peoples. Clarendon Press, Oxford, UK. pp. 17–37.
– There is a tension in international law between the territorial sovereignty of governments and the status of individuals and groups as beneficiaries of human rights. It is being resolved in favour of the state, but it is also being challenged inter alia by claims by and on behalf of indigenous peoples for recognition of their group rights.

56. Flitner, M.; Leskien, D.; Myers, D. 1995. Review of national actions on access to genetic resources and IPR in several developing countries. World Wide Fund for Nature, Gland, Switzerland.
– Reviews recent national laws to implement the CBD and GATT's Trade-Related Aspects of Intellectual Property Rights section. The authors present the views of local NGOs on new legislation in selected countries with high levels of biodiversity.

57. Food and Agriculture Organization (FAO). 1989. Informal innovative systems — legal aspects. FAO Legal Office, Rome, Italy.
– Informal innovation is characterized by the continuous nature of the innovation process; the fact that the author or breeder is not recognized; the fact that the starting material usually comes from the Third World; and freedom of access to the results. There are a number of systems for the indirect or partial recognition of informal innovation, cultural heritage, and folklore. It is hoped that the FAO system for plant genetic resources will protect the rights of informal innovators.

58. Foundation for Revitalisation of Local Health Traditions (FRLHT). 1995. Beyond the biodiversity convention: empowering the ecosystem people. FRLHT, Bangalore, India.
– Summary of discussions and decisions made at a meeting of organizations who are going to field-test the community register format.

59. Fowler, C.; Mooney, P. 1990. Shattering: food, politics and the loss of genetic diversity. University of Arizona Press, Tuscon, AZ, USA.
– Genetic erosion has serious social effects, including mass starvation. Control over the gene pool is shifting from farmers to scientists and heads of industry, whereas political considerations determine agricultural policy with increasing frequency. At the moment, the North is engaged in a struggle with the South for control over plant genetic resources.

60. Gadgil, M. 1987. Diversity, cultural and biological. Tree, 2(12), 369–373.
– Early human populations possessed high levels of cultural diversity dependent on and supportive of high levels of biological diversity. This pattern changed drastically with technological innovations that enabled certain human groups to break down territorial barriers and to usurp the resources of other groups. Traditions of resource conservation can re-emerge when the dominant cultures spread over the entire area and the innovations diffuse to other groups. This could change once again as genetically engineered organisms become an economically viable proposition with the accruing advantages concentrated in the hands of a few

groups. A further drastic reduction in biocultural diversity may ensue.

61. Gadgil, M.; Berkes, F. 1991. Traditional resource management systems. Resource Management and Optimization, 8(3–4), 127–141.

– The Western view that humans are entitled to dominate and use nature at will recognized no limits to the exploration and modification of ecosystems. This view has changed gradually since the mid-19th century. Nevertheless, the science-based techniques of resource management that have since been developed are applicable almost entirely to single-species populations in highly simplified ecosystems. On the other hand, a diversity of traditional cultures has elaborated management systems more consistent with the ecosystem view and current ecological theory. This paper explores the synthesis of traditional and scientific ecology.

62. Gadgil, M.; Berkes, F.; Folke, C. 1993. Indigenous knowledge for biodiversity conservation. Ambio, 22(2–3), 151–156.

– Indigenous knowledge consisting of "diachronic" observations can be of great value and complement the "synchronic" observations on which Western science is based. Indigenous groups are well aware of the importance of biodiversity. Their knowledge base is indefinite and their implementation of conservation involves an intimate relationship with the belief system. Such knowledge is difficult for Western science to understand. However, it is vital that indigenous knowledge is conserved. This should be accomplished through promoting indigenous peoples' community-based resource management systems.

63. Gamez, R.; Piva, A.; Sittenfeld, A.; Leon, E.; Jimenez, J.; Mirabelli, G. 1993. Costa Rica's conservation program and national biodiversity institute, INBio. In Reid, W.V.; Laird, S.A.; Meyer, C.A.; Gamez, R.; Sittenfeld, A.; Janzen, D.H.; Gollin, M.A.; Juma, C., ed., Biodiversity prospecting: using genetic resources for sustainable development. World Resources Institute, Washington, DC, USA; Instituto Nacional de Biodiversidad, San José, Costa Rica; Rainforest Alliance, New York, NY, USA; African Centre for Technology Studies, Nairobi, Kenya. pp. 53–67.

– Tropical biodiversity will continue only to the extent that societies use resources for intellectual and economic development. Doing so requires creative new structures and collaboration among groups that have traditionally been separate, if not opposed, such as biologists and businessmen. The authors claim that, in Costa Rica, a serious attempt to forge such new socioeconomic and "socioecological" collaborations is building bridges between such separate groups.

64. Gannon, P.; Guthrie, T.; Laurie, G. 1995. Patents, morality and DNA: should there be intellectual property protection of the Human Genome Project? Medical Law Journal, 1, 321–345.

– Examines the appropriateness of using existing patent laws to secure protection for the work being carried out in the Human Genome Project. Certain ethical and practical problems are explored. It is suggested that it might be appropriate to consider alternative means of rewarding those involved in unraveling human DNA. An attempt is made to outline some appropriate matters to consider in developing such an alternative.

65. Genetic Resources Action International (GRAIN). 1995. Towards a biodiversity community rights regime. Seedling, 12(3), 2–14.

– As an alternative to IPR, GRAIN argues for a local community rights regime based on heritage, territoriality, and communality, which could be implemented through the CBD and the International Undertaking on Plant Genetic Resources.

66. Glowka, L.; Burhenne-Guilmin, F.; Synge, H.; McNeely, J.A.; Gundling, L. 1994. A guide to the Convention on Biological Diversity. International Union for the Conservation of Nature and Natural Resources, Gland, Switzerland. Environmental Policy and Law Paper, 30.

– A comprehensive analysis of CBD articles by the International Union for the Conservation of Nature's Environmental Law Centre.

67. Gollin, M.A. 1993. An intellectual property rights framework for biodiversity prospecting. In Reid, W.V.; Laird, S.A.; Meyer, C.A.; Gamez, R.; Sittenfeld, A.; Janzen, D.H.; Gollin, M.A.; Juma, C., ed., Biodiversity prospecting: using genetic resources for sustainable development. World Resources Institute, Washington, DC, USA; Instituto Nacional de Biodiversidad, San José, Costa Rica; Rainforest Alliance, New York, NY, USA; African Centre for Technology Studies, Nairobi, Kenya. pp. 159–197.

– Outlines how IPR can be applied to the new technologies, commercial practices, and ethical standards of biodiversity prospecting and discusses the merits of creating new biodiversity prospecting rights. IPR laws are no panacea without the harmonization of intellectual property, environmental protection, and commercial laws. The various IPR mechanisms are explained and analyzed.

68. Golvan, C. 1992. Aboriginal art and the protection of indigenous cultural rights. European Intellectual Property Law Review, 14(7), 227–232.

– The aboriginal art industry is a lucrative one which employs thousands of people. In 1988, retail sales amounted to $18.5 million. A number of court cases have been concerned with the protection of the right to prevent others from exploiting these works of art. An organization now exists to manage the copyright claims of Aborigines. The author suggests legislative measures that would eliminate time limitation from copyright and recognize civil rights that could function alongside copyright.

69. Gray, A. 1990. Between the spice of life and the melting pot: biodiversity conservation and its impact on indigenous peoples. International Work Group for Indigenous Affairs, Copenhagen, Denmark. Document 70.
– Indigenous peoples account for most of the world's cultural diversity and tend to inhabit areas of the world with the greatest biodiversity. Nevertheless, many advocates of conservation believe that the interests of indigenous peoples are best served by tying them more closely to the world economic system. "Green capitalism" is another top-down approach harmful to conservation and likely to lead to further exploitation of indigenous peoples. The way for indigenous peoples to protect biodiversity is through the recognition of their rights to their territories. Furthermore they should be able to control the marketing of their commodities and receive respect and recognition for the benefits of their knowledge.

70. Greaves, T., ed. 1994. Intellectual property rights for indigenous peoples: a sourcebook. Society for Applied Anthropology, Oklahoma City, OK, USA.
– The rights of indigenous societies to control the use of their cultural knowledge by outsiders has become an issue of global importance. This book includes both cases where indigenous groups have asserted these rights and analyses of the legal and political contexts for such rights.

71. Green College Centre for Environmental Policy and Understanding. 1993. Seminar on intellectual property rights, indigenous cultures and biodiversity conservation, 14 May 1993. Green College Centre for Environmental Policy and Understanding, Oxford, UK.
– Report of a seminar at which participants discussed IPR with reference to indigenous peoples, pharmaceutical research, and the conservation of biodiversity.

72. Greengrass, B. 1991. The 1991 Act of the UPOV Convention. European Intellectual Property Review, 13(12), 466–472.
– The vice-secretary-general of the Union for the Protection of New Varieties of Plants (UPOV) explains the 1991 revision of the UPOV convention, which is compared with the 1978 version of the convention.

73. Gupta, A.K. 1993. Creativity, innovation, entrepreneurship and networking at grassroots level. Society for Research and Initiatives for Sustainable Technologies and Institutions (SRISTI), Ahmedabad, India.
– The key objectives of SRISTI are to strengthen the capacity of grassroots-level innovations and inventors engaged in conserving biodiversity to protect their IPR by experiment; to add value to their knowledge; to evolve entrepreneurial ability to generate returns from their knowledge; and to enrich their cultural and institutional basis of dealing with nature.

74. Gupta, A.K. 1994. Dilemma in conservation of biodiversity, ethical, equity and moral issues: a review. Society for Research and Initiatives for Sustainable Technologies and Institutions, Ahmedabad, India.
– Critical review of attempts by institutions to deal with equity issues relating to biodiversity prospecting and ethnobiological research.

75. Gupta, A.K.; Patel, K.; Patil, B.L. 1992. Conserving diversity for sustainable development: the case of plants of insecticidal and veterinary medicine importance. Indian Institute of Management, Ahmedabad, India. Working Paper, 1003.
– The authors are engaged in documenting local technical innovations and ecological systems. This work indicates the considerable potential for building on peoples' knowledge for developing sustainable techniques. A case is made for redefining the framework for biodiversity conservation to include traditional knowledge.

76. Harhoff, F. 1991. Indigenous rights between law and sociology: internationalising soft norms in a hard context. North Atlantic Studies, 1(2), 64–70.
– Identifies certain aspects of dogmatic legal science relevant to the study of binding norms beyond traditional hierarchy of legal sources. Argues that recognition of the right of indigenous peoples to self-determination in international law will depend on the international community's willingness to accept modifications to the principle of sovereignty.

77. Hayson, V.; Richstone, J. 1987. Customizing law in the territories: proposal for a task force on customary law in Nunavut. Inuit Studies, 11(1), 91–106.
– For some time Inuit in the Northwest Territories (NWT) have been demanding its division and the creation of a new territory to be known as Nunavut, in which Inuit would constitute the majority. This paper provides a brief summary of recent constitutional development in the NWT and focuses on a proposal by the Nunavut Constitutional Forum to integrate customary law within the overall justice system in the future territory. This proposal calls for the establishment of a task force on customary law to study and report on how the justice system could be modified to do this.

78. Hendrickx, F.; Koester, V.; Prip, C. 1993. Access to genetic resources: a legal analysis. Environmental Policy and Law, 23(6), 250–258.
— Analyzes Article 15 of the CBD, which deals with access to genetic resources, and contains a detailed discussion of the concept of prior informed consent in the context of the convention.

79. Herle, A. 1994. Museums and shamans: a cross-cultural collaboration. Anthropology Today, 10(1), 2–5.
— Describes an innovative collaboration between a Nepalese shaman and a museum. The museum is displaying cultural artifacts selected, stored, and exhibited in a culturally sensitive manner following the shaman's advice. Particularly sacred objects are held on deposit, not owned, by the museum. The museum will help the shaman's people set up their own museum and archives in Nepal.

80. Human Genome Organization (HUGO), Europe. 1994. The Human Genome Diversity (HGD) Project. Summary document incorporating the HGD project outline and development, proposed guidelines, and report of the international planning workshop held in Porto Conte, Sardinia, Italy, 9–12 September 1993. HUGO, London, UK.
— Explains the aims and importance of the Human Genome Diversity Project and summarizes deliberations of a planning workshop that covered scientific aspects, ethical issues, and an overall plan.

81. International Union for the Conservation of Nature and Natural Resources (IUCN); United Nations Environment Programme (UNEP); World Wide Fund for Nature (WWF). 1991. Caring for the earth: a strategy for sustainable living. IUCN, UNEP, WWF, Gland, Switzerland.
— Follow up to the 1980 World Conservation Strategy which contains a list of goals to achieve "sustainable development." Sections of the book deal with principles and actions for sustainable living, and actions to implement the "strategy for sustainable living."

82. Inuit Circumpolar Conference (ICC). 1992. Principles and elements for a comprehensive Arctic policy. McGill University, Montreal, PQ, Canada.
— The ICC has identified and elaborated the principles and elements necessary for an Arctic policy that ensures the environmental integrity of the region and the survival of Inuit values and cultural identity. The report compiles principles approved at ICC general assemblies and Arctic policy conference workshops.

83. Jabbour, A. 1983. Folklore protection and national patrimony: developments and dilemmas in the legal protection of folklore. Copyright Bulletin, 18, 10–14.
— Concerns about folklore relate to issues of authentication, expropriation, compensation, and the erosion of the health and vitality of folk cultures. An intellectual property framework cannot resolve certain dilemmas. One of the main problems concerns the relationship of the world's traditional cultures to nation states. Other avenues need to be explored, such as appellations of origin.

84. Jacobs, J.W.; Petroski, C.; Friedman, P.A.; Simpson, E. 1990. Characterization of the anticoagulant activities from a Brazilian arrow poison. Thrombosis and Haemostasis, 63(1), 31–35.
— Research by Merck scientists on an arrow poison used by an Amazonian tribe confirms its anticoagulant properties.

85. Janzen, D.H.; Hallwachs, W.; Gamez, R.; Jimenez, J.; Sittenfeld, A. 1993. Research management policies, permits for collecting and research in the tropics. In Reid, W.V.; Laird, S.A.; Meyer, C.A.; Gamez, R.; Sittenfeld, A.; Janzen, D.H.; Gollin, M.A.; Juma, C., ed., Biodiversity prospecting: using genetic resources for sustainable development. World Resources Institute, Washington, DC, USA; Instituto Nacional de Biodiversidad, San José, Costa Rica; Rainforest Alliance, New York, NY, USA; African Centre for Technology Studies, Nairobi, Kenya. pp. 131–157.
— Research in the field can yield major benefits, and a national system of permits helps allocate both these benefits and research costs within and between countries. Such a system also helps ensure that research does not destroy its own raw materials. Specifically, a research agreement should be required for any research in any wildland that is conserved or used for its biodiversity. It is argued that national sovereignty considerations should not prevent the state from issuing bioprospecting concessions to private concerns.

86. Jodha, N.S. 1992. Common property resources: a missing dimension of development strategies. World Bank, Washington, DC, USA. Discussion Paper, 166.
— Common property resources (CPRs) tend to be disregarded in rural development strategies. However, in areas like the dry regions of India, CPRs could be made an effective component of rural development strategies. There is an urgent need for the rehabilitation and development of CPRs as productive community resources by donor agencies.

87. Johnson, M., ed. 1992. Lore: capturing traditional environmental knowledge. Dene Cultural Institute, Hay River, NWT, Canada, and International Development Research Centre, Ottawa, Canada.
— The importance of traditional environmental knowledge relates to resource management, conservation, development planning, and

environmental assessment. Comanagement can establish appropriate institutional relationships, thereby helping to facilitate the integration of traditional knowledge and Western science to deal better with environmental problems. Results of a workshop on documentation and application of traditional ecological knowledge through community-based research are presented.

88. Johnston, B.R., ed. 1994. Who pays the price? The sociocultural context of environmental crisis. Island Press, Covelo, CA, USA.
– Collection of articles exploring the relationship between human rights and environmental problems and demonstrating that social justice environmentalism is a growing worldwide phenomenon.

89. Joyce, C. 1994. Earthly goods: medicine-hunting in the rainforest. Little, Brown and Co., Boston, MA, USA.
– Describes bioprospecting, past and present. The present-day search for rainforest species of value to the pharmaceutical industry is seen as part of a "radical" experiment to preserve remaining forests by demonstrating the value afforded by conservation.

90. Juma, C. 1989. The gene hunters: biotechnology and the scramble for seeds. Princeton University Press, Englewood Cliffs, NJ, USA, and Zed Books, London, UK.
– Examines the implications of advances in biotechnology and the conservation of genetic resources for the Third World in general and Africa in particular. It is argued that new techniques, unlike earlier technological revolutions, are applicable to small-scale, labour-intensive production and thus offer Africa a significant opportunity to transform its economy.

91. Kamstra, J. 1994. Protected areas: towards a participatory approach. Committee for the International Union for the Conservation of Nature and Novib, Amsterdam, Netherlands.
– Effective local participation in protected areas is unsatisfactory. Governments must provide the legal framework to enable local people to have an effective voice. Cooperation between development and conservation organizations must be enhanced.

92. Kate, K. 1995. Biopiracy or green petroleum? Expectations and best practice in bioprospecting. Overseas Development Administration, London, UK.
– Bioprospecting will not provide sufficient financial incentives to conserve the world's biodiversity. Nevertheless, bioprospecting is not inherently exploitative, and can benefit biodiversity-rich countries. Recommendations are provided for actions and strategies by plant collecting institutions and governments that wish to promote bioprospecting. These actions and strategies should ensure that benefits are shared fairly between companies, governments and local communities in biodiversity-rich regions of the world.

93. Kemf, E., ed. 1993. The law of the mother: protecting indigenous peoples in protected areas. The Sierra Club, San Francisco, CA, USA.
– Uses case study approach to offer a vision of how to design and implement conservation projects to provide for the well-being of local peoples, wildlife, and the land itself.

94. Khalil, M.H.; Reid, W.V.; Juma, C. 1992. Property rights, biotechnology and genetic resources. African Centre for Technology Studies, Nairobi, Kenya. Biopolicy International Series, 7.
– Synthesis of papers and discussions from an African regional consultation on the biodiversity conservation strategy program of the World Resources Institute, the International Union for the Conservation of Nature and Natural Resources, and the United Nations Environment Programme.

95. King, S.R. 1994. Establishing reciprocity: biodiversity, conservation and new models for cooperation between forest-dwelling peoples and the pharmaceutical industry. In Greaves, T., ed., Intellectual property rights for indigenous peoples: a sourcebook. Society for Applied Anthropology, Oklahoma City, OK, USA. pp. 69–82.
– The question is no longer whether forest-dwelling people and indigenous peoples should benefit from products developed on the basis of their knowledge and forest management technology, but rather how to provide these benefits in the most fair and effective way. Benefits from the author's company, Shaman Pharmaceuticals, are provided in accordance with the expressed needs of the local people as well as their contribution to natural products research. It is argued that benefits should be immediate and include acknowledgment of the intellectual contribution of indigenous peoples.

96. Kingsbury, B. 1992. Self-determination and "indigenous peoples." In Proceedings of the 86th annual meeting. American Society of International Law, Washington, DC, USA. pp. 383–394.
– Customary international law recognizes a right of self-determination, and claims to this right come more and more often from non-state groups such as indigenous peoples. It is argued first that self-determination need not entail the option of separate statehood; second, that self-determination must be understood in terms of process and political legitimation; and third, that "statehood" should not be seen as a single outcome.

97. Kloppenburg, Jr, J.R. 1988. First the seed: the political economy of plant biotechnology.

Cambridge University Press, Cambridge, UK.
— The emergence of the new biotechnologies and of large corporations that produce both seeds and chemicals for the agriculture industry is a significant recent phenomenon. In spite of a dependence on the plant genetic resources of the South, the economic and political power of these corporations and of Northern governments has ensured that they continue to enjoy free access to these resources.

98. Kloppenburg, Jr, J.R. 1988 (ed.). Seeds and sovereignty: the use and control of plant genetic resources. Duke University Press, Durham, NC, USA.
— Contributions deal with the history of plant genetic resource transfer, the politics of ownership, access and control of these resources, and the various measures that could be taken to ensure that benefits from their exploitation are shared fairly.

99. Kloppenburg, Jr, J. 1991. No hunting! Biodiversity, indigenous rights and scientific poaching. Cultural Survival Quarterly, 15(3), 14–18.
— The value of Third World genetic resources is very high. Northern agricultural development is the result of the free transfer of these resources. Biotechnology is increasing the value of these resources, yet the South is not benefiting. Indigenous people must become more aware of this situation, and their property rights must be respected for benefits to be shared fairly.

100. Kloppenburg, Jr, J.; Gonzales, T. 1994. Between state and capital: NGOs as allies of indigenous peoples. In Greaves, T., ed., Intellectual property rights for indigenous peoples: a sourcebook. Society for Applied Anthropology, Oklahoma City, OK, USA. pp. 163–177.
— Explains the advantages and drawbacks for indigenous peoples of forging alliances with NGOs, and examines the trade-offs in these alliances that indigenous peoples must weigh.

101. Kothari, A. 1994. People's participation in the conservation of biodiversity in India. In Krattiger, A.F.; McNeely, J.A.; Lesser, W.H.; Miller, K.R.; St Hill, Y.; Senanayake, R., ed., Widening perspectives on biodiversity. International Union for the Conservation of Nature and Natural Resources, Gland, and International Academy of the Environment, Geneva, Switzerland. pp. 137–145.
— One aspect of the growing crisis of biodiversity depletion in India is the increasing alienation of people from the very biological resources on which their lives depend. Therefore, community control over natural resources must be restored.

102. Krattiger, A.F.; McNeely, J.A.; Lesser, W.H.; Miller, K.R.; St Hill, Y.; Senanayake, R., ed. 1994. Widening perspectives on biodiversity. International Union for the Conservation of Nature and Natural Resources, Gland, and International Academy of the Environment, Geneva, Switzerland.
— A collection of papers presented at the 1993 Global Biodiversity Forum. The papers deal with implementation of the CBD at international, national, and local levels.

103. Laird, S.A. 1993. Contracts for biodiversity prospecting. In Reid, W.V.; Laird, S.A.; Meyer, C.A.; Gamez, R.; Sittenfeld, A.; Janzen, D.H.; Gollin, M.A.; Juma, C., ed., Biodiversity prospecting: using genetic resources for sustainable development. World Resources Institute, Washington, DC, USA; Instituto Nacional de Biodiversidad, San José, Costa Rica; Rainforest Alliance, New York, NY, USA; African Centre for Technology Studies, Nairobi, Kenya. pp. 99–130.
— The increase in bioprospecting and the importance of conserving sources of genetic and biotechnological resources means that contracts have to be developed to ensure the return of benefits to the supplier countries and their citizens. Benefits should be both immediate and long term.

104. Laird, S. 1994. Natural products and the commercialization of traditional knowledge. In Greaves, T., ed., Intellectual property rights for indigenous peoples: a sourcebook. Society for Applied Anthropology, Oklahoma City, OK, USA. pp. 145–162.
— Describes three scenarios in which traditional knowledge is transferred to commercial interests and the types of benefits and levels of control over this process that are retained by the communities.

105. Laird, S. 1995. Access controls for genetic resources: the assertion of sovereignty. World Wide Fund for Nature, Gland, Switzerland.
— The CBD gives governments the right to impose conditions on access to biological resources. Governments are now putting in place national systems of access control, and recent developments in this area are examined. Institutions and communities often deal directly with collectors of biological resources. Existing research and commercial agreements and codes of conduct and declarations are analyzed in terms of their compliance with the CBD.

106. Laurie, G.T. 1996. Biotechnology and intellectual property: marriage of inconvenience? In McLean, S.A.M., ed., Contemporary issues in law, medicine and ethics. Dartmouth Publishing, Aldershot, UK.
— The biotechnology industry has encountered practical problems in seeking patent protection, and there is much criticism of patent systems. Many objections to patenting life are of a moral nature, and these will have to be addressed.

107. Leonen, M.; la Vina, A.G.M. 1994. Obstacles to harnessing creativity: Philippine efforts to conserve biodiversity and to use biological resources sustainability. *In* Krattiger, A.F.; McNeely, J.A.; Lesser, W.H.; Miller, K.R.; St Hill, Y.; Senanayake, R., ed., Widening perspectives on biodiversity. International Union for the Conservation of Nature and Natural Resources, Gland, and International Academy of the Environment, Geneva, Switzerland. pp. 179–190.
 – Identifies issues and strategies for broadening participation in implementing the CBD, which requires the recognition of community-based resources and management systems.

108. Lesser, W.H. 1991. Equitable patent protection in the developing world: issues and approaches. Eubios Ethics Institute, Christchurch, New Zealand.
 – Outlines various forms of patent protection and economic arguments for existing laws. Goes on to suggest alternatives for patent law legislation. Concludes with a revised model law derived from a model law produced by the World Intellectual Property Organization.

109. Lesser, W. 1994. An approach for securing rights to indigenous knowledge. International Academy of the Environment, Geneva, Switzerland. Working Paper, 15.
 – Suggests that indigenous peoples discontinue use of the term IPR in place of what the author calls "reserved rights" or "sequestered rights." Access laws and contract arrangements together can ensure that indigenous peoples are fairly compensated. Indigenous groups should be active in the passage of appropriate national laws to implement the CBD.

110. Lesser, W. 1994. Attributes of an intellectual property rights system for landraces. Geneva, International Academy of the Environment, Geneva, Switzerland. Biodiversity/Biotechnology Program, Working Paper R10W.
 – Addresses the IPR situation for landraces to evaluate the applicability of existing IPR laws and characterize the attributes of a new system.

111. Lewin, R. 1993. Genes from a disappearing world. New Scientist, 29 May, 25–29.
 – The Human Genome Diversity Project has touched off a heated debate about genetics, race, and human welfare.

112. Lobo, S. 1991. The fabric of life: repatriating the sacred Coroma textiles. Cultural Survival Quarterly, 15(3), 40–46.
 – The people of Coroma, Bolivia, discovered that some of their sacred textiles had been stolen to become part of the illicit trade in antiquities. Efforts are being made to have them returned from the United States. This case has stimulated awareness in North America of the scale of violations of indigenous peoples' cultural property rights.

113. Loita Naimina Enkiyio Conservation Trust Company (LNECTC). 1994. Forest of the lost child: a Maasai conservation success threatened by greed. LNECTC, Narok, Kenya.
 – The Loita Maasai have protected and conserved their forest for generations and are its custodians according to customary law. However, the county council wants to turn the forest into a reserve for tourism development. The Maasai are fighting in the courts to save their forest. They hope that implementation of Article 8j of the CBD will support them in their struggle.

114. Maddock, K. 1989. Copyright and traditional designs — an aboriginal dilemma. Intellectual Property, 2(1), 7–9.
 – A comparative look at the complex traditional means of protecting intellectual or cultural "property" in aboriginal society, which highlights the integral relationship between aboriginal art, law, and social life.

115. Martin, G.J. 1995. Ethnobotany: a people and plants conservation manual. Chapman and Hall, London, UK.
 – Manual on ethnoecological methodology that addresses the link between ethnoecology, conservation, and community development.

116. McGowan, J. 1991. Who is the inventor? Cultural Survival Quarterly, 15(3), 20.
 – US patent laws do not allow for the protection of discoveries of information known already by indigenous people. The award of patents to two companies based on properties of the neem seed appears to be a contradiction of patent law according to this interpretation.

117. McGowan, J.; Udeinya, I. 1994. Collecting traditional medicines in Nigeria: a proposal for IPR compensation. *In* Greaves, T., ed., Intellectual property rights for indigenous peoples: a sourcebook. Society for Applied Anthropology, Oklahoma City, OK, USA. pp. 57–68.
 – Proposes a contract that would contain provisions for compensating local communities. The specifics of compensation mechanisms and local participation are dealt with in the proposal.

118. McKie, R. 1995. History's bones of contention. The Observer, 16 April, 3.
 – Some museum curators argue that pressure from indigenous peoples to return fossils, human remains, and cultural artifacts is endangering evidence of origins of the human race.

119. McLean, S.A.M.; Giesen, D. 1994. Legal and ethical considerations of the Human Genome Project. Medical Law Journal, 1, 159–175.
 – Identifies ethical, legal, and social implications of the Human Genome Project in various areas, such as human identity, discrimination,

medical confidentiality, data protection, insurance, and IPR.

120. McNeil, R.J.; McNeil, M.J. 1989. Ownership of traditional information: moral and legal obligations to compensate for taking. Northeast Indian Quarterly, Fall, 30–35.
– When knowledge is transferred from indigenous peoples to ethnobotanists and others, the knowledge providers should be better protected by the legal system. It is suggested that existing concepts adopted by legal systems, such as property theory and contract doctrines, provide at least a model, and perhaps a mechanism, for such protection.

121. Mead, A.T.P. 1994. Misappropriation of indigenous knowledge: the next wave of colonisation. Otago Bioethics Report, 3(1), 4–7.
– Explores examples of misappropriation of indigenous knowledge, past and present. It is concluded that global trends in the environmental sciences and medical research may well constitute "the next wave of colonisation."

122. Messenger, P.M. 1989. The ethics of collecting cultural property: whose culture? whose property? University of New Mexico Press, Albuquerque, NM, USA.
_ Focuses on the ethical, legal, and intellectual issues related to the disposition of cultural property, particularly archaeological remains. Contributions from various fields discuss the issues from their unique perspectives and offer constructive suggestions for increasing cooperation. Ways of improving the protection of cultural property and resolving differences regarding cultural heritage issues are also discussed.

123. Milton, K. 1993. Environmentalism and anthropology. In Milton, K., ed., Environmentalism: the view from anthropology. Routledge, London, UK. pp. 1–17.
– Explores the relationship between anthropology and environmentalism, which has emerged as a distinctive social commitment.

124. Minority Rights Group. 1994. Polar peoples: self-determination and development. Minority Rights Group, London, UK.
– Describes the sometimes catastrophic effects on Northern indigenous peoples of the incursions of explorers, mineral prospectors, missionaries, and bureaucrats and outlines the awakening of native political activism and the steps being taken toward indigenous self-determination.

125. Mispireta, M.L. del Rio. 1994. Introducing biodiversity into the decision-making process of the Peruvian government: a utopia? In Krattiger, A.F.; McNeely, J.A.; Lesser, W.H.; Miller, K.R.; St Hill, Y.; Senanayake, R., ed., Widening perspectives on biodiversity. International Union for the Conservation of Nature and Natural Resources, Gland, and International Academy of the Environment, Geneva, Switzerland. pp. 125–131.
– A basic strategy for implementing the CBD in a country like Peru should include rural programs for training, diffusion, and extension of information; an inventory of the country's national patrimony; and the establishment of regional agreements.

126. Moran, A.G., ed. 1994. IPR sourcebook Philippines: with special emphasis on intellectual property rights in agriculture and food. Los Banos College of Agriculture and Management and Organizational Development for Empowerment, University of the Philippines, Los Banos, Philippines.
– This collection of conference papers, other papers, and discussion transcripts deals with local applications and implications of IPR and with ethical and legal dimensions of policy review and advocacy of IPR.

127. M.S. Swaminathan Research Foundation (MSSRF). 1994. Methodologies for recognizing the role of informal innovation in the conservation and utilization of plant genetic resources. MSSRF, Madras, India. Proceedings No. 9.
– Contains arguments for sui generis IPR and crop variety protection measures that resolve problems relating to equity and ethics. Includes a draft law regarding plant breeders' rights that integrates farmers' and breeders' rights in a mutually supportive manner.

128. Mugabe, J. 1994. Technology and biodiversity in Kenya: technological capabilities and institutional systems for conservation. In Krattiger, A.F.; McNeely, J.A.; Lesser, W.H.; Miller, K.R.; St Hill, Y.; Senanayake, R., ed., Widening perspectives on biodiversity. International Union for the Conservation of Nature and Natural Resources, Gland, and International Academy of the Environment, Geneva, Switzerland. pp. 81–92.
– Overview of national technological capabilities for biodiversity conservation in Kenya. Reviews two case studies of institutions engaged in biodiversity conservation: the Kenya Wildlife Service and the National Genebank of Kenya.

129. Nafziger, J.A.R. 1987. Protection of cultural property. California Western International Law Journal, 17, 283–289.
– The United States has various legal mechanisms at its disposal to protect cultural property, both its own and the property of other countries held in the United States. In addition to the Unesco Convention, national and bilateral laws and agreements can be divided into soft laws and hard laws. Improvements could be made by defining the concept of "genuine significance" for a satisfactory compromise

between the national patrimony versus common heritage standpoints.

130. Nettheim, G. 1988. "Peoples" and "populations" — indigenous peoples and the rights of peoples. In Crawford, J., ed., The rights of peoples. Clarendon Press, Oxford, UK. pp. 107–126.
— Many of the claims of indigenous peoples are not specific to indigenous peoples and have recognition in international law. However, they also have their own claims derived from dispossession of their lands and destruction of their culture. Acknowledgment and recognition of land rights along with other claims categorized under the umbrella "self-determination" are, in part, occurring in the Australian and Canadian legal systems. However, more needs to be done.

131. Niedzielska, M. 1980. The intellectual property aspects of folklore protection. Copyright, November, 339–346.
— Searches for a way to apply copyright law to folklore. It may also be necessary to consider the intellectual property field for protection instruments. For example, the use of appellations of origin and unfair competition might be usefully applied.

132. Nijar, G.S. 1994. Towards a legal framework for protecting biological diversity and community intellectual rights: a Third World perspective. Third World Network, Penang, Malaysia.
— Argues that recognition of farmers' and indigenous peoples' rights are essential for biodiversity conservation, and proposes two model laws as a contribution to a new legal framework that would embody such recognition.

133. Oldfield, M.L.; Alcorn, J.B., ed. 1991. Biodiversity: culture, conservation and eco-development. Westview Press, Boulder, CO, USA.
— The dual themes of conservation of biological resources and rural development are explored. Using traditional resource management systems as the basis of study, the contributors assess traditional management of plant and animal diversity, explore the rationale for in situ conservation, and discuss existing and possible linkages between development and conservation.

134. Pacific Concerns Resource Centre (PCRC). 1995. Proceedings of the indigenous peoples' knowledge and intellectual property rights consultation, 24–27 April 1995, Suva, Fiji. PCRC, Suva, Fiji.
— Proceedings of the United Nations Development Programme-sponsored consultation on IPR in which indigenous peoples from the Pacific region met to discuss common concerns related to traditional knowledge, resources, and intellectual property rights.

135. Peralta, E.C. 1994. A call for intellectual property rights to recognise indigenous people's knowledge of genetic and cultural resources. In Krattiger, A.F.; McNeely, J.A.; Lesser, W.H.; Miller, K.R.; St Hill, Y.; Senanayake, R., ed., Widening perspectives on biodiversity. International Union for the Conservation of Nature and Natural Resources, Gland, and International Academy of the Environment, Geneva, Switzerland. pp. 287–289.
— International and national laws should recognize intellectual contributions to the use of genetic resources and cultural expressions.

136. Pimbert, M.P.; Pretty, J.N. 1995. Parks, people and professionals: putting "participation" into protected area management. United Nations Research Institute for Social Development (UNRISD), International Institute of Environment and Development, and World Wide Fund for Nature, Geneva, Switzerland. UNRISD discussion paper, 57.
— Critique of the "parks without people" paradigm of protected areas management. As an alternative, the authors present a new paradigm based on "participation" with local communities.

137. Pinel, S.L.; Evans, M.J. 1994. Tribal sovereignty and the control of knowledge. In Greaves, T., ed., Intellectual property rights for indigenous peoples: a sourcebook. Society for Applied Anthropology, Oklahoma City, OK, USA. pp. 41–55.
— Indigenous peoples in the southwestern United States have found it difficult to prevent others from commercially exploiting their knowledge, cultural property, and sacred symbols. Many of them have concluded that it may be best to enter the market on their own terms and avoid telling the outsider anything.

138. Pleumarom, A. 1994. The political economy of tourism. The Ecologist, 24(4), 142–148.
— International tourism, particularly to destinations in the South, is directed at transforming cultures and economies to promote "development." Because ecotourism and "sustainable" tourism ignore this, they perpetuate patterns of power and dominance that are destructive of the environment and of people.

139. Plotkin, M.; Famolare, L., ed. 1992. Sustainable harvest and marketing of rainforest products. Conservation International and Island Press, Washington, DC, USA.
— Based on papers presented at the conference on the sustainable harvest and marketing of rainforest products held in Panama City in June 1991. The book is divided into the following sections: conserving ethnobotanic information; the potential of nontimber forest products; palms and their potential; plants as medicines; and reaching international markets.

140. Poole, P. 1989. Developing a partnership of indigenous peoples, conservationists, and land use planners in Latin America. World Bank, Washington, DC, USA. Policy, planning, and research working papers — environment.
 − Provides recommendations for working in partnership with indigenous peoples in conservation. Such partnerships require recognition of land rights, incorporation of traditional knowledge into wildlands and native area planning, and greater attention to the economics and resource implications of local activities to harvest wild resources.

141. Posey, D.A. 1990. Intellectual property rights and just compensation for indigenous peoples. Anthropology Today, 6(4), 13–16.
 − Reversing cultural, ecological, and biological diversity loss is urgent. It is necessary to give intrinsic value to forests and natural habitats, recognize the role of indigenous peoples, and develop legal and practical mechanisms to guarantee IPR for traditional knowledge.

142. Posey, D.A. 1994. International agreements for protecting indigenous knowledge. In Sanchez, V.; Juma, C., ed., Biodiplomacy: genetic resources and international relations. African Centre for Technology Studies, Nairobi, Kenya. pp. 119–137.
 − Based on a review of international agreements, it is argued that IPR debates must be translated into practical tools for local communities; this requires that non-Western models of intellectual and cultural property be analyzed to redefine IPR as an entirely new concept. The development of this redefinition must be led by indigenous peoples themselves.

143. Posey, D.A. 1994. International agreements and intellectual property right protection for indigenous peoples. In Greaves, T., ed., Intellectual property rights for indigenous peoples: a sourcebook. Society for Applied Anthropology, Oklahoma City, OK, USA. pp. 223–251.
 − Identifies areas of international law where elements of protection of the rights of indigenous peoples could form the basis for a new system.

144. Posey, D.A. 1994. Traditional resource rights: de facto self-determination for indigenous peoples. In van der Vlist, L., ed., Voices of the earth. Centre for Indigenous Peoples and International Books, Amsterdam, Netherlands. pp. 217–239.
 − Proposes a new integrated rights approach as an alternative to IPR for the protection of traditional knowledge and resources. This approach, traditional resource rights, provides new opportunities for constructive dialogue with indigenous and traditional peoples on their own terms.

145. Posey, D.A. 1995. Indigenous peoples and traditional resource rights: a basis for equitable relationships? Green College Centre for Environmental Policy and Understanding, Oxford, UK.
 − Access to biological resources and benefit-sharing from their use and application are essential elements of the CBD. It has been assumed that IPR would be a key mechanism to implement the CBD in these areas. However, indigenous peoples see IPR as a serious threat to their knowledge and well-being. This paper proposes an alternative concept to IPR: traditional resource rights (TRRs). Also, it provides recommendations for collecting institutions to ensure that their policies do not lead to further exploitation of indigenous peoples.

146. Posey, D.A.; Dutfield, G.; Plenderleith, K. 1995. Collaborative research and intellectual property rights. Biodiversity and Conservation, 4(8), 892–902.
 − Indigenous knowledge is increasingly important in scientific research, and indigenous peoples are becoming politicized in the use, misappropriation, and commercialization of their knowledge and resources. The indigenous movement is now demanding IPR over information obtained through research and just compensation for economic benefits that may eventually accrue. Scientists must develop ethically sound procedures if they wish to carry on such research.

147. Prott, L.V. 1988. Cultural rights as peoples' rights in international law. In Crawford, J., ed., The rights of peoples. Clarendon Press, Oxford, UK. pp. 93–106.
 − Critical analysis of the cultural rights that are often formulated by Third World governments as human rights issues. Policies and laws developed on such a basis are likely to be contradictory. On the other hand, lawyers from developed countries have been slow to act in meeting the concerns of developing countries.

148. Raghavan, C. 1990. Recolonization: GATT in its historical context. The Ecologist, 20(6), 205–207.
 − The chief priority of the industrialized countries in the Uruguay Round was to extend their control over the global economy. In the past, this was achieved through a mixture of colonialism and threats of military intervention. It is argued that today these countries intend to have GATT and the threat of trade retaliation serve the same purpose.

149. Rankin, A. 1995. "Real history" revives Argentina's indians. History Today, 45(6), 8–10.
 − Describes a community-based project to record the oral history of Wichi people and generate maps as a means of supporting a land claim.

150. Redford, K.H.; Stearman, A.M. 1993. Forest-dwelling native Amazonians and the conservation of biodiversity: interests in common or in

collision? Conservation Biology, 7(2), 248–255.
  – The indigenous peoples organization, COICA, proposes a framework for cooperation with environmentalists. It appears that indigenous people and environmentalists define conservation and biodiversity in different ways, with indigenous people focusing more on preservation of general habitat characteristics and exclusion of extensive habitat alteration. In fact, the interests of conservation biologists may not be completely compatible with the agenda of indigenous peoples, argue the authors.

151. Reid, W.V. 1992. Genetic resources and sustainable agriculture: creating incentives for local innovation and adaptation. African Centre for Technology Studies, Nairobi, Kenya. Biopolicy International Series, 2.
  – Current policy regimes fail to promote local innovation or provide incentives for the upstream exploration of potential values of genetic resources. Changes will require acceptance by all countries of new ownership regimes for genetic resources. It is argued that the only lasting solutions to maintaining the genetic resources base of agriculture are in situ conservation, recognition of local and national ownership of genetic resources, and research and investment aimed at informal innovation.

152. Reid, W.V.; Laird, S.A.; Gamez, R.; Sittenfeld, A.; Janzen, D.H.; Gollin, M.A.; Juma, C. 1993. A new lease on life. *In* Reid, W.V.; Laird, S.A.; Meyer, C.A.; Gamez, R.; Sittenfeld, A.; Janzen, D.H.; Gollin, M.A.; Juma, C., ed., Biodiversity prospecting: using genetic resources for sustainable development. World Resources Institute, Washington, DC, USA; Instituto Nacional de Biodiversidad (INBio), San José, Costa Rica; Rainforest Alliance, New York, NY, USA; African Centre for Technology Studies, Nairobi, Kenya. pp. 1–52.
  – The agreement between INBio and Merck sets a precedent in the history of biodiversity prospecting. More and more companies are now screening natural products, and this may provide incentives and funds for conservation, as long as appropriate and effective policies are put in place. This article puts forward some general principles for such policies.

153. Reid, W.V.; Laird, S.A.; Meyer, C.A.; Gamez, R.; Sittenfeld, A.; Janzen, D.H.; Gollin, M.A.; Juma, C., ed., 1993. Biodiversity prospecting: using genetic resources for sustainable development. World Resources Institute, Washington, DC, USA; Instituto Nacional de Biodiversidad, San José, Costa Rica; Rainforest Alliance, New York, NY, USA; African Centre for Technology Studies, Nairobi, Kenya.
  – The proliferation of bioprospecting in the tropics makes it urgent to develop equitable legal arrangements so that the natural environment is enhanced rather than diminished, and developing countries benefit.

154. Ritchie, M. 1990. GATT, agriculture and the environment. The Ecologist, 20(6), 214–220.
  – The US government, backed by corporate interests, is using the General Agreement on Tariffs and Trade to push through drastic measures to deregulate global trade in agricultural and related products. The proposals would devastate small farmers around the world and massively increase the control of big businesses over the production of, and trade in, food and other natural products. The rights of national and regional legislatures to implement environmental and health protection regulations would also be seriously compromised.

155. Rossel, P. 1988. Tourism and cultural minorities: double marginalisation and survival strategies. *In* Rossel, P., ed., Tourism, manufacturing the exotic. International Work Group for Indigenous Affairs, Copenhagen, Denmark. Document 61. pp. 1–20.
  – Highlights some of the social and economic threats of tourism to cultural minorities. Nevertheless, some ethnic groups may well be able to benefit from revenues generated by tourism.

156. Rossler, M. 1993. Conserving outstanding cultural landscapes. The World Heritage Newsletter, 2, 14–15.
  – Reports on the decision of the World Heritage Committee to adopt cultural landscapes under Unesco's World Heritage Convention. Three categories of cultural landscape are defined by the committee.

157. Rubin, S.M.; Fish, S.C. 1994. Biodiversity prospecting: using innovative contractual provisions to foster ethnobotanical knowledge, technology and conservation. Colorado Journal of International Environmental Law and Policy, 5, 23–58.
  – Until recently, biodiversity prospecting has failed to provide conservation incentives. The CBD established certain principles and objectives that biodiversity prospecting contracts might follow. Authors discuss certain contract provisions that might optimize benefits to the host country as well as specific compensation packages, such as those involving technology transfers, royalties, concession fees, etc.

158. Ruppert, D. 1994. Buying secrets: federal government procurement of intellectual cultural property. *In* Greaves, T., ed., Intellectual property rights for indigenous peoples: a sourcebook. Society for Applied Anthropology, Oklahoma City, OK, USA. pp. 111–128.
  – Analyzes legal dilemmas encountered in IPR negotiations between indigenous communities and federal communities arising from legal constraints embedded in US federal law.

159. Rural Advancement Foundation International. 1990. Folkseed: a journalistic overview of the battle over plant genetic resources. RAFI,

Ottawa, Canada.
— Compares the innovations of traditional farmers with those of modern plant breeders, and emphasizes the importance of Third World crop germplasm. It is argued that the extension of IPR protection for folk varieties is playing to the rules of a game "cooked up in Washington" and should not be supported. The overview concludes with a list of traditional farming practices that could be patentable should United States proposals on TRIPs be adopted.

160. Rural Advancement Foundation International. 1993. "Immortalizing" the good Samaritan: patents, indigenous peoples, and human genetic diversity. RAFI, Ottawa, Canada. RAFI communiqué.
— Highlights the human rights implications of the Human Genome Diversity Project. The fears are that genetic information in samples taken from indigenous people could be patentable and commercialized. A demonstration of this likelihood is the village of Limone, Italy, where companies are taking samples and applying for patents. Authors suggest that genetic information could make it possible to devise cheap and community-targeted biological weapons.

161. Rural Advancement Foundation International. 1994. The benefits of biodiversity: 100+ examples of the contribution by indigenous and rural communities in the South to development in the North. RAFI, Ottawa, Canada. Occasional Paper Series 1(1).
— Compilation of data intended to give an insight into the enormous contribution made by the South to the well-being of Northern citizens and the economic benefit of Northern corporations.

162. Rural Advancement Foundation International. 1994. Conserving indigenous knowledge: integrating two systems of innovation. An independent study by the Rural Advancement Foundation International. United Nations Development Programme, New York, NY, USA.
— Identifies issues and trends in IPR systems and argues that the indigenous system of innovation is left unprotected. In view of the inherent unfairness of this situation, the authors suggest various alternatives to IPR.

163. Rural Advancement Foundation International. 1994. The patenting of human genetic material. RAFI, Ottawa, Canada. Communiqué.
— The patenting of human biological material is now the focus of debate over its social, ethical, and political implications. A scientific explanation of human biological materials is given along with a report on activities carried out to oppose the patenting of human cell lines, including those from indigenous peoples.

164. Rural Advancement Foundation International. 1995. Biopiracy update: a global pandemic. RAFI, Ottawa, Canada. Communiqué.
— Provides examples to show the extent to which biological resources and traditional knowledge are being appropriated and patented by corporations. One reason for this is that bilateral bioprospecting agreements sanctioned by the CBD operate beyond the control of source communities and countries.

165. Sanchez, V.; Juma, C., ed. 1994. Biodiplomacy: genetic resources and international relations. African Centre for Technology Studies, Nairobi, Kenya.
— A detailed analysis of the main features of the CBD. The contributions outline specific ways to implement the convention.

166. Sanchez, V.; Juma, C. 1994. Challenges and opportunities for South–South cooperation in implementing the Convention on Biological Diversity. In Krattiger, A.F.; McNeely, J.A.; Lesser, W.H.; Miller, K.R.; St Hill, Y.; Senanayake, R., ed., Widening perspectives on biodiversity. International Union for the Conservation of Nature and Natural Resources, Gland, and International Academy of the Environment, Geneva, Switzerland. pp. 305–307.
— The costs and complexities of adding value to genetic resources with medicinal properties exceed the resources available to developing countries operating individually. The model of research partnerships among the pharmaceutical corporations with research institutions should be emulated in the form of South–South technology alliances.

167. Sarmiento, G. 1994. The new constitution of Colombia: environmental and indigenous peoples' issues. In Krattiger, A.F.; McNeely, J.A.; Lesser, W.H.; Miller, K.R.; St Hill, Y.; Senanayake, R., ed., Widening perspectives on biodiversity. International Union for the Conservation of Nature and Natural Resources, Gland, and International Academy of the Environment, Geneva, Switzerland. pp. 133–135.
— The new Colombian constitution establishes peoples' responsibilities for protecting cultural entities and natural resources, and recognizes the rights of indigenous peoples by legally recognizing their territories.

168. Schuking, H.; Anderson, P. 1991. Voices unheard and unheeded. In Shiva, V.; Anderson, P.; Schuking, H.; Gray, A.; Lohmann, L.; Cooper, D., ed., Biodiversity, social and ecological perspectives. Zed Books and World Rainforest Movement, Penang, Malaysia.
— A biodiversity crisis is being caused by humans. The main area of concern is tropical forests. Conservation must give priority to preserving ecological functions and subsistence uses over schemes to commercialize biological resources for the international market as

advocated by those promoting the "save it, study it, use it" approach.

169. Scoones, I.; Thompson, J., ed. 1994. Beyond farmer first: rural people's knowledge, agricultural research and extension practice. Intermediate Technology Publications, London, UK.
— The purpose of this book is to reveal how agricultural research and extension, far from being discrete, rational acts, in fact form part of a process of coming to terms with conflicting interests and viewpoints, a process in which choices are made, alliances formed, exclusions effected, and world-views imposed.

170. Sedjo, R.A. 1992. Property rights, genetic resources and biotechnological change. Journal of Law and Economics, 35(1), 199–213.
— "Wild" genetic resources have elements of public and private goods. This gives rise to conflicts over the common heritage status of biological resources. As a result, the global genetic resource base is eroding. However, it is difficult to capture genetic resource rents, so countries have little incentive to preserve genetic resources. One possible solution is to enforce property rights. The other is to "internalize externalities" through registration. According to the author, the latter approach is more realistic.

171. Seeger, A. 1992. Ethnomusicology and music law. Ethnomusicology, 36(3), 345–359.
— The author calls on ethnomusicologists to inform themselves better on rights and obligations relating to traditional music. In indigenous communities, songs may be subject to a complex range of rights and obligations, but such songs are often considered public domain, meaning that a Western musician may turn them into his or her intellectual property.

172. Shelton, D. 1995. Fair play, fair pay: strengthening local livelihood systems through compensation for access to and use of traditional knowledge and biological resources. World Wide Fund for Nature, Gland, Switzerland.
— This study is based on three facts: traditional knowledge is being lost as rural groups, particularly indigenous populations, are transformed or disappear; biodiversity is decreasing; and biological resources are increasingly valuable in biotechnology. Therefore, it is equitable to require that indigenous and other people be compensated for transmitting the knowledge that they have acquired and maintained.

173. Shiva, V. 1991. Biodiversity, biotechnology and profits. In Shiva, V.; Anderson, P.; Schuking, H.; Gray, A.; Lohmann, L.; Cooper, D., ed., Biodiversity, social and ecological perspectives. Zed Books and World Rainforest Movement, Penang, Malaysia. pp. 43–58.
— Biotechnology turns biodiversity conservation into conservation of "raw materials" rather than conservation of the means of production of life itself, leading to increasing genetic uniformity. The author advocates diverse agricultural systems, warning of the dangers for biodiversity of the commoditized seed.

174. Shiva, V., ed. 1994. Biodiversity conservation: whose resource? whose knowledge? Indian National Trust for Art and Cultural Heritage (INTACH), New Delhi, India.
— Collection of papers from the 1994 INTACH seminar "Biodiversity Conservation, People's Knowledge and Intellectual Property Rights."

175. Shiva, V. 1994. Farmers' rights and the Convention on Biological Diversity. In Sanchez, V.; Juma, C., ed., Biodiplomacy: genetic resources and international relations. African Centre for Technology Studies, Nairobi, Kenya. pp. 107–118.
— In biodiversity conservation, the most critical actors are local communities. However, their rights have been neglected in intergovernmental negotiations. Farmers' rights, which are the rights of indigenous communities to conserve their resources and regenerate their knowledge of resources, should be respected and considered in development planning.

176. Shiva, V.; Anderson, P.; Schuking, H.; Gray, A.; Lohmann, L.; Cooper, D., ed. 1991. Biodiversity: social and ecological perspectives. Zed Books and World Rainforest Movement, Penang, Malaysia.
— The contributors argue that the roots of biodiversity loss lie in the industrial system of the North. Biotechnology will erode biodiversity by increasing genetic uniformity, and imposing IPR to turn life forms into private property. Therefore, conservationists who support industrial use of biodiversity to add "value" to genetic resources are misguided. Instead they should realize that it is Third World peasants and forest dwellers who are the true conservers of biodiversity.

177. Shutkin, W.A. 1991. International human rights law and the earth: the protection of indigenous peoples and the environment. Virginia Journal of International Law, 31, 479.
— Explores the convergence of environmental and human rights issues as they relate to indigenous peoples, and the capacity of international law to protect peoples and the environment within the context of human rights jurisprudence.

178. Siebeck, W.E.; Evenson, R.E.; Lesser, W.; Primo Braga, C.A., ed. 1990. Strengthening protection of intellectual property in developing countries: a survey of the literature. World Bank, Washington, DC, USA.
— Developing countries are being urged to strengthen intellectual property protection. This literature survey seeks to find out whether developing countries will benefit economically from strengthened IPR regimes. Concludes that information required to provide definitive

answers is lacking and proposes a research agenda to investigate the issues.

179. Sittenfeld, A.; Gamez, R. 1993. Biodiversity prospecting by INBio. *In* Reid, W.V.; Laird, S.A.; Meyer, C.A.; Gamez, R.; Sittenfeld, A.; Janzen, D.H.; Gollin, M.A.; Juma, C., ed., Biodiversity prospecting: using genetic resources for sustainable development. World Resources Institute, Washington, DC, USA; Instituto Nacional de Biodiversidad, San José, Costa Rica; Rainforest Alliance, New York, NY, USA; African Centre for Technology Studies, Nairobi, Kenya. pp. 69–97.

– Biodiversity prospecting is being conducted by the Instituto Nacional de Biodiversidad (INBio) in Costa Rica's conservation areas. The types of collaboration are described as well as the objectives of INBio's work.

180. Soleri, D.; Cleveland, D.; Eriacho, D.; Bowannie Jr, F.; Laahty, A.; Zuni community members. 1994. Gifts from the creator: intellectual property rights and folk crop varieties. *In* Greaves, T., ed., Intellectual property rights for indigenous peoples: a sourcebook. Society for Applied Anthropology, Oklahoma City, OK, USA. pp. 19–40.

– Discusses the disappearance of folk crop varieties and the failure to recognize IPR of indigenous farmers. Explains the work of the Zuni Folk Varieties Project, which was founded to promote the use of folk varieties among the present-day Zuni.

181. Southworth, E. 1994. A special concern. Museums Journal, July, 23–25.

– Assesses the status of human remains in museums of the United Kingdom and presents the World Archaeological Congress's Code of Ethics on obligations to indigenous peoples.

182. Spiwak, D. 1993. Gene genie and science's thirst for information with indigenous blood. Abya Yala News, 7(3–4), 12–14.

– Condemnation of the Human Genome Diversity Project from the viewpoint of indigenous people.

183. Stephenson, D.J. 1994. A legal paradigm for protecting traditional knowledge. *In* Greaves, T., ed., Intellectual property rights for indigenous peoples: a sourcebook. Society for Applied Anthropology, Oklahoma City, OK, USA. pp. 179–189.

– Considers the possibility of using licensing agreements of the type used by software companies as a model for agreements involving the transfer of traditional knowledge.

184. Suagee, D.B. 1994. Human rights and cultural heritage: developments in the United Nations Working Group on Indigenous Populations. *In* Greaves, T., ed., Intellectual property rights for indigenous peoples: a sourcebook. Society for Applied Anthropology, Oklahoma City, OK, USA. pp. 191–208.

– Presents the current agenda of the UN's Working Group on Indigenous Populations. The author argues that IPR should not be seen as a competing priority with other pressing needs, such as land and sovereignty, but a complementary one.

185. Svarstad, H. 1994. National sovereignty and genetic resources. *In* Sanchez, V.; Juma, C., ed., Biodiplomacy: genetic resources and international relations. African Centre for Technology Studies, Nairobi, Kenya. pp. 45–65.

– In the context of the CBD, the author compares and contrasts the demands of the North and the South. Various remedies are proposed to ensure that countries and people in the South benefit from the CBD's elements of national sovereignty over genetic resources and technology transfer.

186. Tickell, O. 1992. Nuts, bucks and survival. Geographical Magazine, August, 10–14.

– Discusses the debate over the "rainforest harvest," specifically the contrasting positions of Survival International and The Body Shop.

187. Unrepresented Nations and Peoples Organization. 1993. Self-determination in relation to individual human rights democracy and the protection of the environment (conference report). UNPO, The Hague, Netherlands.

– Contains a discussion on the concept of self-determination and summaries of comments by members and supporters of the Unrepresented Nations and Peoples Organization.

188. Valentine, P.S. 1993. Ecotourism and nature conservation: a definition with some recent developments in Micronesia. Tourism Management, April, 107–115.

– Presents a narrow definition of ecotourism that requires a two-way link between it and nature conservation. Examples are given of how ecotourism might be used to support nature conservation directly in Micronesia. Concludes with some suggested guidelines for the establishment of ecotourism.

189. van der Vlist, L., ed. 1994. Voices of the earth: indigenous peoples, new partners and the right to self-determination in practice. Centre for Indigenous Peoples and International Books, Amsterdam, Netherlands.

– Presents contributions of representatives of indigenous peoples from around the world at a conference to build support for the demands of indigenous peoples and to help create a sustainable world order that reflects the world's cultural diversity.

190. van Wijk, J.; Cohen, J.I.; Komen, J. 1993. Intellectual property rights for agricultural biotechnology: options and implications for developing countries. International Service for National Agricultural Research, The Hague,

Netherlands.
 – Analysis of the complexities, options, and implications of IPR in relation to national biotechnology strategies.

191. Verma, S.K. 1995. TRIPs and plant variety protection in developing countries. European Intellectual Property Review, 17(6), 281–289.
 – The Trade-Related Aspects of Intellectual Property Rights agreement permits an effective sui generis system. Such a system for developing countries can be modeled broadly on the Union for the Protection of New Varieties of Plants Convention, but economy, ecology, equity, and employment should be considered to promote a sustainable job-led economic growth strategy in these countries.

192. Walden, I. 1993. Intellectual property in genetic sequences. Review of European Community and International Environmental Law, 2(2), 126–135.
 – Discusses the potential and limitations of granting countries IPR over their genetic diversity, which would require these countries to control access to their resources. The author's analysis of legal protection of genetic information though a sui generis system indicates that such an approach could be difficult to achieve.

193. Walgate, R. 1990. Miracle or menace: biotechnology and the Third World. The Panos Institute, London, UK.
 – Explains biotechnology and its potential in the fields of health and food. Most biotechnology is in private hands, but corporations are concerned with making profits. This reality may be harmful to the interests of Third World countries. The main danger for these countries is substitution of new bio-industrial products for existing high-value Southern products. The main benefits may be some technology transfers. Public-sector research is the key to appropriate biotechnology for Third World countries. NGOs and governments can help scientists listen to and learn from the poor so as to develop appropriate technologies.

194. Warren, D.M.; Slikkerveer, L.J.; Brokensha, D., ed. 1995. The cultural dimension of development: indigenous knowledge systems. Intermediate Technology Publications, London, UK.
 – In international development, increasing attention is being paid to the potential of traditional knowledge. The case studies in this volume confirm that local people know a great deal about their environment and that local knowledge must be taken into account in the planning and implementation of development.

195. Weiner, J.G. 1987. Protection of folklore: a political and legal challenge. International Review of Industrial Property and Copyright Law, 18(1), 56–92.
 – Author defines folklore as a starting point for the investigation of recent attempts to protect folklore through legal means. Various possibilities are considered such as copyright law, model laws, and the "paid public domain."

196. Wood, D. 1994. Conservation and agriculture: the need for a new international network of biodiversity and development institutes to resolve conflict. In Krattiger, A.F.; McNeely, J.A.; Lesser, W.H.; Miller, K.R.; St Hill, Y.; Senanayake, R., ed., Widening perspectives on biodiversity. International Union for the Conservation of Nature and Natural Resources, Gland, and International Academy of the Environment, Geneva, Switzerland. pp. 425–434.
 – Argues against the "people without parks" concept of many environmentalists and funding agencies. Instead there should be greater investment in agricultural research including livestock research. Proposes creation of a system of biodiversity and development institutes along the lines of the Consultative Group on International Agricultural Research.

197. Woodmansee, M. 1984. The genius and the copyright: economic and legal conditions of the emergence of the "author." Eighteenth Century Studies, 17(4), 425–448.
 – Traces the 18th century evolution of the notion of authorship Until then, writers were not credited with original thought or regarded as the main creators of a book. Thus the early professional writers were exploited and publishers were seriously affected by reproduction of works. "Authorship" made the interests of writers, the public, and publishers conveniently appear identical.

198. World Commission on Environment and Development. 1987. Our common future. Oxford University Press, New York, NY, USA.
 – This report of the WCED (the Brundtland Report) calls for a marriage of economy and ecology through "sustainable development." It provides a range of proposals to solve critical environment and development problems so that human progress can be sustained without bankrupting the resources of future generations.

199. World Council of Indigenous Peoples. 1993. Presumed dead... but still useful as a human by-product. WCIP, Ottawa, Canada.
 – Strong condemnation of the Human Genome Diversity Project by an indigenous peoples' organization.

200. World Intellectual Property Organization. 1988. Background reading material on intellectual property. WIPO, Geneva, Switzerland.
 – An IPR sourcebook from an organization that administers many IPR conventions, this book provides detailed explanations of all IPR types recognized under Western legal systems.

201. Yamin, F. 1995. Biodiversity, ethics and international law. International Affairs, 71(3), 529–546.
– Suggests that biodiversity conservation issues require us to clarify the moral and ethical foundations of our relations with the natural world and with each other. This may require new theories of ethics and international distributive justice, which would assist in the implementation of the CBD.

202. Yamin, F. 1995. The biodiversity convention and intellectual property rights. World Wide Fund for Nature, Gland, Switzerland.
– Examines the link between IPR and the Convention on Biological Diversity. The author proposes recommendations to ensure that such rights are supportive of and do not run counter to the objectives of the convention.

203. Yamin, F.; Posey, D.A. 1993. Indigenous peoples, biotechnology and intellectual property rights. Review of European Community and International Environmental Law, 2(2), 141–148.
– Reviews the various international organizations, conventions, declarations, and existing IPR rules that could be used to help indigenous people protect their knowledge, folklore, crafts, and biodiversity.

204. Yano, L.I. 1993. Protection of the ethnobiological knowledge of indigenous peoples. UCLA Law Review, 41(2), 443–486.
– Explains the value of ethnobiological knowledge and states that patent law is inadequate to protect such knowledge. Treaties and contracts are other possible mechanisms to protect traditional knowledge, but these have not yet proved effective in ensuring equitable benefit-sharing. The author concludes that patent protection should be extended to include traditional knowledge.

205. Yen, A.C. 1992. The interdisciplinary future of copyright theory. Cardozo Arts and Entertainment Law Journal, 10(2), 423–437.
– There are two conflicting copyright theories. The first is the view that copyright exists to provide economic incentives for the production of creative work; so there is a compromise between authors and consumers. The second is the natural law theory, which postulates a moral right for creative people to benefit from the fruits of their labour. The United States' Supreme Court tends to support the economic argument only. Analysts also generally explain concepts like originality and the idea–expression dichotomy in economic terms. The author is opposed to this view, arguing that considerations of justice and fairness are essential to a complete copyright theory.

206. Young, E. 1995. Third World in the First: development and indigenous peoples. Routledge, New York, NY, USA.
– European colonization has marginalized the "first peoples" in industrialized countries such as Australia and Canada. Modernization, exemplified by state and private development and the "assistance" provided by the state, has disregarded the integrated socioeconomic structures of their communities. The author examines how development has affected these peoples and explores alternative strategies that might be available to them.

207. Yusuf, A.A. 1995. International law and sustainable development: the Convention on Biological Diversity. In Yusuf, A.A., ed., African yearbook of international law (vol. 2). Kluwer Law International, The Hague, Netherlands. pp. 109–137.
– This review of the CBD identifies gaps and conflicts that must be dealt with to make implementation more effective. The adoption of protocols is needed in several areas: for example, ways of sharing knowledge and technologies and protection of indigenous knowledge and practices. Furthermore, it is necessary for our knowledge of biodiversity to be enhanced and for developed countries to honour their financial commitments.

Subject index

The numbers in this index refer only to the entries in the preceding annotated bibliography.

agricultural research 7, 45, 59, 90, 97, 98, 126, 151, 162, 169, 190, 194, 196
appellations of origin 83, 131, 143

biodiversity prospecting (bioprospecting) 6, 29, 45, 53, 67, 85, 89, 90, 92, 95, 99, 103, 134, 152, 153, 157, 164, 165, 174
biotechnology 6, 45, 59, 67, 90, 94, 97, 98, 106, 172, 173, 176, 190, 193
breeders' rights (see Union for the Protection of New Varieties of Plants)

cell lines 1, 18, 163
codes of ethics 46, 74, 105, 145, 181
collaborative research 30, 82, 105, 115, 145, 146, 149
community registers 58, 145
community intellectual rights 92, 132
conservation
 ex situ 7, 59, 102, 115, 133, 207
 in situ 28, 59, 102, 115, 133, 207
Convention on Biological Diversity (CBD) 7, 66, 78, 92, 101, 102, 105, 107, 125, 128, 132, 165, 166, 172, 174, 175, 185, 201, 202, 207
common property 14, 60, 61, 86, 183, 204

contracts 6, 50, 70, 74, 103, 105, 109, 117, 120, 153, 157, 170, 172
copyright 8, 18, 68, 114, 131, 158, 171, 195, 197, 200, 205
cultural expressions/folklore 5, 16, 68, 83, 110, 114, 131, 137, 171, 180, 195, 203, 204
cultural property 52, 70, 79, 82, 83, 112, 114, 118, 121, 122, 129, 137, 143, 144, 147, 172, 181
cultural heritage 52, 57, 65, 70, 82, 122, 129, 131, 143, 144, 147, 156, 174, 184
customary law 77

ecosystems management 14, 32, 33, 51, 60, 61, 62, 69, 75, 86, 87, 101, 121, 133, 136, 174, 194
environment 3, 25, 56, 67, 202

farmers' rights 22, 39, 45, 57, 65, 127, 132
folklore, arts, and crafts, trade in 16, 68, 83, 137, 155
Food and Agriculture Organization (FAO) and plant genetic resources 22, 26, 39, 45, 54, 57, 59, 65, 126, 162

General Agreement on Tariffs and Trade (GATT) 25, 47, 56, 132, 145, 148, 154, 159, 191
genetic resources, trade in 12, 39, 45, 54, 59, 78, 90, 94, 97, 98, 103, 105, 110, 126, 151, 152, 157, 162, 165, 170, 185, 192

Human Genome Diversity Project 1, 28, 80, 111, 121, 134, 160, 163, 182, 199
human rights 19, 31, 35, 55, 70, 88, 130, 143, 144, 172, 177, 184, 189

indigenous peoples and the nation state 4, 10, 34, 55, 76, 83, 88, 96
indigenous rights 10, 19, 31, 35, 55, 70, 76, 95, 130, 142, 143, 144, 177, 184, 189, 203
industrial application (of traditional knowledge) 12, 29, 46, 53, 69, 71, 84, 89, 94, 95, 99, 104, 134, 146, 159, 161, 162, 164
Instituto Nacional de Biodiversidad (National Biodiversity Institute of Costa Rica) 6, 45, 63, 74, 85, 89, 105, 152, 153, 157, 179
intellectual property rights
   appellations of origin 83, 131, 143
   copyright 8, 18, 68, 114, 131, 158, 171, 195, 197, 200, 205
   cultural expressions/folklore 5, 16, 68, 83, 110, 114, 131, 137, 171, 180, 195, 203, 204
   environment 3, 25, 56, 67, 202
   life forms 11, 18, 36, 59, 64, 67, 106, 119, 126, 134, 162, 163, 173, 176, 192
   patents 8, 11, 12, 29, 45, 59, 67, 106, 108, 116, 119, 126, 134, 159, 162, 163, 178, 190, 192, 200
   petty patents (utility models) 67, 108, 200
   trademarks 8, 16, 67, 108, 200
   trade secrets 8, 12, 67, 108, 200
   traditional knowledge 6, 13, 21, 22, 29, 31, 45, 47, 52, 59, 67, 69, 70, 71, 73, 109, 116, 120, 135, 141, 142, 143, 144, 159, 162, 172, 180, 203, 204
international law
   conservation 15, 19, 49, 102, 201

human rights 19, 31, 35, 55, 70, 88, 130, 143, 144, 172, 177, 184, 189
indigenous peoples and the nation state 4, 10, 34, 55, 76, 83, 88, 96
indigenous rights 10, 19, 31, 35, 55, 70, 76, 95, 130, 142, 143, 144, 177, 184, 189, 203
self-determination 34, 35, 38, 70, 76, 96, 124, 130, 142, 143, 144, 145, 187, 189
"soft law" 76, 129, 142, 144

life forms 11, 18, 36, 59, 64, 67, 106, 119, 126, 134, 162, 163, 173, 176, 192

medicinal plants, trade in 9, 17, 41, 95, 104, 139

National Biodiversity Institute of Costa Rica 6, 45, 63, 74, 85, 89, 105, 152, 153, 157, 179
National Cancer Institute (USA) 6, 29, 44, 46, 74, 89, 139, 157
nontimber forest products, trade in 40, 69, 71, 104, 133, 139, 168, 186

patents 8, 11, 12, 29, 45, 59, 67, 106, 108, 116, 119, 126, 134, 159, 162, 163, 178, 190, 192, 200
petty patents (utility models) 67, 108, 200
prior informed consent 66, 78, 105, 132, 172
protected areas 2, 20, 37, 42, 43, 91, 93, 113, 115, 136, 140, 150, 196

self-determination 34, 35, 38, 70, 76, 96, 124, 130, 142, 143, 144, 145, 187, 189
Shaman Pharmaceuticals 6, 29, 74, 89, 95, 139, 157
"soft law" 76, 129, 142, 144
sustainable development 27, 48, 81, 198, 206
tourism 16, 113, 138, 155, 188, 206
trade
   folklore, arts, and crafts 16, 68, 83, 137, 155
   genetic resources 12, 39, 45, 54, 59, 78, 90, 94, 97, 98, 103, 105, 110, 126, 151, 152, 157, 162, 165, 170, 185, 192
   medicinal plants 9, 17, 41, 95, 104, 139
   nontimber forest products 40, 69, 71, 104, 133, 139, 168, 186
trademarks 8, 16, 67, 108, 200
trade secrets 8, 12, 67, 108, 200
traditional knowledge
   ecosystems management 14, 32, 33, 51, 60, 61, 62, 69, 75, 86, 87, 101, 121, 133, 136, 174, 194
   industrial application 12, 29, 46, 53, 69, 71, 84, 89, 94, 95, 99, 104, 134, 146, 159, 161, 162, 164
   intellectual property rights 6, 13, 21, 22, 29, 31, 45, 47, 52, 59, 67, 69, 70, 71, 73, 109, 116, 120, 135, 141, 142, 143, 144, 159, 162, 172, 180, 203, 204
traditional resource rights 65, 92, 144, 145, 146
Union for the Protection of New Varieties of Plants (UPOV) 24, 45, 56, 57, 59, 72, 108, 110, 126, 127, 159, 172, 178, 190, 191

The Authors

Darrell A. Posey is Titled Researcher for the Brazilian National Council for Science and Technology at the Goeldi Museum, Belém, Brazil. He is Director of the Programme for Traditional Resource Rights of the Oxford Centre for the Environment, Ethics, and Society and a Fellow of Linacre College, University of Oxford. Dr Posey was Founding President of the International Society for Ethnobiology and is President of the Global Coalition for Bio-Cultural Diversity, under whose auspices he founded and coordinates the Working Group on Traditional Resource Rights. He was the recipient of the Sierra Club's first "Chico Mendes Award for Outstanding Bravery in Defense of the Environment" and is one of the recipients of the United Nations "Global 500" award.

Graham Dutfield is Research Coordinator for the Working Group on Traditional Resource Rights. He holds degrees in Latin American studies, from Portsmouth University, and environment and development, from Cambridge University. Mr Dutfield has addressed international conferences in India, the Netherlands, and the United Kingdom on issues concerning the resource rights of indigenous peoples and local communities. His work has been published by the International Union for the Conservation of Nature (IUCN) and the journal *Biodiversity and Conservation*.

About the Institution

The International Development Research Centre (IDRC) is committed to building a sustainable and equitable world. IDRC funds developing-world researchers, thus enabling the people of the South to find their own solutions to their own problems. IDRC also maintains information networks and forges linkages that allow Canadians and their developing-world partners to benefit equally from a global sharing of knowledge. Through its actions, IDRC is helping others to help themselves.

About the Publisher

IDRC BOOKS publishes research results and scholarly studies on global and regional issues related to sustainable and equitable development. As a specialist in development literature, IDRC BOOKS contributes to the body of knowledge on these issues to further the cause of global understanding and equity. IDRC publications are sold through its head office in Ottawa, Canada, as well as by IDRC's agents and distributors around the world.

Augsburg College
Lindell Library
Minneapolis, MN 55454